Preface

This is the 5th edition of a book which proved its usefulness by running through four editions in 18 years. The original author Alfred Read, assisted by A. T. Purse, drew on his wide experience, both of law and business, to produce a guide for Company Directors which was at the same time convenient, practical and thorough. The object of this edition is the same but times have changed. The pressure of legislation is greater than it was 20 years ago and interventionism by the state is expanding as much in the field of business law as elsewhere.

The 1967 Companies Act made a swing in this direction, which will be accelerated when the contents of the 1973 Companies Bill ultimately find their way on to the Statute Book. This Bill is useful as an indication of a Government view of good business practice, and compliance with its standards, for example in the field of insider trading, must be commended. These standards are referred to in the appropriate parts of the text. But interventionism did not start with the 1967 Act. The trend towards regulation and disclosure has been continuous since the first major Companies Act of 1862. As far as Directors are concerned, there has been a parallel movement from amateur to professional status. The Executive Director of today might have some difficulty in recognising his relationship with his Victorian predecessor who was described in one case as a country gentleman who could not be expected to understand the accounts!

The modern Director is a professional who is expected to understand not only accounts, but all the other extensive duties which the Law imposes upon him. It is hoped that this book will provide a compact and practical guide to those duties, but it does not shrink from technicalities where the alternative appears to be oversimplification. For the same reason, a good deal of detailed attention is devoted to the Articles of Association which impinge on

Preface

almost every aspect of the Director's responsibilities. Table A is the basis of the Articles of most companies; it appears in full in Appendix B 2 and its provisions are referred to throughout the book in so far as they affect each subject under discussion.

Space has also been given to the recent case law, particularly the *Wallersteiner v Moir* litigation and the *First Re-Investment Trust Ltd.* investigation which seem to indicate that the old questions of Directors' duties are being looked at with a new and more critical eye. Other subjects to receive special consideration include the exercise of Directors' powers, interest in contracts, duties of good faith and skill, insider dealing, disclosure, Directors' Reports, take-overs, rights of minorities, duties of dissenting directors, service contracts, loss of office and Directors' pensions.

Within this framework, the book has been entirely rewritten with the object of presenting the law in a concise and readable form, with extensive use of tabulations and sub-headings; so that when the reader is confronted with a specific problem, for example on loans to Directors, he may quickly turn to the relevant paragraph where he will find first a statement of the general rule, followed by the exceptions and salient points, in a series of short and tabulated sections. A specimen form of Directors' Service Agreement is set out in Appendix A, as an illustration rather than a precedent, as this most important matter naturally requires individual consideration in every case. Finally, the author hopes that accountants and lawyers, as well as Company Directors themselves, may find the book of use, in gathering together in a convenient form, the statutory and common law on this subject.

Acknowledgements are due to: Messrs. Read and Purse, for their kindness and assistance and to the staff of the publishers for their expert help. Mr. M. A. Newman of the Scottish Widows Fund gave the benefit of his practical and detailed knowledge of the difficult and ever changing subject of Directors' Pensions. Lastly, the author is grateful to his clients for the inexhaustible supply of problems which they have presented to him. He has tried to dwell on those matters which have caused the most difficulty in practice.

Peter Loose

London, 5th June 1975.

Foreword

It is arguable that the need for positive and effective business leadership was never greater than it is in Britain today. Indeed much of Western Europe is now experiencing economic difficulties of one sort or another comparable with those of this country.

It remains one of the prime objects of the Institute to encourage professionalism in business, and we are constantly endeavouring to improve the many services offered by the Institute to achieve this end. We are, after all, the only business organisation which caters for directors as individuals.

It goes without saying, therefore, that I welcome the decision to publish a new edition of 'The Company Director'. The functions, powers and duties of directors are increasingly complex and this book does a great deal to clarify the confusing issues. I warmly recommend it.

JAN HILDRETH,
Director-General, Institute of Directors
AUGUST 1975

Contents

Contents

Contents

Contents

Contents

Glossary of Terms and Abbreviations

1948 Act	Companies Act 1948
1967 Act	Companies Act 1967
1973 Companies Bill	A Bill introduced by the Conservative Administration in December 1973 which fell with that Administration in March 1974. It contained many important amendments of company law which are likely to be enacted in due course.
The Acts	1948 and 1967 Acts
A.G.M.	Annual General Meeting
All E.R.	The All England Law Reports
Articles	The internal regulations of the Company
Close Company	A Company where the owners and the directors are substantially the same people; as in the typical Private Company. Not used as a technical term in this book.
Compulsory Winding-Up	Winding-Up (Liquidation) of a Company after a petition to the Court under s.222 1948 Act.
Days	Where a period of days is specified in the Act as the period within which a duty is to be performed, it includes Saturdays, Sundays and Bank Holidays, *unless specifically excluded by the relevant section.*
Debenture	An acknowledgement of a debt by a Company, whether or not secured.
Default Fine	A fine, if not specified, of up to £5 per day while the default continues, under s.440 1948 Act.

Glossary of Terms and Abbreviations

Dept.	Department of Trade
E.G.M.	Extraordinary General Meeting
Extraordinary Resolution	A Resolution specified for certain very limited purposes requiring a 75% majority and (usually) 14 days notice.
Filing	Lodging forms and documents with the Registrar of Companies.
Fixed Charge	A charge on a specific asset e.g. a mortgage of land, which prevents the Company from dealing with that asset without the consent of the chargee.
Floating Charge	A security given by a Company, usually on its whole undertaking, which does not prevent the Company from dealing freely with its assets so long as it continues in business. When business stops or a Receiver is appointed the charge ceases to float and settles or crystallises, as a fixed charge, on the assets owned at that time.
Listed Company	A Company with a quotation (listing) on The Stock Exchange.
Liquidator	The officer appointed to wind up a Company in a Compulsory or Voluntary Winding-Up. The Directors must give way to him.
Majority	A majority of those who *do* vote at a meeting regardless of the total number of qualified voters.
Memorandum	The Company's external affairs document, or charter, containing its powers.
Ordinary Resolution	A Resolution passed by a simple majority; for all purposes other than those for which a Special or Extraordinary Resolution is required by the Acts or the Articles.
Private Company	A Company which restricts share transfers, limits its membership to 50, and prohibits public share issues.
Public Company	Any Company which is not private, whether or not its shares are listed (quoted).

Receiver	An Officer appointed by a holder of a debenture, such as a Floating Charge, when the Company defaults or stops business. His duty is to get in and pay what is owing to the debenture holder, *not* to Wind-Up the Company. The Directors must give way to him.
Registrar	Registrar of Companies, 55-71, City Road, London EC1Y 1BB.
Section (or s.)	Where no date or Act is stated, such references are to the 1948 Act.
Special Notice	28 Day notice *to* the Company of intention to propose certain ordinary resolutions.
Special Resolution	A resolution specified for several important matters by the Acts and requiring a 75% majority.
Table A	The specimen Articles contained in Schedule I of the 1948 Act.
Ultra Vires	Beyond the powers of the Company as stated in its Memorandum.
Voluntary Winding-Up	Winding-Up (Liquidation) of a Company after a resolution of the members, supervised by them if the Company is solvent, (Members' Vol. W/Up) and by the Creditors if not (Creditors' Vol. W/Up). In either case no application to the Court is required.

Table of Cases

Table of Cases

Table of Cases

Table of Cases

Table of Cases

Table of Cases

Table of Cases

Table of Cases

Table of Cases

Table of Cases

Chapter 1

THE COMPANY AND ITS MACHINERY

1-01 Background

This book deals with the functions, powers and duties of company directors. But before turning to the directors themselves, we should look briefly at the legal framework within which they work. What then do the directors direct? The answer, for all practical purposes, is companies limited by shares and registered under the Companies Act 1948, or one of its predecessors, going back to 1844. The Joint Stock Companies Act of that year introduced the principle of incorporation by registration which has been followed ever since. Limitation of liability was achieved by shareholders in 1855 and private companies were set apart from public companies in 1907. Company law was reformed by the Acts of 1862, 1908, 1929 and 1948 and on each occasion, the trend was towards greater disclosure by the company and greater powers of intervention by the State.

The Act of 1967 continued this trend and abolished the privilege of privacy of accounts, hitherto enjoyed by "exempt" private companies. It was not, however, a thorough-going overhaul of company law like its predecessors, but rather an *hors d'oeuvre* of those items from the Jenkins Report of 1962[1] which happened to commend themselves to the government of the day. A Bill to deal with the rest of Jenkins, and indeed to take the law a good deal further along the interventionist road, was introduced in 1973, but fell with the Heath government in 1974. However, the contents of the Bill are likely to be resurrected in the next Act and they contain significant proposals for directors, particularly in regard to "insider trading". Directors may be advised to bear them in mind, even before they are enacted, in as much as they indicate the views of the Department of Trade as to what is good practice. These provisions are therefore noted in the relevant parts of the text.

---

1. *Report of the Company Law Committee under the chairmanship of Lord Jenkins;* Cmnd. 1749 (June 1962).

1-01 Background

The two other strands of reform which are likely to be woven into the next Act, are the proposals of the European Communities[2] and those of the Labour Party[3].

1-02 Types of Company

We have said that, for all practical purposes, we are considering directors of companies limited by shares and registered under the Companies Act 1948[4]. These are not the only types of Company which can exist but they are by far the most numerous and significant and all references in this book are to such companies unless the contrary is stated. The full range of possibilities is:—

(a) *Registered companies limited by shares* in which case the liability of a member is limited to the amount, if any, unpaid on his shares[5] and which in turn are sub-divided into:

   (1) *Private Companies* i.e. those which by their *Articles of Association*

      (a) restrict the right to transfer their shares

      (b) limit their number of members (excluding employees) to fifty

   and (c) prohibit any invitation to the public to subscribe for shares or debentures[6]

   (2) *Public Companies* i.e. all those which are not Private.

(b) *Registered Unlimited Companies,* where the members' liability to contribute is unlimited[7].

(c) *Registered Companies Limited by Guarantee* where his liability is limited to the amount which he has guaranteed to contribute in the event of winding up[8].

---

2. Particularly the *5th Draft Directive* submitted by the E.E.C. Commission on 9th October 1972.

3. *The Community and the Company; Report of a Working Group of the Labour Party Industrial Policy Sub-Committee;* May 1974.

4. Strictly speaking, Companies are now governed by three primary Acts, the *Companies Acts of 1948* and *1967* and the *European Communities Act 1972* (s.9.). These Acts do not form a " code " of Company Law but merely a set of statutory rules and many of the most important principles of Company Law, e.g. as to directors' duties are to be found only in the cases.

5. s.1(2)(a), 1948 Act.

6. s.28, 1948 Act.

7. s.1(2)(c), 1948 Act.

8. s.1(2)(b), 1948 Act.

(d) *Companies* incorporated by *Royal Charter*, e.g. Hudsons Bay Company.

(e) *Companies* incorporated by *special Act of Parliament*, e.g. Transport Authorities, and other Public Corporations.

Types (d) and (e) do not concern us here and of the Registered companies, type (a) must have a share capital and types (b) and (c) may or may not, as their promotors wish. Unlimited companies have the unique privileges of exemption from filing accounts[9] and the right to repay or reduce their share capital without the consent of the Court. Guarantee companies are often members' clubs and other non-commercial institutions.

The registered limited companies on the register at 31st December 1973 were[10]:—

(a)	Public Limited Companies	14,272
(b)	Private Limited Companies	557,347

and the new registrations in 1973 were:—

(a)	Limited	64,512[11]
(b)	Unlimited	165

We are, therefore, dealing here with directors of private and public limited companies and the significant difference between such companies should be briefly looked at before we go on to consider the administrative machinery of limited companies generally.

1-03 Public and Private Companies

As we have seen, a private company is one whose *Articles* restrict transfers, limit the membership to fifty and prohibit invitations to the public to subscribe. All other companies are usually described as "public" companies, although the name is not normally used in the Acts; as far as the Acts are concerned private companies are simply a class of registered companies to which certain special provisions apply. All other companies are governed by the general provision of the Acts—as are private companies except where they are specifically excluded. Thus the Acts put the cart before the horse by treating as exceptions a group of companies which, in fact, make up

---

9. s.47, 1967 Act.
10. Annual Report of the Department of Trade, *Companies in 1973*. (Figures for England and Wales.)
11. All but one of these were Private Companies. For reasons of convenience Public Companies are, in practice, formed as Private Companies and then converted.

more than 97% of the total. Hence the machinery of the Acts, which is designed primarily for the public company, often appears unduly formal and complicated to many of the half-million private companies which use it. The solution might be a separate Act for private companies which could give them the benefits of incorporation and limited liability combined with the informality and flexibility of a partnership.

This has been done in the United States and has been hinted at by governments from time to time[11a]. In the meantime the main distinctions between public and private companies are:—

(a) The private company must contain, in its Articles, the restriction noted above.

(b) The private company is exempt from the requirements as to commencement of business, filing consents of directors, holding of a statutory meeting, and filing a statement in lieu of prospectus[12].

These requirements are also avoided, in practice, by public companies. They are incorporated as private companies and do not convert themselves until they are ready to make a public issue and to file a prospectus. The conversion is a simple process as all that is required is a Special Resolution to delete the three restrictions from the Articles. The Company thereupon becomes a public company.

(c) A private company needs only two members, a public company, seven[13].

(d) A private company need have only one director, (although he cannot also be Secretary). A public company must have two[14].

(e) Regulations as to retirement of directors at the age of seventy apply to public, but not to private companies[15].

(f) Proxies may speak at general meetings of private, but not public companies[16].

11a. White Paper, *Company Law Reform;* Cmnd. 5391 July 1973, para. 34.
12. ss.109, 181, 130 and 48, 1948 Act.
13. ss.1 and 31, 1948 Act.
14. ss.176, 177, 1948 Act.
15. s.185, 1948 Act.
16. s.136, 1948 Act.

(g) Bearer shares and share warrants cannot be issued by a private company as this would conflict with the requirement of restrictions on transfer[17].

Other requirements are applied to companies *listed* on the Stock Exchange itself and these are set out in Appendix E.

Public companies are not, of course, the same as "listed" companies. Listed companies must, by definition, be public companies since their shares must be freely transferable, but the converse is not the case. A company may become public, file its statement in lieu[18] of prospectus, and never take any steps to seek a quotation.

1-04 The Machinery of the Company

The essential components of the registered company limited by shares are:—

(a) *The Memorandum of Association,* stating the name, domicile (England or Scotland), objects, limitation of liability and authorised share capital[19], and subscribed by at least two persons[20].

(b) *Articles of Association* containing the internal regulations of the company and signed by the subscribers to the Memorandum[21]. Registration of Articles is not compulsory, as the specimen Articles known as *Table A* in Schedule 1 of the 1948 Act will apply, except as modified or excluded. However, the Articles of a private company must contain the appropriate restrictions and, in practice, Articles are always registered, even if they say no more than:

> "The Company is a private company and Part II of Table A in the First Schedule to the Companies Act 1948 shall apply to the Company".

---

17. s.28, 1948 Act.
18. s.48, 1948 Act.
19. s.12, 1948 Act.
20. s.1, 1948 Act. If the company were to be formed as a public company, it would require seven subscribers, but virtually all companies are in practice, formed as private companies. This book therefore confines itself to the incorporation procedure for private companies and the additional require-ments for public companies are disregarded. In 1973 only *one* company out of 64,117 was formed as a public company.
21. ss.6–9, 1948 Act.

Part II of Table A incorporates the regulations of Part I, with the addition of the special restrictions required for private companies. See Appendix B.

(c) *Share Capital;* the Authorised or Nominal Capital will be that stated in the Memorandum, but the *Issued* Capital need be no more than the shares (usually two) which the subscribers of the memorandum have agreed to take. Registration is effected by filing the Memorandum and Articles, a Declaration of Compliance with the requirements of the Act (Form 41), and Particulars of the Authorised Share Capital (Form PUC 1)[22] together with registration fee of £50. If all is in order the Registrar of Companies issues a *Certificate of Incorporation*[23] whereupon the company becomes a legal entity separate from its members[24].

(d) *The Members,* who own not the company but their shares in it, and who perform their functions through the medium of the *General Meeting.* However, the general meeting is not a physical manifestation of the company itself, and its rights and powers depend upon the provisions of the Acts and the Articles. The role of the general meeting vis-à-vis the directors is discussed in Chapter 3 below and it will be seen that far from being in control of the companys' affairs, the general meeting may rather be regarded as playing second fiddle to the directors for most purposes.

(e) *The Directors,* who since the Company cannot act in person, are normally entrusted with the duty of managing its affairs. "The business of the Company shall be managed by the Directors", says Article 80 of Table A, but the precise nature of their powers and duties depends upon the terms of the Articles in each case, subject to the over-riding provisions of the Companies Acts. A private company must have at least one director and a public company (unless registered before 1st November 1929) at least two[25].

(f) *The Secretary* is also a compulsory requirement of the Acts and he must not be:—

---

22. Finance Act 1973, Pt. V and Schedule 19. A further form (PUC 2 & 3) is filed when the members actually pay for the shares either at incorporation or afterwards and Capital Duty is paid at 1%.
23. s.13, 1948 Act.
24. *Salomon* v *Salomon & Co. Ltd.* [1897] A.C. 22.
25. s.176, 1948 Act.

    (a) the sole director of the company

or (b) a corporation whose sole director is also sole director of the company

or (c) sole director of a corporation which is itself the sole director of the company[26].

His position is discussed in Chapter 6.

(g) *An Auditor* must be appointed at each Annual General Meeting, although the initial appointment and subsequent casual vacancies may be filled by the directors[27]. He cannot be:—

    (a) an officer or servant of the company

or (b) the partner or employee of an officer or servant

or (c) a body corporate

or (d) a person precluded by (a) or (b) from acting as auditor of a parent, subsidiary or co-subsidiary of the Company[28].

He must be:—

    (a) a Chartered Accountant

or (b) a Certified Accountant

or (c) specially authorised by the Department of Trade[29].

It is the director's duty to check the qualifications of the Auditors, as an unqualified appointment is a nullity and the Department of Trade might then intervene and make the appointment[30]. The importance of the modern Auditor cannot be over-estimated—with Corporation Tax at 52%, the State is, in effect, a majority shareholder in every business and the qualified auditor is its watchdog, whether or not he appreciates his role as a government agent. Without the self-assessing machinery which he provides, the State would have no hope of claiming the lion's share which it now enjoys.

---

26. ss.177, 178, 1948 Act.
27. s.159, 1948 Act.
28. s.161, 1948 Act, s.2, 1967 Act.
29. s.161, 1948 Act, ss.2 and 13, 1967 Act.
30. s.159(3) 1948 Act.

(h) A *Registered Office* is required with effect either from the 14th day after incorporation, or from commencement of business whichever is the earlier[31]. The address must be in England and Wales, or in Scotland, whichever country is chosen as domicile in the Memorandum and details must be filed with the Registrar. The country of domicile cannot be changed. The purpose of the Registered Office is, of course, to provide an address to which communications and proceedings may be addressed since the company cannot be served in person. The posting of documents to the registered office is good service and a company which moves and fails to notify the Registrar, has only itself to blame if judgement is obtained against it in default[32]. The office need not be its place of business and may freely be changed on fourteen days' notice to the Registrar. The company's name must be shown outside, but there is no requirement that the Certificate of Incorporation should be displayed in the office.

(i) The *Common Seal,* along with perpetual succession, is conferred upon the newly incorporated company by s.13(2) of the 1948 Act. A seal containing a diestamped impression of the company's name is then acquired from a law stationer and is usually adopted and impressed in the minute book at the directors' first meeting. It is used for any documents, such as deeds and share-certificates, which are required to be under seal[33] and the procedure for affixing is laid down by the Articles. Table A, Article 113, requires the addition of the signatures of a director and the secretary or a second director[34]. In practice the second signatory is usually the secretary and in that case he must not also sign as Director[35]. The Board can always appoint a deputy or assistant Secretary[36].

1-05 Memorandum of Association. Name

The Memorandum and Articles are of importance to every director.

---

31. ss.107, 108, 1948 Act.
32. s.437, 1948 Act; *A/S Cathrineholm v Norequipment Trading Ltd.* [1972] 2 All E.R. 538.
33. s.32, 1948 Act.
34. Note that Article 113 does not require them to witness the affixing of the Seal, merely to *sign* the document which is sealed.
35. s.179, 1948 Act.
36. s.177, 1948 Act.

He should obtain a copy and make himself familiar with their contents as he is deemed to know what is in them[37].

The Memorandum contains five clauses[38], Name, Office, Objects, Liability and Capital. The Registered Office has already been discussed but the other clauses need more consideration.

The Name

(a) The Company has freedom of choice except that the Secretary of State for Trade (of whose Department the Registrar of Companies is a permanent officer) can refuse a name which he considers *"undesirable"*.[39] The Department's policy is set out in a practice note (c.186) which is revised from time to time and of which the current version appears in Appendix C.

(b) the name must end with the word *Limited,* unless the Department gives permission to dispense with it[40].

To obtain such permission the Company must

(1) restrict its objects to the promotion of art, science, religion, charity or "other useful object" and

(2) prohibit dividends to its members.

(c) Subject to Department of Trade approval, a Company's name may be *freely changed* by Special Resolution (75% majority) of the members[41].

(d) The name must be *displayed*[42]

(1) outside every place of business in a conspicuous position in letters easily legible,

(2) on its seal,

(3) on all business letters, notices, bills, cheques and orders.

(e) The *business letters,* order forms, etc., must also show

(1) place of registration (i.e. England (or London) or Scotland (or Edinburgh)).

(2) registered number

(3) address of registered office (if this is the only address on the stationery, the fact that it is the registered office must be stated).

---

37. Copies can always be obtained through Law Agents or direct from the Registrar of Companies, Companies House, 55-71, City Road, London EC1Y 1BB.
38. s.2, 1948 Act.
39. s.17, 1948 Act.
40. s.19, 1948 Act.
41. s.18, 1948 Act.
42. s.108, 1948 Act.

These requirements were introduced by s.9. *European Communities Act 1972* and the Department's notes on these and the other provisions of s.9. are set out in Appendix C.

(f) If the Company uses a business name *different* from its registered name, it must register it under the *Registration of Business Names Act 1916*. The forms and instructions can be obtained from the Registrar of Business Names at Companies House. His notes for guidance are in Appendix C.

There are, of course, penalties for non-compliance with any of these requirements.

1-06 Memorandum—Objects

If the director looks at the objects clause (clause 3) in his company's memorandum, he will see that it starts with the words "The objects for which the Company is established are:—". Then comes sub-clause (a) which contains a description of activities roughly corresponding to what the Company actually does. This is followed by a long series of further sub-clauses apparently giving the company power to do almost anything under the sun. This form of omnibus objects clause bears no relation to the specimen (Table B) in the First Schedule of the 1948 Act but it has been supported by the Courts[43], and is universally adopted in practice in an effort to avoid falling foul of the dreaded *Ultra Vires* rule. This was originally evolved by the Courts to protect shareholders from having their money invested in business ventures which they had not contemplated. Hence the Courts held that any transaction which was not within the terms of the objects clause or reasonably incidental thereto, was *ultra vires* and could not be enforced, either against[44] or (probably) by the Company[45]. However, its original purpose has long been lost sight of and in recent years the rule has functioned mainly as a trap for unwary third parties, enabling the Company or its liquidator to get out of paying debts freely contracted in good faith[46]. Moreover, if the members of the Company themselves wish to change the objects, it is not difficult for them to do so.[47]

43. *Cotman v Brougham* [1918] A.C. 514.
44. *Sinclair v Brougham* [1914] A.C. 398.
45. *Bell Houses Ltd. v City Wall Properties Ltd.* [1965] 3 All E.R. 427.
46. Re *Jon Beauforte* (*London*) *Ltd.* [1953] 1 All E.R. 634.
47. s.5, 1948 Act.

Jenkins (para. 42) and others have suggested amendments but it was only accession to the E.E.C. which impelled the legislature into action[48]. Section 9 of the *European Communities Act 1972,* provides that the Company can no longer raise the defence of *ultra vires* against a third party if:

(a) the third party acted "in good faith" and

(b) the transaction was "decided on by the directors".

What these expressions may mean is uncertain,[49] to say the least, but what is clear is the fact that the *ultra vires* bogey has been wounded but by no means killed. It is still of significance in relation to the Directors' powers and duties vis-à-vis their own shareholders and this is discussed in Chapter 3 below. Moreover, even in relation to third parties, it may be involved if:—

(a) the company can prove absence of good faith or

(b) if the transaction has not been "decided on by the directors" or

(c) if the third party chooses to rely on it himself. s.9 says nothing about *depriving* him of his existing rights.

1-07 Memorandum—Change of Objects

One of the absurdities of the *ultra vires* rule is the ease with which the members of the Company can change the objects if they choose to do so. Section 5 of the 1948 Act permits change of objects within fairly narrow limits, by Special Resolution (75% majority) and allows objectors with not less than 15% of the whole or any class of the issued capital to apply to the Court within 21 days for cancellation. Objection on the ground that the alteration is *outside* the limits of s.5 can be made by any shareholder however small his holding. But s.5(9) goes on to say that an alteration *cannot be questioned* on this ground unless proceedings are started within 21 days of the resolution.

If, therefore, the members are unanimous, they can change the objects to anything they like, whether within or without the grounds permitted by s.5. No one will object and after 21 days the alteration becomes impregnable. A copy of the Special Resolution and of the

---

48. The amendments had to be made in 1972 to comply with E.E.C. Directive 151, but even then they were botched and a fresh attempt was to be made in cl.5 of the abortive Companies Bill of 1973.

49. See the detailed criticism and analysis in *Gore-Browne on Companies,* supplement to 42nd Edition, p.40.

1-07 Memorandum—Change of Objects

Memorandum as altered, has to be filed within 15 days,[50] but under the E.E.C. accession statute,[51] addititional requirements as to notification of such alterations are imposed:—

(a) the Registrar must publish notice of receipt of the alteration in the London Gazette.

(b) the Company cannot "rely against other persons", on the alteration, unless it had been notified in the Gazette, or the third party had actual knowledge of it.

(c) the third party may extend his period of protection to 15 days after notification in the Gazette if he was "unavoidably prevented" from knowing of the alteration.

(d) a copy of the Memorandum of Association, as amended, must be filed within 15 days, or by 1st February 1973 where the amendment had already been made on 1st January 1973. Where the amendment consists solely of an alteration of objects, this was already a requirement of the 1948 Act[52].

These requirements of s.9 of the *European Communities Act* apply not only to alterations of objects but also to, *inter alia*,

(a) Certificates of Incorporation

(b) Alterations of other parts of the Memorandum (e.g. name or capital) or of the Articles

(c) Notice of change of directors

(d) Annual return

(e) Notice of change of registered office.

The Registrars' notes on compliance with the section are in Appendix C.

1-08 Memorandum—Liability

The liability clause of a registered limited company states: "The Liability of the members is limited"[53]. In a sense, this is superfluous, since once the separate identity of the company is established there is no reason why the members should be liable for the company's debts. Their liability, if any, is to the company itself and is limited, as one would expect, by the terms of their contract

---

50. s.143, 1948 Act; s.5(7), 1948 Act.
51. *European Communities Act 1972* s.9(3)(4)(5) and (6).
52. s.5(7), 1948 Act.
53. s.2, 1948 Act.

with the company. They have taken shares and they must therefore pay for them—hence their liability is limited to the amount unpaid on those shares. This will include a Share Premium if the shares have been allotted to them on those terms, since the premium forms part of the company's capital[54].

The only exception to the principle of limited liability derives from the rule that if the minimum membership falls below seven (public) or two (private), for more than six months, every member who knows of this is severally liable for debts contracted during that time[55].

Limited and unlimited companies may re-register as unlimited and limited respectively under the procedure provided by the 1967 Act[56]. These procedures were introduced because of the abolition of the "exempt private company" by that Act. The attitude of the legislature and of the Jenkins Committee was that limited liability was a privilege to be paid for in the form of public disclosure of one's accounts. Hence private companies were offered a simple choice—limited liability with disclosure or unlimited liability with privacy.

1-09 Memorandum—Share Capital

The Memorandum must state the amount of share capital and its division "into shares of fixed amount"[57]. Thus "no par value" shares, are not permitted, though often recommended[58]. The amount stated in the memorandum is, of course, the *authorised* or *nominal* capital, and is simply the amount which the company is authorised to issue. It must be distinguished from:—

(a) *Issued* Capital—that part of the authorised capital actually issued to members

(b) *Paid-up* Capital—that part of the issued capital which has actually been paid for. It is this alone which attracts the 1% Capital Duty under the Finance Act 1973.

(c) *Uncalled* Capital—that part of the issued Capital not yet called up.

---

54. s.56, 1948 Act.
55. s.31, 1948 Act.
56. ss.43, 44, 1967 Act.
57. s.2(4), 1948 Act.
58. Jenkins Committee, para 34.

(d) *Reserve* Capital—that part of the uncalled Capital which the company has resolved not to call up except on winding-up[59]. Not to be confused with *Capital Reserves* which are reserves set aside in the balance sheet as not being available for dividend.

(e) *Loan* Capital—which is not capital at all, but borrowings, often secured by debentures. The debenture-holders are not members but creditors of the company and the borrowings do not form part of the company's capital.

(f) *Preference* Capital—shares issued or unissued, with priority over the ordinary shares as to dividend and/or capital. In practice often regarded as analogous to debentures, especially as they may be redeemable[60], but totally different in legal terms in that their holders are members of the company, whose holdings form part of the company's capital. Their security is in all respects, inferior to that of the debenture holders, although they may have rights to participate in a surplus on winding-up.

(g) *Stock*—is simply fully paid issued shares consolidated and expressed as units of currency. Conversion into stock is likely to be abolished in the next Companies Act[60a].

Occasionally the Memorandum also divides the shares into classes, preferential, ordinary, deferred, etc., and sets out their rights, but this is more usually done in the Articles.

Alterations of the Capital clause are of two kinds:—

(a) *Increase of Capital,* sub-division, conversion into stock or consolidation may be simply effected by Ordinary Resolution of the members (bare majority)[61]. The Resolution and a Notice of Increase is filed within 15 days[62].

(b) *Reduction of Capital,* is a more drastic step and is closely supervised since it conflicts with one of the fundamental principles of Company Law—the preservation of the Company's Capital for the benefit of the creditors. Reduction is only possible if:—

---

59. s.60, 1948 Act.
60. s.58, 1948 Act.
60a. cl.34 *Companies Bill* 1973.
61. s.61, 1948 Act and Art.44, Table A.
62. s.63, 1948 Act.

(a) authorised by the Articles as under Article 46, Table A, and

(b) effected by Special Resolution (75% majority) and

(c) confirmed by the Court.

If the proposed reduction affects creditors, as when capital is being returned to shareholders, then they have the right to object and the Court will want to see them protected before confirming the reduction[63].

1-10 Articles of Association—Generally

While the memorandum regulates the Company's dealings with the outside world and may be described as its Charter, the Articles control its internal affairs and are more in the nature of Bye-Laws. For most purposes they are of more daily concern to the director than the Memorandum and he should take particular note of their contents. Companies have almost complete freedom in their choice of Articles and from them alone can the director ascertain his powers and the procedures which he must follow. He will usually find that his company, if public or listed, will have a complete set of special Articles drafted to meet its specific requirements. If it is a private company, however, it is likely to adopt Part II Table A[64] with some modifications.

Table A is set out in Appendix B and the Director will usually find that the greater part of it applies to his company but that certain of its Articles have been expressly excluded and replaced with special ones. He can assume that all of the Articles in Table A apply except where they are *specifically excluded* by his own Articles[65].

The director should, however, note the date of incorporation of his company which is usually stated on the front cover of the Memorandum and Articles. If it is earlier than 1st July 1948[66] then Table A in the preceding Companies Act (1929) will apply to his company unless excluded. This does not differ greatly from the 1948 Table A, but there are some differences, for example, as to capitalisation of reserves and issue of bonus shares, and he should

---

63. *Re Lucania Temperance Billiard Halls (London) Ltd.* [1965] 3 All E.R. 879.
64. Specimen Articles in Schedule 1, 1948 Act (See also Appendix B2). Table A, Pt. II incorporates the whole of Part I except for Articles 24 and 53.
65. s.8(2), 1948 Act.
66. s.8(2), 1948 Act.

obtain the 1929 Table A from the law stationers. In all cases, therefore, a company which does not exclude Table A altogether, is governed by that version of Table A which was in force at the date of its incorporation. The only exception is where the Company has subsequently passed a Special Resolution adopting all or part of a later version. In that case there should be a copy of the Special Resolution in the Articles and the amendment should be incorporated in the text. Unfortunately, this is not always done, and the newly appointed director should, in any event, make a company search to show him all the resolutions which have been passed and any other information on his company's file. The full table of relevant dates for Table A is as follows:—

Date of Incorporation	*Table A applies in the Companies Act of:*
From 1st July 1948 to the present	1948
From 1st Nov. 1929 to 30th June 1948	1929
From 1st April 1909 to 31st Oct. 1929	1908
From 1st Oct. 1906 to 31st March 1909	S.R.80.596/L15
From 1862 to 30th Sept. 1906	1862

A pre-1948 company which is changing its Articles should normally take the opportunity of excluding the old version of Table A entirely and adopting all or part of the current version.

1-11 Articles of Association—Features

The Articles govern almost every aspect of the directors' activities and the relevant provisions of Table A and other common articles are noted throughout the text. However, certain characteristic features may usefully be summarised:—

(a) The Articles (and Memorandum) have the effect of a *covenant or contract, signed and sealed* by every member[66a].

(b) The director as such, is not a party to the contract but it *can be enforced*

   (i) by the company against any member, e.g. to refer a dispute to arbitration[67].

66a. s.20, 1948 Act.
67. *Hickman v Kent or Romney Marsh Sheep-Breeders Ass.* [1915] 1 Ch. 881.

    (ii) by any member against the company, e.g. to compel the company to record his vote[68].

    (iii) by one member against another, e.g. to compel another member to buy his shares[69].

(c) The Articles *do not themselves form a contract* with the director *qua* director, but they may form the basis of the director's service contract and provide evidence of its terms, e.g. as to salary[70]. As such they are always liable to alteration by the members (see below).

(d) The Articles are *freely alterable* by Special Resolution of the members (75% majority)[71], subject to certain restrictions:—

    (i) The alteration must not conflict with the Memorandum. This is not likely to occur, in any event, with the modern form of memorandum which does not contain class rights or anything beyond the requirements of the Act.

    (ii) The alteration is subject to the terms of the 1948 Act, e.g. (a) s.22—it must not increase a member's liability without his consent.

        (b) s.72—it must not vary class rights without following the procedure of the section which gives the right to object to 15% of the class members.

        (c) s.210—it must not conflict with any alteration made by the Court under the procedure provided by this section for relief against oppression.

    (iii) alteration must be *bona fide* for the benefit of the company as a whole, i.e. not discriminatory against a particular group of shareholders[72], nor "malicious" in intent[73]. However, the burden of proof of bad faith is heavy and in most of the cases the objector has failed to discharge it. The fact that the majority will, in practice, be the beneficiaries of the alteration is not enough[72], and the Courts have been reluctant to

---

68. *Pender v Lushington* [1877] 6 Ch. D.70.
69. *Rayfield v Hands* [1958] 2 All E.R. 194.
70. *e.p. Beckwith* [1898] 1 Ch. 324.
71. s.10, 1948 Act.
72. *Greenhalgh v Arderne Cinemas Ltd.*]1950] 2 All E.R. 1120.
73. *Sidebottom v Kershaw Leese & Co.* [1920] 1 Ch. 154.

overturn a majority vote even where the relative voting power of the objectors is being diminished[74].

(iv) an alteration may be a breach of contract with a third party, e.g. where it conflicts with a managing director's service agreement. He cannot prevent the alteration but he is entitled to damages[75].

The Memorandum and Articles (and any alterations) are on the file at Companies House, and may be inspected and copied by anyone[76].

1-12 The Role of the Director

Where, then, does the director stand on this corporate stage and what part does he perform? In fact, he plays several parts. The company is an artificial person but it cannot function without human agents. Those agents are the directors, and as company law evolved at a comparatively late stage in the history of English law, elements from other branches of the law were called in aid to define an office which was unique and which did not fit entirely within any of them.

These elements are discussed in the text but they include:—

(a) *Agency:* The director is acting not on his own behalf but on that of the company. Therefore, he is, in some respects, an *Agent* and has some of the rights and duties which characterise the Principal and Agent relationship, e.g.

(i) On contracts within his authority, it is normally the company and not the director who is liable[77].

(ii) if he exceeds his authority he may be liable to a third party for breach of warranty of authority[78].

(iii) like other agents he must account to his principal for any personal profit made by him out of his position[79].

---

74. *Rights & Issues Investment Trust Ltd. v Stylo Shoes Ltd.* [1964] 3 All E.R. 628.
75. *Southern Foundries Ltd. v Shirlaw* [1940] 2 All E.R. 445.
76. s.426, 1948 Act. This applies to all documents kept by the Registrar. The search fee is still 5p. The copying fee is also still 2½p per folio of 72 words but this is disregarded in practice as the Registrar supplies photocopies and charges accordingly.
77. *Elkington & Co. v Hurter* [1892] 2 Ch. 452.
78. *Firbank's Exors v Humphreys* [1886] 18 Q.B.D. 54.
79. *Industrial Development Consultants Ltd. v Cooley* [1972] 2 All E.R. 86.

And yet he differs from other agents in that he himself, in conjunction with his co-directors, is in control of the affairs of his own principal, and that principal is itself restricted in its freedom of action by the *ultra vires* rule.

(b) *Trusteeship:* Directors are often described as Trustees and this is certainly true in the sense that

(i) any assets in their hands are held on trust for the company[80].

(ii) their powers must be exercised for the benefit of the company, e.g. they must not issue shares for the purpose of maintaining their control[81].

(iii) they are in a fiduciary position and their personal interests must not conflict with their duties to the company[82].

It will be noted that their beneficiaries are not the members but the company itself[83]. But they differ from Trustees in the conventional sense in that:

(i) the trust property is not vested in them, they are agents and not principals.

(ii) their duties of management usually involve the running of what must, in some ways, be a speculative business.

(iii) their duties of skill and care are probably lower than those of ordinary Trustees, whose function is to hold and administer investments.

(c) *Master and Servant:* A non-executive director who confines his role to that of attending board meetings is not an employee[84] but a full time executive director is employed by the company and for many purposes his position is similar to that of other employees. This is envisaged by the 1948 Act itself which uses the words "any director holding a salaried *employment* or office in the company" in s.54(1)(b). In this situation the director is wearing two hats, one as a member of the board and one as an employee of the board. It is the

---

80. *Selangor United Rubber Estates Ltd. v Cradock (No.3)* [1968] 2 All E.R. 1073.
81. *Piercy v S. Mills & Co. Ltd.* [1920] 1 Ch. 77.
82. *Scottish C.W.S. Ltd. v Meyer* [1958] 3 All E.R. 66.
83. *Percival v Wright* [1902] 2 Ch. 421.
84. *Boulting v A.C.T.A.T.* [1963] 1 All E.R. 716.
85. *Re Lee, Behrens & Co.* [1932] 2 Ch. 46.

failure to keep these two capacities separate which has led to confusion in some of the cases.

(d) *Independent Contractor:* In so far as the director is rendering services for reward he must accept the burden of skill and care which falls on all such persons. In his case the level of the duty was pitched very low in the leading authority[86], but it has probably risen in recent years, particularly where highly qualified directors are appointed to perform executive duties. Thus, there seems no reason why a Chartered Accountant appointed as Finance Director should not be expected to show the same objective standard of skill and care as if he were engaged to do the work as a private practitioner.

1-13 Who are the Directors?

The appointment of directors is discussed in the next chapter but it must be borne in mind that the word is not confined to those who have been properly appointed. It may, in fact, have several meanings:—

(a) A person duly appointed in accordance with the Articles and not subsequently disqualified by any provision in the Articles. He is a director for all purposes.

(b) A person appointed, but with some defect in his appointment; so far as third persons are concerned his acts are validated by s.180 of the 1948 Act.

(c) A person never appointed at all, either properly or improperly, but nevertheless, performing the functions of a director. This *de facto* director is converted into a director for the purposes of the 1948 Act, by s.455:—"director includes any person occupying the position of director by whatever name called." The far-reaching consequences of these provisions should not be underestimated. Their effect is that such a person incurs all the responsibilities and penalties imposed by the Act while at the same time having none of the authority of a proper appointment. Hence, he may find himself liable not only to statutory penalties and to third parties, but also to the company itself for inter-meddling in its affairs.

---

86. *Re City Equitable Fire Insurance Co. Ltd.* [1925] Ch. 407.

These definitions of the word "director" have nothing to do with the filing of notice of the appointment with the Registrar.[86a] Status as a director is not dependent upon such filing—failure to comply is an offence punishable by a default fine (£5 per day[87]) but it does not invalidate the appointment. The presence or absence of the director's name on the company's file may, however, be relevant to the question of whether a person has been "held out" as a director to third parties[88]. Note that s.200 offers a further definition of a "constructive" director for the purposes of that section—namely "a person in accordance with whose directions or instructions the directors of a company are accustomed to act"[89].

1-14 Who are the Officers?

The word "officer" will often be found in the Acts when a person is being fixed with liability for company offences. Thus s.200, 1948 Act, requiring registration of Directors and Secretaries, says that "the company and *every officer* of the company who is in default shall be liable to a default fine". This is the characteristic language employed by the Act for the enforcement of its requirements. Several points may be noted:—

(a) s.455 of the 1948 Act, provides that "officer includes" a *director, manager* or *secretary*. Thus the definition is not exhaustive but will inevitably comprise all those engaged in management at a senior level, whatever they may be called. An auditor is an "officer" for some purposes but not for others but normally a person employed as an independent professional such as a Solicitor or Accountant, does not fall within the definition[90].

(b) How then does an officer become liable to criminal proceedings and a default fine? He does so, if he "knowingly and wilfully authorises or permits the default refusal or contravention mentioned in the enactment"[91].

(c) What is the default fine itself? Unless some specific penalty is mentioned in the relevant sections, the fine is not more than £5 per day, for as long as the default continues[92].

86a. s.200(4), 1948 Act.
87. s.440, 1948 Act.
88. See Chapter 3 below (para 3–15).
89. s.200(9)(a).
90. *Carter's Case* (1886) 31 Ch. D.496.
91. s.440(2) 1948 Act.
92. s.440 (1), 1948 Act.

Chapter 2

APPOINTMENT OF DIRECTORS

2-01 Articles Decide

A Company, like any other artificial creature, can function only through its human agents, and those agents are "Directors", by whatever name they may be called[1]. How, therefore, are they appointed and by whom? The answer lies in the Articles of Association, as English Law gives almost complete freedom to the promoters of a Company in their choice of machinery for this purpose. The only exception is where two or more directors are to be proposed for election to a public Company[2]. Thus the Act does not say that Directors must be appointed by the Members in general meeting, although it does say that they may always be *removed* in this way, no matter what the Articles may provide[3]. The enquirer must, therefore, look at the Articles and what he is likely to find is summarised below.

2-02 Appointment of First Directors

The machinery for appointing the first directors is likely to be one of the following:—

(a) *Nominated by Subscribers*

   Article 75 of Table A provides that they will be appointed in writing by the Subscribers of the Memorandum or a majority of them and that their number will be decided likewise. This is, perhaps, the procedure most commonly found in practice. If the article does not refer to a majority of the subscribers, they must all sign the appointment[4]. In practice

---

1. s.455, 1948 Act.
2. s.183, 1948 Act see below.
3. s.184, 1948 Act.
4. *Re Great Northern Salt Co.* (1890) 44 Ch. D.472.

this is likely to happen in any event as there are usually two subscribers.

(b) *Named in the Articles*

The Articles themselves may name the first directors (and the Secretary) and in that event their appointment dates from the incorporation of the Company.

(c) *Appointed by the First Meeting of Members*

If the Articles are silent, the first meeting of members can appoint directors. The subscribers become members *ipso facto* on incorporation[5] and, although the Act does not say so, they can appoint directors by a bare majority on an ordinary resolution[6].

Articles 92 and 97 of Table A expressly provide for the appointment of directors by ordinary resolution of the members and this is the general practice, unless the Articles contain special provisions of the type illustrated below.

(d) *Special Provision in the Articles*

The Articles can provide for any other procedure as an alternative to Article 75 of Table A. Thus they may allow the Directors to be nominated in writing by some specified person or company. The latter would be appropriate to the case where a Company was forming a subsidiary and wanted to control appointments of directors without having to hold meetings. In such cases the nominee takes office immediately by virtue of the nomination itself[7].

2-03 Appointment of Subsequent Directors

When the first board has been appointed and the company is a going concern, subsequent appointments are again governed by the Articles, with one exception. This is s.183 of the 1948 Act which provides that two or more directors of a *public* company cannot be proposed by a single resolution without unanimous consent.

The following are examples of Provisions found in Company Articles:—

---

5. s.26, 1948 Act.
6. *York Tramways v Willows* (1882) 8 Q.B.D. 685.
7. *British Murac Syndicate v Alperton Rubber Co.* [1915] 2 Ch. 186.

(a) *Appointment by Ordinary Resolution of Members in General Meeting*

Article 97 of Table A provides that:—

> "the Company in general meeting may appoint any person to be a director either to fill a casual vacancy or as an additional Director".

The Article does not specify an ordinary resolution but this is implied from the absence of a reference to any other type of resolution. Moreover ordinary resolutions are expressly prescribed by this Part of Table A for other purposes, e.g.:—

> Where a dismissed director is replaced (Art. 97), or where the number of directors is increased, or reduced (Art. 94).

This is the procedure most commonly found in practice, and the ordinary resolution requires a bare majority of those entitled to vote and *who do vote* at a general meeting of the Company. This does not mean that specially loaded voting rights may not be exercised on such a resolution. They are as permissible here as on other matters[8].

2-05

(b) *Restrictions on the Members' Right to Appoint*

Article 97 is usually accompanied by Article 93 which is intended to prevent the members from giving too much of a shock to the Board at General Meetings. Article 93 provides that no-one (except retiring directors or nominees of the Board itself) shall be proposed for appointment unless notice of the proposal signed by a member and by the prospective director, has been left with the Company at least three days (and not more than twenty-one) before the meeting.

For Companies "listed" on the Stock Exchange, certain provisions must be included in the Articles and these are set out in Appendix E. Amongst them is a requirement that the minimum period for notice under Art. 93 of Table A, should be seven rather than three days[9].

Public Companies are subject to the additional restriction of s.183 whereby two or more Directors must not be proposed by

---

8. *Re N.F.U. Development Trust Limited* [1972] 1 W.L.R. 1548.
9. *Stock Exchange Requirements: Sched. VII* Para. D.5.

a single resolution unless this is agreed unanimously by the Meeting. Thus the members cannot be presented with a situation where they have to choose all or none.

Although an appointment in contravention of s.183 is void, acts done in good faith by the Director may be validated by s.180 (see para 2-17 below).

2-06

(c) *Nomination by Specified Parties*

The Articles (although not Table A) sometimes provide that the majority may appoint (and remove) Directors in writing. This may be useful where a Company is a subsidiary or there are very few members so that there may be inconvenience or difficulty in holding meetings. Similar provisions can be made for the right of holders of specific blocks of shares to nominate a proportion of the Board. Cumulative voting rights of this type are common in the United States where they ensure that minorities have a voice on the Board. They are unknown to English Company Law, where in the absence of special Articles, 51 % of the members can appoint 100 % of the Board.

There is no reason, however, why such rights should not be given by the Articles and there is much to be said for the greater use of such rights. For example in the typical case of an "incorporated partnership" with two or three equal share-holders, one party may be denied representation on the Board if the other or others choose to absent themselves from meetings or succeed in voting down his nominee. The only remedy is then an expensive, protracted and uncertain expedition to the Chancery Division[10]. This could be avoided if the Articles gave to each party the right to appoint his specified number of representatives, in writing.

2-07

(d) *Appointment by the Directors*

Article 95 of Table A, which is useful and is normally adopted, enables the Directors (by a majority vote):—

---

10. *Re Lundie Bros. Ltd.* [1965] 2 All E.R. 692. *Re Westbourne Galleries Ltd.* [1972] 2 All E.R. 492.

    (i)   to fill casual vacancies

    (ii) to add to the Board

They must not exceed the maximum number specified by the Articles and their nominees retire at the next A.G.M. when they may be re-elected. They are not counted in the number of Directors who retire by rotation in the usual way, (Article 89). Public Companies must provide for such retirement and submission for re-election by the members at the next A.G.M.[11]

The power to fill casual vacancies does not apply to retirement by rotation or by effluxion of time as this cannot be "casual", but there is nothing to prevent the Board from making an appointment under their power to add to their number, if the General Meeting does not elect. (Article 95, Table A.)

There is nothing to prevent the Articles from giving the Directors the sole power to make appointments, i.e. to the exclusion of the General Meeting, but a residuary power remains with the members and such an Article will not take away their powers at all unless it so provides in the clearest terms[12].

2-08

(e) *Appointment of Successors or Alternative Directors*

There are three possibilities to be considered here:—

    (i)   The Articles or any agreement may (although not commonly) allow a Director to *assign* his office. In that case the assignment is of no effect until approved by a special resolution (75% majority) of the Company (s.204, 1948 Act). This section overrides any agreement or Article to the contrary.

    (ii) likewise an Article may allow a Director to nominate his *successor*.

If this may properly be construed as something other than an assignment, s.204 would not apply.

---

11. *Stock Exchange Requirements Sched. VII* Pt. A. Para D3
12. *Worcester Corsetry v Witting* [1936] Ch. 640.

(iii) the Articles may allow a Director to appoint an *Alternative* to act in his absence. This is certainly not affected by s.204 and is a useful provision in the typical private company where the Directors are the proprietors. It is not, however, in Table A and a clearly worded Article will be required.

N.B. None of these powers are appropriate to Public Companies where, in any event, the Members must have the power to remove any Director at any time by Ordinary Resolution[13].

2-09 Number of Directors

(a) *The Companies Act 1948* requires a minimum of *two* for a Public Company and *one* for a Private Company s.176.

(b) Within these requirements the *Articles* are free to make any provisions which may be desired and whether as to maximum or minimum or both. Table A provides as follows:—

  (i) that the number (and names) shall first be determined in writing by the subscribers of the Memorandum or a majority of them.

Article 75

  (ii) that thereafter the number may be increased or reduced by *ordinary resolution* of the members, i.e. the power is out of the hands of the Directors themselves.

Article 94

(c) *An alternative* form of Article specifies both a maximum and minimum number of Directors but there is little to be said in its favour unless the members wish to restrict the powers of the Board. As in the case of qualification shares, the main effect of such an Article is to provide an unnecessary stumbling block if it is noticed, or an embarrassment if it is overlooked.

(d) *Effect of non-compliance* with such Articles is as follows:—

  (i) If there are too many Directors, the appointments of the supernumaries are void but their acts done in good faith may be valid under s.180. On discovering the defect they must cease to act until the permitted number is increased and they are reappointed.

---

13. *Stock Exchange Requirements. Sched. VII* Part A. Para D4.

(ii) If there are *too few*, e.g. because the number falls below the minimum, Article 100 of Table A (which is usually adopted) allows the survivors to act for the purpose of increasing their number or calling a General Meeting, *but for no other purpose.* Innocent third parties may not be prejudiced[14].

N.B. Where a private company has only one Director, he cannot also be Secretary (s.177(1)), and there is no doubt that the idea of one-man management is viewed with some disfavour. Private Companies subject to the *Protection of Depositors Act 1963* must have two Directors and the privilege of having a single Director is likely to be abolished entirely in the future[15].

2-10 Who can be a Director?

Generally, anyone unless he is disqualified for some specific reason. Thus, there is no qualification imposed by the law itself and therefore the following (amongst others) can be appointed Directors unless the Articles forbid it:—

(a) a minor, i.e. a person aged less than 18

(b) another Company

(c) a person of unsound mind

(d) an alien

(e) a Director of another Company

(f) a non-member

(g) the Secretary (except where there is only one Director).

2-11 Disqualified by Law

The following are disqualified by the Law itself:—

(a) *an undischarged bankrupt,* unless authorised by the Court[16]. He is also prohibited from taking part in the management, directly or indirectly, so cannot escape this section by hiding behind his wife. Penalty: two years or £500 fine or both.

---

14. *British Asbestos Co. v Boyd* [1903] 2 Ch. 439.
15. See Clause 41 of the *Companies Bill 1973*.
16. s.187, 1948 Act.

(b) *a person prohibited by the Court*[17]. Such an order (for a period not exceeding five years) can be made against anyone convicted of a company offence or found guilty of fraud or misconduct in connection with a Company. The offender cannot then act as a Director or participate in management without leave of the Court. Penalty: two years or £500 fine or both.

  Note that there is a loophole here as the period runs from the date of *conviction* and not from release from prison[18]. Thus the offender could serve his disqualification period while sitting peacefully in his cell, and be free to promote and manage companies as soon as he emerges from the prison gates.

(c) *The Auditor of the Company* or of any Company within its group may not also be a Director, Secretary or employee of the Company[18a]. Nor may he be the partner or employee of such a person[19].

(d) the *Secretary cannot* be *Sole* Director of a private company[20]; and where something (such as the execution of a document) has to be done by the Director and the Secretary, the same person cannot act in both capacities.

(e) *A Clergyman* cannot be a Director[21]

(f) *A person of seventy years* or more cannot be appointed Director of a *Public* Company (or of its subsidiary) unless:—

  (i) the Articles provide otherwise

  or (ii) the appointment is approved in general meeting by an ordinary resolution of which "special notice", stating his age, has been given (s.185). For "special notice", which is a technical term, see Chapter 7 below.

2-12 Disqualified by the Articles

The Articles can impose any qualification that may be desired such as that a Director must be a shareholder or teetotal or

---

17. s.188, 1948 Act.
18. *R v Bradley* [1961] 1 All E.R. 669.
18a. s.161, 1948 Act.
19. s.161, (2)(b).
20. s.178, 1948 Act.
21. s.29. *Pluralities Act 1838.*

2-12 Disqualified by the Articles

British[22].   One must bear in mind that such qualifications cannot necessarily be overridden by the majority.   51 % will serve to appoint a Director but 75 % is required to alter the Articles.

2-13 Qualification Shares

Typical requirements in the Articles are those relating to *Share Qualification.*

No such qualification is imposed by Table A, or by the Act itself and there is little to be said in favour of such a requirement. Where it is found in the Articles, it is usually nominal, and then serves no purpose except as a nuisance.   This is particularly so in Private Companies where a qualification share is allotted to an employee director and it is left outstanding after his employment has ceased.   In the case of Public Companies, qualification shares are not a requirement of the Stock Exchange.

Table A (Article 77) provides that there is *no* shareholding qualification unless fixed by general meeting (i.e. by a bare majority), but where such a qualification is fixed or specified in the Articles, the position is as follows:—

(a) *Two months' grace.*   The Director must have his qualification Shares within a period of not more than two months[23]. *A shorter* period may be specified by the Articles, but if not, the two months' period applies. The period runs from the date of appointment, and in the case of a Poll, this is the date when the Poll is ascertained and not the date of the meeting[24].

(b) *Effect of Failure to Qualify.*   Where qualification Shares are required and the Director either fails to acquire them within the specified period (not exceeding two months) or ceases at any time to hold them, he forthwith *vacates office* (s.182(3)). The Articles (Table A, Art. 88(a)) usually repeat this provision.

(c) *Effect of Vacation of Office under s.182(3).*   Where a Director vacates office because of s.182 the effect is as follows:—

  (i)   If he continues to act as Director he is liable to a fine of £5 per day during the default (s.182(5)).

22. *Govt. Stock Co. v Christopher* [1956] 1 All E.R. 490.
23. s.182, 1948 Act.
24. *Holmes v Keyes* [1958] 2 All E.R. 129.

(ii) If he acts inadvertently in this way the Court can relieve him from liability under s.448[25].

(iii) his contract to serve as Managing Director at a salary is invalidated, but he may have a claim on a *quantum meruit* for fair remuneration for work actually done in that capacity[26].

(iv) In the absence of a quantum meruit claim he has no right to Director's remuneration under the Articles and may have to repay what he has received[27].

(v) Acts done *before* disqualification remain valid[28].

(vi) Acts done *after* disqualification by a person who continues to be held out as and to act as a *de facto* Director are valid as regards both third parties and members (s.180)[29], unless they know of the defect[30].

(vii) The disqualified Director cannot be reappointed until he has his qualification shares (s.182(4)).

2-14 Meaning of Share Qualification

This depends upon the Articles although s.182(2) provides that bearer shares will not suffice. Thus the Director must be on the Register.

The following points have been decided and will apply in the absence of contrary provisions in the Article:—

(a) A *joint* holding will qualify[31].

(b) A *Trustee* holding e.g. under a settlement will qualify even if the Articles require a holding "in his own right", since the company does not recognise the Trust, and can safely treat him as the owner[32].

(c) Conversely a purely equitable right to the shares will not suffice if someone else's name is on the Register[33].

---

25. *Re Barry & Staines Linoleum* [1934] Ch. 227.
26. *Craven-Ellis v Canons Ltd.* [1936] 2 All E.R. 1066.
27. *Brown & Green Ltd. v Hays* (1920) 36 T.L.R. 330.
28. *Re International Cable Co.* (1892) 66 L.T. 253.
29. *Dawson v African Consolidated Land & Trading Co.* [1898] 1 Ch. 6.
30. *Morris v Kanssen* [1946] A.C. 459.
31. *Grundy v Briggs* [1910] 1 Ch. 444.
32. *Sutton v English & Colonial Produce Co.* [1902] 2 Ch. 502.
33. *Spencer v Kennedy* [1926]Ch. 125.

(d) A *Representative* holding e.g. as Executor or Liquidator will not qualify since here the Company must recognise the representative capacity[34].

(e) The source of the qualification shares does not matter[35], but if they are a gift from a promoter or vendor there may be a liability for breach of trust[36].

(f) The cost of the shares *must not be lent* or given to the Director by the Company[37]; although there is no objection to the provision of qualification shares in a subsidiary, since here they are held on trust for the parent and the director thus receives no financial benefit. In these circumstances a director normally signs a Declaration of Trust.

(g) Where the share qualification is increased, the Director is not thereby disqualified but must obtain his increased holding within a reasonable time[38].

(h) Where the Articles require the qualification *before* taking office, e.g. "no person shall be appointed *unless* etc.", the Director cannot take advantage of the period of grace[39], but the period will apply unless the Articles specifically exclude it[40].

(i) S.181 requires, *inter alia,* that qualification shares must be taken or guaranteed before a Director is appointed or advertised in a Prospectus of certain public Companies. However, the Section has been nullified in practice, as it does *not apply* to a company which was private *before* it was public—and almost all public Companies are now formed in this way.

The 1973 Companies Bill was to have repealed the Section together with other redundant provisions such as s.109 (Trading Certificate) and s.130 (Statutory Meeting).

2-15 Other Disqualifications in the Articles

Table A, Article 88 removes a Director from office on the occurrence of any of the following events:—

---

34. *Boschoek Proprietary Co. v Fuke* [1906] 1 Ch. 148.
35. *Re Hercynia Copper Co.* [1894] 2 Ch. 403.
36. *Re London & S.W. Canal* [1911] 1 Ch. 346.
37. ss.54 and 190, 1948 Act.
38. *Molineaux v London Birmingham & Manchester Insurance Co.* [1902] 2 K.B. 589.
39. *Channel Collieries Trust v Dover Railway Co.* [1914] 2 Ch. 506.
40. *Re International Cable Co.* (1892) 66 L.T. 253.

(a) failure to obtain or keep *qualification shares* under s.182 (discussed above), or passing the A.G.M. after reaching the retirement age of seventy under s.185. This Section only applies to Public Companies and only to them if their Articles do not exclude it.

(b) becoming *bankrupt* or making an arrangement with creditors. Becoming bankrupt implies the making of an Adjudication Order and the undischarged bankrupt is in any case prohibited from acting by s.187. The making of an arrangement with Creditors may be an Act of Bankruptcy under s.1(i)(a) *Bankruptcy Act 1914* but does not necessarily result in Bankruptcy proceedings. In this respect, therefore, Article 88 (b) goes beyond s.187.

(c) *being prohibited* by order of the Court under s.188, because of Company fraud or misconduct. See para 2-11 above.

(d) becoming of *unsound mind*

(e) *resigning* by notice in writing

(f) *being* absent from Board Meetings without permission, for more than six months.

Other grounds for disqualification are often found in the Articles and these are discussed in Chapter 9.

The effect of all these Articles is automatic removal from office and thus the purported appointment of a disqualified person would be a fruitless exercise. The Board cannot waive the disqualification[41].

2-16 Aliens

English Company Law imposes no restrictions on the appointment of an alien as Director. However, his nationality must be stated on

(a) the Register of Directors, (s.200(2)(a)).

(b) the particulars filed with the Registrar of Companies, (s.200(4)), and

(c) letterheads catalogues etc. (s.201.(1)) on which the Company's name appears, unless he is an E.E.C. National in which case he is exempted by the *Companies (Disclosure etc.) Order 1974.*

41. *Re Bodega Co.* [1904] 1 Ch. 276.

In his capacity as an employee he must, of course, comply with the regulations in force from time to time, which govern the right of aliens to work in the U.K. If he is a shareholder, he must also comply with the Exchange Control regulations, if resident outside the scheduled Territories.

2-17 Defects in Appointment

A director must:—

(a) have been properly appointed and

(b) not have been subsequently disqualified by the operation of the Articles or the Law.

If, for any reason, he does not satisfy these requirements the question arises of his own position and whether third parties can rely on his acts.

Several factors may be relevant;

(a) **S.180 1948 Act,** provides that "the acts of a director or manager shall be valid notwithstanding any defect that may afterwards be discovered in his appointment or qualification". Thus a technical defect such as a Director's temporary parting with his qualification shares will not invalidate a call made by a Board of which he was an essential member[42]. However, in *Morris v. Kanssen*[43] the House of Lords restricted the effect of the section by drawing a rather difficult distinction between a defective appointment on the one hand (to which s.180 would apply), and a situation where there is "no appointment at all", on the other. This seems to mean that s.180 will only help a third party where the defect is technical or procedural (such as insufficient notice of the meeting[44], but one must bear in mind that the activities in *Morris v. Kanssen* were of a fraudulent nature and the third party who sought to rely on s.180 knew that there was something wrong. This is very different from the situation where the third party is unaware of the defect and in those cases the Court would probably help him even though the Director was, technically, out of office at the time he acted[45].

42. *Dawson v African Land Co.* [1898] 1 Ch. 6.
43. *Morris v Kanssen* [1946] A.C. 459.
44. *Briton Medical Life Association v Jones* (1889) 61 L.T. 384.
45. *British Asbestos Co. v Boyd* [1903] 2 Ch. 439.

(b) *Article 105* of Table A contains a similar provision and it should be noted that both Article 105 and s.180 apply to defects "afterwards" discovered. This means that the existence of the *defect* itself must not be known at the time of the appointment, although the parties may have known of the *facts* which cause the defect[46].

(c) *Minutes* recording the appointment at General or Board Meetings are regarded as valid until the contrary is proved, (s.145(3)).

(d) Quite apart from s.180, if the position of an innocent third party is that he is dealing with persons who are *held out* by the Company as Directors, he may hold the Company responsible for their acts on the normal principles of Agency[47].

(e) Such a *de facto* Director is likewise subject to all the duties and liabilities of a properly appointed Director under the provisions of s.455:— "any person occupying the position of director by whatever name called."[48]

(f) An injunction may be obtained to prevent the *de facto* Director from continuing to act[49].

(g) The acts of the Director or of the meetings which he attended may be ratified by a properly constituted Board or Meeting[50].

(h) The defect in the appointment may be the fact that the Director himself has *not consented to* it. Strangely enough, this is an eventuality which the Act has not considered as there is no requirement for formal consent before appointment (except under s.182 which never applies). Nor does the new Director have to sign the Register or the notification to the Registrar. Common sense requires, however, that a person must not be appointed to an office without his consent, and in such circumstances he would be treated as *renouncing* office when he discovered it, even though his appointment satisfied all the requirements of the Act and the Articles.

46. *Channel Collieries Trust v Dover Railway Co.* [1914] 2 Ch. 506.
47. *Hely-Hutchinson v Brayhead Limited* [1968] 1 Q.B. 549.
48. *Re New Par Consols (No. 1)* [1898] 1 Q.B. 573.
49. *Cheshire v Gordon Hotels* [1953] Times 13th Feb.
50. *Re Portuguese Copper Mines* [1890] 42 Ch.D. 160.

2-17 Defects in Appointment

(i) Following logically from the principle that innocent third parties should normally be protected, is the rule that those (whether Directors or third parties) who know of the defect when entering into a transaction, cannot subsequently complain of it or rely upon it[51].

2-18 Publicity

It is the object of the Act that members and third parties should always be able to ascertain who are the officers of a Company. This object is achieved in several ways:—

(a) the *Company* must keep its own Register at the Registered Office under s.200 1948 Act. This must contain the following details of Directors (including *de facto* Directors (s.200(9)):—

    (i) full name and any former name

    (ii) usual residential address

    (iii) nationality

    (iv) business occupation

    (v) other directorships (except for parent or subsidiary companies or fellow subsidiaries)

    (vi) date of birth if subject to s.185 (i.e. if a Public Company or a subsidiary—unless excluded by the Articles).

Items (i) and (ii) must also be included in the Register in respect of the *Secretary*. The penalty in default is a fine of £5 per day. This Register must be open to inspection to members (free) and the public (not more than 5p) during normal business hours (s.200(6)). In default there is a fine of £5 and the Court may order inspection (s.200(7) and (8)).

(b) The same particulars of these officers and of any changes must be filed with the Registrar of Companies within fourteen days (s.200(4) and (5)).

By s.9(3) of the *European Communities Act 1972*, the Registrar must publish these particulars in the London Gazette. S.9(4) of the same Act appears to provide that the Company cannot rely on a change of Directors as against third parties until the date of such publication or actual notice to the third party.

---

51. *Tyne Mutual Association v Brown* (1896) 74 L.T. 283.

The penalty for non compliance with s.200 is a fine of £5 per day (s.200(7)).

(c) *The Annual Return* must contain the contents of the Register at the date of the Return (s.124 1948 Act).

(d) *Letter Headings,* circulars, catalogues, etc., must set out:

    (i)   the Director's christian names (or initials) and surname

    (ii) any former names

    (iii) nationality *if not British* (unless an E.E.C. national: see below)

(s.201)

The penalty in default is a fine of £5, but the Department of Trade may grant exemption "if special circumstances exist". The nationality of a Director who is a subject of any of the member states of the E.E.C. *need not be stated,* by virtue of the *Companies (Disclosure of Directors' Nationalities) Exemption Order 1974.*

Chapter 3

POWERS OF DIRECTORS

3-01 Articles Define Powers

A company must have directors whether it appoints them or not, in that those who actually manage its business will be "occupying the position of director" and so regarded as directors by the law[1]. The only exception might be a company which is managed by the members *en bloc*, but even they would probably fall within the definition. Thus, there would be a board of directors and a body of members even though the composition of both were identical[2].

Such an identity of ownership and management is common in small family companies, though the reverse is usually true of listed companies. There will be directors, therefore, in every company, whether *de facto* or *de jure*; what then is their power to direct? The answer to this question is not to be found in the Acts, which are not a code of company law, but a set of rules to govern certain limited aspects of that law. The Acts impose many liabilities on directors, and many restrictions on their activities, but nowhere do they say what the directors *may* do.

This is, therefore, a matter which the legislature has left to the company to decide for itself, and as it is an internal question, it will be dealt with in the Articles of Association. The question is described as an internal one because it is essentially one of a division of powers within the organs of the Company. The Company itself has the powers given to it by law and by its Memorandum, within the ambit of the *ultra vires* rule. The Articles decide how those powers are to be allocated between such organs as the company has established for its management. The company must have a general meeting of members which has statutory powers and a general

---

1. s.455, 1948 Act.
2. This situation has been more realistically appreciated in the United States where some close companies are allowed to dispense with a board of directors altogether.

residuary authority, but it enjoys wide freedom as to what other functionaries there will be and as to the allocation of powers between them.

Thus the Articles may, as does Table A, Article 80, delegate the general power of management to the directors, or they may specify the powers which the general meeting and directors are to have and give residuary powers to one or the other, or they may entrust the management to a single managing director or to a named person (who will then become a *de facto* director by virtue of s.455), or indeed, to a complete outsider, such as a management or service company.

Thus all, or nearly all, depends on the Articles and the newly appointed director should make it his first task to examine their contents. He must bear in mind, however, that the ultimate residuary authority does rest with the general meeting of members, in the sense that a company, like Parliament, cannot deprive itself of the right to reverse or repeal what it has done in the past. Thus, Articles can can always be changed by Special Resolution (75% majority), though the nature of the voting rights themselves are, in turn, a legitimate subject for the Articles, which can, in effect, decide what 75% shall mean by giving weighted votes to specified shares or on specified circumstances[3].

3-02 Limitations on the Articles

We have noted that the members in general meeting have certain statutory and residuary powers and these are independent of and unaffected by anything which may be in the Articles. What are these limits on the company's freedom to regulate its internal affairs by its Articles?

They include the following:—

(a) an *Increase* in the Authorised capital must be carried out by resolution of the members[4].

(b) a *Reduction* in issued capital can only be carried by Special Resolution (75% majority) of the members[5], with the consent of the Court.

---

3. *Bushell v Faith* [1970] 1 All E.R. 53.
4. s.61(2), 1948 Act. Note that this does not concern the power to issue or *allot* the shares which is often in the hands of the directors. (Table A, Art. 80, leaves it to them by implication but there is usually a Special Article to that effect.
5. s.66(1), 1948 Act. Note that a reduction of unissued authorised capital serves no purpose and would never be carried out in practice.

(c) Alteration of the *Memorandum* of Association can only be carried out:—
   (i) as to the *name* by Special Resolution with consent of the Department of Trade[6].
   (ii) as to the *objects* clause by Special Resolution[7].
   (iii) as to the *liability* clause by consent of *all* the members when changing from limited to unlimited[8] and by Special Resolution when changing from unlimited to limited[9].
   (iv) as to the *Capital* clause by increasing or reducing in the way referred to in (a) and (b) above.

(d) Alteration of the *Articles* of Association can only be carried out by Special Resolution[10].

(e) Voluntary *Liquidation* of the company must be started by:—
   (i) *Ordinary* Resolution where its period of existence is limited by a provision in the Articles
   or (ii) *Special* Resolution for any purpose
   or (iii) *Extraordinary* Resolution where unable to continue because of insolvency[11].

(f) Directors can be *removed* from office by Ordinary Resolution of the members regardless of anything in the Articles[12]. This does not mean that other methods of removal, such as by Special Resolution or by co-directors or by a named individual, are excluded; merely that the Ordinary Resolution procedure can be used in any event.

(g) Every Annual General Meeting of the members *shall* "appoint an *auditor*"[13]. The directors and the Department of Trade have the right to make temporary or casual appointments but the members' right to appoint at the A.G.M. cannot be taken away. The effectiveness of this right is another matter, and is discussed in Chapter 7 below.

---

6. s.18(1), 1948 Act.
7. s.5(1), 1948 Act.
8. s.43, 1967 Act.
9. s.44, 1967 Act.
10. s.10, 1948 Act.
11. s.278, 1948 Act. An Extraordinary Resolution requires the same majority (75%) as a Special Resolution and the only practical difference is that it can be called on 14 instead of 21 days' notice.
12. s.184, 1948 Act.
13. s.159(1), 1948 Act.

(h) The *Annual General Meeting* itself is a compulsory require-ment[14] in each calendar year. The Act does not, however, specify anything that is to be done at the A.G.M. In practice the Accounts are presented to it but this is not essential, as any general meeting will serve to receive them[15].

The *calling* of a General Meeting is also obligatory for the directors if they are requested to do so by one-tenth of the paid up voting capital, regardless of anything in the Articles[16].

(i) The right to demand a *Poll* at general meetings cannot be excluded by the Articles, so long as the demand is made by at least:—

    (i) five voting members

or (ii) one-tenth of the voting rights

or (iii) one-tenth of the voting paid up capital.

Moreover, Proxies have the same rights as members for this purpose[17].

(j) The right to appoint a *Proxy* cannot be denied by the Articles to any member entitled to attend and vote[18]. This right must be stated in the notice calling the meeting and the proxy document cannot be required to be lodged more than two days in advance of the meeting.

(k) *Reorganisations* are provided for by special machinery in the 1948 Act, which is independent of anything in the Articles. This includes:—

    (i) *Reconstruction under s.287* whereby a company may go into a members' liquidation and pass a Special Resolution to exchange the company's assets directly for shares in another company.

    (ii) A *Scheme of Arrangement* under s.206 whereby a compromise or arrangement can be made binding on all the parties affected where agreed to by 75% in value and a majority in number at a meeting summoned by the Court, provided the scheme is then sanctioned by the Court. This procedure can be used where some

---

14. s.131, 1948 Act.
15. s.148, 1948 Act says that the directors shall "lay before the company in general meeting a profit and loss account"... etc.
16. s.132, 1948 Act.
17. s.137, 1948 Act.
18. s.136, 1948 Act.

variation of creditors' or shareholders' rights is the only solution to a difficulty and the Court has wide powers to take any steps necessary to implement the scheme.

(iii) *Compulsory Purchase of dissentients' shares under s.209.* This is a procedure designed to facilitate orthodox take-over bids, by enabling a bidder who has obtained 90% acceptances, to acquire the remainder compulsorily on the same terms. There are stringent conditions which must be strictly complied with.

(1) The *Appointment of Inspectors* by the Department of Trade is an important weapon in the armoury of shareholder protection and one which cannot be interfered with by the Articles.

(i) Under s.164, 1948 Act, the Department *may* appoint inspectors "to investigate the affairs of a company" on the application of either: 200 members or one-tenth of the issued shares[19].

(ii) Under s.165(a) the Department *must* appoint such inspectors if:
either the company passes a Special Resolution to that effect or the Court so orders.

(iii) Under s.165(b) the Department *may* appoint on its own initiative if it has grounds for suspicion.

(iv) Under s.172 the Department *may* appoint inspectors on its own initiative and *must* do so at the request of the members specified in (i) above, to report on *control ownership* of shares.

(v) Under s.32 of the 1967 Act, the Department *may* appoint inspectors if they suspect (e.g. on complaint from members) that Section 25, 27 or 31 of 1967 Act have not been complied with. These sections relate to the prohibition of option dealing and the notification of interests by directors and their families.

(vi) Under s.109 of the 1967 Act, the Department *may* require production of *company papers* and accounts[20].

19. ss.164, 165, 1948 Act. This can be, for shareholders, a useful and effective alternative to hazardous and expensive litigation. In 1973, 408 applications were received and 98 approved. The most interesting recent investigation was that in connection with the National Group of Unit Trusts — see below.

20. Of the 93 applications for investigation which were accepted by the Department in 1973, 81 were under s.109.

This again may be instituted at the request of members and may be a preliminary to investigation under the 1948 Act.

The Department has wide powers of search and entry under these provisions and there are severe penalties on directors or officers who withhold or suppress information[21].

(m) Control over certain *payments to directors,* is taken out of their hands, regardless of anything in the Articles:—

   (i) Remuneration cannot be paid to them as a *Tax free* sum or a sum expressed to be net of the current rate of tax. If this is done, the net sum becomes a gross payment and is thus itself subject to tax[22].

   (ii) *loans* to directors or guarantees of such loans are prohibited except in certain limited cases[23].

   (iii) *compensation* for loss of office must be approved by the members (i.e. by an ordinary resolution)[24].

   (iv) *payments* to directors in connection with a sale of assets or shares must also be approved by the members[25].

(n) *Assignment of Office* by a director to a third party, even if in pursuance of a provision in the Articles, is of no effect unless approved by a Special Resolution[26].

(o) Attempts in the Articles to *relieve* directors, from liability for default or negligence are of no effect[27].

(p) the *accounting duties* of directors as to the form and presentation of accounts, cannot be modified by the Articles[28].

3-03 Powers in the Articles: Table A

Having considered some of the limitations on the scope of the Articles, we can now see how powers are distributed, in practice,

---

21. ss.109–118, 1967 Act.
22. s.189, 1948 Act.
23. s.190, 1948 Act.
24. s.191, 1948 Act.
25. ss.192–194, 1948 Act. These sections are discussed in Chapter 9.
26. s.203, 1948 Act. It will be seen that the required majority (75%) is greater than that required for the appointment of a director in the ordinary way. Thus in practice s.203 can always be circumvented if the director can get a bare majority of support for his proposed assignee.
27. s.205, this section applies to any officer or auditor and includes provisions in contracts as well as in the Articles.
28. ss.147–149, 1948 Act as amended by 1967 Act.

between the directors and the general meeting of members. Every director must look at his own company's Articles but he will usually find, at least in a private company, that they incorporate the whole or the greater part of the Specimen Articles provided in Table A to the First Schedule of the 1948 Act[29]. The 1948 Table A is set out in Appendix B, but in this chapter we can take note of some of its salient features[30]. Most of them are then discussed separately in the relevant part of the text.

(a) Article 80 provides that "the business of the company *shall be managed by the directors*". This is, perhaps, the foundation stone of Table A, as upon it is built the management structure of the Company. If Article 80 is adopted, as it usually is, then all powers of management except those specifically reserved by the Act or by other Articles, will be in the hands of the directors. The members "cannot themselves usurp the powers which by the Articles are vested in the directors"[31]. In these circumstances it is not true to say that the general meeting of members is in control of the company. It can alter the Articles by Special Resolution, or dismiss the directors by Ordinary Resolution, but what it cannot do is to tell the directors how to run the company's affairs[32]. The relationship between the Board and the general meeting is discussed further in paragraph 3-06 below.

(b) Article 2 provides that *Share Rights* and restrictions such as preferences to dividend or capital (usually known as "Class Rights"), shall be fixed by the *members* by Ordinary Resolution in general meeting. Note that this does not mean that the members decide when and to whom and at what price shares will be issued. This more important decision is one of the residuary matters left to the directors by Article 80[33].

(c) Article 4 provides that class rights may generally be *varied* with the consent of three-quarters of the members of the class.

---

29. Table A is generally regarded as a well-drafted precedent which has not become obsolete. The Specimen Memorandum, on the other hand (Table B), has been out of date for sixty years.
30. The director of a post-1948 company when looking at his own Articles should bear in mind that these provisions of Table A will automatically apply unless specifically excluded; s.8(2), 1948 Act.
31. *John Shaw & Sons (Salford) Ltd. v Shaw* [1935] 3 All E.R. 456; per Greer L.J.
32. *Scott v Scott* [1943] 1 All E.R. 582.
33. In practice a special article usually gives the directors an express power to issue shares.

(d) Article 10 *prohibits financial assistance* for the purchase of the company's shares, except to the very limited extent permitted by the Act[34].

(e) Article 44 allows *increase* of authorised share capital by Ordinary Resolution of the members.

(f) Article 46 allows *reduction* of share capital by Special Resolution subject to the consent of the Court[35].

(g) Article 49 allows the *directors* to call extraordinary general meetings whenever they think fit, and also at the request of members specified in the Act[36].

(h) Article 55 requires the *Chairman* of the board to preside at general meetings.

(i) Article 75 provides that the *first directors* shall be nominated by the subscribers to the Memorandum of Association.

(j) Article 76 leaves *remuneration* of the directors to be fixed by the members in general meeting (i.e. ordinary resolution).

(k) Article 77 requires *no qualification* shareholding for directors and leaves it to be fixed, if at all, by a general meeting.

(l) Article 79 delegates all the company's *borrowing powers* to the directors, including power to give mortgages or security of any kind but *limits* the borrowing to the amount of the company's issued capital, unless consent of a general meeting (ordinary resolution)[37].

(m) Article 81 allows directors to appoint attorneys for the company to act in the company's name.

(n) Article 84 requires disclosure of director's *interest in contracts* and provides rules for his dealing with the company (discussed in Chapter 4 below).

(o) Article 85 allows the directors to determine how *cheques* and bills of exchange are to be signed.

(p) Article 87 allows directors to pay *gratuities* or *pensions* to retired salaried directors.

---

34. s.54, 1948 Act.
35. s.66, 1948 Act.
36. 1/10 of paid-up voting capital; s.132, 1948 Act.
37. Third parties are not concerned with this restriction unless they have express notice that the limit is being exceeded. Article 79, and *Royal British Bank v Turquand* (1855), S.E & B. 248.

(q) Article 88 provides for *disqualification* of directors in cases of removal by members, bankruptcy, orders of Court, insanity, resignation or six months' absence, without leave, from board meetings.

(r) Article 89 provides for *resignation* of all directors at the first A.G.M. and thereafter of one third-of the board at yearly intervals, with eligibility for re-election[38].

(s) Article 93 *restricts nominations* for the board (except by the directors themselves) to cases where notice is given to the company by a voting member not less than three or more than twenty-one days before a general meeting.

(t) Article 94 allows the general meeting by Ordinary Resolution to *increase* or *reduce* the *number* of directors and to decide their rotation.

(u) Article 95 allows the *directors* to fill *casual* vacancies on the board or to appoint additional directors—within the limits fixed by the subscribers or by the company, but Article 97 extends this power also to the general meeting of members.

(v) Article 96 allows the members to *remove* a director at any time by Ordinary Resolution[39].

(w) Article 98 allows the directors to regulate their *meetings* as they think fit; questions are to be decided by a majority of votes with a casting vote for the chairman. Any director may call a meeting at any time. Quorum is two unless the directors fix any other number (Art. 99). They elect their own chairman (Art. 101).

(x) Article 100, allows directors to *continue to act* despite vacancies, but where the number falls below the quorum the survivor or survivors may act only to increase the number or call a general meeting.

(y) Article 102 allows *delegation* by the directors to such member or members of the board as they think fit.

(z) Article 106 allows resolutions to be signed by all the directors, without the need for a meeting[40].

---

38. Article 91. In the case of closed private companies, there is much to be said for deleting this Article as it serves little purpose except as a nuisance.
39. This applies anyway by virtue of s.184, 1948 Act.
40. The Act also permits a one-man-board for private companies and formal meetings are clearly unnecessary in such cases; s.176, 1948 Act.

(aa) Articles 107–109 allow the board to appoint a *Managing Director* upon such terms and with such of their powers as think fit.

(bb) Article 110 requires the board to appoint the *Secretary*

(cc) Article 114 permits *dividends* to be
  (i) *declared* by the *general meeting* (i.e. Ordinary Resolution) but
  (ii) not to *exceed* the amount recommended by the *directors*[41].

(dd) Articles 123–127 require "true and fair" *accounts* to be kept and presented by the directors, as do Sections 147–149 of the 1948 Act. The directors decide if and to what extent the members may see the books (Article 125).

(ee) Articles 128–129 allow for *capitalisation of profits* and *issue of bonus shares*. The *general meeting* must so resolve but it can only do so on the directors' recommendation.

(ff) Article 130 requires the appointment of *Auditors* in accordance with the Acts[42], which in turn impose the duty on the general meeting with power to the directors to make interim appointments.

(gg) Article 136 *indemnifies* directors and other officers against liability incurred in defending proceedings (civil or criminal) provided:—
  (i) they are successful
  or (ii) relief is granted to them by the Court under s.448, 1948 Act[43].

3-04 Private Companies: Table A, Part II

Part II of Table A provides specimen regulations for *private companies*. It does this by incorporating the whole of Table A, Part I with certain modifications. These are:—

(a) The omission of *Article 24* of Part I whereby the directors' power to refuse share transfers is limited to partly paid shares. This Article is replaced by Article 3 of Part II.

---

41. This is the classic example of separation of powers by the Articles and means that the members even by a unanimous vote, cannot exceed the directors' recommendation. The question is discussed paragraph 3–09 below.
42. ss.159–161, 1948 Act and s.14, 1967 Act.
43. This Article does not conflict with s.205, 1948 Act, which we have already noted, as the section expressly allows an indemnity in these terms.

(b) The omission of *Article 53* of Part I which fixes a quorum of three members present in person (i.e. not proxies) for general meetings. This is replaced by Article 4 of Part II.

(c) Article 2 of Part II contains the *restrictions* which make the company a private company and are required by s.28 of the 1948 Act, namely:

   (i)   restricting share transfers as specified in Article 3 below,

   (ii) limiting members, excluding employees, to fifty,

   (iii) prohibiting invitations to the public to subscribe,

   (iv) prohibiting bearer·share warrants.

(d) Article 3 of Part II provides that "the Directors may, in their absolute discretion and without assigning any reason therefor, *decline to register* any transfer of any share whether or not it is a fully paid share"[44].

(e) Article 4 of Part II fixes the *quorum* for general meetings at two members—present in person or *by proxy*.

(f) Article 5 of Part II allows resolutions in writing to be *signed* by all the voting members, without the need for a general meeting[45].

3-05 Earlier Versions of Table A Still Apply

As we have seen, the 1948 Table A applies only to:

(a) companies formed after 1st July 1948 (in so far as they do not exclude it) and

(b) older companies which specifically adopt it.

It may, therefore, be worth repeating that, before looking at the Articles, a director should note his company's date of incorporation, since upon this may depend the version of Table A which will govern his duties[46]. If he finds that his company is subject to one of the earlier versions, he will usually be advised to recommend the adoption of the current version at the next convenient opportunity.

---

44. This unfettered discretion is usually restricted in practice by a special Article permitting transfers in specified cases, e.g. within the membership or within the family.

45. In many copies of Table A, the reader will see an additional Article (No. 6) of Part II allowing the directors to require information from members. This related solely to status as an "exempt private company" and was repealed when that status was abolished by Schedule 8 Part III of the 1967 Act.

46. A Table of the respective dates and versions of Table A appears in para. 1-08.

This is not a difficult or expensive operation[47], involving as it does, merely the passing and filing of a Special Resolution, and it is usually in the Company's interests to have the latest edition, if it is to have Table A at all. As it has developed, Table A has moved towards greater freedom and flexibility and it may be regarded as an expression of the government's view of the best practice available at the time of its enactment[48].

Assuming, then, that the director finds that he is governed, for the time being, by an earlier version of Table A, what are the major differences which he should beware of? Articles 5–7, 16, 28, 31, 66, 71, 73, 78, 81–85, 87, 93, 106, 109–112, 119–120, 128–129, 135 and the whole of Part II, in the 1948 Act, have no direct equivalent in the Tables of 1908 and 1929. Let us look at some of the differences:—

(a) Article 5 (1948) expressly provides that the issue of new shares ranking *pari passu* with existing *preferred* shares, is not a variation of their class rights. This is not in the earlier Tables and the directors would certainly want the protection of such a clause before making a new issue.

(b) Article 28 (1948) allowing the company to *charge a fee* of not more than 12½ pence on registration of probate or any document other than a transfer is not found in the earlier Tables. *They do* provide however for such a fee on registration of a transfer as does Article 25 (1948).

(c) Article 66 (1948) provides that *objections* to the qualification of a voter can only be made at the relevant meeting and not afterwards. The Chairman's decision is final. This is only found in the 1948 Table A.

(d) Article 7 (1948) contains a "two-way" *proxy* form for use at general meetings and Article 73 preserves its validity in the event of death, insanity, revolution, etc. These are not found in the earlier versions.

(e) Article 78 is only found in the 1948 Act and allows directors to have an *appointment* or *interest* in subsidiary or associated companies without having to account for fees or other benefits, "unless the company otherwise direct". In the latter case the

---

47. Though it has become more expensive since s.9 of the European Communities Act 1972 required printed copies of the amended Articles to be filed. See Appendix G(d).
48. *Re Marshall, Fleming & Co.* [1938] S.C. 873.

director would become subject to the general law concerning private benefits, discussed in Chapter 4 below.

(f) Article 81 (1948) entitles the directors to *delegate* widely by power of attorney, including the power for the attorney himself to sub-delegate[49]. This is not found in the earlier versions of Table A.

(g) Article 84 (1948) contains important regulations on *directors' interests in contracts* which are discussed in Chapter 4 below. This Article replaces and mitigates the severity of Article 72 of the 1929 Table A. Directors must beware of Article 72, or its predecessors, if their company is subject to the older versions of Table A, since it *automatically disqualifies them from office,* if they have any interest in a contract with the Company, *unless* the company consents in general meeting.

(h) Article 87, another important feature of the 1948 Table A, allows directors to pay *pensions and gratuities* to their salaried colleagues on retirement.

(i) Article 93 of the 1948 Table A, also introduced the rule that *nominations to the board* by members of the company must be lodged between three and twenty-one days before the meeting.

(j) Article 106 (1948) allowed board resolutions to be *signed by all the directors* instead of passed at a meeting.

(k) Article 109 (1948) allows *delegation to a Managing Director.* This was not in the pre-1948 Articles, but may have been implied from the power, which they did contain, to *appoint* such a director (Table A, 1929, Art. 68). No managing director should accept office unless Article 109, or a similar provision is adopted, since there is no general power, apart from the Articles, to appoint and delegate to him[50].

(i) Article 110 (1948) requires the appointment of a *Secretary* by the directors, upon such terms as they think fit[51].

(m) Article 120 (1948) allows the general meeting to pay a dividend or bonus *in specie* or by way of paid-up shares or debentures.

---

49. Not to be confused with the power to delegate to Committees of themselves in Article 102 (1948), which is also in the Tables of 1929 (Art. 85) and 1908 (Art. 91).

50. *Boschoek Proprietary Co. Ltd. v Fuke* [1906] 1 Ch. 148.

51. This was not in the previous version of Table A since the appointment of a Secretary was not made mandatory at all until s.177 of the 1948 Act.

The directors' role is restricted to the resolving of difficulties with regard to fractional amounts and valuations. Note that under the pre-1948 Table A, there is no such power and dividends *must* be paid in cash[52].

(n) Articles 128–129 (1948) allow the *capitalisation of profits* and issue of *bonus shares,* by the general meeting, on the recommendation of the directors. This power is not in the earlier forms of Table A and must therefore be inserted before a pre-1948 company can take this step. The practical effect of such a situation is that the directors will need a 75% vote of the members (to alter the Articles) instead of a bare majority.

(o) The whole of Part II of the 1948 Table A, containing the *private* company provisions, is absent from the pre-1948 models. Thus a private company formed between 1908 (when such companies were introduced) and 1948 *must* have special Articles adopting the restrictions prescribed for such companies[53].

3-06 Private Company Variations on Table A

Having considered the main features of Table A, we can now turn to some of the variations which are made in practice. The director of a private company is likely to find that his company has adopted Table A but with modifications. These modifications tend to fall into a pattern as most private companies use standard forms of Articles adopting and amending Table A, which are supplied by law stationers after settling by Counsel. The object of the amendments is usually to increase the freedom of action of the directors and common features of these forms may be noticed.

(a) Certain clauses of Table A are often excluded. Amongst these are Articles 24 and 53 (excluded by Part II of Table A itself), 75 (leaving first directors to be nominated by subscribers), the Proviso to Article 79 (restriction on borrowing powers), 87 (payment of pensions) 88, (requiring all directors to sign the minute book), 96 (removal from office), 97 (power of general meeting to fill casual vacancies on the board), 126

---

52. *Wood v Odessa Waterworks Co.* (1889), 42 Ch.D. 636.
53. s.28 in the 1948 Act. See para. 3-04 above.

(appointment of Auditors), and Part II Article 3 (directors' complete discretionary power to refuse to register transfers)[54].

(b) The *issuing of shares* is usually placed expressly in the hands of the directors, *subject* often to a proviso that new shares must first be offered pro-rata to existing shareholders[55], unless the general meeting decides otherwise. A common form is:— "The shares shall be under the control of the directors who may allot ... as they think fit". This does not mean that the directors have a free hand, however, as they are always subject to an overriding obligation to use their powers for the benefit of the company rather than for themselves or for any group of individuals[56].

(c) The *company's lien* (or charge) for debts owing to the company is often extended to *fully* paid shares. Table A limits this to partly paid shares[57], but such shares are rare and a lien on fully paid shares is clearly of more practical use in a private company where the members are likely to become indebted to the company. Article 12 of Table A gives the company the right to sell the members' share if his debt is not paid.

(d) *Restrictions on transfer* in private companies are often expanded far beyond the simple provisions of Table A. It will be remembered that Article 3 of Part II left complete discretion to the directors but most private companies prefer their shareholders to enjoy the right to transfer their shares within clearly defined limits. Any form of restriction meets the statutory requirements for a private company.

Provisions commonly found in such Articles are:

(i) a right to transfer freely to other members,

(ii) a right to transfer within a member's family,

(iii) a right of pre-emption for other members, i.e. involving an offer to them before the selling member can offer his shares elsewhere.

---

54. There must be some restriction on transfer but this usually takes a less extreme form in practice.
55. Note that this pro-rata entitlement is not a requirement of the 1948 Table A, though it is in the earlier models.
56. *Bamford v Bamford* [1969] 1 All E.R. 969. This important subject is discussed in Chapter 4 below.
57. Table A, Article 11. Listed companies cannot have a lien on fully paid shares since this would restrict freedom of transfer.

    (iv) (occasionally) a right to transfer within members of a particular trade or profession.

    In most of these cases Article 3 of Table A Part II is not deleted but remains in reserve to give directors a discretion over all transfers which do not fall within the specified categories.

(e) The maximum and minimum *number* of directors is often specified. One director will suffice for a private company[58] and even if a minimum of two or three is fixed, the Articles may provide that a sole survivor can function for all purposes.

(f) *Borrowing powers* are almost invariably extended by deleting the proviso to Article 79 of Table A, which limits the directors' borrowing to the amount of the issued capital. The normal practice is to delegate *all* (i.e. unlimited) borrowing powers to the directors. This is clearly necessary if the directors of £100 companies are to have any effective borrowing powers, but whether it is desirable is another matter. It may perhaps be said that those who lend large sums to under-capitalised companies have only themselves to blame, but the day of reckoning for £100 companies may be at hand in the form of a compulsory minimum paid-up capital[59].

(g) The rules as to *director's interests in contracts* are often relaxed in private company Articles, enabling him to vote on such contracts and to retain the profit which he earns. This may be logical in a director-controlled company although it may not appear so to outside shareholders (i.e. those who are not members of the controlling group).

(h) Power to appoint *alternate directors* is often taken, so as to enable members of the board to appoint attorneys, as it were, to speak and act on their behalf, if they are unable to attend to business themselves.

(i) *Executive directors* may also be provided for in the Articles. They are the converse of the *de facto* directors mentioned in the Act[60], in that they are directors in *name* but not in fact.

---

58. s.176, 1948 Act.
59. This was provided for in the 1973 Companies Bill. The figures were left blank but it is believed that they were to be the comparatively modest amounts of £1,000 for private and £10,000 for public companies.
60. s.455, 1948 Act.

The Article usually allows for their designation as Executive, Special, Regional or Local directors by the board and should expressly state, if that is the intention, that they are *not* directors for the purposes of the Acts.

(j) *Accounting and Auditing* duties are usually extended by the Articles to cover the requirements added by the 1967 Act[61].

(k) *Retirement* at 70 under s.185, 1948 Act, is often expressly excluded as is the three year rotation period of Table A[62]. In director-controlled companies, retirement by rotation is little more than a nuisance and may well be dispensed with. An alternative is to specify named as directors Life or Governing directors, but this is more often found in pre-1948 companies[63].

(l) *Share Transfer forms* do not require the signature of the transferee, and a special Article is often inserted to record this and to make it clear that Article 22 of Table A is no longer applicable in this respect[64].

(m) Power to pay *pensions* may be extended to directors who have not held salaried office—thus going beyond Article 87, Table A.

3-07 Listed Company Variations on Table A (Compulsory)

At the end of 1973, there were 15,576 public companies in England, Wales and Scotland[65], of which 3,429 were "Listed" on the Stock Exchange. Directors of Listed companies will find that the Articles contain differences of two kinds from those in Table A, Part I[66].

(a) those arising from the requirements of the Stock Exchange,

(b) those adopted by the company to meet its particular requirements.

In this paragraph we look at the requirements of the Stock Exchange and thus at variations on Table A which will be found

---

61. ss.13–14, and 16–22, 1967 Act.
62. Articles 89–92, Table A, 1948.
63. Life Directors appointed after 18th July 1945 can always be removed in any event by ordinary Resolution under s.184, 1948 Act.
64. s.1 Stock Transfer Act, 1963.
65. Almost exactly the same as in 1964, when the number was 15,251.
66. Adoption of Part I of Table A (i.e. excluding the private company requirements of Part II) is sufficient to constitute a public company but in practice, a full set of special Articles is always adopted.

in the Articles of all Listed Companies[67]. The source of these requirements is as follows:—

(a) The London Stock Exchange and the Midlands, Western, Northern and Scottish Exchanges were unified into *The Stock Exchange* on 31st March 1973. This is the prescribed stock exchange for the purpose of the Companies Act 1948 (ss.38, 39, 417 & 418)[68].

(b) The requirements of the Stock Exchange are set out in a publication called *Admission of Securities to Listing* issued by authority of the Stock Exchange and periodically up-dated[69].

(c) This contains, *inter alia*:—

    (i) explanatory information

    (ii) the "Listing Agreement" which applicants must enter into[70], and which takes the form of a resolution of the board.

    (iii) the City Code on Takeovers and Mergers

    (iv) Appendix 34 to the Rules and Regulations of the Stock Exchange. This specifies in detail the procedure for admission to the List, the contents of the prospectus and (Schedule VII, Part A), a set of provisions which must be incorporated in the company's Articles[70].

Both the Listing Agreement and the Compulsory Articles are set out in Appendix E below, but we are concerned here with the Articles. In a Listed Company, these *must* provide (*inter alia*):—

(a) that *transfers* of fully paid shares will be free of any restriction and will be registered without fee.

(b) that *Share Certificates* will be sealed and issued free in the case of loss or transfer of part of a holding.

(c) that *unclaimed dividends* will not be forfeited until twelve years after declaration.

(d) that *borrowing powers* of the directors, in respect of the company and others within its group, shall not exceed an

---

67. The expression "Listed" to describe the admission of securities to the Official List, replaced "quoted" in June 1972.
68. *Companies (Stock Exchange) Order 1973* (S.I. 1973 No. 482)
69. Obtainable from the Quotations Dept., P.O. Box 119, The Stock Exchange, Throgmorton Street, London, EC2P 2BT.
70. Copy in Appendix E.

ascertainable amount, without the consent of the general meeting. Thus the director of a listed company will always find in the Articles *some* limit on his borrowing powers.

(e) that a director will not vote on any contract where he has an interest[71].

(f) that casual appointments to the board must submit themselves for re-election at the next A.G.M.

(g) that the company will have power, in general meeting, to remove any director, including a managing director, by ordinary resolution at any time, but without prejudice to any right to damages which he may have[72].

(h) that a period of at least seven days be available during which nominations to the board can be made, and that the deadline for lodging nominations with the company be no earlier than seven days before the meeting.

(i) that a *printed copy* of:
  (i) director's report,
  (ii) balance sheet,
  (iii) profit and loss account,
  (iv) all documents required to be annexed shall be sent to every member at least twenty-one days before the general meeting[73].

(j) that the *share capital structure* be stated in the Articles together with class rights, if any.

(k) that *non-voting shares* be described as such[74], as must shares with restricted voting rights.

(l) that *Proxies* must be capable of being "two-way".

3-08 Listed Company Variations on Table A (Optional)

We have noted some of the provisions which directors of all Listed companies will find in their company's Articles. We can now

---

71. The Articles may provide exception to this, but if so they must be approved by the Committee on Quotation of the Stock Exchange.

72. This would be the case in any event under s.184, 1948 Act, but this provision means that it must be expressly stated in the Articles.

73. These are statutory requirements s.158 (1948 Act), s.24 (1967 Act), Many additional items of information are required by the Listing Agreement, see Appendix E.

74. Such shares are now out of favour and future issues were to have been prohibited by cl. 21, 1973 Bill.

turn to some of the other modifications on Table A which they are likely to find in practice.

(a) *Table A* is usually excluded entirely and replaced by a complete set of Articles, drafted to meet the company's specific requirements, although re-introducing many of the clauses of Table A.

(b) There will, in the usual way, be a *multiple objects clause* in the Memorandum containing many sub-clauses, each of which is described as independent. The directors should be given power in the Articles to pursue or discontinue any one of these branches of business as they think fit.

(c) *Class rights* should be specified, including rights on winding-up.

(d) *Variation of class rights* should also be provided for, requiring a specified majority (usually 75 %) of the members of the class[75]. with a quorum of at least one-third of the class[76].

(e) *Issuing of Shares* is usually entrusted to the directors, subject to the directions of the General Meeting, but in any event, the Listing Agreement (cl.16) requires the directors to get the consent of the General Meeting before any shares are issued for cash, otherwise than to existing equity shareholders. Further restrictions on directors' powers in this field were proposed for all companies in cl. 55 of the 1973 Companies Bill.

(f) Power to pay underwriting and other *Commissions* is usually taken, within the limits of the Acts[77].

(g) There may be *discretionary powers* to refuse to register transfers but only in respect of *partly paid* shares[78].

(h) *Forfeiture* at the discretion of the directors may be allowed but only for *non-payment of calls,* and the procedure must be strictly complied with[79]

(i) Power to *increase* or re-arrange capital by Ordinary Resolution and to reduce by Special Resolution in the manner prescribed *by the Act* will usually be granted to the general meeting, often with wide discretion to the directors to resolve problems in regard to joint holders or fractional amounts.

---

75. As provided by Table A, Article 4.
76. This is required by the Stock Exchange; where one member holds all the class shares, he can constitute a meeting on his own. *East v Bennett Bros. Ltd.* [1911] 1 Ch. 163.
77. The limit is 10 % of the issue price—s.53, 1948 Act.
78. The Articles must provide that fully paid shares are free of resrictions and not subject to any lien.
79. see Table A, Articles 33–36.

(j)   Procedure for calling and conducting *General Meetings* may be left to Table A (Articles 47–61) but it may be useful to provide that where a meeting is requisitioned[80] by members, no business shall be conducted beyond that stated in the requisition.

(k)   Provisions for *Voting Rights* should specify the circumstances in which preference or other classes of shares have the right to vote.

(l)   *Qualification shares* may be required for directors in which case they must obtain them within two months or such less period as is stated in the Articles, otherwise they vacate office[81].

(m)   *Remuneration* of directors may be stated by reference to a global sum which they are to divide up as they think fit or as a percentage of profits.   Such remuneration is for the usual non-executive part-time services[82].

(n)   Remuneration for full time *executive directors* should be provided for quite separately, with full power to the board to appoint and pay them within their discretion.

(o)   Power to pay *gratuities and pensions* should also be widely drawn so as to apply to former directors and officers of all categories.

(p)   s.185, of the 1948 Act (*retirement at 70*) applies to public companies but *may* be excluded by the Articles if the members so desire.

(q)   *Qualification shares* may be fixed by the Articles or Table A; Article 77 may be followed leaving the qualification, if any, to be fixed by the members in General Meeting.

(r)   Detailed provisions as to Directors' *interest in contracts* will usually be found providing *inter alia*, for:—
  (i)   exemption from disqualification,
  (ii)   exclusion from voting or quorum,
  (iii)   retention by him of his profit,
  (iv)   permission to vote and be counted in a quorum for the purpose of fixing pension schemes and terms of employment (other than his own service contract),

---

80. s.132, 1948 Act.
81. s.182, 1948 Act.
82. Remuneration is discussed in Chapter 8, below.

(v) relaxation of this Article by Ordinary Resolution of the members.

(s) The Board may be allowed to appoint *local managers or "directors"* and *local boards* with such delegated duties as the board may decide.

(t) Special provisions will usually be included for the appointment and remuneration of the *Managing Director,* and other executive, departmental and branch directors as well as the Chairman and Vice-chairman.

3-09 Effect of Articles—Dominance of the Board

Having looked at examples of Articles both in Table A and elsewhere, what can we conclude about the separation of powers which the Articles invariably prescribe? One feature which immediately strikes the eye is the supremacy of the *constitution* of the company (the Acts and case law combined with the Memorandum and Articles) over the organs of the Company which that constitution creates. The situation is analogous to that in a Federal as opposed to a Unitary State. It is neither the Federal nor the provincial governments, nor the courts, which are supreme, but the constitution itself. So with a company, neither the general meeting nor the board of directors is the ultimate authority. That authority is the company's constitution which may be changed certainly, but until it is so changed, it cannot be overridden by any one of the company's organs.

Thus, although the members may regard the company as "their company" because they own it, they cannot override or usurp the powers which the directors have been given by the Articles. They can, of course, change the Articles by Special Resolution[83] or change the directors by Ordinary Resolution[84] but, until they do so, they must yield to the authority which the directors have been given[85].

To take an important example, the Articles normally include Article 114 of Table A which says that dividends may be:—

(a) *declared* by the *members* in general meeting
    but

---

83. s.10, 1948 Act.
84. s.184, 1948 Act.
85. "A company cannot by ordinary resolution dictate to or overrule the directors in respect of matters entrusted to them by the Articles" *Bamford v Bamford* [1970] Ch. 212 at p.220 per Plowman J.

(b) shall not exceed the amount, if any, *recommended by the directors.*

Thus, the directors decide whether there may be a dividend and if so, how much. The members may take it or leave it, but they cannot initiate it. So a unanimous resolution by all of the members to declare a certain dividend will be of no effect whatsoever unless the directors approve it[86]. This principle applies equally to all the exclusive powers which the directors may be given, including the general power in Article 80 of Table A to manage the business of the company. So a resolution of the members that the company should not acquire some leasehold premises could be disregarded by the directors who had already decided to the contrary[87]. Article 80 is so wide that the members' powers are effectively limited to those specifically given to them, such as the power to remove directors or to increase capital. The directors are thus the repositories of all residuary powers and, as such, have become the dominating element in the corporate machinery, as has occurred in most constitutions of the federal or power-sharing type.

3-10 Dominance of the Board—Exceptions

Two exceptions may be worth noting to the general principle that the members must keep to the place which the articles have allotted to them:—

(a) If the directors *will not act,* either from choice, or because of a dispute or lack of quorum, the general meeting may do so, e.g. to appoint an additional director[88] or to sue[89].

(b) Article 80 makes the directors' powers subject "to such regulations—as may be prescribed by the company in general meeting". This is a difficult provision but it is probably limited to procedural matters and would not enable the members to interfere with the directors' substantive powers[90].

3-11 Borrowing Powers

We should look separately at one of the more important powers that are given specifically to directors—quite apart from the general

---

86. *Scott v Scott* [1943] 1 All E.R. 582.
87. *Salmon v Quin & Axtens Ltd.* [1909] A.C. 442.
88. *Barron v Potter* [1914] 1 Ch. 895.
89. *Marshall's Valve Gear Co. Ltd. v Manning Wardle & Co. Ltd.* [1909] 1 Ch. 267.
90. *Thomas Logan v Davis* [1911] L.T. 914.

sweeping-up power under Article 80. The usual position with regard to borrowing powers is as follows:—

(a) The *Memorandum* will contain a power for the *company* to borrow and to give security of all kinds[91]. The power will be implied in any case, in a trading company[92].

(b) The *Articles*, if adopting Table A, Article 79, will allow *directors* to exercise all the company's powers.

(c) *Private* company Articles often delete the proviso to Article 79, but if it is not deleted, then the directors' borrowings cannot exceed the *issued capital* of the company, without the consent of the general meeting.

(d) *Listed* company Articles *must* restrict the directors' powers to an ascertainable amount, e.g. paid-up capital, unless the members' consent is obtained[93].

The importance and frequency of company borrowings is such that every director will want to ensure that both loan and security are within the powers both of the company and the board. If not, he may find himself liable both to the lender for breach of warranty of authority and to the company for breach of duty. He will also bear in mind the strict obligation to *register* charges (mortgages, debentures, floating charges, etc.) with the Registrar of Companies within 21 days of their creation[94]. Registration is usually effected by the lender, who loses his security if he is out of time, but it is equally in the interest of the company itself since default leads to a liability to a fine and the *loan becomes immediately repayable*[94]. Thus a fixed loan for twenty years can be converted overnight into one repayable on demand, merely through inadvertence or a delay in the post. If the twenty-one day limit is not met, the only hope is an application to the Court for an extension of time under s.101, but this itself may involve difficulties with other securities[95]. The

---

91. Though it will often lack the power to guarantee the debts of associated companies, and a change in the objects clause may be called for by banks and other lenders in such cases.

92. *General Auction Estate Co. v Smith* [1891] 3 Ch. 432.

93. As will be seen in the discussion of *ultra vires* below in this chapter, third parties are not usually concerned with these limits but this is small consolation to the director who has exceeded his powers.

94. s.95, 1948 Act. Strictly speaking "creation" means the date when the charge is executed even though the advance and the dating of the document occur later. This only adds to the dangers of this notorious section, *Esberger & Son Ltd. v Capital & Counties Bank* [1913] 2 Ch. 366.

95. *Watson v Duff Morgan & Vermont (Holding) Ltd.* [1974] 1 All E.R. 794.

importance of complying with s.95 cannot be too strongly emphasised. Treasury consent is not normally required for borrowings (or share issues) except that for issues exceeding £3 million, the *timing* of the issue must be approved by the Bank of England[96].

3-12 Powers Exercised Collectively

The directors do not enjoy individual rights to act on behalf of the company, as do partners, and the general rule is that they must act *collectively* as a board[97]. Article 98 of Table A provides that:—

(a) they may meet as they think fit,

(b) any director may call a meeting or require the secretary to do so[98],

(c) each director has one vote, and all questions are decided by a simple majority, with a casting vote for the chairman, if necessary.

Thus an individual director is not, as such, entitled to bind the company although, in practice, there may be exceptions to the general rule, which we can now consider:—

(a) the Articles (as Article 102 of Table A) may entitle the board to *delegate* to such one or more directors as they think fit,

(b) the Articles may expressly confer individual management powers on a named director or on the managing director. (Table A, Article 109 does not do this, but leaves it to the board to decide what powers the managing director shall have),

(c) so far as third parties are concerned, managing directors are normally "held-out" as having authority to bind the company regardless of the actual extent of their delegated powers, and even if they have not been formally appointed at all[99],

(d) an individual may be so effectively in control of a company that he will be regarded as having actual or ostensible authority to act on its behalf[100],

(e) Article 106 of Table A allows the directors to dispense with a board meeting altogether where a resolution is signed by all of them.

96. *Control of Borrowing (Amendment) Order 1972* (S.I. 1972 No. 1218)
97. *Re Haycraft Gold Reduction Co.* [1900] 2 Ch. 230
98. Meetings are considered in detail in Chapter 7 below.
99. *Hely-Hutchinson v Brayhead Ltd.* [1968] 1 Q.B. 549
100. *Ford Motor Credit Co. v Harmack, The Times* 7th July 1972 (C.A.)

In general, it may be said that business practice is at variance with the law on the question of the directors' duty to act collectively as a board. In practice, business men do deal with a single director whether or not he is the Managing Director and whether or not he has any delegated powers. They treat him as they would a partner in a professional firm. It may be that they run some risk in doing so; although the Court might be able to help them by the "holding-out" principle. This has now been extended even to the Secretary who is regarded as having ostensible authority to bind the company on "administrative" matters, such as the ordering of office equipment and hire cars[101]. The law had tended in the past to regard the Secretary as a person of insignificance with no authority whatsoever, long after the time when he had developed into a most important officer, often playing a larger role than some of the individual directors. As a last resort, a third party whose contract is repudiated by the board, may have a claim against the offending director for *breach of warranty of authority*[102].

It may be noted that a director may have an individual right to inspect the company's books and accounts at all times by virtue of s.147 of the 1948 Act.

3-13 Delegation of Powers

As we have seen, directors may not delegate their powers unless specifically permitted to so do and such permission is granted by Article 102 of Table A. Article 102, or an expanded version, is always likely to be adopted and the usual position is as follows:—

(a) The directors may *delegate* to one or more of themselves as they think fit (Article 102). There is no legal objection to a Committee of one[103].

(b) The board cannot deprive itself of the right to *revoke* a delegation of powers (although such revocation might amount to a breach of contract with a managing director as we shall see below).

(c) The board may appoint a *Managing Director* with such powers and on such terms as it thinks fit (Articles 107–109).

---

101. *Panorama Developments (Guildford) Ltd. v Fidelis Furnishing Fabrics Ltd.* [1971] 3 All E.R. 16.
102. *Firbank's Executors v Humphreys* [1886] 18 Q.B.D. 54.
103. *Re Fireproof Doors Ltd.* [1916] 2 Ch. 142.

3-13 Delegation of Powers

Thus in any specific case, a director must consider first the extent of delegation permitted by the Articles and second, the extent to which it has actually taken place. If the first is adequate, the second may well be presumed in practice as there may be a *de facto* Managing Director even if no formal appointment has been made[104]. However, it is clearly in the interests of all parties to have the delegation expressly made, and any director who is to be given specific responsibilities, whether as Managing Director, or otherwise, should ask his board for the appropriate resolution to be passed and minuted.

The special questions arising from the *removal* of the Managing Director are discussed in Chapter 9 below, but it must always be borne in mind that the *extent* of his powers, as of any other director or committee, are entirely at the discretion of the board who may make exclusions or impose limits as they think fit[105], subject to the terms of his service agreement.

Thus, if the service agreement or resolution specifies, as it commonly does, that the managing director shall perform such functions as the board may assign to him, he may not be able to complain if they decide to confine him exclusively to one of the subsidiaries[106].

3-14 Directors Exceeding Powers: (1) *Ultra vires* the Company

Having ascertained the extent of his powers, our director can now consider the consequences, if he exceeds them. There are two levels at which this may occur, the first limited by the powers of the company itself, and the second by those of the board. In this paragraph, we are concerned with acts which are *ultra vires* the company itself, that is beyond the powers stated in the Memorandum, or reasonably ancillary thereto; although it should be noted that in either case there is a breach of the director's duty to the company which may lead to a liability on his part to compensate the company, if it suffers loss. What, then, is the position where a director enters into a contract which is *ultra vires* the company as where he borrows money for a business which the company is not authorised to carry on?[107]

---

104. *Freeman & Lockyer v Buckhurst Park Properties Mangal Ltd.* [1964] 1 All E.R. 630.
105. A specimen of a Director's Service Agreement appears in Appendix A.
106. *Harold Holdsworth & Co. (Wakefield) Ltd. v Caddies* [1955] 1 All E.R. 725 (House of Lords).
107. *Re Jon Beauforte (London) Ltd.* [1953] 1 All E.R. 634, where the lenders were excluded from proving in the company's liquidation.

(a) The contract is prima facie *void* and cannot be ratified even by the unanimous vote of all the members[108].

(b) An important exception to the general rule was created by Section 9(1) of the *European Communities Act 1972*, whereby:

    (i) in favour of a person dealing with a company *in good faith*.

    (ii) any transaction *decided* on by the directors

    (iii) shall be deemed to be *within the powers* of both the company and the directors.

Moreover, the third party is presumed to be acting in good faith and is under no obligation to enquire as to the powers of the company or the directors[109]. To this extent, the section overturned the old principle that third parties are deemed to have notice of all public documents including the Memorandum and Articles.

(c) If s.9. does not apply, then the contract cannot be enforced against the company (or more usually, the company's liquidator, since a company which intends to continue in business is hardly likely to plead *ultra vires* as a means of getting out of its contracts). Thus a bank's claim was rejected in the liquidation of a company whose object was to provide services for the Festival of Britain and which then took up pig-breeding as its sole business[110].

(d) S.9. only applies, in any event, for the benefit of third parties, and so it will not protect the company where the *company itself* seeks to enforce an *ultra vires* contract. Whether the third party can plead *ultra vires* on the part of the company is something which has never been firmly established, but if a contract is void it is difficult to see why the company should be able to enforce it if the other party cannot[111].

---

108. *Ashbury Rly. Carriage Co. Ltd. v Riche* (1875) L.R. 7 H.L. 653.
109. This section was an attempt to implement E.E.C. Directive 151 of 9th March 1968 and creates as many difficulties as it solves. For example, what is meant by "decided on by the directors" and "dealing...in good faith", in this context? It is difficult to understand why the draftsman did not take the opportunity to abolish *ultra vires* altogether as far as the outside world was concerned, leaving it merely as a restriction as between the members and the board.
110. *Introductions Ltd. v National Provincial Bank Ltd.* [1969] 1 All E.R. 881.
111. This defence succeeded for the third party in *Bell Houses Ltd. v City Wall Properties Ltd.* [1965] 3 All E.R. 427, though the decision was later reversed on other grounds.

3-14 Directors Exceeding Powers: (1) *Ultra vires* the Company

(e) as between the directors and their shareholders, an *ultra vires* act is a breach of duty (which can be restrained by injunction) whether falling within s.9. or not[112].

(f) the directors may be liable to an injured third party for breach of warranty of authority[113].

The absurdity of the *ultra vires* rule even in its present truncated state, is compounded when one considers how easy it is to change the objects clause, so as to extend the objects, or even (in effect) to eliminate the *ultra vires* rule altogether. This was done in the case of *Bell Houses Ltd. v City Wall Properties Ltd.*[114] by the simple expedient of empowering the company to carry on "any other trade or business whatever which can *in the opinion of the board of directors* be advantageously carried on . . . ". The procedure for alteration of the objects which requires a Special Resolution (75% majority) is discussed in Chapter 1, para. 1-06 above. In the meantime, *ultra vires* lives on and the motto must be "Caveat Director"[115].

3-15 Directors Exceeding Powers: (2) *Ultra vires* the Board

The second type of *ultra vires* situation in which a director may find himself is where his act is within the powers of the *company*, but beyond those of the *board*, or indeed beyond his own authority as a single member of that board. The position here is as follows:—

(a) As the transaction is within the power of the company, it can be *ratified*[116] by ordinary resolution of the members in general meeting.

(b) If it is merely beyond the authority of a *single* director, it may be ratified by the board in the same way.

(c) The *"Turquand"* rule may apply[117]. This provides that if a transaction is not inconsistent with the *external* public

---

112. *Parke v Daily News Ltd.* [1961] 1 All E.R. 695.
113. *Chaples v Brunswick Building Society* [1881] 6 Q.B.D. 696.
114. [1966] 2 All E.R. 674.
115. in *Re New Finance & Mortgage Co. Ltd.* [1975] 1 All E.R. 684, the suppliers of petrol to a filling station had their proof rejected by the liquidator as being *ultra vires* the objects of a Finance Company. Fortunately, the Court was able to overturn the liquidator's decision by bringing the trade within the description "and merchants generally" in the objects clause.
116. *Bamford v Bamford* [1969] 1 All E.R. 969.
117. *Royal British Bank v Turquand* (1856), 6 E. & B. 327.

documents (Memorandum and Articles, Special Resolutions, etc.) of a company, an outsider is not concerned with *internal* irregularities. Thus if the directors are entitled to borrow with the authority of an ordinary resolution of the members, the outsider may assume that they have obtained it. He cannot so do, however, if he *knows* of the irregularity or if he is an *insider*, e.g. a director[118].

(d) S.9(1) of the *European Communities Act 1972* applies, just as it does to contracts which are *ultra vires* the company itself. Unfortunately, the same problems also apply, including the requirement that the transaction must be "decided on by the directors". See para. 3-14 above.

(e) The company may be bound by the contract if it has "*held out*" the director as having authority to make a contract of that type[119]. This is important for third parties, because the legal restrictions on the authority of individual directors are widely disregarded in practice; innocent outsiders inevitably find themselves dealing with people who have been put in a position to make contracts, whether or not they have been authorised or indeed appointed as directors at all. Fortunately, the Courts are taking note of the realities of these situations, as in *Ford Motor Credit Co. v Harmack*[120] where the affairs of three companies were so intermingled that the dominant shareholder was to be regarded as having authority to act for any of them. Thus, where the board allowed one of its members to represent himself as being in the position of a Managing Director they and the company were bound by indemnities and guarantees which he signed[121].

(f) The director(s) who have exceeded their authority are in the same position as where they have exceeded the powers of the company itself. Thus they will have a potential liability to

---

118. *Morris v Kanssen* [1946] A.C. 459.

119. *Freeman & Lockyer v Buckhurst Park Properties (Mangal) Ltd.* [1964] 1 All E.R. 630.

120. *The Times* 7th July 1972 (E of A) Note also Lord Denning's remarks in *Wallersteiner v Moir (No. 1)* [1974] 3 All E.R. 217. "they were just the puppets of Dr. Wallersteiner ... I am of the opinion that the Court should pull aside the corporate veil and treat these concerns as being his creatures —for whose doings he should be and is responsible."

121. *Hely-Hutchinson v Brayhead Ltd.* [1968] 1 Q.B. 549.

the company for breach of duty[122], and to the third party for breach of warranty of authority.

3-16 Validity of Directors' Acts

Technical defects in the qualifications or appointment of a director are corrected for the benefit of third parties by s.180 of the 1948 Act and Article 105 of Table A (which is usually adopted). Both provide that his acts are not invalidated by any defects which might be *afterwards* discovered in his appointment or qualification, and Article 105 extends the protection to acts of the board or of committees. Some features may be noted:—

(a) Acts done in relation to *members* as well as outsiders are validated as where calls were made by an unqualified director[123].

(b) They do not cover cases where there has been no appointment at all, as where a person, who had never been appointed, purported to attend a board meeting and to appoint another director[124].

(c) They do not validate acts which could not have been done even by a properly appointed director, such as the appointment of an unqualified director as managing director[125].

Other procedural matters may be noted here:—

(a) In High Court proceedings a company must appear by counsel and not in person by its managing director[126].

(b) Directors may, however, appear as the company in person in Magistrates Courts.

(c) Proceedings started without authority by a director may be ratified by the liquidator on winding-up[127].

---

122. Unless the members resolve not to sue them (which they can always do even though they cannot ratify the *ultra vires* contract) or unless the Court gives relief under s.448, 1948 Act, if they have acted honestly and reasonable and ought fairly to be excused.
123. *Dawson v African Consolidated Land Co.* [1898] 1 Ch. 6
124. *Morris v Kanssen* [1946] A.C. 459
125. *Craven-Ellis v Canons Ltd.* [1936] 2 K.B. 403
126. *Frinton & Walton U.D.C. v Walton & District Sand & Mineral Co. Ltd.* [1938] 1 All E.R. 649.
127. *Danish Mercantile Co. Ltd. v Beaumont* [1951] 1 All E.R. 925.

(d) By s.36 of the 1948 Act, documents or proceedings may be authenticated by a director, secretary or authorised officer and do not require the Common Seal.

(e) By s.32(1)(a) of the 1948 Act, contracts required by law to be in writing under *seal* may be made on behalf of the company under its common seal (e.g. Leases or Conveyances of land)[128].

(f) By s.32(1)(b) and (c) of the 1948 Act, contracts which between "private persons" are made in writing or by word of mouth may be likewise made for the company by "any person acting under its authority express or implied".

(g) Article 113 of Table A provides that the seal shall be affixed and the document signed by a director and countersigned by the Secretary or by a second director or some other nominee of the directors. The Article does not require them to *witness* the sealing.

(h) S.74 of the *Law of Property Act 1925* provides that sealing is valid in favour of a purchaser if attested by a director and the secretary or his deputy. In that case, the purchaser does not need to consult the Articles. Note the importance of the act of sealing however:— there is a presumption that the document e.g. an underlease, takes effect at once even though the directors may have thought that it would not do so until completed and handed over by their solicitor[129].

(i) By s.33 of the 1948 Act, bills or promissory notes bind the company, if signed "in the name of or by or on behalf or on account of the company by any person acting under its authority".

By s.108(4) of the Act any officer who signs without stating the company's full name becomes personally liable to the third party. The only permitted abbreviation appears to be "Ltd." for "Limited", although where the third party is himself responsible for the incorrect statement of the name, he cannot rely on it in enforcing personal liability against the signatory[130].

---

128. "Contracts" in the usual sense of the word do not have to be under seal and thus can be made in writing or by word of mouth under s.32(1)(b) and (c).
129. *D'Silva v Lister House Development Ltd.* [1971] 1 All E.R. 858.
130. *Durham Fancy Goods Ltd. v Michael Jackson (Fancy Goods) Ltd.* [1968] 2 All E.R. 987.

3-17 Comment and Reform: Two Tier Boards

We have seen that the board of directors is, in practice, the dominating element in the corporate structure, even though the members retain the ultimate sanction in the form of their right to remove and replace directors at any time by ordinary resolution, under s.184 of the 1948 Act. It has been suggested that these rights may be more apparent than real, in the sense that the rounding up of 51% of the votes in a widely dispersed public company is a herculean (and expensive) task. The directors, on the other hand, are in control of the proxy machinery and in effect, of their own remuneration. Thus it is said that the board will tend to evolve into a self-perpetuating and self-remunerating oligarchy. Moreover, even in private companies the right to remove directors can be effectively blocked by loaded voting rights as was done in *Bushell v Faith*[131].

Against this it may be objected that there are many checks and balances to prevent the assumption of excessive power by the directors:—

(a) The right of the members to decide the composition of the board by ordinary resolution is paramount, whether or not they choose to exercise it. There is no limit to what a determined shareholder may achieve, even if he remains in a minority[132].

(b) New appointments made by the board itself, invariably have to seek re-election at the next A.G.M.

(c) Details of remuneration must be disclosed in the accounts and the Directors' Report.

(d) The Department of Trade has wide powers under sections 164–175 of the 1948 Act and 35–42 of the 1967 Act to investigate the affairs of a company and it may exercise these powers at the request of a single shareholder.

(e) The Jenkins Committee, whose 1962 report is still not fully translated into legislation, favoured greater disclosure but

---

131. [1970] 1 All E.R. 53. However this case was to have been overruled by Cl. 44 of the 1973 Companies Bill which also shifted the balance of power towards the members in some other respects e.g. by restricting the directors' power to issue shares and sell the assets (Cl. 54-57).

132. In *Wallersteiner v Moir (No. 2)* [1975] 1 All E.R. 849. Mr. Moir, a small shareholder, pursued the controlling director to the Court of Appeal, recovered £234,773 for his company and secured an indemnity for his own costs.

not the imposition of restrictions on business freedom "which would seriously hamper the activities of honest men in order to defeat an occasional wrongdoer". The Committee pointed out that "The Act provides shareholders with powerful weapons provided they choose to use them and even if practical considerations make them difficult for the small investor to wield, the same cannot be said of the institutional investor"[133].

Nevertheless, the debate on the powers of directors continues, with particular reference to the larger companies. Criticism here often concentrates on two points; first, that boards of directors tend to be dominated more and more by full-time executives who are more concerned with their own position than the interests of the shareholders, and second, that the interests of workpeople are not represented on the board.

The remedy, it is suggested, is the introduction of the "two-tier" board structure such as exists in certain European countries (notably in Germany where it originated) and which it has been proposed in the E.E.C. Fifth Draft Directive should be made mandatory throughout the European Economic Community. Under this system a large company is required to have two boards of directors, a supervisory board appointed by the shareholders and employees in defined proportions, and a management board appointed by the supervisory board and responsible to it. On certain matters the management board cannot act without the consent of the supervisory board and no one can be a member of both boards.

Opponents to the introduction of this system into United Kingdom legislation point out that, in so far as there is any force in the charges levelled at present British practice, other remedies are available and are to be preferred to the cumbersome and time-wasting structures proposed. Shareholders already have the weapons which we have noted and it can hardly be said that employees are without a voice, at least when they have a powerful Trade Union to speak for them[134].

---

133. Report of the *Company Law Committee* Cmnd. 1749, para. 106.
134. Two-tier boards do not appear in the 1973 Conservative Companies Bill and although they are advocated in the Labour Party Green Paper, "The Community and the Company" (1974), the worker-representative would only be allowed to emerge through Trade Union machinery. Thus, unorganised workers who might have most to gain from two-tier boards, would be excluded from participation. As the Labour Party, rather quaintly, puts it: "We do not consider that the answer lies in permitting direct election by employees..." Perish the thought!

3-17 Comment and Reform: Two Tier Boards

The argument about compulsory two-tier boards is essentially one of flexibility against conformity. After all, the existing single-tier structure could incorporate worker representation and it seems to cater equally well for the three alternative forms of company management which are found in practice. First, the traditional, *non-executive* board which directs but does not manage. All the directors are non-executive and management is in the hands of senior executives under the supervision of the board;[135] a two-tier board in all but name but with the freedom to change if circumstances require.

Second, the *mixed* board, which unites outside directors with one or more senior executives, usually including a Managing Director. This has been found to work in practice and is common amongst Listed companies, but it does have the disadvantage (if such it be) of combining two roles in the same individuals. The executive directors share responsibility for the supervision of management, of which they themselves form part.

Third, the *close* company board where management, supervision and indeed ownership coincide in the same persons. This is characteristic of the 600,000 private companies in the U.K. and is one of the factors which makes them so different an animal from the typical public company. The opponents of compulsory two-tier boards would therefore say that all the advantages of these boards can be achieved without imposing a rigid and formalistic framework upon our companies. Be that as it may, the two-tier board is here to stay and all E.E.C. members will be bound by the provisions of the Fifth Directive when, and if, it is enacted by the Council of Ministers.

---

135. A notable example of this type of board in U.K., is that of the Prudential Assurance Co. Ltd.

N.B. An amended draft of the European Companies Statute has been proposed by the E.E.C. Commission – see Bulletin of the European Communities Supplement 4/1975.

Chapter 4

DUTIES OF DIRECTORS

4-01 Source of Duties

The duties of directors derive from their position in relation to the Company, as it has been evolved by the Courts[1]. We should, therefore, briefly analyse their position before turning to the duties themselves. It is an amalgamation of several elements:—

(a) *Agent*, in that the director acts not on his own behalf but on that of the Company.

(b) *Trustee,* in that he controls assets and exercises powers for the benefit of the company and not for himself.

(c) *Employee,* in that an executive, paid director is in a similar position as regards rights and duties, to that of any other employee.

(d) *Professional Adviser,* in so far as he is rendering services for reward (even as a non-executive fee earner) he must accept the burden of skill and care which falls on independent contractors of this type[2].

The Director does not fall entirely within any of these categories since his function is unique but his duties derive from principles applicable to them, and break down into two broad divisions—those of *good faith* and those of *skill and care*. Virtually every duty or liability (including breaches of the Companies Acts) can be seen to fall under one of these headings.

A useful and authoritative guide to the practical and ethical aspects of this subject is published by the Institute of Directors as *Guidelines for Directors.*

---

1. Their position is not defined or stated in the Acts, although the 1973 Bill made a start in that direction by stating their general duty of good faith in Cl. 52. See also para. 1-12.
2. These aspects of the Directors' position are also considered in para. 1-12 above.

4-02 Duties to Whom?

The general rule is that directors' duties are owed to the *Company* and not to individual shareholders[3]. This leads inevitably to the question—how is the Company to enforce those duties when the directors control the company's affairs? This is a question to which English Law has not found a truly satisfactory answer, although the bringing of a *derivative action* by a minority shareholder is an established possibility[4]. The duty, then, is owed to the Company and in the case of failure, it is to their own board that the members must primarily look to enforce it. By the same token, the Company, in the form of the general meeting, can usually ratify, or indeed pardon, the defaults of a director, although questions will naturally arise where the director uses his own shareholding to secure the passing of an Ordinary Resolution to that effect[5]. However, unless there is a "fraud on the minority" the Court will not normally interfere with the Director's proprietorial right to vote his own shares[6].

When being told that his duty lies to the Company our director may reasonably ask what is meant by "the Company"—does it mean the present shareholders exclusively, or is he entitled to have regard to the long term welfare of the artificial creature itself? And what of its employees, customers, creditors, associate companies and indeed the community at large? This question raises many difficulties but some guidelines may be indicated:—

(a) *Dividends.* The most obvious conflict is that between the maximisation of dividends and the retention of profits to meet the Company's own requirements. Here the director is entitled and bound to exercise his business judgement in striking a balance between two legitimate but competing demands[7].

(b) *Employees.* So far as employees, creditors and others are concerned, the law imposes no general duty upon directors[8]

---

3. *Percival v Wright* [1902] 2 Ch. 421.
4. *Wallersteiner v Moir (No. 2)* [1975] 1 All E.R. 849.
5. As in *Hogg v Cramphorn Ltd.* [1966] 3 All E.R. 420 where the Court excluded certain wrongfully issued shares from voting on the ratification resolution. See Chapter 5 below.
6. *Northern Counties Securities v Jackson Steeple & Co.* [1974] 2 All E.R. 625.
7. See Megarry J's remarks in *Gaiman v National Association for Mental Health* [1970] 2 All E.R. 362. "The interests of some particular section or sections of the (Company) cannot be equated in those of the (Company) and I would accept the interests of both present and future members of the (Company) as a whole as being a helpful expression of a human equivalent".
8. See *Parke v Daily News* [1962] 2 All E.R. 929.

but it is clearly a matter of "enlightened self-interest"[9] to have regard for their welfare and to conduct the company "as a good citizen", in that, thereby, the directors are likely to serve most effectively the interests of the present and future members of the Company.

(c) *Companies Bill.* Cl.53 of the 1973 *Companies Bill* specifically provided that "the matters to which the Directors of a Company are entitled to have regard in exercising their powers shall include the interests of the Company's *employees* generally as well as the interests of its members."

(d) *Nominees.* Where a director is a *nominee* of a parent company, or a shareholder or creditor, he must bear in mind that there is no such thing as a *delegate* director in English law. Every director has exactly the same responsibility to the Company as a whole and if he neglects that responsibility in the interests, or on the orders, of his principal he will be guilty of a breach of duty. Thus, he must not starve a subsidiary out of business merely because it suits the parent company to do so[10], nor must he be guided by the interests of the group as a whole, at least where the subsidiary has separate creditors[11].

This principle is widely disregarded in practice and nominee directors often see themselves simply as watchdogs for those who put them on the board. They are wrong, and before accepting office they should remember that the law expects them to devote their loyalty to the Company as a whole.

4-03 Duty of Good Faith

Essentially; the director's duty is to act *bona fide* in the interests of the company and to use his powers for the purposes for which they were conferred. It will be seen that these are not necessarily the same things. A director will be acting *bona fide* if he genuinely considers that he is acting in the company's interest and the test is

---

9. *Guidelines for Directors* (Institute of Directors 1973); the reader is referred particularly to the wide discussion of these questions of boardroom practice on pp. 25–29.
10. *Scottish Co-op. Wholesale Society v Meyer* [1958] 3 All E.R. 66.
11. *Charterbridge Corporation v Lloyds Bank Ltd.* [1969] 2 All E.R. 1185.

thus subjective[12].   But while still acting in this belief, he may nonetheless use his powers for a purpose for which they were not
intended.   In this case there is no bad faith but there is a breach of
duty and this time the test is objective.   A characteristic example of
the second type of situation is where directors issue shares, not to
raise capital needed by the Company but, for example, to forestall
a takeover bid[13].

We now have an expression of the official view of this duty, in
the attempt to state it in Clause 52 of the 1973 Companies Bill:—

"52 (1)   a Director of a company shall observe *the utmost good
faith* towards the company in any transaction with it or
on its behalf and shall act honestly in the exercise of the
powers and the discharge of the duties of his office.

(2)   a Director of a company shall not make use of any money
or other property of the Company or of any information
acquired by him *by virtue of his position*, . . . to gain
directly or indirectly an *improper advantage* for himself
at the expense of the Company."

This was not an attempt at an exhaustive definition and indeed it
was manifestly not so.   The words "at the expense of the company"
are narrower than the existing law since the director can be liable to
account for a personal profit whether or not it was at the expense of
the Company[14].

We can now look at some examples.

4-04 Trustees of Powers

The director's duty is to use his powers for the purposes for which
they were intended, that is for the benefit of the company as a
whole and not for any "collateral purpose"[15].   The Court will not
interfere in the exercise of the director's discretion or business
judgement[16], and must therefore be satisfied that the purpose is
unauthorised.   Thus the power to issue shares must be used for the
purpose of raising capital for the Company and not by way of
defence to a takeover bid[16a].

---

12. Re *Smith & Fawcett Ltd.* [1942] 1 All E.R. 542.
13. As in *Hogg v Cramphorn Ltd.* [1966] 3 All E.R. 420.
14. *Regal (Hastings) Ltd. v Gulliver* [1942] 1 All E.R. 378.
15. Re *Smith & Fawcett* [1942] 1 All E.R. 542.
16. *Pergamon Press v Maxwell* [1970] 2 All E.R. 809.
16a.   General duties on a bid are considered in paras. 5-05 and 5-16 below, where
the provisions of the City Code are also noted.   Extracts appear in
Appendix D.

In *Bamford v Bamford*[17] the directors issued 500,000 shares to another party for precisely such a purpose. It was held that the allotment was voidable if not *bona fide* in the interests of the company, but since the Company was the party injured, it could, after full disclosure, ratify the allotment by Ordinary Resolution at a general meeting. The case illustrates that:

(i) honesty or good faith is not enough,

(ii) misuse of powers, even in the honest belief that it is in the company's interests, will be a breach of the duty of skill and care; even if not of the duty of good faith,

(iii) the company, provided there is no fraud, can usually ratify the unauthorised act by Ordinary Resolution[18].

The director's duties in this most important area of the issuing of shares have come into question on a number of other occasions. There has been little doubt that they did not appreciate their over-riding obligation, which was to raise capital for *the needs of the Company* and for no other purpose. Some of these cases are instructive:—

(a) In the *Savoy Hotel Investigation*[19], the Inspector reported that the directors had made an "invalid use of the powers of management" where they sought to put properties out of reach "of the speculator's grasp" by issuing shares to trustees of a staff benevolent fund.

(b) In the *National Group of Unit Trusts Investigation*[20], the Inspectors reported, *inter alia*, that the directors (who controlled a majority of the shares) made a Rights issue, knowing that many of the outside shareholders would be unlikely to take it up. The result was to dilute the outside interests still further and thus to reduce their share of profit on a forthcoming sale (which the directors did not disclose). The Inspectors accordingly concluded that the directors were in breach of duty.

Both (a) and (b) were investigations by the Department of Trade under their statutory powers.

---

17. [1969] 1 All E.R. 969.
18. Even perhaps in the case of the use of the directors' powers for the direct benefit of themselves, as where they acknowledged a statute-barred debt due to one of them. *Re Gee & Co. (Woolwich) Ltd.* [1974] 2 W.L.R. 515.
19. Second Report. June 14th 1954 (HMSO).
20. Report on First *Re-Investment Trust Limited* and other companies, published by Department of Trade 1974 (HMSO).

(c) In *Hogg v Cramphorn* [1966] 3 All E.R. 420 the directors, fearing a bid, issued shares to trustees for the benefit of the employees, confidently expecting that the trustees would support them in the coming struggle. They honestly believed that they were acting in the best interests of the Company but it was held that they had misused their powers and were thus in breach of duty. The issue could be ratified by general meeting but the new shares must not be voted.

(d) In *Howard Smith Ltd. v Ampol Petroleum Ltd.*[21] a bid was again pending and this time the directors were in the minority. The majority (55%) said they would reject the bid, whereupon the directors promptly issued sufficient shares to the bidder to reduce the objectors below 50% and thus to enable the bid to succeed. The Privy Council held that the issue of shares could be set aside on grounds of improper purpose even though:

(i) there was no element of self-interest
    and

(ii) the company *did* need new capital

the primary purpose was to facilitate the bid and this was sufficient to invalidate the directors' decision.

The lesson to be derived from these examples is that directors are trustees of their powers and must exercise them for the purposes for which they were given, that is for the benefit of the company as a whole. If they knowingly use their powers for other purposes they break their duty of good faith and if they do so unknowingly they break their general duty of skill and care.

4-05 Trustees of Assets

Just as directors are trustees of the powers entrusted to them so it is with the Company's property. The ownership of the assets is not vested in the Directors so that in this respect they differ from the trustees of, for example, a Will or a Settlement. However, the assets are in their hands and under their control and they have all the duties of Trustees in their dealings with them. Thus, if they dispose of the assets without consideration and merely because they have been ordered to do so by the majority shareholder who nominated them, they will have a liability for misapplication which can

---

21. [1974] 1 All E.R. 1126.

be enforced by the minority shareholders[22]. This principle applies to any disposal or use of the company's property which is unauthorised or not *bona fide* in the interests of the Company.

In these circumstances the directors must repay what they have misappropriated, whether or not they acted honestly. For example:—

(a) where they apply assets for an *ultra vires* purpose[23],

(b) where they pay compensation for loss of office without disclosure to the members under s.191, 1948 Act[24],

(c) where they pay dividends out of capital[25],

(d) where they provide financial assistance for the purchase of the company's own shares in breach of s.54, 1948 Act[26].

We may note that "property" or "assets" bears an extended meaning for the purpose of the director's duties as Trustees. The trust extends to:—

(a) assets which are *received* by the directors in circumstances which oblige them to hold for the Company's benefit, as where they are paid commission by third parties on company contracts[27],

(b) inventions, discoveries, technical or confidential information acquired by directors in the course of business[28],

(c) business advantages, such as opportunites to enter into contracts, which directors obtain by virtue of their position whether or not the Company could have taken advantage of them[29].

---

22. *Selangor United Rubber Estates Ltd. v Cradock* (No. 3) [1968] 2 All E.R. 1073.

23. *Re Claridge's Patent Asphalte Co. Ltd.* [1921] 1 Ch. 543.

24. *Re Duomatic Ltd.* [1969] 1 All E.R. 161.

25. *Re Sharpe* [1892] 1 Ch. 154.

26. "Every director who is a party to a breach of s.54 is guilty of a misfeasance and breach of trust, and is liable to recoup to the company any loss occasioned to it by the default." *Wallersteiner v Moir (No. 1)* [1974] 3 All E.R. 217 per Lord Denning M.R. at p. 239.
Lord Denning also gave a useful guide to directors on the interpretation of this notorious section: "You look to the Company's money and see what has become of it. You look to the Company's shares and see into whose hands they have got. You will then soon see if the company's money has been used to finance the purchase."

27. Even if the Company itself could never have received commission, *Boston Deep Sea Fishing Co. v Ansell* [1889] 39 Ch.D. 339.

28. *Cranleigh Precision Engineering Ltd. v Bryant* [1965] 1 W.L.R. 1243.

29. Even where the third party would not have placed the contract with the Company because of his personal objection to it. *Industrial Development Consultants Limited v Cooley* [1972] 2 All E.R. 162.

4-05 Trustees of Assets

It will be seen that cases of this type also illustrate the principle that a director must not make an unauthorised personal profit out of his position. This question is discussed below but it is really the other side of the same coin. The director as trustee is liable if he misapplies the Company's assets: and if he misapplies them into his own pocket he is equally liable on the alternative ground that he must not use his position to enrich himself[30].

4-06 Trustees of their Position: Personal Profit

Flowing naturally from the director's position both as Agent and as Trustee is the rule that he must not make a personal profit from his position, beyond what he receives in the form of authorised remuneration. The leading case of *Regal (Hastings) Ltd. v Gulliver* is worth noting as it indicates the width and strictness of the rule[31]. In that case a company owned a cinema and wished to purchase two others with a view to selling all three as a going concern. It formed a subsidiary to buy the two additional cinemas but could only afford to contribute £2,000 of the required share capital of £5,000. Accordingly the remaining 3,000 shares were taken up by the directors. The shares in both companies were sold off and the profit on the subsidiary's shares (2,000 being sold by the Company and 3,000 by the Directors) amounted to £2.80 per share. The new owners of the parent company then caused it to sue the directors for the profit which they had made and it was held by the House of Lords that they must repay.

The case teaches many hard lessons in the sphere of directors' duties, including the following:—

(a) the fact that they acted in good faith and that the company itself could not have subscribed for the shares was no defence. The directors' opportunity came to them *because* of their position and this was sufficient to require them to "disgorge" their profits,

(b) there was no merit in the claim because it benefited only the buyers who were presumably content with the price which they had agreed to pay for the shares. So the recovery of the directors' profit came as an unmerited windfall. If anyone was to benefit it should have been the original outside

---

30. *Regal (Hastings) Ltd. v Gulliver* [1942] 1 All E.R. 378.
31. [1942] 1 All E.R. 378.

shareholders who *sold* their shares at a price which did not reflect that part of the profit which the directors were eventually required to pay over. This is a problem which can always arise where a Company changes hands after some breach of duty has occurred but before any proceedings are taken,

(c) directors should therefore bear in mind that what they do today, confident in the knowledge that the general meeting will support them, may fall tomorrow under the hostile scrutiny of strangers or indeed of a liquidator or inspector. All their actions should therefore be decided by the criterion of whether they will stand such scrutiny[32],

(d) where directors do have majority support at the general meeting, there is nothing to prevent them submitting proposals of the *Regal* type for ratification by the members by Ordinary Resolution. This will protect them in the future provided there is no fraud on the minority[33]. Thus, in a later case, the directors escaped liability where they had been confirmed in office by the company *after* it was aware of the facts[34],

(e) the very harshness of *Regal*, strengthens its value as a guideline for directors. If they retain or account for profits or benefits on the principles of that case they are unlikely to be open to attack; and if in doubt they should seek approval of an Ordinary Resolution at the next general meeting.

Examples of Personal Profits

Other illustrations of this principle may be noted:—

(*a*) *Conflict of Interest*

Phipps v Boardman[35] indicated the continuing authority of *Regal*. In that case a trust held shares in a company and an opportunity arose to acquire further shares. The shares were not an authorised investment, and so one of the trustees and the trust solicitor acquired the shares for themselves. It

---

32. The Inspectors' report on the *National Group of Unit Trusts Investigation* [1974] (First Re-Investment Trust Ltd. and other companies) describes some hair-raising examples of failure to apply this test.
33. One of the many galling features of *Regal* for the directors is that they were apparently in a majority and so could have had their share purchase ratified if they had troubled to do so.
34. *Lindgren v L. & P. Estates Co*. [1968] 1 All E.R. 917.
35. [1966] 3 All E.R. 721 (House of Lords).

was held, as in *Regal* that they must account to the trust for their profit, but the additional factor of conflict of interest was present, as is always likely when an opportunity is presented to the Company and the directors must decide whether the Company will take it. In *Phipps*, the conflict derived from the fact that the defendants could not advise impartially as to whether the trust should seek, from the Court, the power to acquire the shares itself.

There were indications in *Phipps* that information acquired by a director, while acting as such, might not always give rise to an obligation of this type, but there would have to be evidence of full disclosure and rejection of the opportunity by the Company. Moreover, if the director was involved in the board decision to reject, his burden of proof would be correspondingly greater.

(b) *Ratification Insufficient*

To the general principle that a director may keep his personal profit where it is ratified by the members in general meeting, there must clearly be an exception where the directors are themselves in the majority and use their votes to pass the resolution. Otherwise the minority could be expropriated at will. Thus in *Cook v Deeks*[36] the directors used their position to obtain in their own names a contract which should have benefited the Company. They passed an Ordinary Resolution to the effect that the Company should have no interest in the contract, but the Privy Council held that nonetheless the contract "belonged in equity to the Company and ought to have been dealt with as an asset of the Company". Unanimous approval by *all* members would be a different matter[37].

(c) *Fees from Subsidiaries*

Where a director is put on the board of a subsidiary or in some other position where he receives fees or benefits, as a result of the action of his company he is prima facie liable to account for them on the principles discussed above. However Article 78 of Table A allows such a director to retain his fees unless the Company (that is—the members by Ordinary Resolution) otherwise direct.

---

36. [1916] 1 A.C. 554.
37. *Re Gee & Co. (Woolwich) Ltd.* [1974] 2 W.L.R. 515.

(*d*) *Post-retirement profits*

In *Industrial Development Consultants Ltd. v Cooley*[38] the director failed to get a contract for the Company but was then asked by the customer if he would take it up in his private capacity. He then got himself released from his service contract on the grounds of ill health, took up the contract and, not surprisingly, found himself ordered to pay over his profit to the Company. There was a clear case of conflict of interest and the opportunity to get the contract arose out of his position as director. If he had vacated his office *before* receiving the approaches which led to the contract the position might have been different, as fiduciary duties cease on termination of the trustee relationship[39].

(*e*) *"Bribes"*

It naturally follows from these rules that benefits paid to the director by third parties in connection with the company's affairs, must be accounted for. This applies particularly, at the time of incorporation, to payments from promoters or sellers of property to the Company[40], to takeover bids and to payments from contractors[41].

To encapsulate the philosophy of these cases, one might take the proposition of Lord Hodson in *Phipps v Boardman*[35]

"No person standing in a fiduciary position, when a demand is made upon him . . . to account for profits acquired by him by reason of his fiduciary position and by reason of the opportunity and knowledge, or either, resulting from it, is entitled to defeat the claim upon any ground save that he made the profits with the knowledge and assent of the other person."

4-07 Trustees of their Position: Interest in Contracts: Principles

Where a director has a personal interest in a contract with his company, he is clearly placed in a situation where questions of conflict of interest, personal profit and breach of fiduciary duty are bound to arise. The law has, therefore, been active in this field

---

38. [1972] 2 All E.R. 162.
39. *Nordisk Insulin Laboratorium v C. L. Bencard* [1953] 1 All E.R. 986.
40. *Re London & South Western Canal Co.* [1911] 1 Ch. 346.
41. *Boston Deep Sea Fishing Co. v Ansell* [1889] 39 Ch.D. 339.

since the development of commercial companies in the mid-nineteenth century. The main features are as follows:—

(a) The general rule is that a director *must not* have such an an interest[42] unless:

  (i) he discloses it under s.199, 1948 Act (see below)

and (ii) the Articles permit it

or (iii) it is ratified by Ordinary Resolution of the members,

(b) the *effect* of a breach of this rule is that

  (i) the director must *account* for the profit made

and (ii) the contract is *voidable* if the company chooses to avoid it[43],

(c) the rule applies to *interests of any kind* (however small) including:

  (i) a partnership in a firm

  (ii) a shareholding in a company[44]

and to any other situation where a conflict of interest may arise

(d) *disclosure* of interest in a contract or proposed contract is required by s.199 of the 1948 Act which provides that

  (1) the director must disclose the *nature* of his interest at *a meeting of the board*,

  (2) this must be the *first* meeting at which the contract is considered or (if later) the first meeting after he acquires his interest,

  (3) a *general* notice of interest in a company or firm will suffice provided he takes steps to have it read at the next meeting,

  (4) *penalty* in default of not more than £100,

  (5) without prejudice to any *rule of law*, restricting such interests (namely the general rule discussed above).

Thus, compliance with the section does not *of itself* validate the contract; the director still needs ratification by general meeting or some enabling provision in the Articles.

(e) In practice *the Articles* do normally contain such an enabling provision and Table A, Article 84 requires that:

---

42. *Costa Rica Rly Co. Ltd. v Forwood* [1900] 1 Ch. 746.
43. *Aberdeen Rly Co. v Blaikie Bros.* [1854] 2 Eq. Rep. 1281 (H. of L.).
44. *Transvaal Lands Co. v New Belgium Land Co.* [1914] 2 Ch. 488.

(1) The director shall *declare* his interest in accordance with s.199

(2) He will *not* vote or be counted in a quorum, when the contract is considered, *except* where

    (a) He is being indemnified against company obligations which he has taken on himself

or   (b) the company is giving security to the third party in respect of such obligations

or   (c) the director is taking or underwriting shares or debentures in the Company

or   (d) his interest is solely as *shareholder* or officer in another company.

(3) He may hold any other *office of profit* with the Company (as the board may determine) and *may contract* with the company.

(4) He may be counted in the *quorum* when his office is considered and may *vote* on any appointment other than his own.

(5) He or his firm may act in a *professional* capacity for the company and be paid accordingly[45].

The effect of Article 84 is to enable the director to contract with the company and keep his profit *provided* he complies with the Article and with s.199 as to disclosure, voting and quorum[46]. The statutory authority of Table A makes it clear that there is no objection, in principle, to the relaxation of directors' liabilities in this way and special Articles may well go beyond Article 84, as where a director is permitted even to vote and be counted in the quorum on his own contract[47]. However, the Article must be strictly complied with and the burden of proof will lie on the director himself[48]. Moreover s.199 itself cannot be excluded and the director must be prepared to show, if necessary, that the contract was a fair one and entered into by the company with competent advice and full knowledge of the circumstances[49].

---

45. Neither he nor any partner or employee can be *Auditor* (s.161, 1948 Act; s.2, 1967 Act).

46. *Costa Rica Rly Co. Ltd. v Forwood* [1901] 1 Ch. 746.

47. Such an Article is clearly desirable in single-family companies where all the members of the Board would otherwise be disqualified.

48. *Gray v New Augarita Porcupine Mines Ltd.* [1952] 3 D.L.R. 1 (Privy Council).

49. "full and frank disclosure" *Fine Industrial Commodities Ltd. v Powling* [1955] 2 All E.R. 707.

4-08 Interest in Contracts: Features

We have looked at the principles governing directors' interests and seen that in practice the severity of the rule is mitigated by Article 84 or variations on it. Some other features should be noted

(a) *Ratification*

In the unlikely event that the rule is not relaxed by the Articles, the Director, in addition to disclosing under s.199, must get the contract approved by the members in general meeting. For this purpose the directors may vote their own shares[50], so long as this does not amount to a "fraud on the minority"[51].

(b) *Listed Companies*

In *Listed* companies the Articles *must* exclude the directors' right to vote, where he has a "material" interest[52]. Exceptions may be specified in the Articles but they require the consent of the Quotations Committee.

(c) *Failure to comply*

Where a director fails to disclose, or fails to comply with the specific terms of the saving Article, the contract does not become void but two consequences follow:—

(i) if it is not too late to do so, the contract may be *rescinded* by the Company

and (ii) the director must account for his profit[53].

(d) *Additional Disclosure*

We have seen that disclosure under s.199 is to the *board* only, but further requirements were added by the 1967 Act:

(i) s.16(1)(c) requires the Directors' Report to give particulars of "significant" contracts in which a director had a "material" interest (except service contracts). The words "material" and "significant" leave some discretion for the directors as compared with s.199 which requires disclosure of *all* interests however trivial,

---

50. *Northern Counties Securities v Jackson Steeple & Co.* [1974] 2 All E.R. 625.

51. As in *Cook v Deeks* [1916] 1 A.C. 554 (Privy Council); "fraud" in this sense means "oppression" rather than "criminal deception" which is its normal connotation.

52. Appendix 34, Stock Exchange Rules: Schedule VII. The word "material" limits the effect of this requirement; the general law applies to interests of any kind.

53. *Hely-Hutchinson v Brayhead Ltd.* [1968] 1 Q.B. 549.

(ii) by s.16(1)(d) the report must also disclose directors' benefits in connection with the acquisition of shares,

(iii) s.23 requires every director to take reasonable steps to comply with the above. Penalties in default,

(iv) by s.26, Contracts of Service (except where terminable without compensation within twelve months) must be open to inspection by the members.

(e) Extent of Disclosure

As we have seen s.199 is not restricted to "material" interests in contracts and it requires the "nature" of the interest to be declared. What does this mean?—surely that the director must do more than say "I declare an interest in this contract". He must go further and say what form his interest takes, whether he is an owner, shareholder, or director of the contracting party and (if relevant), what is the *extent* of his personal stake[54]. Unfortunately the section confuses the issue by providing (s.199(3)) that a general notice of membership in a specified company shall be sufficient notice of interest in all future contracts with that company. This is all very well for the situation where the director has given a general notice that he has shares in a large listed company. No doubt this will serve adequately for any contracts which his company may make in the future. But what of the case where he is in control of the third party and stands to make a very large personal profit from the transaction under discussion. Can he rely on a general notice of an (unspecified) interest which he gave years earlier, and allow the contract to go through without saying a word. The answer must be "no" and the reason must lie in his wider duty of good faith. He may have complied with s.199 but the general fiduciary duty requires him to go further and to inform the Board of the specific facts which he knows to be relevant to their decision[55].

---

54. *Gray v New Augarita Porcupine Mines Ltd.* [1952] 3 D.L.R. 14 (Privy Council) where Lord Radcliffe said "if it is material to their judgement that they should know not merely that he has an interest but what it is and how far it goes then he must see to it that they are informed".

55. This was certainly the view of the Inspectors in the Investigation in connection with the *National Group of Units Trusts* (First Re-Investment Trust Ltd.) (Dept. of Trade 1974). In a situation of this type they pointed out that a general declaration was "almost valueless". "Only a full and specific declaration could have enabled the other directors to appreciate the significance of the decisions they were being called upon to make."

(*f*) *Procedure*

An example of the procedure followed in one public company may be useful.

(i) directors give *general notice* of all their directorships and shareholdings in other companies under s.199 and s.200 of the 1948 Act,

(ii) at each board meeting the *chairman* draws attention to s.199 and requests disclosures under that section of any interest in contracts on the agenda.

(iii) directors disclose specifically, any *material* interest in contracts either on the agenda or otherwise pending.

This procedure faces the problem discussed in paragraph (e) above, that general *disclosure* under s.199 is not enough and that *specific* disclosure of *material* interests is also required. The Institute of Directors (*Guideline for Directors* pp. 24–25) refers also to the practice of requiring a director to leave the meeting and to abstain from voting even at general meetings, whenever a matter is discussed in which he is remotely interested. Moreover, the director should not in any circumstances enter into a contract where abnormal personal gain accrues to him. In other words, full disclosure and compliance with the Articles is not a passport to contractual freedom. It is only the first test which a contract must pass, the second being the overriding duty of good faith. The director will meet this requirement only if the contract is one which he could justify to the members at a general meeting after all the facts were disclosed.

(*g*) *Reform*

The Jenkins Committee had noted some of the weaknesses of s.199, particularly the restriction of the duty of disclosure to cases coming before the board when in practice many contracts were never brought before the board. Amendments were included in the 1973 Companies Bill and are noted here as an indication of what the Administration regarded as good practice. They are likely to be the minimum requirements of the next Bill.

(i) The nature of the interest must be disclosed *whether or not* it comes before the board.

(ii) A general notice must state the *facts*, by reason of which the director is interested in certain contracts, and must be given *before* contracts of that type are first considered.

(iii) Directors' interests are extended to include those of his family, i.e. spouse and minor children including step-children and adopted children[56].

4-09 Contracts with the Company: Other Restrictions

Apart from the general question of interest in contracts there are other statutory restrictions on the company's dealings with its directors:

(a) *Loans* to directors are usually prohibited[57].

(b) *Tax free* payments to directors are prohibited and any agreement to make such a payment is treated as an agreement to pay the sum stated, but *subject* to deductions of tax, i.e. as though the net sum were a gross sum[58].

(c) *Compensation* for loss of office requires disclosure and approval by the members, i.e. by Ordinary Resolution[59].

(d) *Disclosure* of remuneration and compensation for loss of office is required in the accounts[60].

(e) *Service Agreements* or details, if not in writing, must be available for inspection by any member, unless terminable without compensation within twelve months[61]. This is also a requirement of the Stock Exchange Listing Agreement during the A.G.M. period and, in addition, contracts for *ten* years or more must be approved by Ordinary Resolution[62].

(f) The *Directors' Report* must disclose any contract of *significance* in which a director has a *material* interest together with his shareholdings and any special company arrangements for share-acquisition[63].

(g) Dealing in *options* is prohibited in the case of listed companies[64].

(h) *Interests* of the directors in securities of the company or its associates must be notified to the company and recorded in its register[65].

---

56. *Jenkins Report* para. 99; *Companies Bill 1973* Cl. 47.
57. s.190, 1948 Act, discussed in Chapter 8 below.
58. s.189, 1948 Act.
59. s.191, 1948 Act.
60. s.196, 1948 Act; s.6, 1947 Act, discussed in Chapter 8.
61. s.26, 1967 Act.
62. *Admission of Securities to Listing.* Sched. VIII, Part A.
63. s.16, 1967 Act.
64. s.25, 1967 Act. See Chapter 5 below.
65. ss.27–29, 1967 Act.

4-10 Competition

One would expect that a director would be prevented by his fiduciary obligations from competing with his company, as he would if he were a partner[66]. However, this is not necessarily the case and the position appears to be as follows:

(a) He may accept a directorship in a competing company[67], and (presumably) may compete directly on his own account[68].

(b) However, the nature or extent of his duties may exclude such activity either by implication or expressly. This would particularly be the case where he is a full-time executive[69].

(c) Moreover, his role as a competitor must, by definition, involve a risk of a conflict of interest and thus of a breach of his fiduciary duty. In the event of such a breach the Court might restrain him by injunction from continuing to act in both capacities[70].

(d) Aside from the general duty of good faith, the competing director is also exposed to attack by the members on the ground of oppression[71], "if he subordinates the interests of the one company to those of the other"[72]. In practice it is difficult to see how a man can sit on the boards of two directly competing companies and still do justice to both of them.

(e) Covenants against competition after vacation of office, which may appear in the director's service agreement are subject to the general rules concerning restraint of trade and are discussed in Chapter 8. A director who is wrongfully dismissed is usually freed from such covenants in any event[73].

4-11 Confidentiality

One of the inevitable difficulties which a competing director finds himself faced with is that of conflict with his wider duty of

---

66. Partnership Act 1890, s.30.
67. *London & Mashonaland Exploration Co. Ltd. v New Mashonaland Exploration Co. Ltd.* [1891] W.N. 165.
68. *Bell v Lever Bros.* [1932] A.C. per Lord Blanesburgh at p.195.
69. *Hivac Ltd. v Park Royal Scientific Instruments Ltd.* [1946] 2 All E.R. 350.
70. Although the *Mashonaland* case (Note (67) above), appears to suggest the contrary.
71. s.210, 1948 Act, see Chapter 5 below.
72. *Scottish Co-op Society Ltd. v Meyer* [1959] A.C. 324 per Lord Denning at p. 368.
73. *General Billposting Co. Ltd. v Atkinson* [1909] A.C. 118.

confidentiality. How does he avoid giving the rival business the benefit of confidential information which he has acquired as a director?

The duty of confidentiality itself forms part of the duty of good faith and restricts the director from using, either during or after his term of office, anything which belongs to the company for his own purposes. Property, in the normal sense, is clearly included, but also intangible property in the form of trade secrets[74], lists of customers, company documents and other confidential information[75]. One would expect that knowledge of an impending takeover bid would fall within this category so that directors who speculated on such knowledge would have to account for their profits. However, insider trading, although unacceptable in practice, is still ostensibly permitted by the law, at least until *Percival v Wright* is repealed or reversed[76].

In *Baker v Gibbons*[77], it was held that the duty in respect of confidential information applied "with particular force" (as one would expect) to a director as compared with other employees and agents. But the duty was not broken by the director in this case who, after dismissal, recruited some of the company's selling agents to join his own competing business. He had simply memorised their names and addresses and had not stolen any documents or confidential information. Moreover the Court is always reluctant to interfere, at the request of an employer, with the efforts of a former employee to earn his living.

4-12 Duty of Skill and Care: Principles

We have been looking at duties which fall within the general category of good faith; a largely negative obligation to do nothing which conflicts with the Director's duty to his company. But what of the positive side? What is a director expected to do to *promote* the company's welfare. Very little—might be the cynic's reply and this would not unfairly represent the view of the Courts, at the time when the law was being developed[78]. This largely derives from the

---

74. *Cranleigh Precision Engineering Ltd. v Bryant* [1965] 1 W.L.R. 1293   Outside confederates may also be made subject to an injunction on this ground.
75. *Printers & Finishers Ltd. v Holloway* [1964] 3 All E.R. 54.
76. [1902] 2 Ch. 421.   Insider Trading is discussed in Chapter 5 below.
77. [1972] 2 All E.R. 759.
78. See the remarks of Neville J. in *Re Brazilian Rubber Plantations* [1911] 1 Ch. 425.   "A Director is not bound to take any definite part in the conduct of the company's business but so far as he does undertake it he must use reasonable care in its despatch."

nineteenth-century business atmosphere, when directors rarely acted in an executive capacity. They were often amateurs in the sense that they had no specialised knowledge of the company's business and saw themselves rather as country gentlemen, who attended board meetings from time to time and relied on their paid executives to run the company. It is hardly surprising that the Courts could not expect much from them and that the standards applied appear to have little relevance to the modern duties of the highly paid fully professional executive director of today. In fact the old cases are less absurd than they seem, if one bears in mind that they deal almost entirely with non-executive or "outside" directors. Different standards will naturally be applied to the professionals, who are employees as well as members of the board.

The early cases culminated in *Re City Equitable Fire Insurance Co.*[79] in 1925 where Romer J. submitted three propositions which continue to serve as the primary authority on this subject:—

(a) *A Subjective Test of Skill*
A director need not exhibit in the performance of his duties a greater degree of skill than may reasonably be expected from a person of *his* knowledge and experience.

(b) *Periodical Attendance*
He is not bound to give continuous attention to the affairs of the Company. His duties are of an *intermittent* nature to be performed at periodical board meetings. He is not bound to attend all such meetings though he ought to whenever he reasonably can.

(c) *Delegation to Executives*
He is entitled to trust an official to perform such duties as can properly be entrusted to him in accordance with the Articles.

In *Re City Equitable,* what had happened was a catastrophic fraud by the Managing Director, who had been given a free hand by his colleagues. He had concealed the fraud by showing items in the balance sheet as "loans at call" and "cash in hand" but the directors never enquired where they were. In fact the loans were mainly to himself and the cash included £73,000.00 in the firm of stockbrokers of which he was a partner. It was held that the co-directors were negligent, although in this case they were protected

---

79. [1925] Ch. 407.

by one of the Articles which made them liable only for wilful neglect or default. Such Articles are now prohibited by s.205, 1948 Act.

These propositions are manifestly intended for the non-executive director and, despite their undemanding and lenient tone it by no means follows that their usefulness is exhausted[80]. For example, as the qualifications of directors, and business and accounting knowledge generally, have developed, so will the subjective test in paragraph (a) have become more severe. If the duty is to exhibit the skill of a person of "*his*" knowledge and experience, this must mean that the Chartered Accountant on today's board bears a much heavier responsibility than the "country gentleman" of 1883 who, it was held, could not be expected to understand the company's accounts![81] Indeed his duty of skill and care must surely be equal to that which would be expected of him if he were acting in a professional capacity for a client. Let us now turn to some of the implications of these principles.

4-13 Duty of Skill and Care: Examples

(a) *Cheque Signing*

In *Re City Equitable* the following tests were suggested:

(i) In the absence of suspicious circumstances a director who is asked to sign can trust the officers as to whether it is properly required and whether it is duly applied for the stated purpose.

(ii) He should satisfy himself as to an authorising resolution, either in advance or by way or confirmation.

(iii) Such resolution should preferably specify payees and amounts.

Clearly these suggestions will be impracticable for large companies but, even there, the proper procedure for delegating powers must be followed in accordance with the Articles.

Directors are justified in handing a cheque to their Solicitor and relying upon him to see that it is put to its proper use[82].

---

80. They were applied as recently as *Huckerby v Elliott* [1970] 1 All E.R. 189.
81. *Re Denham & Co.* (1883) 25 Ch.D. 752 where he was exonerated from blame for paying a dividend out of capital.
82. *The New Mashonaland Syndicate, Re* [1892] 3 Ch. 577.

(b) *Investments*

Romer J. also suggested that

(i) each director is responsible for ensuring that funds are properly invested, except in so far as delegation of the duty may be permitted by the Articles,

(ii) safe custody of the securities may properly be entrusted to an appropriate full-time officer such as manager, accountant or secretary.

(c) *Professional Advice*

Directors are entitled to rely on qualified professional advice where appropriate, and indeed may be obliged to do so, for example to get an independent valuation of a property offered to them as a mortgage security[83].   Having obtained the advice they must exercise their own judgement but they are not expected to be experts themselves unless they were appointed as such.   "A director of a life insurance company does not guarantee that he has the skill of an actuary or of a physician."[84]

(d) *Diligence*

Romer J's statement that the director's duty is to attend board meetings whenever, in the circumstances, he is reasonably able to do so, may well be too lenient for modern requirements. It may be said that if a director cannot attend regularly he ought not to accept office and if he does not attend, how can he ensure that responsibilities are properly delegated and that there is nothing to attract suspicion.   "It should be understood that a director consenting to be a director, has assumed a position involving duties which cannot be shirked by leaving everything to others."[85]

Moreover the position is quite different where the director assumes a specific responsibility for a particular task or degree of attendance whether by way of service contract or otherwise. In that case his responsibility express or implied is a matter of contract like that of any other employee or agent.   It may

---

83. *Fry v Tapson* (1884) 28 Ch.D. 268.
84. Romer J. in *Re City Equitable*.
85. *Drincqbier v Wood* [1899] 1 Ch. 406 per Byrne J.

go so far as to include a positive duty to take the initiative in pursuing business opportunities even to the extent of changing to some other *intra vires* business[86].

(e) Negligence

The general principle here is said to be that directors cannot be held liable for "errors of judgement". Thus in *Dovey v Corey*, bad debts had been included in the balance sheet on an assurance by a manager that they were good. As a result dividends were paid out of capital. A (non-managing) director was sued for negligence but the House of Lords exonerated him. "The business of life could not go on if people could not trust those who are put in a position of trust for the express purpose of attending to details of management."[87]

However, where they fail to meet the *City Equitable* standard of care, by failing to show the skill one would expect of people of their experience and qualifications, there will be a liability for negligence[88]. Moreover the presence of a service agreement may well imply an obligation to satisfy an objective standard of reasonable skill and care[89].

4-14 Duty of Skill and Care: Reliance on Others

Romer J. suggested that directors were entitled to rely on the relevant officers in the absence of suspicious circumstances, and directors have escaped liability on this principle in *Dovey v Corey*[88] and other cases. The same holds true for reliance on a properly delegated sub-committee of the board[90].

Likewise the default of one director does not necessarily impose liability on the others[91]. However, failure to supervise or enquire where there are suspicious circumstances or other reasons for doing so, may involve the innocent director in the breach of duty; for example where the Chairman signed a minute and reported to the

---

86. *Fine Industrial Commodities Ltd. v Powling* [1955] 2 All E.R. 707.
87. [1901] A.C. 1, 477 per Lord Halsbury L.C.
88. e.g. on a reckless sale of assets; *Re New Travellers' Chambers Limited* (1895) 12 T.L.R. 529.
89. *Lister v Romford Ice & Cold Storage Co. Ltd.* [1957] A.C. 555 (House of Lords).
90. *Land Credit Co. of Ireland v Lord Fermoy* (1870) 5 Ch. App. 763.
91. *Huckerby v Elliot* [1970] 1 All E.R. 189 where the director failed to enquire whether a gaming licence had been obtained but had no reason to be suspicious.

general meeting on an *ultra vires* investment effected by his colleagues[92]. And where he is, in fact, supervising a delegated task he cannot claim that he did not know what was going on[93].

The question of a director's responsibility for the defaults of his colleague was examined in detail by the Inspectors who investigated the companies owning shares in the National Group of Unit Trusts Ltd.[94] and their report indicated some of the limitations of the *Dovey v Corey* principle. The investigation dealt with a complicated series of interlocking investment companies but, as far as the co-directors were concerned, the question boiled down to this. Were they responsible for the default of a colleague who dominated the board, who bought and sold investments at will, and who submitted his decisions for ratification merely as a formality? The answer of the Inspectors was—yes. To a co-director who tried to rely on *Dovey v Corey* and *Re City Equitable,* they pointed out that it was not a case of being entitled to trust a delegated officer, but of failure to exercise his *own* duty of care by applying his own judgement to the merits of the dealings which were submitted for ratification. He failed in his duty by his continued participation in a system of management under which investment changes were approved without proper consideration. All the co-directors were found wanting in this respect and even those who had raised their voices in protest were told that this was not enough. Continued participation in a system which he knows to be unsatisfactory will thus fix a director with part of the responsibility for the consequences. "In fulfilment of his duty of due care in the company's affairs, a non-executive director should apply to the problems before the Board a conscientious and independent standard of judgement, free of involvement in the daily affairs of the company. When such directors are mere "yes-men" to the Chairman, they fail to fulfil this function."[95]

4-15 Consequences of Breach of Duty

What steps are open to the company or others where there has been a breach of one or more of these duties?

---

92. *Re Lands Allotment Co.* [1894] 1 Ch. 617. He will have a right of contribution from those responsible, *Ramskill v Edwards* (1885) 31 Ch.D. 100.
93. *Dept. of Health & Social Security v Wayte* [1972] 1 All E.R. 255 where a director who had gone out of office on liquidation was made liable for National Insurance contributions which should have been paid while he was a director.
94. Report on *First Re-Investment Trust Ltd.* and other companies: Dept. of Trade 1974.
95. Dept. of Trade report, p. 108.

(*a*) *Company to Sue*

Primarily the company is the party to sue, as it is the company to whom the duties are owed. However, if for some reason the company cannot or will not sue (for example because the wrongdoer controls it) one or more shareholders can bring a *derivative action* in their own name but on behalf of the Company[96].

(*b*) *Liquidation*

After the company has gone into liquidation the Liquidator may bring proceedings under s.333 1948 Act for *misfeasance,* for any breach of duty involving misapplication of assets.

(*c*) *Measure of Damages*

The damages to be claimed will be either the *loss* suffered by the company or (in cases where loss to the company is irrelevant as in a claim for personal profit) the *profit* made by the director. In liquidation the Court may restrict the claim to the amount required to pay the debts[97].

The director cannot *set-off* any debt owing from the Company to him[98].

(*d*) *Defendant*

Proceedings may be brought against

(i)   a *de facto* director
(ii) a retired director[99]
(iii) the estate of a deceased director[100]
(iv) a bankrupt director

(*e*) *Limitation of Actions*

After *six years* actions are barred by the *Limitation Act 1939* except for fraud, fraudulent breach of trust or the recovery of trust property which has passed through his hands[101].

---

96. *Wallersteiner v Moir (No. 2)* [1975] 1 All E.R. 849
97. *Re Home & Colonial Insurance Co.* [1930] 1 Ch. 102.
98. *Re Anglo-French Co-operative Society* (1882), 21 Ch.D. 492.
99. *Curtis's Furnishing Stores Ltd. v Freedman* [1966] 2 All E.R. 955.
100. Except, probably, in liquidation where s.333 seems to require a personal order against the director himself.
101. ss.2, 19, *Limitation Act 1939.*

4-16 Other Personal Liabilities

It may be convenient to summarise here some of the other liabilities which may affect directors.

(a) *Contracts:* Where a director enters into a contract on behalf of his company with proper authority to do so, he incurs no liability to the other party since he is merely acting as the Company's agent. There are, however, a number of circumstances in which he will risk *personal* liability, and these are now considered.

(b) *Personal Liability:* Where the director contracts without disclosing the company's interest, the other party may hold him liable. Moreover, if he signs or authorises any:

   (i)   Bill of Exchange,

   (ii) Cheque,

or (iii) Order for money or goods

in which the company's *name* is not mentioned he is under s.108 1948 Act *personally liable* to the third party if the Company does not pay and also subject to a fine of £50.00. The full and correct name must be stated and the only permissible abbreviation is "Ltd."[102] Thus, the description "M. Jackson (Fancy Goods) Ltd." would not do for "Michael Jackson (Fancy Goods) Ltd." although in the case where this arose, the plaintiffs could not rely on the error, as they were themselves responsible for it[103].

Certain statutes may also impose personal liability on the Director if the company fails to comply with the statutory requirements, for example payment of National Insurance contributions. An order can be obtained, even after the Company is in liquidation, against the director who was in office at the time of the default[104].

(c) *Breach of Warranty or Authority*

We have said that the directors do not normally incur personal liability for company contracts. But where he purports to make a contract which fails to bind the company and which the company repudiates, he may be liable to the

---

102. *F. Stacey & Co. Ltd. v Wallis* (1912), 106 L.T. 544.
103. *Durham Fancy Goods Ltd. v Michael Jackson (Fancy Goods) Ltd.* [1968] 2 All E.R. 987.
104. *Dept. of Health & Social Security v Wayte* [1972] 1 All E.R. 255.

third party on the ground of breach of *warranty of authority*[105]. As the name indicates, this liability is based on the assumption that the director has *warranted* to the third party that he has the authority to enter into the contract. If it then turns out that it is beyond the powers either of himself, or of the board, or of the company itself, he has broken that warranty and is liable accordingly. Examples may be noted:

(i)   Where the director negotiates a loan which puts the total borrowing beyond the company's limit[105].

(ii) Where directors induce the bank to pass cheques in the absence of a proper mandate[106].

It may be noted that these are both cases where the third party had no reason to think that the position was different from that represented by the director. But where the lack of authority is apparent from the Memorandum or Articles, it might be objected that the third party is presumed to know this and cannot complain. Fortunately for those who have to do business, it is unlikely that this objection would be sustained. The director who misrepresents his powers as they are stated in the public documents should be liable to a third party who has been thereby induced to enter into a contract. He should not escape merely because the third party failed to inspect (and understand) the Memorandum and Articles[107].

Moreover, the likelihood of having to rely on this remedy against the individual directors is itself lessened by two developments which tend to save contracts from being repudiated on the ground of lack of authority:—

(i)   the "*holding out*" principle whereby the company will itself be liable in most cases where the director is allowed to deal with third parties in a way which would normally imply authority to enter into such contracts[108].

and (ii) s.9 of the *European Communities Act 1972*, whereby directors' powers "shall be deemed to be free of any limitation under the memorandum or articles" which the third party is under no obligation to inspect.

---

105. *Chaples v Brunswick Permanent Building Society* [1881] 6 Q.B.D. 696.
106. *Cherry & McDougall v Colonial Bank of Australasia* (1869) L.R. 3 P.C. 24.
107. *West London Commercial Bank v Kitson* (1883) 12 Q.B.D. 157 where the directors were personally liable for accepting a bill of exchange even though the Memorandum showed that they had no power to do so.
108. *Hely-Hutchinson v Brayhead Ltd.* [1968] 1 Q.B. 549

Unfortunately this section is bedevilled by its restriction to transactions "decided on by the directors", which if it means anything at all, must presumably involve a decision by the board or a properly delegated committee. And yet this is precisely what is lacking in the situation which the section was intended to cover[109].

(d) *Torts*

The basic principle of separate corporate entity[110] means that it is generally the company alone which can sue or be sued for torts (civil wrongs such as negligence, trespass, libel, deceit) which are alleged to have been done to or by it. Thus the directors will not have *personal* liability merely because the wrongful act could only be done on their authority[111]. But if it can be proved that they were actively involved in directing or procuring the wrongful act, they may be jointly liable with the company[112]. The extent to which the company itself is liable for the torts of the director, depends on the ordinary principles of an employer's vicarious liability for the action of servants committed in the scope of their employment. If a tort falls within this category and is committed by a director in a position of authority (whether actual or implied), the company will be liable[113]. It might be thought that an *ultra vires* act could never be within the scope of employment, but if the board commit a tort in the course of pursuing an *ultra vires* object, it could hardly be right to deny the injured party his right of compensation from corporate funds merely on this ground[114].

(e) *Company Crimes*

The Company can be prosecuted for the crimes of directors, if the relevant statute is construed as extending liability to employers[115], despite the fact that it is clearly impossible for the company to have a guilty intention or *mens rea*. However, for such criminal liability to be imposed, it seems that

---

109. See Chapter 3 para. 3-14. The government realised the defects of s.9 and had a further shot at the target in s.5 of the 1973 Companies Bill. Unfortunately this has not been enacted.
110. *Salomon v Salomon & Co. Ltd.* [1897] A.C. 22.
111. *British Thomson-Houston Co. v Sterling Accessories Ltd.* [1924] 2 Ch. 33.
112. *T. Oertli A-G. v E. J. Bowman (London) Ltd. and others* [1956] R.P.C. 282.
113. *Rudd v Elder Dempster & Co. Ltd.* [1933] 1 K.B. 566.
114. *Campbell v Paddington Corporation* [1911] 1 K.B. 869.
115. *Pearks, Gunston & Tee Ltd. v Ward* [1902] 2 K.B. 1.

there must be evidence of active involvement in the crime by those actually managing the company's affairs, whether properly appointed directors or not[116].

Thus an intention to deceive by the secretary and branch manager were held to be sufficient to make the company liable where they were the responsible officers in the area of activity in which the offence occurred[117]. What the Court is doing therefore is to attribute the mental state of the directing officers to the Company itself.

Needless to say, any director who is responsible for the commission by the company of a crime (or a tort) may well be liable to his own company for breach of duty, unless he can get relief from the Court[118].

Moreover, where a company gives an undertaking in the course of proceedings and then breaks it a director may also find himself personally liable for contempt[119].

4-17 Criminal Liabilities

Despite the principle of a separate corporate identity established by *Salomon v Salomon & Co.* there are many provisions in the Companies Acts and elsewhere which impose personal liability on directors as well as on their companies.

The opportunities for committing a breach of the Acts, are truly abundant (over 80 sections create offences) and the consequences horrifying. The practice of the Department of Trade has been to abstain from prosecution except in flagrant or protracted cases or offences which have been fraudulent or damaging to others. But the risk is always present, and should be borne well in mind by those who are asked to serve as directors of companies with which they may have little influence or regular contact.

The characteristic mechanism of the Act consists of the imposition of a duty, such as that to file the *Annual Return*[120], accompanied by the sanction that: "the company and *every officer* of the company who is in default shall be liable to a default fine."

---

116. *Tesco Supermarkets Ltd. v Nattrass* [1971] 2 All E.R. 127.
117. *Moore v Bresler Ltd.* [1944] 2 All E.R. 515.
118. *Selangor United Rubber Estates Ltd. v Cradock* (No. 3) [1968] 2 All E.R. 1255.
119. *Biba Ltd. v Stratford Investments* [1972] 3 All E.R. 1041 where the unfortunate director was a Solicitor who had no responsibility for day-to-day management.
120. s.126, 1948 Act. Out of a total of 3,407 prosecutions in 1973, 3,355 were in respect of this and the related section, 127 which requires the annexing of the accounts and Directors' report. There were 1,523 convictions.

The effect of such a provision is that:

(1) A director (as an Officer) is liable if he knowingly and wilfully authorises and permits the default[121],

and

(2) the fine is £5.00 for *every day of the default,* unless some other amount is specified in the section.

Moreover, many sections also include a liability to imprisonment and this may range from six months for failure to prepare and file the Directors' Report[122] to *Life,* for impersonating a shareholder in an attempt to obtain his shares[123].

Apart from the default fines for failure to comply with formal requirements of the Act, there are other even more serious penalties in respect of offences which contain an element of fraud or non-disclosure:

(a) *Destruction or falsification,* alteration or disposal of documents or being privy thereto, can be punished by up to two years' imprisonment and/or a fine[124].

(b) Similar penalties apply to officers of a company being *wound up*[125].

(c) A *False Statement* made knowingly in any return, report, certificate, balance sheet, etc., is a criminal offence[126].

(d) Payment of *dividends out of capital,* as well as being a breach of duty, may amount to a criminal conspiracy as may any agreement to use the company's assets dishonestly, that is for a purpose which they could not honestly believe to be in the interests of the company[127].

(e) Publishing by an Officer of a *misleading or false statement* with intent to deceive, is an offence punishable with up to seven years' imprisonment[128].

The statement has to be false "in a material particular" and it may be so if it is misleading as a whole even though there is no specifically false statement.

---

121. *Beck v Board of Trade Solicitor* (1932), 76 Sol. J. 414.
122. s.23, 1967 Act.
123. s.84, 1948 Act.
124. s.113, 1967 Act.
125. s.329, 1948 Act.
126. s.438, 1948 Act.
127. *R. v Sinclair* [1968] 3 All E.R. 241.
128. s.19(1) *Theft Act 1968.*

Thus, in the leading case of *R. v Lord Kylsant* a prospectus said quite truthfully that dividends had been paid every year between 1921 and 1927. What it did not say was that the company had made trading losses during each of those years and had only been able to keep up its dividends out of non-recurring exceptional items following the end of the war. The implication was that the company had been trading profitably and this was a statement false in a material particular[129].

(f) Inclusion of a *misleading statement* in a *Prospectus* is a separate offence under s.44, 1948 Act, committed by anyone who authorised the issue of it, punishable by a fine of £500, and up to two years' imprisonment unless he proves

    (1) reasonable belief in its truth

or (2) that it was immaterial.

Note that no intention to defraud is necessary.

(g) *Fraudulently* inducing a person to *acquire securities* leads to liability under the *Prevention of Frauds (Investment) Act 1958* s.13 as amended by the *Protection of Depositers Act 1963* s.21; and s.1 of the latter imposes liability for fraudulently inducing a person to *invest money* on *deposit*.

(h) *Liquidation* is the occasion for other criminal liabilities (ss.328 to 334, 1948 Act) and the Court (in a compulsory liquidation) may direct the liquidator to institute a prosecution or refer to the Director of Public Prosecutions[130].

Unfortunately the costs come out of the assets and such a prosecution should only be ordered against the wishes of those entitled, if they have a duty to prosecute, as good citizens[131].

(i) *The Director's Burden of Proof* in these cases will depend partly upon the words of the governing section; whether, for example, they include "knowingly" "fraudulently" or "wilfully" and whether they impose a presumption of guilt which the director has to disprove. There are several alternatives:

    (i) The typical offender, as in s.126, 1948 Act (filing of Annual Return), is "every officer of the Company who is in default". This is defined by s.440 as "any officer . . . who *knowingly and wilfully* authorises or permits the

---

129. *R. v Lord Kylsant* [1932] 1 K.B. 442.
130. s.334, 1948 Act.
131. *Re London & Globe Finance Corporation* [1903] 1 Ch. 728.

default . . . ' ". This is an important safeguard for the non-executive director and means that he cannot be made liable unless he had some direct involvement in and knowledge of the offence or deliberately shut his eyes to what was going on. Thus he was excused in a case where he did not learn of a failure to file an allotment contract until after the default had occurred and then attempted to correct it[132].

Since it is clearly impracticable, especially in a large company, for all the directors to supervise compliance with the statutory requirement, this section confirms the general principle, that having appointed officials (particularly the secretary) whom they reasonably believe to be competent, they should not be personally liable for their defaults, in the absence of grounds for suspicion[133].

(ii) Some sections expressly incorporate this principle, for example s.23, 1967 Act which makes a director liable for failing to take "all reasonable steps to secure compliance" with the duties in respect of the Directors' Report. He has a defence if he can show "that he had reasonable grounds to believe and did believe that a competent and reliable person was charged with the duty of seeing that the said section" was complied with.

(iii) Some sections go further and *presume* guilt on the part of the director for the company's offence unless he can prove the contrary, or that he took all the steps, which he should have done, to prevent it[134].

(iv) Some statutes impose a joint criminal liability on the director and the company where an offence is proved to have been committed with his consent or connivance, or is attributable to his neglect[135].

(v) The winding-up provisions (ss.328–334) impose a particularly formidable set of criminal penalties for directors, mainly in connection with concealment or alteration of documents or information, or failure to co-operate with

---

132. *Beck v. Board of Trade Solicitor* (1932), 76 Sol. J. 414.
133. *Huckerby v Elliott* [1970] 1 All E.R. 189.
134. e.g. Borrowing (Control and Guarantees) Act 1946 Sched. 3(4).
135. e.g. Deposit of Poisonous Wastes Act 1972, s.6.

the Liquidator. An attempt by a director to procure the cancellation of a debt owing from him to the company was held not to be a criminal transfer under these sections[136].

4-18 Relief from Liability

(1) *By Ratification*

A director who has committed an offence or breach of duty, may, nevertheless, escape liability in certain circumstances.

Three possibilities are open to him:—

(a) Ratification by the members in general meeting.

(b) Indemnity in the Articles or by agreement.

(c) Relief by the Court.

Ratification by General Meeting

We have already seen that a breach of duty, if not *ultra vires* the company, may be pardoned or ratified by an Ordinary Resolution of the Members[137], or by their unanimous approval (whether at a meeting or not)[138].

The qualifications on this principle are that:

(i) the director can vote his own shares[139], unless to do so would be a fraud on the minority, as in some cases where the director directly or indirectly controls the meeting[140],

(ii) he must in any event have acted honestly, so that the breach should have been one of the duty of skill and care rather than that of good faith[141].

Examples of breaches which *can be ratified* in this way:

(i) alloting shares for the wrong purpose,

(ii) failing to disclose an interest in a contract,

(iii) obtaining a secret profit, without damaging the company,

---

136. *R. v Davies* [1954] 3 All E.R. 335.
137. *Hogg v Cramphorn Ltd.* [1966] 3 All E.R. 420 and see para 4-02 above.
138. *Re Gee & Co. (Woolwich) Ltd.* [1974] 2 W.L.R. 515.
139. *Northern Counties Securities Ltd. v Jackson Steeple & Co. Ltd.* [1974] 2 All E.R. 625.
140. *Cook v Deeks* [1916] 1 A.C. 554.
141. As in the takeover cases such as *Bamford v Bamford* [1969] 1 All E.R. 969, where the directors believed (though wrongly) that they were acting in the interests of the company in using their share-allotting powers to fend off the bid

(iv) negligence or lack of diligence[142].

Examples of *non-ratifiable* breaches:

(i) those involving an element of fraud or lack of honesty[143],

(ii) *ultra vires* or unlawful acts e.g. payment of dividends out of capital[144],

(iii) acts requiring a special procedure, e.g. the passing of a special resolution,

(iv) infringement of the personal rights of members, e.g. refusal to register share transfers for an improper purpose[145],

(v) "fraud on the minority" as where the directors seize a business opportunity for themselves when it should have belonged to the company as in *Cook v Deeks*[140]. Contrast *Regal (Hasting) Ltd. v Gulliver*[146], where the company could not have taken the opportunity in any case, and so the directors could have had their share purchase ratified if only they had thought of it. Excessive remuneration of controlling directors may also fall within the category of "oppression" or "fraud on a minority"[147].

4-19 Relief from Liability

(2) *By the Articles s.205*

Exemption from liability was frequently conferred upon the directors by the Articles and indeed the *City Equitable* directors, although negligent, escaped by means of such an Article. However, the law was subsequently changed and s.205 of the 1948 Act now declares that any Article (or contract) is *void* in so far as it *exempts* or *indemnifies* any officer or auditor for liability for

(a) negligence

(b) default

(c) breach of duty

(d) breach of trust

---

142. A good illustration is *Pavlides v Jensen* [1956] 2 All E.R. 518 where a minority shareholder alleged that a mine had been sold, not fraudulently, but at an under value. It was held that this could be ratified by the general meeting even though the directors were in the majority.

143. *Atwool v Merryweather* (1867) L.R. 5 Eq. 464n.

144. *Flitcroft's Case* (1882), 21 Ch.D. 519.

145. *Re Smith & Fawcett Ltd.* [1942] 1 All E.R. 542

146. Para. 4-06 above.

147. *Re Jermyn Street Turkish Baths* [1971] 3 All E.R. 194.

The only qualification is that the Article or contract may allow the Company to indemnify him against costs incurred in either
(a) *successfully* defending himself
or (b) *obtaining* relief from the Court.

Table A, Article 136 duly gives an indemnity in these terms.

It will be seen that the section only prohibits an *exemption* from liability and there is no objection to a *reduction* in the extent of the *duty,* subject to compliance with statutory requirements, and (presumably) the director's primary duty of good faith[148].

Examples of such a reduction are to be found in
(a) *Article 78,* Table A, which allows a director to keep benefits accruing to him from associate companies,
and
(b) *Article 84,* Table A which allows him to keep his profit from contracts with the company, provided he declares his interest and does not vote; and indeed allows even the restrictions on quorum and voting to be suspended or relaxed by Ordinary Resolution.

4-20 Relief from Liability

(3) *By the Court*
Even if a director is found in breach of duty or trust or otherwise in default, he may yet escape personal liability if the Court decides that he has acted, *honestly* and *reasonably* and ought *fairly* to be excused[149].

Note that all three requirements must be present, the first two being matters to be proved and the third being a matter for the Court's discretion. Failure on any one count will thus be sufficient to deprive the director of relief[150].

Examples of the workings of s.448:—
(a) The apprehensive director need not wait for proceedings to be brought against him, as he can take the initiative in applying to the Court for relief (s.448(2))

---

148. This was itself to have become a statutory requirement in Cl. 52 of the 1973 Companies Bill.
149. s.448, 1948 Act.
150. As in *Re J. Franklin & Son Ltd.* [1937] 2 All E.R. 43, where the directors had wrongfully paid out the company's money. A misfeasance summons (s.333) was taken out by the liquidator and the Court refused to grant them relief.

   (b) Relief has been given for:

      (i) *ultra vires* acts when carried through in good faith and on legal advice[151],

     (ii) *failure to get approval* for remuneration as required by the Articles[152],

    (iii) *failure to take qualification shares*[153],

   (c) opposition to the granting of relief by the members is not conclusive[154].

   (d) Relief has been refused.

      (i) where directors allowed an unqualified person to make up a quorum for fixing their remuneration[155],

and (ii) where they neglected their obligation to get approval for compensation for loss of office for a dismissed director[156],

and (iii) where they misapplied company funds by slavishly following the orders of the controlling shareholder[157].

Finally we may note that directors also have the usual right to the protection of the *Limitation Act 1939* after *six years*, except where:

   (a) there is a fraud, in which case the time does not run until it is or should have been discovered,

and

   (b) where the director has the company's property, in which case time does not start to run at all.

---

151. *Re Claridges Patent Asphalte Co. Ltd.* [1921] 1 Ch. 543.

152. *Re Duomatic Ltd.* [1969] 1 All E.R. 161.

153. *Re Barry & Staines Linoleum Ltd.* [1934] Ch. 227.

154. *Re Gilt Edge Safety Glass Ltd.* [1940] Ch. 495.

155. *Re J. Franklin & Son Ltd.* [1937] 2 All E.R. 43

156. s.191, 1948 Act, *Re Duomatic Ltd.* (above). It is interesting to see that both these refusals related to breach of duty in respect of *remuneration*.

157. *Selangor United Rubber Estates Ltd. v Cradock (No. 3)* [1968] 2 All E.R. 1073.

Chapter 5

RELATIONS WITH SHAREHOLDERS

5-01 Transfer of Shares

One of the duties of the board is to register share transfers (when duly stamped) and in the case of *Listed* companies, they will have no discretion, as fully paid shares must be transferable without restriction. However, as we have seen private companies must, by s.28 of the 1948 Act, restrict the right to transfer their shares. What then are the duties of the directors of a private company when a share transfer is presented to them for registration? All depends upon the Articles which will contain the restrictions, but directors should remember that in the absence of some impediment they must register a duly stamped transfer accompanied by the share certificate and the prescribed fee (if any). The stamp duty is at present 2% on the consideration, but under the *Stock Transfer Act 1963,* the transfer can be in the form specified in that Act and does not need the signature of the transferee. This is the form now used invariably by stockbrokers. Thus the *prima facie* right to have his shares transferred rests with the shareholder[1] and it is for the directors to show why it should be denied in any particular case.

When they refer to the Articles, the directors will usually find restrictions of two kinds:—

(a) a power for directors, "in their absolute discretion and without assigning any reason therefor" to decline to register any transfer[2] and

(b) power for the members to transfer freely within the membership or the family, but with a right of pre-emption for insiders before there is a transfer to an outsider.

Articles frequently combine the two forms of restriction in such a way that the directors' powers under (a) will only come into play

---

1. *Lindlar's Case* [1910] 1 Ch. 312.
2. Table A. Pt. II Art. 3.

if the possibilities in (b) have been exhausted and a transfer to an outsider is in prospect.

They must, of course, satisfy themselves that a transfer submitted under (b) complies with the relevant Article but the exercise of their discretion only arises under (a) and it is here they may be in need of guidance.

The following factors may be relevant:—

(a) Their primary duty is to exercise their discretion (like all other powers) in the interests of the company[3].

(b) The burden of proving bad faith or improper purpose, lies on the person alleging it. It was held that this burden was not discharged in a case where a surviving (50%) director and shareholder refused to register a transfer unless half of the shareholding was sold to him. It was held there was nothing to show that he was not acting in the company's interests[3].

(c) Where the Article is as wide as Table A, Part II Article 3, the directors would be well advised to give no reason for their refusal. If they give none, there is nothing to be attacked[4].

(d) Their duty is to act in good faith in the interests of the company, with due regard to the member's right to transfer his shares, and fairly to consider the matter at a board meeting. Thus, if they take no action at all, the transfer must be registered[5].

(e) They must give notice of refusal within *two months* (s.78, 1948 Act), otherwise they are liable to a default fine, and the transferee will usually be entitled to demand registration[6]. Cl.20 of the *Companies Bill 1973* would have reduced the period to 28 days and *required* the directors to state the grounds for refusal, *regardless* of anything in the Articles.

(f) The remedy for a disgruntled member is to apply to the Court for *rectification* of the register, under s.116, 1948 Act; not for a winding-up[7].

3. *Re Smith v Fawcett Ltd.* [1942] 1 All E.R. 542
4. *Re Bede S.S. Co.* [1917] 1 Ch. 123.
5. *Moodie v W. & J. Shepherd* (*Bookbinders*) *Ltd.* [1949] 2 All. E.R. 1044.
6. *Re Swaledale Cleaners Ltd.* [1968] 3 All E.R. 619.
7. *Charles Forte Investments Ltd. v Amanda* [1963] 2 All E.R. 940.

(g) *Transmission* on death, bankruptcy or liquidation of a member gives rise to two consequences:—

    (i) The company must accept the Probate etc., as evidence of the right of the representative to deal with the shares (ss.76 and 82, 1948 Act).

    (ii) This does not mean that the company must accept the representative as a *member*. If he applies for registration as such, the directors have the same right to decline as they would have had in the case of the original member himself (see Table A, Art. 30).

On death of a joint holder, the survivor becomes the sole member.

5-02 Compulsory Acquisition of Shares

We have noted the directors' responsibilities in connection with the restriction of share transfers. What powers may they enjoy in the opposite direction—that of *compelling* share transfers? There are several possibilities:—

(a) *Lien.* The Articles may give them a lien (or charge) on shares for any debts due from the members to the company. In that case the Articles usually give also a power of *Sale,* at the directors' discretion, with further power to execute a transfer. Table A Articles 11–13, contain such provisions but are restricted to *partly* paid shares[8].

However the special Articles of private companies often extend this to fully paid shares, which is clearly of more practical use to the company, in view of the rarity of partly paid shares.

(b) *Compulsory Transfer.* The Articles may also provide that a member *shall* transfer his shares on specified terms in the event of:

    (i) his bankruptcy

or (ii) breach of some regulation of the company. Transfer under (i) cannot be resisted by the Trustee in Bankruptcy unless he can show unfairness in the price. It is not therefore inherently objectionable[8a]. A resolution by the

---

8. They have to be so restricted in *Listed* Companies.
8a. *Borland's Trustee v Steel Bros. & Co. Ltd.* [1901] 1 Ch. 279.

directors (or members) for compulsory transfer under (ii) will be enforceable if *bona fide* in the interest of the company as a whole, as where it is used to get rid of a competing shareholder[9].

It will not be *bona fide*, however, if the objective is simply to expropriate the minority[10] or to force a sale without reference to the needs of the company[11].

(c) *Deprival of Pre-emptive Rights*

A shareholder may be deprived of his pre-emptive rights (i.e. his rights to have first refusal in respect of the shares of the other members) by an alteration of the Articles, since every shareholder takes the risk that such alterations may be made—provided the change is made *bona fide* and is not a fraud on the minority[12].

5-03 Insider Dealing *Percival v Wright*

We look now at the director's position and his obligations where he is himself buying or selling shares in his own company. The law on this difficult subject is generally thought to be out of date and this is not surprising since it derives from one highly criticised decision by a Court of first instance in 1902, *Percival v Wright*[13]. In this case, a group of shareholders approached the directors and asked them to purchase their shares. The directors did so without disclosing that a sale of the company's business was pending which put a far higher value on the shares than that which the directors were paying. It was held that:—

(a) the directors' duty was owed to the company and not to the shareholders individually.

(b) there had been no misrepresentation or unfair dealing and it was the members who had approached the directors.

(c) therefore the transaction would not be set aside.

Absurd as it may be and below even the lowest standards of conduct which we would now accept, *Percival v Wright* is still the law. Whether its continued authority is due to the rarity of

9. *Sidebottom v Kershaw Leese & Co.* [1920] 1 Ch. 154.
10. *Brown v British Abrasive Wheel Co.* [1919] 1 Ch. 290.
11. *Dafen Tinplate Co. Ltd. v Llanelly Steel Co.* [1920] 2 Ch. 124.
12. *Greenhalgh v Arderne Cinemas Ltd.* [1950] 2 All E.R. 1120.
13. [1902] 2 Ch. 421.

its facts or to the reluctance of minority shareholders to risk bankruptcy in seeking to get it overruled is not known. What is known is the view of the 1973 Government and the Department of Trade—they would treat such conduct on the part of the directors as a criminal offence[14].

Moreover, it might well be that *Percival v Wright* would be decided differently today in any event, on the principle of *Regal (Hastings) Ltd. v Gulliver,* in that the directors had derived a personal profit from information acquired by them as directors. As we have seen, absence of damage to the company is irrelevant and the inside information may be regarded as company property which they have used[15]. It would be the company which would reap the reward and not the shareholders who sold their shares, but this would be better than nothing and at least the shareholders who pursued the matter could expect an indemnity for their costs on the basis of *Wallersteiner v Moir*[16]. Moreover, it may be argued that it is right that the company should benefit because it is the company's property (the inside information) which has been used and the members as a whole should share in the proceeds.

5-04 Insider Dealing: The Companies Bill 1973

Having attempted to see *Percival v Wright* in its modern context we may now seek to draw some conclusions:—

(a) Clearly, there can be no objection in principle to the owning, and therefore the buying and selling, of shares by a director. Otherwise, what would be the point of a share qualification?

(b) What is objectionable is share dealing by a director when he is at an *advantage* over the other party by virtue of his inside information. This is where his difficulty arises because there must be very few occasions when a director does *not* have such inside information and is not therefore at an advantage. He must surely satisfy himself, if he can, that the information would not affect a prudent buyer or seller—

---

14. *Companies Bill 1973* ss.12–16. There is little doubt that Insider Trading will be prohibited in the next Companies Act.
15. see para. 4-06 above.
16. (No. 2) [1975] 1 All E.R. 849.

i.e. is *not price-sensitive,* and only then can he feel free to deal.

(c) As we have seen, even with *Percival v Wright* as an authority, dealings in breach of these principles could give rise to liability to the company on the ground of personal enrichment.

(d) Moreover during the period of limbo, with insider dealing destined to become a criminal offence the prudent director must surely take note of the standards which were put forward in the *Companies Bill 1973* and see whether his conduct will meet them.   In so far as they affect directors, they were as follows[17]:—

Companies Bill 1973

(a) A director must *not deal* in his company's shares if
  (i) he has *price sensitive* information, and
  (ii) it is *not* generally *available* (i.e. the *Percival v Wright* situation).

(b) He must not deal in shares in *another* company if his information relates to transactions affecting both his company and the other (i.e. the director of a bidding company must not deal in shares in the "target").

(c) He must not use *agents* to deal on his behalf.

(d) He must not *pass on* his inside information (i.e. *tips*) if the shares are Listed and he has reason to think the "Tippee" will deal.

(e) The *"Tippee"* if an associate (e.g. relative, partner or employee) of the "Tipper", must not deal.

(f) the *company* must not deal when any director or employee is precluded.

(g) *Exception:* dealing is allowed if the main purpose was not to make a profit or avoid a loss as where he had to sell to pay income tax or repay a creditor.

(h) *Further exceptions* where a director acts solely:
  (i) to acquire qualification shares
or (ii) in a share option or incentive scheme
or (iii) as agent (not having given advice to the principal)
or (iv) as underwriter

---

17. *Companies Bill 1973* Cl. 12–16.

or (v) as Trustee of a Pension Fund

or (vi) as Personal Representative, Liquidator, Receiver or
         Trustee in Bankruptcy.

(h) The *Penalties* for contravention of these provisions were to
    have been imprisonment for up to *seven* years, and or a fine,
    combined with a liability to compensate the "outsider" for
    any loss (Cl.15).

These provisions of the Bill were undoubtedly far reaching and
stringent, and compliance with them should be enough to satisfy
the most disgruntled "outsider"[18]. The object, of course, is to ensure that all parties to a transaction shall deal on the basis of
equal availability of information. If strictly adhered to, they are
bound to make it very difficult for a director to deal in his
company's shares at all, except where he falls within one of the
exceptions. After all, when is a director not in possession of price
sensitive inside information? He must inevitably know more than
outsiders, even if the effect of his knowledge on the market price
may usually be slight. The logical consequence would appear to be
that implementation of these clauses would impose a *positive duty*
to *disclose* information on the part of the director. In the case of
sales on the Stock Exchange, this is impossible except by means of
publication in the press, but it is otherwise where the parties are
face to face. So in sales or purchases of shares in private companies,
there might develop a *duty to communicate*[19], which would turn the
Contract into one of utmost good faith (*uberrimae fidei*) like an
insurance contract. The civil liability to compensate could perhaps
be excluded by the contract but this is not possible in respect of
the criminal liability.

5-05 Insider Dealing: Practice

We have observed the two opposite ends of the legal spectrum
in the form of *Percival v Wright* and cl.12–16 of the *Companies Bill
1973*; what then are directors doing in practice, and what should
they be advised to do?

(a) They may be recommended to follow the rules of the 1973 Bill
    which we have just discussed. This must be sound advice,

---

18. There seems little doubt that they will be enacted at the next reform; they
    were proposals of a Conservative Government and other administrations are
    not likely to be less stringent. This comment applies equally to the other
    provisions of the Bill, most of which were of an "interventionist" nature
    and imposed greater obligations upon the company and its directors.
19. As alleged in *Arenson v Arenson* [1973] 2 All E.R. 235.

if difficult to take. There is something to be said for getting used to it before it is enacted.

(b) In *Listed Companies* they will often have house rules which will give them some guidance, for example as to abstaining from dealing during a prescribed period before the announcement of the results.

(c) The Institute of Directors in *"Guidelines for Directors"* pp.20–21, indicates practical and ethical standards:—

   (i) "Never buy shares in a company of which you are a director on the strength of inside information not available to the general body of shareholders or without thinking of the possible consequences for the company or indeed yourself when you may wish to sell. It is self-evident that damage can come about through it being known that directors are *selling* and, moreover, it is just as wrong to sell shares on inside information (the inference being that things are not going too well) as it is to buy them."

   (ii) Few things can more rapidly impair a company's investment status than being labelled as "a directors' company", i.e. one where the directors are in the habit of dealing in their own shares.

   (iii) The principle of willing seller dealing with willing buyer only applies when both deal with *identical* knowledge.

   (iv) There should be a *close season* for dealing of a few weeks before and after publication of the results or of any price sensitive information.

(d) Where *Mergers or Takeovers* of Public Companies are concerned the *City Code* prescribes a code of practice, not enforceable by law but widely observed, as a form of self-discipline administered by the Panel on Takeovers and Mergers[20].

   It includes the following Rules in relation to Insider Dealing:

Rule 30: No dealings of any kind may be made in the shares of the offeree company by anyone (other than the offeror) who is *privy* to the preliminary discussions or intentions of the parties between,

---

20. *City Code on Takeovers and Mergers* (June 1974), issued by the City Working Party and obtainable from The Issuing Houses Association, Roman Wall House, 1–2 Crutched Friars, London EC3N 2NJ. See also Appendix D.

(i)   the time when there is reason to suppose that an approach or offer is *contemplated*

and

(ii) the *announcement* of the approach or offer or of the termination of discussions.

Rule 31: Subject to Rule 30, and other Rules of the Code, dealings must be notified *daily* to the Stock Exchange, the Panel and the Press.

In addition *General Principle 5* contains an overriding obligation on all parties "to prevent the creation of a false market" in the shares of either company. This can only be achieved if information is equally available to all and if, in the absence of such equality, those with information abstain from dealing. *Practice Note No. 7* (June 1974) applies this principle in conjunction with Rule 30, as follows:

(1)   After an announcement of a bid has been made, a further duty not to deal falls upon the offeror and those who may be privy to discussions or intentions with regard to *termination* of the offer, before the announcement of termination.

(2)   The offeror, although usually entitled to deal under Rule 30, may not do so if normal business standards forbid, e.g. where he has been given confidential price sensitive information by the offeree.

The Stock Exchange has issued its own guidelines for Takeovers and Acquisitions; these incorporate the City Code and the objective is the maximum of disclosure, including disclosure of directors' interests[21].

(e)   A general *duty of disclosure* to members was discussed by Department of Trade inspectors recently in an investigation under s.165(b) of the 1948 Act[22]. They pointed out that although a director's duties are owed to the company, there must be an implication in the "information" sections of the Act that directors should supply to shareholders all the information concerning the company's affairs *which they might reasonably expect* to receive, particularly when they are being invited to vote on a resolution in General Meeting. The Inspectors made the interesting point that this interpretation is supported by the Act itself in s.165(b) where Inspectors may

---

21. *Admission of Securities to Listing,* Chapters 4 & 5.
22. Report on *First Re-Investment Trust Ltd.* and other companies. Dept. of Trade; H.M.S.O. 1974.

be appointed if the Department of Trade considers "that its members have not been given all the information with respect to its affairs *which they might reasonably expect*". Does not this imply a general duty to give information which goes beyond the specific obligations in regard to the Accounts, Directors' Report, Shareholdings and other matters?

It has certainly been held, in the case of a takeover, that directors in supplying information and making a recommendation, have a duty to their own shareholders to be honest and not to mislead[23].

5-06 Option Dealings

The first move towards statutory regulations of insider trading (which is, incidentally, favoured by the Takeover Panel itself) was made in 1967 with the prohibition of *Option Dealing* by directors of *Listed* companies. Ss.25 and 30 of the *Companies Act 1967* provide that:—

(a) the buying of an option to
    (i) call for delivery (a "call" option)
or (ii) make delivery (a "put" option)
or (iii) to call or put, as he elects (a "double" option)
       of *Listed* shares or debentures in his company or an associated company, is a *criminal* offence by the director.

(b) the *penalty* is imprisonment for up to two years or a fine or both.

(c) "*director*" includes a person whom the directors are accustomed to obey.

(d) *Spouses* and *minor* children are equally prohibited, although they may escape liability by proving that they had no reason to believe that their spouse or parent was a director (s.30).

(e) The prohibition does *not* apply to an option to *subscribe* for share (i.e. from the company itself) or to the purchase of *convertible* debentures. Thus the section does nothing to prevent share-option schemes as a form of remuneration, although details must be disclosed under s.16(1)(d) of the 1967 Act in the Directors' Report.

(f) If it appears that there has been a contravention of s.25, the Department of Trade may order an investigation (s.32).

---

23. *Gething v Kilner* [1972] 1 All E.R. 1164.

Option dealing is, in the ordinary way, a straightforward piece of gambling but it is difficult to refute the argument that there is no difference in principle between using inside information to deal in options and using it to deal in the shares themselves.

5-07 Disclosure. (1) Directors' Share Interests

The philosophy of the 1948 and 1967 Companies Acts was that standards of conduct and fair dealing in the affairs of companies could be maintained not so much by *regulation* as by *disclosure*. It was thought, for example, that directors would not deal improperly in their company's shares if their dealings were reported and thus became subject to comment and criticism by the members. As we have seen, the "disclosure" philosophy is tending, in some areas, to yield to the "regulatory" approach, but the importance of disclosure has not diminished. Many obligations are imposed on directors, in this respect, and we may look first at the position with regard to their own shareholdings, and its relevance to the monitoring of insider dealings.

The duty to *disclose directors' shareholdings* is enforced by the following requirements of ss.27–29 of the 1967 Act[23a].

(a) Every director *must notify* his company of his interests in its shares or debentures.

(b) Written notice must be given within *14 days* of his becoming a director if he already owns the shares; otherwise, within 14 days of his acquiring the interest (or of his learning of it, if later).

23a. What follows is an attempt to state the effect of these sections (which replaced s.195 of the 1948 Act) in a condensed and reasonably comprehensible form. They are so elaborate and exhaustive that one may sympathise with the following exchange which occurred in the House of Commons Standing Committee:—

Mr. J. T. Price: "Does anybody seriously believe that all these complicated provisions are capable of being enforced or observed ... It is just academic nonsense."

The Chairman: "What has been selected for discussion can hardly be called nonsense."

In fact, Mr. Price was nearer the truth than he may have realised. The drafters of these sections tied themselves into so many knots that they eventually produced a piece of literal nonsense. S.28(11) provides that delivery of shares to a person's order in fulfilment of his purchase contract is deemed to be an event as a result of which he *ceases* to be interested in them. So when he gets the contract note he becomes "interested" but when the executed transfer and share certificate arrive, his interest ceases! So much for those who are determined to leave no loophole unstopped!

(c) 14 days' notice must also be given of any *change* in his interests (sale, purchase, contract, rights issue from an associate, etc).

(d) The notice must state the number, amount and class of the shares or debentures and the *price*.

(e) *Contravention* or making a false or reckless statement may be punished by up to *two years'* imprisonment or a fine or both.

These requirements are backed up by a formidable array of definitions and extensions, of which we may summarise the following:—

(a) *Interests to be notified* (s.28)

(i) "Interest" is *not excluded* by reason of remoteness, or the manner in which it arises, or restrictions on it.

(ii) Interest in *Trusts* are thus included (except discretionary trusts).

(iii) Interests of a *company* are included where the director controls its management or one-third of the voting power.

(iv) He is interested as soon as he enters into a *contract* to purchase, and as soon as he has a right to call for delivery.

(v) Control of any *right* enjoyed by the shares is included.

(vi) A *joint* interest is included.

(vii) Interests in *unidentifiable* shares are included (e.g. where they form part of a trust holding).

(viii) Interest as a *Trustee* (except a bare Trustee) is included.

(b) *Interests which need not be notified*[24].

(i) Interests in *reversion* or remainder under a trust (i.e. where someone else is entitled to the income.)

(ii) *Discretionary Interests* under a trust.

(iii) Interest as a *bare* trustee (i.e. where the beneficiary can call for delivery at any time, such as where the director is a mere nominee.)

(iv) A *Unit Trust* holding.

(v) Interest as a *Proxy*.

(vi) A right of *pre-emption* under the Articles.

---

24. Some of these exemptions are contained not in the Act but in *Regulations* made by the Department of Trade under their authority in s.27(1) 1967 Act.

(vii) Interest as a Trustee or beneficiary of certain *Superannuation* and *Retirement* schemes[25].

(viii) Interests of a director of a *wholly owned subsidiary,* where he is also a director of the parent which maintains its own register (see below).

(ix) Interests of a director of a wholly owned subsidiary in shares of a *foreign* holding or associate company.

(c) *Wives and Children*

S.31, extends these duties to the interests of spouses and minor children of the director. Moreover, he must give the 14 days' notice in respect of the grant or exercise of any right for them to *subscribe* for shares or debentures in the company. Children includes step-children and adopted children.

(d) *The Notice.* The notice required by s.27 must be given in writing and must *state* that it is given in fulfilment of the obligations under the section[26]. The time limit, as we have seen, is 14 days from,

(i) the day after the director's *appointment* in the case of existing interests,

(ii) the day after the *"event"* in the case of subsequent events,

(iii) the day after he became *aware* of it, in cases where he was unaware at the time of (i) or (ii).

(e) *The Register.* S.29 requires the company to keep a register of the notices given under s.27,

(i) The information must be recorded within *3 days* of receipt[27].

(ii) It must be *indexed* unless it is itself in the form of an index; the forms commonly used for the notices can themselves serve as a loose-leaf index.

(iii) Entries for each name must be in chronological order.

(iv) The company must *itself* record the information where it grants a right to subscribe and where the grant is

---

25. Under ss.208, 221 and 224 *Income & Corporation Taxes Act 1970.*
26. The Publishers supply forms which comply with these requirements (See Appendix F).
27. This excludes Saturdays, Sundays and Bank Holidays as does the 14 day limit, under s.27 (ss.29(4) and 27(12)).

exercised. This does not apply to spouses and children as in their case the director must give the usual notice.

(v) *Inspection* must open to members (free) and the public (5p). The register must be at the Registered Office, or where the register of members is kept and in the latter case, notice of the address must be given to the Registrar. The register must also be available for inspection at the A.G.M. *Anyone* can require *copies* to be supplied within *10 days* at a price of 10p per 1,000 words (s.29(10)).

(vi) *Penalties* for contravention of s.29 are *default fines* and the court can order inspection and the supply of copies.

(vii) *Inspectors* may be appointed by Department of Trade to investigate suspected contraventions of s.27 (s.32). The power to appoint Inspectors under s.172 of the 1948 Act for investigating ownership and control, can also be used to look into share dealings.

(viii) By s.16(1)(e) of the 1967 Act the *Directors' Report* must include particulars of the directors' interests as recorded in the s.29 Register.

Three points may finally be noted:

(a) It will be seen that the all-embracing arms of s.27 may even overlap, so that the total extent of the interests notified may exceed the number of issued shares. For example, if a director and his wife hold 100 shares jointly on trust for two of their children, four separate notices would have to be given and so the register would show a total of 400 shares.

(b) The duty to notify under the 1967 Act is *not* in any way restricted to *listed* or *public* companies. It applies in its full severity to all companies however small and however closely held. The director of a one-man company must thus give notice to himself. Contrast sections 25 (option dealing) and 33 (notification by 10% shareholders) which apply only to *listed* companies.

(c) Sections 27–29 are so complicated and far reaching that the only safe advice which can be given to a director is—when in doubt, give the notice!

5-08 Disclosure: (2) Inspection of Documents

An important aspect of the principle of disclosure and of the relations between board and members, is the right of the latter to *inspect* many important documents and registers. Clearly, this is not so effective as the right to *receive* information but the existence of the right to inspect must be an influence on those whose papers may be inspected.

To summarise, the 1948 Act gives shareholders a right to inspect:—

(i)   the minutes of *general meetings* (s.146)

(ii) the register of *members* (s.113(1))

(iii) the register of *debenture* holders (s.87)

(iv) the register of *charges* (s.105)

(v)   the register of *directors* and secretaries (s.200(6))

(vi) the *statement of affairs* submitted to the Official Receiver in a Winding-Up (s.235(6)).

The 1967 Act allows them to inspect:—

(i)   the *Auditors'* report on the accounts (s.14(2))

(ii) directors' *service contracts* or memoranda thereof (s.26)

(iii) the register of *directors' interests* (s.29)

(iv) the register of *10% shareholders* (s.34).

Moreover, it has been held that:—

(i)   members taking action against the company are entitled to see reports obtained on behalf of the company unless protected by privilege[28].

(ii) where directors hold shares as Trustees they are not obliged, for that reason, to disclose information acquired as directors[29].

So far as the other books and documents of the company are concerned (including ledgers and accounts), the members have *no rights* of inspection except what the Articles permit. Article 125 of Table A leaves it to the directors to decide if, when and to what extent inspection shall be allowed, and provides that no member shall have any right of inspection except as conferred by:—

(i)   statute or

(ii) the directors or

(iii) the general meeting.

---

28. *W. Dennis & Sons Ltd. v West Norfolk Farmers etc. Co.* [1943] Ch. 220.
29. *Butt v Kelson* [1952] 1 All E.R. 167.

5-08 Disclosure: (2) Inspection of Documents

When a member specifically asks for information which does not fall within any of the specified categories, the directors should not, of course, divulge anything which they would not communicate to the members as a whole.

5-09 Disclosure: (3) Inspection of Registers

Some of the rights of inspection noted above deserve special mention, apart from the register of directors' interests which we have considered in paragraph 5-07. We look first at the *Register of Members,* s.110, 1948 Act.

(a) This is required to show:
   (i)   names and addresses and shareholdings of each member,
   (ii) date of entry as a member,
   (iii) date of termination of membership.

(b) The register may be bound or loose leaf and must be indexed (if more than 50 members) unless it constitutes an index in itself. It is *prima facie* evidence of its own accuracy (s.118).

(c) It must be kept at the Registered Office or at the office of a Registrar if made up by him.

(d) *Inspection* must be allowed during business hours to any member (without charge) and to anyone else (5p), and *copies* of any part must be furnished to any one who so requests *within 10 days* on payment of 10p per hundred words (s.113, 1948 Act, s.52(2), 1967 Act).

(e) It may be *closed* for up to 30 days per year by advertisement to that effect.

(f) The register may be *rectified* by the Court if anyone alleges that a name is wrongly entered, or omitted or not removed, (s.116, 1948 Act).

(g) *No notice of any trust* can be entered (s.117, 1948 Act) so that the company is always free to deal only with the registered proprietor[30]. Thus if a vendor of shares has delivered the transfer and share certificate to the purchaser but is still unpaid, he cannot make the company take notice of his lien[31]. The only way in which someone off the register can protect himself is by service of a *"Stop Notice"*. He files an affidavit

---

30. Also stipulated by Article 7, Table A.
31. *Langen & Wind Ltd. v Bell* [1972] 1 All E.R. 296

and notice in the High Court and serves copies on the company. This entitles him not to any priority but to an *eight day* notice of any transfer, during which he must apply to the Court for an injunction[32].

5-10 Register of 10% Shareholdings in Listed Companies

In an effort to prevent the accumulation of large shareholdings by stealth, without the knowledge of the board or the other members, s.33 of the 1967 Act introduced a new obligation to disclose, so that such shareholders might no longer withhold their identity by the use of nominees[33]. The mechanism of the section is as follows:—

(a) The section applies, essentially, to companies with *Listed* capital and to classes of capital carrying full voting rights.

(b) (i) A person who *becomes* interested in 10% of such a class or

 (ii) a 10% holder who *increases* or *decreases* his holding, above that level, and

 (iii) A 10% holder who *sinks* below 10% must *notify* the company in writing of that event and of his holding after it.

(c) A 10% holder when the shares *become listed* must notify.

(d) The notice is to be given within *14 days* of the day after the obligation has arisen.

(e) "*Interest*" is as defined by s.28 for the purpose of directors' interests (see para. 5-7 above), i.e. including most *beneficial and trustee interests* but *excluding*:

 (i) Life Interests.

 (ii) Lenders taking security.

 (iii) Others prescribed by the Department of Trade, e.g. Public Trustee, and certain corporate Trustees[34] and Pension Scheme Trustees.

---

32. *Rules of the Supreme Court* Ord. 50, 11–14.
33. Where Listed companies are themselves the buyers of shares, they have a general duty under Cl. 4(a) of the *Listing Agreement* to notify the Stock Exchange of any "material acquisitions".
34. Regulations S.I. 1968, No. 864 and 1970 No. 1373 and Pension Schemes under *Income and Corporation Taxes Act 1970* ss.208, 221 and 390.

(f) *Penalties* in default, of up to two years' imprisonment or a fine or both.

(g) A *Register* (s.34) of these shareholdings must be kept by the board on lines almost identical to the register of directors' interests, i.e. at the same place, made up in the same manner (within 3 days) and entries do not fix the company with notice of third party rights (s.34(4)). This is because people giving notice may not be on the register (as where their shares are held by nominees) and the company might thus become involved in notice of a trust contrary to s.117 of the 1948 Act. The same is true of the Register of directors' interests (s.29(6)). The register must be open to inspection by all parties during business hours for not less than two hours per day, and copies supplied in the usual way (s.34(7)). However, information as to the holdings of a company incorporated or trading outside the U.K. will be excluded from inspection if the board consider disclosure of information harmful and the Department of Trade consent under s.3(3) or 4(3) of the 1967 Act. There are fines of £500 and default fines for breach of s.34.

(h) where the occurrence of the event giving rise to the obligation is *not known* at that time, the 14 day period does not start until the day after it becomes known[35].

5-11 Register of Directors and Secretaries

Section 200 of the 1948 Act requires a register of directors and secretaries to be kept by the Company as follows:—

---

35. s.33(5), At this point, the draftsman of the 1967 Act having created so extensive a duty, now found himself faced with the problem of innocent shareholders who might become guilty of a criminal offence by accident. Accordingly he moved into a fairy-tale world where there are stages of knowledge and ignorance which may determine the date on which the obligation arises. Thus, the shareholder's ignorance may derive from one or more sources:—

(a) He may know that he has 10% or that his 10% holding has changed (e.g. where a rights issue has been overlooked).

(b) He may not know that the company has come within the section, i.e. that a quotation has been granted.

(c) He may not know that his particular shares have become "relevant", i.e. that full voting rights have been granted.

(d) He may know of the "event" but not that it increases his holding to 10%, e.g. where his holding has changed several times in quick succession.

Then the general rule is that the obligation arises only when *all these sources of ignorance have ceased* and it must be performed 14 days after the last relevant item came to his knowledge.

(a) the Register must be kept at the *Registered Office* and be open for inspection during business hours for not less than two hours per day for members, without charge, and for others at a charge of 5p.

(b) For an *individual* director it must state his name, any former names, his residential address, nationality[36] occupation, and other directorships (except of parent or subsidiary companies or fellow subsidiaries),

(c) For a *Corporate* director, it must state its corporate name and registered office.

(d) These particulars must be *notified* to the Registrar of Companies within 14 days of the appointment of the first directors or of any change in the directors or secretary.

(e) Every *public* company must record the date of birth of its directors. For the purposes of section 200 it is *"subject"* to the retirement-at-70 section, (185) even though its Articles may exclude it.

(f) Similar particulars of *Secretaries* must be given, except that their *age, occupation* and *directorships* of other Companies are not required.

(g) Penalty in default is a fine of £5 per day (s.200 (7)).

(h) The current state of the register must be recorded in the *Annual Return* under sections 124 and 125. This has to be filed with the Registrar within 42 days of the Annual General Meeting (s.126).

5-12 Accounts

Pre-eminent amongst the directors' responsibility to their shareholders is the preparation and submission of Accounts. A compact and authoritative summary both of the statutory requirements and of the best practice is to be found in the booklet, *Financial and Accounting Responsibilities of Directors*[37], and we shall confine ourselves here to a brief summary of the general duties prescribed by the Acts.

---

36. A non-British director need not state his nationality if he is a citizen of an E.E.C. member state: *Companies* (*Disclosure of Directors' Nationalities*) *Exemption Order* 16th January 1974.

37. Published jointly by the *Institute of Chartered Accountants* in England and Wales and by the *Institute of Directors*; obtainable from the Institute of Directors at 10, Belgrave Square, London S.W.1.

5-12 Accounts

These are as follows:—

(a) *Books of Account* must be kept with respect to

   (i) all receipts and payments

   (ii) all sales and purchases

   (iii) assets and liabilities

   and must give a *true and fair* view of the company's affairs and explain its transactions (s.147, 1948 Act). Wilful default or failure to take all reasonable steps to comply, exposes directors to a penalty of six months imprisonment or a fine of £200, *unless* they can prove that they reasonably believed that a competent and reliable person was charged with the duty and in a position to carry it out (s.147(4) 1948 Act). This does not mean that they are exonerated from their general duty of care under the principles of *Re City Equitable Fire Insurance Company*. This duty requires them to display the normal degree of skill and diligence in the manner in which tasks are delegated and supervised.

(b) Penalties are also imposed in *winding-up,* on every officer of a Company where proper books have not been kept during the preceding two years, unless he proves that he acted honestly and ought to be excused (s.331, 1948 Act).

(c) A *profit and loss account* and *balance sheet* must be laid by the directors before the company in general meeting[38], once in every calendar year. This must likewise give a true and fair view of the profit or loss and state of affairs respectively and must be made up to not more than nine months before the meeting, or twelve months before it, when the Company has interests abroad (s.148, 149, 1948 Act).

   These accounts must comply with the detailed requirements of the Eighth Schedule of the 1948 Act as amended and consolidated in the second schedule of the 1967 Act. The directors' duty to comply with these requirements and the penalties for failure are stated in similar terms to those in respect of books of account in paragraph (a) above.

(d) Requirements particularly affecting *directors* are the inclusion in the accounts of:—

---

38. It does not have to be the A.G.M. but unless it is, the accounts annexed to the Annual Return will become out of date.

(i)   loans to officers (s.197, 1948 Act)

(ii) directors emoluments (s.196, 1948 Act and s.6, 1967 Act) (see para. 8-06 below)

(iii) waived emoluments (s.7, 1967 Act)

(iv) salaries of employees exceeding £10,000 p.a. (s.8, 1967 Act)

(e)   Groups of companies attract special requirements which are intended to ensure that the shareholders of the parent company get substantially the same information that they would have received if the business was being carried on by a single company, operating through a number of branches or departments.   This is achieved as follows:—

  (i)   A company with subsidiaries must lay before the members both its own accounts and *group accounts* giving a true and fair view of the state of affairs and profit or loss of the company and subsidiaries, as a whole, so far as concerns the members of the parent company (ss.150–152, 1948 Act).

  (ii) The group accounts are to be *consolidated*, i.e. combining the accounts of the holding and subsidiary companies into a single set of accounts, unless the directors believe that equivalent information can be given in some other way that may be readily appreciated by the members.   So the directors have considerable discretion as to the way in which the group information is presented, particularly in the use of more than one set of consolidated accounts supplemented by explanatory statements (s.151(2), 1948 Act).

  (iii) Group Accounts are *not* required where the company is itself a wholly owned subsidiary of a U.K. company or
  the directors consider that (1) such accounts would be impracticable, misleading or of no real value, or would involve undue delay or expense, or (2) the result would be harmful to the business, or (3) the respective businesses are so different that they cannot be treated as a single undertaking (s.150(2), 1948 Act).

    Grounds (2) and (3) require the consent of the Department of Trade, and the duties and penalties in respect of group accounts follow the pattern set out in paragraph (a) above.

(f) Particular disclosure duties in respect of *associated companies* and *investments* were imposed by the 1967 Act as follows:—

    (i) S.3, requires particulars of *subsidiaries* unless the directors consider that this would involve "excessive length", in which case the list can be confined to those "principally affecting" the profit or loss or assets; or that the disclosure would be harmful in which case Department of Trade agreement must be obtained[39]. The latter ground applies equally to sections 4 and 5 below.

    (ii) S.4 requires *substantial shareholdings* (other than subsidiaries) to be disclosed where the reporting company holds.

        (1) more than 10% of any class

        or

        (2) where the shareholding in another company exceeds 10% of the assets of the *reporting* company.

    (iii) S.5 requires disclosure of the *holding company*, if the reporting company is a subsidiary. Since this is not always a matter that can be definitively stated, the section says that it shall be the company "regarded by the directors as being the company's ultimate holding company".

    (iv) Schedule 2, paragraph 5A requires information as to *unquoted investments* in equity shares, unless their value is *estimated* by the directors and stated in the accounts[40].

(g) *Listed Companies* will have accounting duties in addition to those imposed by the Acts. These are in paragraphs 8 and 9 of the Listing Agreement which appears in Appendix E below.

(h) *Turnover* was required to be disclosed by Schedule 2, paragraph 13A of the 1967 Act, by every company whose figure exceeded £250,000[40a] or was a holding or subsidiary company. Turnover was not defined but the Jenkins Report (paragraphs 381–397) recommended: "the total amount receivable by a company in the ordinary course of business for goods sold or supplied

---

39. 30 applications were made in 1973 and 26 approved.
40. The Department of Trade can change the accounting requirements from time to time by statutory instrument (s.454, 1948 Act).
40a. See footnote 38.

by it as a principal, and for services supplied by it". It is usually suggested that inter-group sales would be shown separately so as to facilitate a true and fair view and their elimination on consolidation.

(i) S.155 of the 1948 Act requires the Balance Sheet to be *signed* by *two directors* (unless there is only one) and there must be annexed to it

(i) the profit and loss account

(ii) group accounts so far as not incorporated

(iii) the auditors' report (s.156)

(iv) the directors' report (s.157)

A copy of every balance sheet to be laid before the general meeting together with the annexed documents, must be sent to every member and every debenture holder, at least 21 days before the meeting. Any member or debenture holder is also entitled to a copy on demand (s.158, 1948 Act s.24, 1967 Act). If, as is usually the case, the meeting is the Annual General Meeting an Annual Return must be filed within 42 days, which must have annexed to it[41] a certified copy of the balance sheet and the documents annexed (s.127, 1948 Act). If the meeting is not the A.G.M. the accounts will be attached to the next Annual Return to be filed. The accounts are then placed on the company's file and are available for public inspection. Consequently, care should be taken to exclude any detailed trading or management accounts, which do not form part of the statutory accounts and which are intended to be kept private. The penalty in default of filing is a fine of £5 per day, but it is interesting to note that the obligation to annex the accounts is in respect of "every balance sheet *laid* before the company . . . during the period to which the return relates". If, therefore, no A.G.M. has been held and no balance sheet laid, a director cannot be convicted of this particular offence[42].

Moreover, by a concession the Department of Trade will accept, in lieu of accounts, a statement from non-trading companies either that they have not traded since incorporation or not since the last annual return and that the balance sheet remains as it was[43].

---

41. Unless the company is unlimited (s.47, 1967 Act).
42. *Stockdale v Coulson* [1974] 3 All E.R. 154.
43. Department of Trade Announcement, June 1971.

5-13 Directors Report

This is a document which by definition is the particular concern of the board and deserves special attention[44].

Originally a short and formal addition to the accounts, it was much expanded by the 1967 Act.

The general requirement, imposed by s.157 of the 1948 Act, was that the directors should attach to every balance sheet a report with respect to

(i)   the *state* of the Company's affairs

(ii) the amount, if any, recommended for *dividend*,

(iii) the amount, if any, proposed to be carried to *reserves*,

(iv) any *change* in the nature of the business of the company or of its subsidiaries or investments, in so far as material for the appreciation of the state of the company's affairs by the members and not harmful to the business.

The penalty imposed on a director for failing to take all reasonable steps to comply, is six months imprisonment (if wilful failure) or a fine of up to £200. It is a defence to prove (as in the case of the accounting duties) that the director had reasonable grounds to believe that a competent and reliable person was charged with the duty and in a position to carry it out (s.23, 1967 Act).

In practice, directors tended to say nothing about the company's state of affairs leaving the accounts to speak for themselves. Thus, the report was confined to a brief statement in respect of dividend, reserves and changes in the business. It was on this modest foundation that the 1967 Act erected a substantial structure of disclosure requirements. Sections 15–24 of the Act required the following additional matters to be dealt with in the report:—

(a) a list of the *directors* during the year (s.16(11)),

(b) the *principal activities* of the company and its subsidiaries and any *significant changes*[45] in those activities during the year (s.16(1)),

---

44. It is the sole responsibility of the directors, and although the Auditors may assist in its preparation, they do not Audit the report. Their certificate does not cover it except where the directors take advantage of s.163 of the 1948 Act and include accounting information in the Directors' Report instead of in the accounts. It is not to be confused, of course, with the *Chairman's Report* which is not a statutory document and is used for a general review.

45. It has been suggested that "significant" may mean "not insignificant", i.e. of some importance though not necessarily of major or decisive importance.

(c) *significant changes* in *fixed assets* in the year; and in the case of *land,* where the market value differs *substantially* from Balance Sheet value, the difference must be *indicated,* if in the opinion of the directors, it is of such *significance* as to require the attention of the members to be drawn to it (s.16(1)(a))[46],

(d) details of *share and debenture issues* during the year and the *reasons* for those issues (s.16(1)(b)),

(e) details of *directors' interests in contracts* must be given if the contract is *significant* and the director's interest is *material*[47]. This does not apply to service contracts (dealt with by a separate register under s.26) nor where his sole interest is as a director (as opposed to shareholders) of another company (s.16(1)(c)),

(f) particulars of company *arrangements* whereby directors acquire *benefits* in the form of shares or debentures in *any* company. Note that this applies to any benefits, however trivial and regardless of whether they are included in the accounts as part of the directors' remuneration (s.16(1)(d)),

(g) particulars of directors' *shareholdings* as notified under sections 27–29, at the beginning and end of the year and thus including debenture holdings and the interests of spouses and children. Details must be given even if the holdings are small or non-existent. If the director has specified, in the register, that

---

46. The effect (with regard to holdings of land) of this sub-section, which may constitute a record for the assembly of so many indefinable words within a single paragraph, is to leave the responsibility to the directors. They are not obliged to have a valuation each year but their duty is to consider the question of value, probably on a break-up basis, and to set this against all the other relevant factors including planning permission, taxation, costs of relocation, employment and even the consequences of liquidation. If a "substantial" difference in the total value of their land and buildings then emerges, they should disclose it, but they are entitled to draw the members' attention to these other factors. "Substantial", like "significant", must mean something more than trivial but need not amount to a major or decisive shift in value. Thus 1% is no doubt not substantial, but 30% probably is. Where the line is drawn is a matter for the directors' discretion but if they have honestly and seriously considered the matter and made their decisions, it would be very difficult to show that they had not complied with the section.

47. The paragraph does not include contracts with *subsidiaries* but directors can hardly be advised to take advantage of this omission. The Stock Exchange have remedied it in the case of listed companies and have also provided that any contract in which the directors' interests is material and which amounts to more than 1% of the company's total purchases or sales, or net assets (in the case of a capital transaction) shall be a *"contract of significance"*. Moreover "interest" is extended to spouses and children as in s.28 (Stock Exchange Notice No. 8471—19th August 1971).

part of his holding is as trustee and part beneficial, this should be repeated (s.16(1)(e)),

(h) particulars of any other matters *material* for the appreciation of the state of the company's affairs by the members, not being, in the opinion of the directors, harmful to the business (s.16(1)(p)),

(i) substantially *differing classes* of business within a company require a statement by the directors of:—

(1) the division of turnover between them

and

(2) the profitability or otherwise of each. A holding company must state similar information for the group as a whole and the £250,000 cut-off applies, as it does to the statement of total turnover in the accounts, for all except holding or subsidiary companies. The question of substantial difference is again left to the directors and it has been suggested that they should be looking at horizontal rather than vertical business structures.

Thus they would tend to apportion activities in different lines of business, such as sales of cars and sales of motor-cycles, rather than attempt the almost metaphysical task of apportioning profit to the successive stages of a vertical operation (s.17, 1967 Act).

The Stock Exchange also requires a geographical analysis where there is trading outside the U.K. (Listing Agreement paragraph 9(b)).

(j) *Employees and Wages* must be the subject of a special reference in the report, if the company (or group) has an average over the year of at least 100 employees.

The directors must state:—

(a) the average number employed by it in each week.

and

(b) the *aggregate* remuneration paid to the employees for the year.

Remuneration includes bonuses but not benefits in kind, and overseas workers are excluded (s.18, 1967 Act).

(k) *Political or Charitable* contributions must be disclosed, if the total exceeds £50. The report must state:—

(1) the *amount* given for each purpose,

(2) the *name* of the donee and the amount given for political purposes where it exceeds £50 in any one case.

(3) the *name* and amount given, where the donee is a political party and the amount exceeds £50.

Group information must be given by a holding company and "political purposes" includes a gift to someone, known to be carrying on or proposing activities likely to affect support for a political party, i.e. whether the gift itself is made for those activities or not[48].

Charitable donees need not be stated.

(1) *Exports* must be reported by companies or groups where they *supply goods* and *turnover* is £250,000 or more.

They must then state

(1) the amount of goods exported from U.K.

or

(2) if none — a statement of that fact.

It has been suggested that the phrase "the supplying of goods" should be construed with some discretion, so that absurd or minimal figures should not have to be stated by a Company where the supplying of goods is a negligible part of their business. The basis for the figure should presumably be the same as that used in calculating the total turnover.

Goods exported as an agent are disregarded and the Department of Trade can dispense with the requirement if it is in the national interest (s.20, 1967 Act),

(m) *Comparative* figures for items in the Directors' Report are not required except in respect of information which would otherwise have been required in the accounts (s.22, 1967 Act).

5-14 Auditors' Report

Every company must have an auditor and his qualifications for appointment are noted in paragraph 1-04(g) above. His position in relation to the directors and the company may be summarised as follows:—

---

48. It is questionable whether the taking of advertising space in a political journal is a political donation.

(a)   He reports to the *members* on the accounts and every balance sheet, profit and loss account and group account presented during his appointment.   The report must be annexed to the accounts, read at a general meeting and be open to inspection by any member[49].

(b)   the report must *state*

   (1)   whether the accounts have been properly prepared in accordance with the Acts

   (2)   whether they give a true and fair view.

(c)   if they are are not satisfied or have failed to obtain the information they require, they must say so[50].

(d)   They perform their duty by forwarding their report to the secretary.   They are not responsible for presenting it to the members[51].

(e)   They have a right of *access* at all times to the books and papers and to such *information* and *explanation* from the directors and officers as they consider necessary[52].   If this is not forthcoming, they should qualify their report.

(f)   They have the right to *attend*, speak at, and be notified of any general meeting[53].

(g)   Their *obligations* briefly are

   (1)   to *acquaint* themselves with their duties under the Articles and the Acts,

   (2)   to *report* to the members on the accounts in the specified form,

   (3)   to *investigate* whether accounts have been kept and whether the balance sheet and profit and loss account have been prepared in accordance with the Acts,

   (4)   to act *honestly* and with the *care and skill* that would be expected nowadays from a man of their professional qualifications[54].

---

49. s.14, 1967 Act.
50. s.14(4) and 14(6) 1967 Act.
51. *Re Allen Craig and Co.* (*London*) *Ltd.* [1934] Ch. 483.
52. s.14(5), 1967 Act.
53. s.14(7), 1967 Act.
54. *Re Thomas Gerrard & Sons Ltd.* [1967] 2 All E.R. 525, which indicated that for this purpose, the standards might be proved by the relevant Statement on Auditing published by the Institute of Chartered Accountants in England and Wales.

When valuing shares, as an Auditor may be asked to do under the terms of the Articles, he must take *reasonable care* in the interest of third parties if he knows that his professional skill is being relied on[55]. He may expressly disclaim responsibility in giving this advice, but this will not protect him when a representation is made fraudulently[56]. Where he is required to value as *expert* and not as arbitrator, the court will not normally entertain an action for negligence in the giving of his opinion[57].

5-15 Dividends

The power sharing aspects of this important subject have been considered in paragraph 3-09 above. As we have seen, the usual Article (114 of Table A) provides that "the company in General Meeting may declare dividends but no dividend shall exceed the amount recommended by the directors". Thus the dividend is the joint responsibility of board and members but the control and initiative remain firmly with the directors—as it must in a case where there are so many inhibiting factors to be considered. Amongst these are the following:—

(a) Dividends cannot be paid out of *capital*[58].

(b) Article 116, Table A, provides that dividends shall be paid only out of *profits*. This is indeed implied by the law in any event, but the definition of profits has never been entirely free from doubt; nor can it be since the charging of expenses to capital or revenue account must at times be a business question, which only the directors can decide in the light of the circumstances[59].

(c) The cases had established that:—

    (1) losses of *fixed* capital need not be made good[59],

    (2) losses of *circulating* capital (e.g. stock-in-trade) during the year must be made good. This is inevitable, in any case with a properly prepared profit and loss account,

55. *Hedley Byrne & Co. Ltd. v Heller & Partners Ltd.* [1963] 2 All E.R. 575.
56. *Commercial Banking Co. of Sydney v R. H. Brown & Co.* [1972] 126 C.L.R. 337.
57. *Arenson v Arenson* [1973] 2 All E.R. 235.
58. *Re Walters' Deed of Guarantee* [1933] Ch. 321.
59. *Lee v Neuchatel Asphalte Co.* (1889) 41 Ch.D. 1.

(3) even *revenue* losses of previous years need not necessarily be made good[60],

(4) uncapitalised *profits* of previous years may always be distributed[61],

(5) a *realised surplus* on capital may be distributed[62] as it is a profit,

(6) even an *unrealised* capital surplus arising on a *bona fide* revaluation may be distributable[63].

(d) Some of these authorities, particularly (3) and (6) above, have been questioned and are manifestly contrary to business prudence. Directors now have authoritative guidance as to better practice in these grey areas in the form of section 72 of the *Companies Bill 1973*, which attempted a definition of *profits available for dividend* as follows:—

(1) Profits should be the combined total of revenue profits and realised capital profits after *deduction* of revenue losses and realised capital losses. Thus any losses brought forward into the accounts must first be absorbed.

(2) *Realised* capital profits should not be distributed unless the directors are satisfied that the remaining capital assets after payment of the dividend are at least equal to book value.

(3) *Unrealised* capital *profits* may only be treated as profits for the purpose of paying up new bonus shares. Thus such profits cannot be paid out in the form of dividends, nor in writing off past losses or paying up debentures or issued shares.

(4) *Capital* assets are defined as any assets other than *current* assets.

(e) Where dividends are paid out of capital, the directors who are responsible, are jointly and severally *liable* to the company[64]. They may claim an indemnity from any shareholder who *knew* of the default[65].

60. *Ammonia Soda Co. v Chamberlain* [1918] 1 Ch. 266.
61. *Re Hoare & Co. Ltd.* [1904] 2 Ch. 208.
62. *Lubbock v British Bank of S. America* [1892] 2 Ch. 198.
63. *Dimbula Valley (Ceylon) Tea Co. Ltd. v Laurie* [1961] 1 All E.R. 769.
64. *Flitcroft's Case* (1882) 21 Ch.D. 519.
65. *Moxham v Grant* [1900] 1 Q.B. 88.

(f) The directors are not usually entitled to *back date* dividends by re-opening the accounts of previous years[66].

(g) Apart from the question of payment out of profits, the directors usually have a discretion as to the amount (if any) to be set aside to reserves. Article 117 of Table A gives them such authority[67].

(h) A further limiting factor on the directors' discretion is the power of the Treasury to restrict ordinary dividends under the *Counter Inflation Act 1973*, s.10. This power was exercised, so as to limit dividend increases in 1973–74 to 5% and in 1974–75 to $12\frac{1}{2}$%.

(i) Dividends must be paid in *cash* unless the Articles otherwise provide[68] and Article 120 Table A allows payment *in specie* or by way of paid up shares or debentures. However, the issue of shares *in lieu* of dividends was made taxable as income in 1975.

5-16 Takeovers and Mergers

Directors involved in such situations will naturally take specialist advice, but it may be useful to draw attention to some of the main features of the takeover scene.

(a) The general duty of the board is their usual one of acting *bona fide* in the interests of the company as a whole. Where an offer for shares is being made, it is not the company but the shareholders, whose interests are primarily at stake; thus the directors must not seek to put assets out of the shareholders' reach[69] nor to block the bid by an unnecessary share issue[70]. Since the director's duty is owed to the company and not to the members, these rules are explained on the basis that the directors must use their powers only for the purposes for which they were conferred, but what is really being protected is the members' right to sell their shares, in a manner which realises the full value of the company's assets.

---

66. *Northern Counties Securities Ltd. v Jackson Steeple & Co. Ltd.* [1974] 2 All E.R. 625.
67. This aspect of the subject is discussed in *Guidelines for Directors* (Institute of Directors) pp. 28–31.
68. *Wood v Odessa Waterworks Co.* (1889) 42 Ch.D. 36.
69. *Savoy Hotel Investigation* (s.165(6), 1948 Act) H.M.S.O. 1954.
70. *Hogg v Cramphorn Ltd.* [1966] 3 All E.R. 420.

(b) The Acts make no special provision for the conduct of bids except for s.209, 1948 Act which enables the bidder to acquire compulsorily in certain circumstances the shares of a dissenting minority, not exceeding 10%, and sections 192–194 whereby payments made to the directors must be disclosed and approved by the members.

(c) However, the directors' duties of good faith and honesty must inevitably come under sharper scrutiny when a bid is made or impending, in that his status as a director is at stake and the result is bound to affect his personal position. A particularly scrupulous adherence to the recommended standards of conduct is therefore expected. These ethical standards are surveyed in the *Institute of Directors'* booklet and include

(1) the right of the shareholders to all available information before deciding whether to sell,

(2) the avoidance of "leaks" before public announcements are made,

(3) the complete suppression of questions of personal interest,

(4) the avoidance of the need for "death-bed repentances" which indicate only that directors have not done their job in the past,

(5) the desirability of following the procedure of the *City Code*,

(6) the importance of taking advice even in the earliest and most tentative stage of the discussions in case they breach the Code or make some other mistake, before they have realised it,

(7) the need for special care and advice where the directors control the company and commit themselves to a particular offer. They must avoid situations where they may deprive the other shareholders of a better offer from another source,

(8) an absolute prohibition on *dealings* by anyone, whether director or otherwise, with inside information,

(9) the avoidance of *warehousing*, or joining with others in acquiring blocks of shares in listed companies amounting to less than 10% individually, but more in aggregate and thus defeating the notification provisions of s.33, 1967 Act.

71. *Guidelines for Directors*, pp. 41–54.

(d) The *City Code*[72] applies primarily to listed companies and will be followed by all directors of such companies. It has no legal force, but violations may be subject to private reprimand and public censure or, in a flagrant case, exclusion from the securities market. The administering, consultative and disciplinary authority is the Panel on Takeovers and Mergers, whose duty is "the enforcement of good business standards, not the enforcement of the law".

Although designed for securities, quoted on the Stock Exchange, the Code also applies to unquoted public companies and its general principles are of wide application.

These are, in essence:—

(1) The spirit as well as the letter of the Code should be observed.

(2) It must be accepted that observance of the code will *restrict* the freedom of the parties involved.

(3) Shareholders must have sufficient *information* and *time* to make their decision. No relevant information should be withheld.

(4) Once a *bona fide* offer has been made or is believed to be imminent, the board of the offeree company must do nothing which might *frustrate* the offer or deprive the members of an opportunity to decide on the merits, *without* their consent in general meeting[73].

(5) The object of all parties must be to avoid the creation of a *false market* in the shares of either company.

(6) A Board which is approached should normally seek competent *outside advice*.

(7) Rights of control must be exercised in *good faith* and there must be no oppression of a minority.

(8) All shareholders of the same class must be *treated similarly*.

---

72. *The City Code on Takeovers and Mergers* issued by the City Working Party, June 1974 and as amended. Copies can be obtained from the Secretary, Issuing Houses Association, 1–2 Crutched Friars, London E.C.3N 2NJ.

73. Such consent should always be obtained when a question arises which may involve a ruling of the Panel so that the members may share the responsibilities: Panel's statement *Re St. Martin's Property Co. Ltd.* and the *Proprietors of Hays Wharf Ltd.* 5th April 1974.

(9) If an offer is made to one or more shareholders, any subsequent general offer must be on *no less favourable* terms.

(10) Information must not generally be furnished to some shareholders *unless* it is made available to all.

(11) Directors shall, in advising shareholders, act *only in their capacity* as Directors and not have regard to their personal or family shareholdings or their personal relationships with the companies.

(12) Any document or advertisement addressed to shareholders shall require the same standard of care as if it were a *Prospectus* under the 1948 Act.

(e) Although the director's duty is owed primarily to the company and not to the members, General Principles 11 and 12 of the City Code, indicate areas where a direct duty to the shareholders will arise. When the directors address advice or recommendations directly to the members, they must take responsibility for what they say. Thus in a case where directors sent out a recommendation but omitted to mention an adverse report from the stockbrokers, it was held that they owed a duty towards their own shareholders "to be honest and a duty not to mislead"[74]. Moreover, any dissenting shareholder could properly complain if he were wrongfully subjected to compulsory purchase under s.209, 1948 Act as a result of such a breach of duty.

A personal duty to the shareholders will also arise if the directors hold themselves out to the shareholders as their agents for the purpose of negotiating a takeover or amalgamation[75].

(f) *The Stock Exchange* Regulations will apply to any listed Company engaged in a takeover but these now incorporate the City Code.

(g) *The Monopolies and Mergers Act 1965* gives wide powers to the Department of Trade who may refer to the Monopolies Commission, any bid which is pending or completed within the last six months if

---

74. *Gething v Kilner* [1972] 1 All E.R. 1164.
75. *Allen v Hyatt* (1914) 30 T.L.R. 444, where they had to account for their personal profit on the resale of the shares. *Percival v Wright* did not apply because of their position as implied agents for the shareholders.

(1) it will create or strengthen a "monopoly", i.e. control of *one-third* of the U.K. trade in any goods or services.

or (2) the assets to be taken over exceed £5 million in value.

Having made the reference, the Department of Trade may make a "standstill order" until the Commission's report is issued.

The Department may then prohibit or even dissolve the merger if it has already taken place. These powers are so sweeping that a clearance is usually sought in advance, where the bid will fall within the terms of the Act[76].

(h) Finally we may note that in any *Takeover or Merger* the directors on either side must bear in mind section 54 of the 1948 Act, which prohibits a company from giving *financial assistance* "for the purpose of or in connection with" the purchase of its own shares or those of its holding company. This provision, deriving from the fundamental hostility of the Law to unlawful reductions of capital, was introduced in 1928 to restrain those who sought to acquire control of a company by the use not of their own money but of that of the company itself. It did not succeed; the penalty was a nominal fine of £100 and the section became notorious for its ineffectiveness. It was observed by the law-abiding and disregarded by those who either did not know or did not care what it meant. There is no doubt that it is not always easy to say whether a transaction falls within the section but a helpful guide was offered to directors by Lord Denning in *Wallersteiner v Moir*[77]; "you look to the company's money and see what has become of it. You look to the company's shares and see into whose hands they have got. You will then soon see if the company's money has been used to finance the purchase".

This case illustrates that the courts are beginning to put some teeth into s.54 in the form of a personal liability, on the part of directors, for loss caused by the use of the company's assets for unlawful purposes. The resulting civil liability, which can be enforced by any shareholder by means of a derivative action, may be a far more effective sanction than

76. The Department of Trade issued *Mergers a guide to Board of Trade Practice*, in 1969.
77. [1974] 3 All E.R. 217.

the criminal penalties[78].   Directors must therefore be on their guard against any proposals for purchase (or sale) which seem to fall within Lord Denning's guidelines.   If the company's money ends up in the hands of the buyer of the shares, no matter how long the journey or how realistic the puppet companies or how numerous the circular cheques, they should beware[79].

5-17 Oppression

This is a subject which directors may regard as irrelevant to their own position, but they should be aware of the bad cases, in as much as they give an indication of the positive standards which are expected by the courts.   The question usually arises where the directors are, or represent, the majority and the minority are complaining of unfair treatment.   Typical grounds for complaint might be that the majority are paying themselves the whole of the profits in the form of directors' remuneration, or that they are using their position to further private business interests instead of those of the company.

This is a large subject but we may note the major features.

(a) The Rule in *Foss v Harbottle*[80] is that minority shareholders cannot generally sue for wrongs done to the company or complain of irregularities in the conduct of its internal affairs[81]. But this does not apply where the act is illegal or *ultra vires* or a "fraud upon the minority", or requires something beyond an ordinary resolution.

(b) A *"fraud on the minority"* may arise where some wrong is done to the company and the majority will not allow an action to be brought[82]; particularly if the wrongful action amounts to a misappropriation of assets or opportunities which ought to belong to the company[83], and is not something

---

78. Cl. 108 of the *1973 Companies Bill* proposed an unlimited fine and up to two years imprisonment.
79. See also *Selangor United Rubber Estates Ltd. v Cradock (no. 3)* [1968] 2 All E.R. 1073 where it was held that the fact that the company had made the invalid loan contrary to s.54 did not prevent it from suing the directors for their breach of trust in getting the Company into such a situation.
80. (1843) 2 Hare 461.
81. Since the majority could correct the defect by going through the correct procedure. *Bentley-Stevens v Jones* [1974] 2 All E.R. 653.
82. As in *Cook v Deeks* [1916] 1 A.C. 554 where the directors wrongly appropriated profitable contracts for themselves.
83. *Menier v Hooper's Telegraph* (1874), L.R. 9 Ch. App. 250.

which might be ratified by the majority in general meeting[84]

In such cases a minority shareholder may sue the offending directors in a *derivative action,* on behalf of the company to enforce right derived from it[85]

(c) The ultimate remedy for an oppressed shareholder is to petition the court for a *compulsory winding-up* under section 222(f) of the 1948 Act on the ground that it is *just and equitable* to do so. Orders have been made where:—

    (1) the basic object has failed

    (2) the business is illegal or fraudulent

    (3) the company is in substance a partnership and there is deadlock or a complete breakdown of confidence[86]

    (4) there is an underlying obligation to allow the petitioner to participate in management, which has been broken[87]

    (5) there has been a repudiation of basic obligations contained in the Articles or a Shareholders' Agreement[88]

However, a compulsory winding-up may clearly be a protracted and unsatisfactory remedy for oppression in many cases and an alternative was offered by s.210 of the 1948 Act.

(d) *Relief for Oppression* under s.210 may be granted by the court to a member who shows that "the affairs of the company are being conducted in a manner oppressive to some part of the members (including himself)". This remedy should be especially appropriate for persistently oppressive conduct which does not amount to a fraud on the minority — such as the deliberate with-holding of dividends. There have been few reported cases, but the presence of the remedy is itself a source of strength to dissatisfied shareholders, and a reminder to the board of the direction in which their responsibilities lie. The essential elements are:—

    (1) there must be *oppression* and facts which justify a *"just and equitable"* winding-up.

    (2) such a winding-up would *unduly prejudice* those who are being oppressed.

---

84. *Bamford v Bamford* [1969] 1 All E.R. 969.
85. *Wallersteiner v Moir* (No. 2) [1975] 1 All E.R. 849, at p. 857.
86. *Re Yenidje Tobacco Co. Ltd.* [1916] 2 Ch. 426.
87. *Re Westbourne Galleries Ltd.* [1972] 2 All E.R. 492.
88. *Re A. & B. C. Chewing Gum Ltd.* [1975] 1 All E.R. 1017.

      (3) the court may then make an order to *terminate* the oppression either

by   (i)   regulating the company's affairs in the future

or   (ii) by ordering one side to buy the other out

or (iii) by ordering the company to buy out one side (reducing capital accordingly)

or (iv) by altering the Articles

or   (v) by making such other order as it thinks fit.

      (4) the oppression must be in respect of the petitioners position as a *member*[88a] and not as a director or employee[89]

      (5) *"oppressive"* means a "burdensome harsh and wrongful" course of conduct, and "must import that the oppressed are being constrained to submit to something which is unfair to them as a result of some over bearing act or attitude on the part of the oppressor"[90]

      (6) Examples of successful applications under s.210 have been cases of

      (i) *"freeze out"* of the minority where the directors, on the orders of the holding company, sought to destroy the company's business, in the interests of another subsidiary which was wholly owned. The majority were ordered to buy out the minority's shares at a fair price[91]

     (ii) *disregard* of the management powers of the board by a former controlling shareholder, who continued to treat the business as his own, even though the majority of the dividend carrying shares had been given to his sons. He was ordered not to interfere except in accordance with board decisions[92]

The successful cases under s.210 have been few and the failures more numerous, as the courts have taken a restrictive view of the section. It is likely to be strengthened, but even in the present state of the law, its importance and that of the "just and equitable" ground of winding up lies in the deterrent rather than in the punishment itself. It was intended

---

88a. *Re Bellador Silk* [1965] 1 All E.R. 667.

89. In that case he may still get a "just and equitable" winding-up as in *Re Westbourne Galleries*, above.

90. *Re Jermyn St. Turkish Baths Ltd.* [*1971*] 3 All E.R. 184.

91. *Scottish Co-op Wholesale Soc. v Meyer* [1958] 3 All E.R. 66.

92. *Re H. R. Harmer Ltd.* [*1958*] 3 All E.R. 689.

as a check on unbridled and oppressive use of majority power and there is no doubt that minorities use the existence of the section for this purpose.   Its value can be particularly great in private companies where minority shareholdings are virtually unsaleable, except to the very people who are in control, and where the minority might otherwise be at the mercy of an unscrupulous board.   Since the cost of litigation may often be a more significant factor than any other[93], it may be noted that the Department of Trade, may petition under s.210 after an investigation.

(e) *Investigation by the Department of Trade* is a final hazard which may have to be faced by the board, where disgruntled shareholders turn to the Department instead of to the courts[94].   The Department *must* appoint Inspectors if:—

(1) The company resolves by Special Resolution (s.165(a) 1948 Act)

(2) The court so orders (s.165(a), 1948 Act)

It *may* appoint if

(3) 200 members or 10% of share-holders apply, (s.164, 1948 Act)

(4) it suspects (on the application of any member or of none) fraud, oppression, misconduct, or the withholding of reasonable information from the members (s.165(b) 1948 Act)

(5) there is good reason to investigate ownership and report on membership and control, (s.172(1), 1948 Act).

It *must* appoint if

(6) 200 members or 10% of shareholders apply for an enquiry into the ownership of particular shares or debentures (s.172(3), 1948 Act)

It *may* appoint if

(7) there appear to be contraventions of ss.25, 27 or 31 of the 1967 Act, (option dealing and notification of interests) (s.32, 1967 Act).

---

93. *In Wallersteiner v Moir No. 2* [1975] 1 All E.R. 849, it was pointed out that the minority shareholder who pursued a defaulting director for ten years, and apparently reduced himself to penury in the process, could not get *Legal Aid* because his was a derivative action on behalf of the company which was not eligible.   He was awarded an indemnity from the company.

94. In 1973, 408 applications were made and 93 approved.   It is interesting to see that the applications made by the minority shareholder in *Wallersteiner v Moir* were rejected.

It *may* itself

(8) require information as to ownership from anyone reasonably believed to be interested (s.173, 1948 Act),

(9) impose restrictions on shares or debentures where there is unwillingness to disclose information (s.174, 1948 Act),

(10) require production of documents (s.109, 1967 Act).

The Inspectors have wide powers to examine witnesses, call for documents, investigate related companies and require assistance from officers and agents. The report may lead to proceedings by the Department,

(1) for winding-up on the "just and equitable" ground (s.35, 1967 Act)

(2) for an order on the ground of oppression under s.210(2), 1948 Act,

(3) for civil claims in the name of the company against directors or others (s.37, 1967 Act),

(4) for criminal conviction for offences against the Companies Acts or otherwise under the provisions of the relevant statute.

It has been held that although the inspectors are not judges, they must, in view of the consequences of their report, act fairly and give a hearing to anyone who is to be criticised or condemned[95]. In practice such persons are usually represented by counsel and the report is usually published. The effect of the extended powers given by the 1967 Act is that the Department of Trade can carry out an informal investigation by using its own powers to call for papers and information, without making a formal appointment of an outside Inspector. One of the difficulties of the 1948 provisions was that the Department was naturally reluctant to make such an appointment, as the publicity would inevitably damage the company even if nothing untoward was discovered. The Department had been criticised for acting only in response to press comment[96].

---

95. *Re Pergamon Press Ltd.* [1970] 3 All E.R. 535.

96. Even so, the most interesting post-1967 investigation, that into the *First Re-Investment Trust Ltd.* and other companies owning shares in the National Group of Unit Trusts, only came about after critical articles in the Investors Chronicle (H.M.S.O. 1974, paragraphs 187–195).

Chapter 6

RELATIONS OF DIRECTORS WITH ONE ANOTHER

6-01 Disagreement on the Board. Majority decides

We have seen that directors act collectively as a board, though the power to delegate is usually given to them by the Articles (paras. 3-12, 3-13 above).

Questions of their relations with one another do not normally arise unless there is disagreement or default or some allegation of personal liability.

What is the position where disagreements occur—as they inevitably will?

The Articles usually provide (Table A, Art. 98) that questions at Board Meetings[1] shall be decided by a *majority* of votes, each director having one vote. Thus the primary rule is that disagreements are resolved, if necessary, by a simple counting of heads, the Chairman having a casting vote in the event of a tie. The size of the shareholding which the director may control or represent, is therefore irrelevant and the legal status and responsibility of every director is exactly the same. This is something which has to borne in mind in private family companies where the controlling or founding director may be required by the Court, if necessary, to pay due respect to the rights of his colleagues[2].

6-02 Responsibilities of dissentients. *First Re-Investment Trust Ltd.*

Conversely, the other directors must beware of becoming "yes" men to a dominant chairman or managing director as they, too, run the risk of liability for breach of duty, if they fail to play their proper part. The reality of this danger was vividly illustrated in the Inspectors' report in the Case of *First Re-Investment Trust Ltd.* and other

---

1. The procedure at meetings is discussed in Chapter 7 below.
2. By an order under s.210; *Re H. R. Harmer Ltd.* [1958] 3 All E.R. 689. See para. 5-17 above.

companies[3] where an entire board of a quoted company was found wanting on this score. The Co-directors were all experienced City business men and yet they allowed themselves to get into a situation where they were acting as "rubber stamps" to the investment decisions of the chairman, who entirely dominated the board.

As a result the chairman was enabled to buy assets for himself at a price which represented only a fraction of their true value. The Chairman knew this; offers had already been made, which he did not disclose, and shortly afterwards the assets were re-sold by him at their full value. All the members of the board were found to be in breach of duty, but the report is particularly instructive in indicating the degree of responsibility in each case.

(a) The *Chairman* was acknowledged to be the dominant director; it was he who had the personal interest in the transactions, and he was found to have knowingly broken his duties of good faith and skill and care, and to be guilty of grave mismanagement.

(b) his *deputy* or "confidential adjutant" was the only other director who knew the true story, but he claimed to be totally subordinate with a status no higher than that of a clerk. "He stated that he had never learned the duties of a director nor read any book or paper of any kind concerning directors' duties . . ." "he had never formed any independent judgement on the matters under inquiry; and that he did not understand the significance of his actions, in particular that they were capable of constituting breaches of his duty as a director"[4]. His Counsel argued that on the basis of the *City Equitable* standard, and having regard to the director's own knowledge and capacity, he was not in breach of duty. The Inspectors rejected this; he knew the facts and must have known that breaches of duty were being committed. Moreover, when the chairman failed to make a proper disclosure of his interest at the board meeting, it was the deputy's duty to remedy the omission. A painful prospect indeed for someone who saw himself merely as a confidential clerk, but the Inspectors concluded that nothing less was expected of him. He was accordingly found to have been knowingly guilty of the same

---

3. *Dept. of Trade* 1974 (H.M.S.O.) paras. 241–324.
4. para. 242.

breaches of duty as the chairman even though the degree of blame was less.

(c) the *third* director did not know of the chairman's plans and said that he would have been horrified if he had known. Moreover, he had become increasingly unhappy about the autocratic style of management and the "rubber-stamp" function of the board and he had criticised it. His Counsel claimed that on the principles of *Re City Equitable* and *Dovey v Corey*, he was not negligent and was entitled to rely on the chairman on matters properly delegated to him. But the Inspectors pointed out that when being asked to *ratify* the chairman's investment decisions at the board meetings, he could not escape his duty to exercise his own judgement. Although acting in good faith, he had therefore failed to meet the required standard of *skill and care*.

The Inspectors went on to indicate the positive steps which they thought he should have taken:—

(i) *Criticism* he had expressed, but the very fact that he did so, should have alerted him to the need for full scrutiny.

(ii) *Formal protests*, recorded in the minutes, should have been the next step, followed by

(iii) *threat of resignation* and resignation itself if the situation was not remedied. The director said he did not resign because he felt he could improve matters from within; but this was not good enough for the Inspectors. They pointed out that to justify such a view he must have been able to point to genuine improvements in the system, and these had not occurred.

He was therefore in breach of duty.

(d) the *fourth* director was also ignorant of the scheme and had been equally dissatisfied with the chairman's style of management. He had taken his opposition to the point of resigning from two of the other companies in the group on the ground that "he was being asked to be a rubber stamp". Moreover, in the present case he was the only director who sought an explanation of the share price at any board meeting. When asked why he did not resign from the Company under investigation, he replied: "I was foolish enough to think that I could change things. I thought that there were glimmers of light coming". The Inspectors accepted his sincerity but pointed out that he could not escape criticism for his *continued participation* in this system of management. This should be tempered because of the firm line which he had taken with the other companies and because he had, at least, questioned the chairman in the present case—but he was still in breach of his duty of skill and care.

It will be noted that the conduct of these four directors attracted criticism at four different and descending levels, but in each case it was sufficiently blameworthy to amount to a breach of duty. The lesson seems clear—silence is never enough. A director, however minor or subordinate his role, has a *positive* duty to apply his own judgement to company matters. If he is not satisfied he must speak up; then he must record a formal objection in the minutes, and if things still do not change, he must resign. Otherwise he will bear some of the responsibility for defaults in which he has no part and which he may even have opposed[5].

6-03 Remedies: (1) Action in Board Meeting

Having considered the extent of his responsibilities, our director must now decide what to do if he finds himself in disagreement with the policy of his colleagues[6].

(a) The first and most obvious step is to raise the matter in a board meeting. If no meeting is in prospect, he should ascertain from the articles whether he has the right to convene a meeting of the directors. Under Article 98 of Table A a director *may* and the secretary on the requisition of a director *shall,* at any time, summon a meeting of the directors. This Article is commonly adopted, but there is, naturally, no certainty that the other members will attend.

If a director raises the matter in dispute at a board meeting and he is outvoted, he must consider whether he will accept the position or whether he will take further action and, if so,

---

5. As in *Ramskill v Edwards* (1885) 31 Ch.D. 100 where a director, who signed a cheqne for an unauthorised loan, was held liable, even though he had protested.
6. See also *"Guidelines for Directors"* (Institute of Directors), pp. 57–58.

what steps are open to him.   His decision must largely depend upon the degree of importance which he attaches to the question.

On all but the most important questions a Director who has been overruled by his colleagues should accept the decision of the majority. He may regret that he has been unable to make his point; he may even feel resentful that his advice is not being followed, but nevertheless he should bear in mind that in deferring to the wishes of the majority he may be doing what is best for the Company and that the interests of the Company should take precedence over his own feelings.

In certain circumstances, however, he is justified in refusing to accept the decision of his colleagues and in taking further action. Indeed, it may not only be his right, but his duty to do so as we have seen in paragraph 6-02 above.   For example, he may consider that he has not been given a fair hearing before the Board, and in that event possibly his best course of action is to circulate to his colleagues a full memorandum setting out his views, so that the matter may be reconsidered.

More serious is the case where a Director considers that some action proposed by the majority is illegal, or not in accordance with the standards of conduct which should be observed.   Even where he is unable to criticise it on grounds of illegality or as being contrary to business ethics, he may consider that the action proposed will have results which will be so detrimental to the interests of the company that, if persisted in, he cannot take any responsibility for it.

As has been emphasised elsewhere in this book, a director occupies a fiduciary position in relation to the Company.   If, therefore, he knows that the Board are intent upon a course of action which in his view is illegal, or will be disastrous, he is not fully discharging his duties if he merely votes against the proposal at a Board meeting. He should, of course, do this and insist on his objections being recorded in the minutes, but having done so he must then consider whether any further action on his part is called for, such as insisting on the company's legal advisers being consulted.

6-04 Remedies: (2) Action in General Meeting

If his opposition is unsuccessful, and he feels that the question is so serious as to justify an open conflict with the rest of the board, a director can also ventilate the matters in dispute at a general meeting of the company.

If he controls, or can count on the support of, a substantial proportion of the total voting power, this may prove an effective method of dealing with the matter. It is true that it is not competent for a General Meeting to reverse any decision taken by the board, or lay down a course of action which the board must follow in relation to matters which under the articles are vested in the Board (see para. 3-09), but no board of directors can for long carry out a policy against the expressed wishes of the shareholders.

The form in which the matter could be raised is a resolution that the meeting has no confidence in the policy being carried out by the board, or a resolution for the appointment of a shareholders' committee (possibly with an independent chairman), to investigate the question; or a resolution for the removal of directors and the appointment of others in their place; or, in cases where an investigation is required, a special resolution under section 165, 1948 Act, for the appointment of an inspector by the Department of Trade. Proper notice of any resolution must be given in accordance with the Act and the Articles, and in the case of a resolution for the removal of directors, this must be "special notice" as required by section 184[7].

The provisions of section 140, regarding the circulation of members' resolutions and statements on requisition, are useful in such circumstances. The general meeting may be the Annual General Meeting of the company or, if the director cannot wait until the next A.G.M., but can control, or enlist the support of, members holding not less than one-tenth of the paid up shares, he can have an Extraordinary General Meeting called under the provisions of Section 132, 1948 Act (see para. 7-02 below).

6-05 Remedies: (3) Resignation

If reference to a general meeting is impracticable, or is unsuccessful, a director can signify his opposition by resigning from the board, and

---

7. See Chapter 9 below.

in some cases this is the best course he can adopt[8].   In such circumstances it may be that, in fairness to the shareholders, he should
publish a statement setting out his reasons for the step he is taking.

On the other hand, a director who finds himself in this position
should consider carefully before he decides to resign, and in making
his decision he should try to put personal preferences on one side and
assess what is in the best interests of the company.   He may come to
the conclusion that more harm will result from his departure than
if he remains on the board and endeavours to put things right.   In
that case he may find himself being asked, in due course, to show
that he has been able to improve the situation by staying on the
board.   If he cannot see any signs of such an improvement he should
again consider whether to resign[8].

Sometimes a Director who is taking a line opposed by the majority,
will find himself under strong pressure from his fellow-directors to
resign.   This may take the form of a threat to use majority voting
power in a general meeting to pass a resolution for his removal from
office under the provisions of the Articles or under section 184 of
the 1948 Act[7].

No doubt most directors in this position would, if they considered
only their personal preferences, choose to resign rather than be
removed, with all the publicity and unpleasantness which the latter
may resolve.   Nevertheless, in this as in other matters, a director
should have regard to the interests of the company and this may
lead him to the conclusion that he should not give way.   After all,
if his opponents carry out their proposal to move a resolution for his
removal under section 184, he will have the right of having a statement
circulated to the members and it may well be his duty, in all the
circumstances, to refuse to resign so that his opponents will have to
make good their threat before the shareholders in general meeting,
when he will be able to put his side of the case.

6-06 Remedies: (4) Inspection by Department of Trade

Where a director considers that the actions of his colleagues
involve serious irregularities, it may be that his best course of action
is to invoke the intervention of the Department of Trade who have

---

8. And indeed it may be his duty to do so if he is not to be saddled with
   the responsibility for what his colleagues are doing (see para. 6-02 above.)

power under sections 164 and 165 of the 1948 Act to appoint inspectors to carry out an investigation of a company's affairs and under section 172 to appoint inspectors to investigate the ownership of the shares of a company. These powers have been summarised in paragraph 5-18 above but it may be useful to re-examine them in relation to the position of a dissatisfied director.

Under section 164 the Department of Trade may order an investigation into a company's affairs on the application of not less than 200 members or members holding not less than one-tenth of the issued shares. In the case of a company not having a share capital, the application must be by not less than one-fifth of the members. The application must be supported by such evidence as the Department of Trade may require for the purpose of showing that the applicants have good reason for requiring the investigation and the Department may, before appointing an inspector, require the applicants to give security, to an amount not exceeding £100, for payment of the cost of the investigation. The names of the complainants and the nature of the charges made are not disclosed to the directors of the company.

Proceedings under section 164, therefore, may be appropriate where a director can obtain sufficient support from other shareholders and the matters complained of are sufficiently grave to warrant the appointment of an inspector.

Irrespective of any application by members, the Department of Trade also have the power to appoint inspectors under section 165, as amended by section 38 of the 1967 Act. This provides that the Department *must* order an investigation if the company, by Special Resolution[9], or the Court, by Order, declares that the company's affairs should be investigated by an inspector appointed by the Department and the Department *may* do so if it appears that the Company's business is being conducted or has been conducted in a fraudulent, unlawful or oppressive manner or its members have not been given all the information with respect to its affairs which they might reasonably expect (s.165(b)).

In appropriate cases, therefore, disclosures of irregularities to the Department of Trade may result in an investigation by an inspector

---

9. In the case of *First Re-Investment Trust Limited* (para. 6-02 above) the board passed a resolution requesting the Department to appoint inspectors and the Department then exercised its discretionary power under s.165(b).

appointed by the Department, and as the Department have the right to publish an inspector's report, to petition for the company to be wound up, to apply for an Order under section 210, or to bring civil proceedings on behalf of the company, the provisions for enabling a company's affairs to be investigated are a powerful deterrent to malpractice.

Under section 172, the Department may appoint an inspector to investigate and report on the membership of a company and otherwise with respect to the company for the purpose of determining the true persons who are or who have been financially interested in the success or failure (real or apparent) of the company, or able to control or materially to influence the policy of the company.

6-07 Remedies: (5) Application to the Court

Sometimes a director, in his capacity as a member of the company, can obtain the assistance of the Court against his fellow directors.

This is, however, limited by the rule that so long as nothing fraudulent or *ultra vires* is being done, the Court will not generally interfere in the internal affairs of a company, but will leave it to the members to settle according to the wishes of the majority under the rule in *Foss v Harbottle*[10]. In that case, two members tried to bring an action on behalf of themselves and the other members against the directors to require them to make good losses sustained as a result of the directors selling their own land to the company for more than it was worth. This would, of course, be a breach of duty, but it was held that as there was nothing to prevent the Company itself from taking action, the action must fail. In other words, if the Board would not sue, it was up to the majority, if they so wished, to remove the directors and appoint others who would take action.

The majority must have their way, at least if the act complained of is one that they could ratify[11].

To this rule there must be exceptions, if there is to be any effective remedy at all for wrongdoing, and the exceptions are:—

    (a) Where the act amounts to a *"fraud on the minority"* as in *Cook v Deeks*[12] where the offending directors took some profitable contracts for their own benefit.

---

10. (1843) 2 Hare 461.
11. See para. 4-18 above.
12. *Cook v Deeks* [1916] 1 A.C. 554.

(b) Where the wrongdoers prevent the company from taking action in such circumstances that the minority are allowed to bring a *derivative action* against them. In this situation the company is still the true plaintiff, as required by *Foss v Harbottle*, but it is put in motion by the minority. They bring the action in their own name but in reality on the company's behalf. The need for this type of remedy was explained by Lord Denning M.R. in *Wallersteiner v Moir* (No.2) [1975] 1 All E.R. 849 at p. 857. "The rule" (*Foss v Harbottle*) "is easy enough to apply when the company is defrauded by outsiders. The Company itself is the only person who can sue. Likewise when it is defrauded by insiders of a minor kind, once again the company is the only person who can sue. But suppose it is defrauded by insiders who control its affairs—by directors who hold a majority of the shares— who then can sue for damages? Those directors are themselves the wrongdoers. If a board meeting is held, they will not authorise proceedings to be taken by the company against themselves. If a general meeting is called they will vote down any suggestion that the company should sue them themselves. Yet the company is the one person who is damnified. It is the one person who should sue. In one way or another some means must be found for the company to sue. Otherwise the law would fail in its purpose. Injustice would be done without redress."

(c) Where the act complained of is *illegal* or *ultra vires*. In that event, the court will take action, whether by injunction or otherwise, at the request of any director or shareholder[13].

(d) Where the act requires something more than the consent of a simple majority of the members, e.g. a special resolution (75 %), then the *Foss and Harbottle* principle does not apply and any *director* or *member* can apply to the court to prevent it[14].

(e) Where a director is being *wrongfully excluded* from the board by his colleagues he may:
  (i) Apply to the court for an *injunction*[15].
 or (ii) Apply for a *compulsory winding up* on the "Just and

13. *Stephens v Mysore Reefs (Kangundy) Mining Co.* [1902] 1 Ch. 745.
14. *Baillie v Oriental Telephone Co.* [1915] 1 Ch. 503.
15. *Hayes v Bristol Plant Hire Ltd.* [1957] 1 All E.R. 685.

Equitable" ground, if the exclusion amounts to a fundamental breach of an agreement between the shareholders[16].

but *NOT* (iii) seek relief from *oppression* under s.210 of the 1948 Act since the oppression is in his capacity as a director and not as a shareholder as required by s.210[17].

(f) If his personal rights as a *shareholder* are being denied, for example where the other directors are refusing to record his vote at general meetings, a director, or any other shareholder may ask the court to enforce them[18] or seek an order under s.210 (see para. 5-17 above).

(g) If the Court considers that *justice* demands further exceptions to *Foss v Harbottle* then it may be that they will made. The case of *Heyting v Dupont*[19] and Lord Denning's remarks in *Wallersteiner v Moir* seem to indicate that solutions will be found if a strict application of *Foss v Harbottle* would otherwise result in a wrong without a remedy[20].

6-08 Remedies: (6) Winding Up

In an extreme case a director might feel that, having regard to the extent of the disagreement among the members of the board, the only solution is to put the company into liquidation. This may occur in a private company, particularly where it has some of the characteristics of a partnership.

If the necessary three-fourths majority can be obtained for the passing of a Special Resolution to wind up, the liquidation can be carried out as a voluntary winding up and, provided a declaration of solvency can be made, it can be a members' voluntary winding up so as to be under the control of the shareholders[21].

If, on the other hand, the three-fourths majority is not available, the director must consider whether an application to the court for an order for compulsory winding up would be likely to succeed.

16. *Re A. & B. C. Chewing Gum Limited* [1975] 1 All E.R. 1017; see also the question of *removal* from office as opposed to *exclusion* from board meetings in Ch. 9 below.
17. *Elder v Elder & Watson Ltd.* (1952) S.C. 49.
18. *Pender v Lushington* [1877] 6 Ch.D. 70.
19. [1964] 2 All E.R. 273.
20. Cl. 70 of the 1973 *Companies Bill* replacing s.210 of the 1940 Act would have allowed the Court to specifically authorise a derivative action in the name of the Company by such persons and on such terms as the Court might direct.
21. s.283, 1948 Act.

As we have seen, one of the grounds upon which the Court has jurisdiction to make such an order is that the Court is of the opinion that it is "just and equitable" that the company should be wound up and it is on this ground that the director will have to rely.

He will only succeed, however, if his case is strong. The following grounds have been successful:—

(a) The main object of the Company has failed

(b) The business is *fraudulent* or illegal or non-existent

(c) There has been *oppression,* as where the controlling directors have persistently refused to supply accounts or information[22].

(d) The company is, in substance, *a partnership* and the "partners" have become *deadlocked* or unable to continue the management[23].

(e) One party is *excluded* from the directorship or from management and the facts show an obligation to allow him to participate[24].

(f) Some *fundamental term* of an agreement between the parties is repudiated[25].

These cases, culminating in *Westbourne Galleries* and *A. & B. C. Chewing Gum* have undoubtedly strengthened the position of a minority director in a partnership situation or where there is some form of contract between the parties. If he finds himself at odds with his colleagues, as not uncommonly happens in private companies, he now has a powerful deterrent against summary dismissal.

22. *Loch v John Blackwood Limited* [1924] A.C. 783.
23. *Re Yenidje Tobacco Co. Limited* [1916] 2 Ch. 426 where the two 50–50 shareholders and directors could not agree about anything. Winding up was ordered even though the company was still profitable.
24. *Re Westbourne Galleries* [1972] 2 All E.R. 492.
25. *Re A. & B.C. Chewing Gum Limited* [1975] 1 All E.R. 1017.

Chapter 7

MEETINGS

7-01 Shareholders' Meetings—Annual General Meetings

Directors are actively involved with meetings of two kinds, general meetings of shareholders and board meetings of the directors. Both law and procedure are important and directors must be familiar with the main features.

The holding of an *Annual General Meeting* (A.G.M.) of the members is an obligation imposed by the 1948 Act as follows:—

(a) s.131 requires the meeting to be held in every *calendar* year and not more than *fifteen* months after the last one. The object is to ensure that the members have at least one opportunity in every year to hear and to question their directors.

(b) A *new* company may omit the A.G.M. in its first and second calendar years, *provided* the first A.G.M. is held within *eighteen* months of incorporation, (s.131(1)).

(c) The *procedure* is governed mainly by *Articles 47–74* of Table A, which are usually adopted. Article 52 provides, in effect, that the *business* of the A.G.M. is

    (i) declaration of *dividend*

    (ii) consideration of *accounts*

    (iii) consideration of *directors'* and *auditors'* reports

    (iv) *election* of directors

    (v) appointment and remuneration of *auditors*

    (vi) *special* business, i.e. any other business. If the Accounts are not ready for the A.G.M. the meeting should still be held so as to comply with s.131. All the other business can be dealt with and the meeting then adjourned to a later date, when the accounts will be presented. Alternatively the meeting can be closed and an A.G.M. called to receive the accounts.

(d) The *duty* to call the A.G.M. is that of the directors under their general management powers in Article 80, Table A. If they *default,* the *Department of Trade* on the application of any member may call it on such terms as the Department thinks fit including, if necessary, a direction that one member in person or by proxy, shall constitute the meeting (s.131(2)).

(e) The *penalty* for default or failure to comply with the the requirements of the Department is a fine of £50 on the company and every officer in default (s.131 (5)).

(f) In addition to the requirements of the Act and the Articles, the A.G.M. is usually the occasion for the *Chairman's Report* on the accounts and prospects of the company, and for members' questions.

  The Chairman's Report although normally circulated with the accounts is not a statutory or formal document and so can be used for any desired purpose. Thus he can explain items in the accounts or indeed, correct misleading impressions which the statutory information might otherwise create. For example some companies, without disclosing personal information, state the amount of tax which a typical tax-payer would have to meet, in respect of the directors' remuneration[1].

(g) Special business of any kind may be taken at the A.G.M., for example in regard to alterations of share capital, issuing of new shares, alterations of the Articles, approval of directors' compensation, incentive schemes, borrowing powers. The nature and details of such matters as *special business* must be specified in the *notice* calling the meeting, (see para. 7-05 below).

7-02 Extraordinary General Meetings

Any other general meeting is an *Extraordinary General Meeting* (E.G.M.) and the following provisions apply:—

(a) The *directors* (by Article 49, Table A) may call such a meeting whenever they think fit[2].

---

1. Listed companies are subject to additional requirements in regard to the A.G.M. under the *Listing Agreement*, paragraphs 2, 5 and 11 (see Appendix E below).
2. As with all their other powers, the directors must use this power in good faith. *Pergamon Press Ltd. v Maxwell* [1970] 2 All E.R. 809.

(b) If there are not, in the U.K., sufficient directors to form a quorum, then *any director* or any *two members* may call an E.G.M. as though they were the board (Article 49).

(c) The directors *must* call an E.G.M. on the requisition of the holders of not less than *one-tenth* of the paid up voting capital, *regardless* of anything in the Articles (s. 132, 1948 Act).

    The requisition must
    (i)   state the objects of the meeting
    (ii) be signed by the requisitionists
  and (iii) be deposited at the registered office.

(d) If the directors *do not* call the meeting requested under s.132, within 21 days, then the requisitionists or the holders of more than half of their voting rights may call it themselves within three months (s.132(3)). Their expenses must be paid by the company which must deduct it from the remuneration of the defaulting directors[3].

(e) If the Articles "do not make other provision", then *two* or more members holding one-tenth of the issued share capital may call a meeting themselves and bear the cost (s.134(b) 1948 Act). This section appears to have little effect, as the Articles invariably do make other provision as where Table A Art. 49, allows a director or any two members to call a meeting when there is no quorum of directors in the U.K.

(f) If it is *impracticable* to call an E.G.M. in any of these ways, then the *court* may call a meeting on such terms as it thinks fit— including a direction, if necessary, that *one member* in person or by proxy, shall constitute the meeting. The court will use this power where minority shareholders (by deliberately absenting themselves) are using the quorum requirements to deny the majority the right to cast their votes[4].

(g) All business at an E.G.M. is *Special Business,* which must be specified in the Notice. Moreover the notice will be confined (in the case of a requisition from members under s.132) to the matters stated in the requisition[5].

---

3. s.132 does not say when the meeting must be *held*; merely that it must be *called* within 21 days. So the directors may call it for any date they choose, though no doubt an excessively remote date would be an abuse of their powers.
4. *Re El Sombrero Ltd.* [1958] 3 All E.R. 1. and *Re H. R. Paul and Son Limited* (1973) 118 Sol. J. 166.
5. *Ball v Metal Industries* (1957) S.C. 315.

7-03 Class Meetings

Where the capital of a company is divided into different classes of shares, it is usually provided in the articles that the rights attached to that class (such as the rate of preferential dividend) may be varied with the consent of an Extraordinary Resolution passed at a seperate general meeting of the holders of the shares of that class, (Table 4, Art 4.)

Such a variation of rights can, however, be reviewed by the Court under section 72 of the 1948 Act, which contains provisions to deal with cases where a variation clause operates unfairly. The section provides that holders of not less than 15 per cent of the shares affected, being persons who did not consent to or vote in favour of the resolution, may, within twenty-one days, apply to the court to have the variation cancelled and in that event the variation will not be effective unless it is confirmed by the Court. The court will not allow a variation if it is satisfied, having regard to all the circumstances of the case, that it would unfairly prejudice the shareholders of the class concerned, but if not so satisfied. it must confirm the variation.

Class rights are not "varied" and so the provisions of s.72 do not apply where

(a) the voting rights of other shares are altered, under the Articles[6],

or (b) new shares of the same class are issued[7].

These cases reduce the effectiveness of s.72 as it is obvious that where there are two classes, each with equal voting rights, the position of one is just as much affected by a strengthening of the other class as by a weakening of itself. However, it is possible that an objector might have a right to complain on the general principle of lack of good faith, without the need to bring himself within s.72 at all[8].

7-04 Communications between Shareholders

Section 140 of the Act gives members representing not less than one-twentieth of the total voting rights, or not less than 100 members holding shares on which there has been paid up an average sum per member of not less than £100, the right to require the company:

---

6. *Greenhalgh v Arderne Cinemas Ltd.* [1951] 2 All E.R. 1120.
7. *White v Bristol Aeroplane Co. Ltd.* [1953] 1 All E.R. 40.
8. *Re Holders Investment Trust Ltd.* [1971] 1. W.L.R. 583.

(a) to give to the members notice of a resolution which it is proposed to move at the next annual general meeting; this must be lodged with the company six weeks before the meeting.

(b) to circulate to the members entitled to notice of any general meeting a statement of not more than 1,000 words with respect to the business of the meeting; this must be lodged one week before the meeting.

The members must deposit with the company a sum reasonably sufficient to meet the company's expenses in giving effect thereto, and the Court may excuse the company from circulating matter which is defamatory.

7-05 Notice of General Meetings

The question of notice is governed partly by the 1948 Act and partly by the Articles.

(a) s.133 provides that, despite anything in the Articles,
   (i) an A.G.M. requires at least *twenty-one* days' written notice
   (ii) an E.G.M. requires at least *fourteen* days' written notice, unless a Special Resolution is to be proposed, in which case *twenty-one* days' notice is required. In practice twenty-one days' notice is normally given for all meetings.

(b) By Article 50 of Table A this must *clear* notice exclusive of both the day of service and the day of the meeting.

(c) *Shorter* notice may be accepted by
   (i) *all* the members entitled to attend and vote in the case of the A.G.M.,
   (ii) a majority in number and 95% in value in the case of an E.G.M.[9]

These provisions are particularly useful for private companies with a small membership, and can be used, if desired, to dispense with the need for notice altogether. The members must be made aware, however, that resolutions are being passed, if that is the case[10].

9. ss.133(3), 141(2), 1948 Act.
10. *Re Pearce Duff and Co. Ltd.* [1960] 3 All E.R. 222.

(d) *Service* of Notice is to be given to *every member* under s.134 the 1948 Act, unless the Articles provide otherwise. Article 134 of Table A requires service upon,

    (i) *every member* except those who have not supplied a registered address. Service by ordinary prepaid post is sufficient and is deemed to have been effected twenty-four hours later (Art. 136).

    (ii) every *personal representative* of a dead member,

    (iii) the *Trustee in Bankruptcy* of a bankrupt member

    (iv) the company's Auditor.

The Articles may exclude certain classes such as preference shareholders, from the right to notice. Accidental omissions are excused by Article 51 of Table A, but this does not include an error of law, such as believing that unpaid vendors were no longer members[11]. However, a procedural irregularity, such as the absence of formal board authority for the meeting, which the majority could cure by going through the proper processes, will not entitle an objector to an injunction[12].

(e) *Contents* of the notice are prescribed as follows:—

    (i) *Article 50* of Table A requires it to specify the *place, day, hour,* and in the case of *special* business, the *general nature* of that business[13]. As we have seen, all business at an E.G.M. is special business[14], as is all business at an A.G.M. apart from the business specified in Article 52 (paragraph 7-01(c) above).

    (ii) The A.G.M. must be *specified* as such in the notice calling it.

    (iii) The *exact wording* of *special* and *extraordinary* resolutions must be set out in the notice which must also specify the type of the resolution (s.141, 1948 Act).

---

11. *Musselwhite v C. H. Musselwhite & Son Ltd.* [1962] 1 All E.R. 201.
12. *Bentley-Stevens v Jones* [1974] 2 All E.R. 653.
13. Thus if the business is "to elect new directors", additional resolutions to elect new directors can be proposed at the meeting. *Choppington Collieries Ltd. v Johnson* [1944] 1 All E.R. 762.
14. Special business must be stated fairly, so as to enable a member to decide whether he should attend. Thus a notice of a resolution for the approval of some improperly paid remuneration was insufficient where it failed to state the amount (£44,876), *Baillie v Oriental Telephone Co. Ltd.* [1915] 1 Ch. 503.

(iv) The notice *must* state with reasonable prominence, the right of every member to appoint a *proxy,* who need not be a member (s.136, 1948 Act).

7-06 Special Notice

Special Notice has nothing to do with notice in the normal sense of notice to the members. It is a technical term used in s.142 of the 1948 Act for a *notice to the company* to be given by a party who proposes to move certain types of Ordinary Resolution at the next general meeting. The procedure is as follows:—

(a) Special Notice has to be given of intention to propose Ordinary Resolutions:—

    (i) to remove a director (s.184, 1948 Act),

    (ii) to appoint a new *auditor* or not to appoint a retiring auditor (s.160, 1948 Act),

    (iii) to appoint a director aged over 70 (s.185, 1948 Act).

(b) The intending proposer of *such* resolutions must give his Special Notice *to the Company* not less than *twenty-eight days* before the meeting. The company must then notify the members either with the notice of meeting or (if that is not practicable) by advertisement or in any other manner permitted by the Articles, not less than *twenty-one days* before the meeting. If the directors call the meeting less than twenty eight days after the Special Notice is served on them, the notice is still valid. It may be noted that the result of the 28 day requirement is that shareholders who wish to propose the removal of a director or auditor at the A.G.M. must serve their Special Notice *before* they have seen the accounts and the directors' report.

(c) The Special Notice may be left at or posted to the Registered Office (s.437, 1948 Act).

7-07 Quorum

The *Quorum* (Latin for "of whom") means the minimum number of members whose presence is necessary in order that business may legally be transacted. The requirements with regard to general meetings are as follows:—

(a) In so far as the articles do not make any other provision, s.134(d) of the 1948 Act provides that the quorum shall be:

(i) *two members personally* present for a private company.

(ii) *three* members personally present for a public company.

Thus proxies do not count for this purpose.

(b) The usual Articles in fact require

(i) *three* members in person for a public company (Table A, Art. 53)

and (ii) *two* members in person or by *proxy* for a private company so that, in practice, proxies are normally counted for this purpose in private companies.

(c) All that is required is that the quorum should be present at the *beginning* of the meeting, when it "proceeds to business"[15]. However there must be at least *two* members present throughout the meeting[16].

(d) *One* person cannot constitute a meeting[16] except:

(i) at a class meeting where he holds all the shares of a class[17],

and (ii) where the Court or the Department of Trade order otherwise under s.135 or 131 of the Act. Subject to this requirement, one individual may count as more than one member if he holds shares in two or more capacities, as where he has both a private holding and a trust holding[18].

(e) A representative of a corporate shareholder counts in the quorum[19], but not an executor or administrator of a deceased shareholder, unless he has been registered as a member (Table A, Art. 32).

(f) If there is no quorum within half an hour of the due time, the meeting is (by Article 54 of Table A)

(i) dissolved if convened on the requisition of members,

---

15. *Re Hartley Baird Ltd.* [1954] 3 All E.R. 695.
16. *Re London Flats Ltd.* [1969] 2 All E.R. 744.
17. *East v Bennett Bros. Ltd.* [1911] 1 Ch. 163.
18. *Neil M'Leod and Sons Ltd., Petitioners* (1967) S.C. 16.
19. When appointed by resolution of that corporation (s.139 1948 Act). If the corporate shareholder is in liquidation, the *liquidator* (where there is no committee of inspection or direction from the Court or creditors) may make the appointment himself (*Hillman v Crystal Bowl Amusements* [1973] 1 All E.R. 379).

(ii) otherwise *adjourned* for one week (or as the directors may determine). At the adjourned meeting the *members present* shall form a quorum[20]. If minority shareholders use the quorum requirements to frustrate the wishes of the majority, by deliberately absenting themselves from meetings, the court will resolve the problem by calling a meeting under s.135, 1948 Act[21].

7-08 Chairman

The Chairman's role is of obvious importance and it may fall to the lot of any director.

(a) *Article 55* of Table A requires that the Chairman of the Board[22] shall take the chair at general meetings or, if he is unwilling or not present within fifteen minutes, the directors may appoint any one of themselves. Failing that the members present may elect any one of their number (Art. 56).

(b) If there is no provision in the Articles, the members may elect any member as chairman (s.134, 1948 Act).

(c) The Chairman's duties are:—

   (i) to preserve order,

   (ii) to conduct the proceedings in the proper manner,

   (iii) to allow shareholders to have a reasonable opportunity to speak, but then to propose, if he thinks fit, that the discussion be terminated[23],

   (iv) to see that the sense of the meeting is fairly ascertained, if necessary by means of a properly taken show-of-hands or poll,

   (v) to decide incidental questions such as the validity of proxies.

(d) By Article 60 of the Table A, the Chairman has a casting Vote in the event of a tie, either on a show of hands or a poll.

(e) Adjournment is not within his sole discretion but Article 57 of Table A allows him to adjourn the meeting, *with its consent* (i.e. by a majority) and he must do so if the meeting so directs.

---

20. "Members" includes a sole surviving member *Jarvis Motors (Harrow) Ltd. v Carabott* [1964] 3 All E.R. 89.
21. *Re H. R. Paul and Sons Ltd.* (1973) 118 Sol. J. 166.
22. He is often referred to as the Chairman of the Company but under Table A, there is no such office.
23. *Wall v London and Northern Assets Corporation* [1898] 2 Ch. 469.

Only the unfinished business may be dealt with at the adjourned meeting and no notice is needed unless it is thirty days or more later. Apart from Article 57, he may adjourn on his own authority in the case of disorder or order the removal of anyone present who persists in acting in a disorderly manner after being asked to withdraw. If the Chairman purports to adjourn improperly, the members may elect another Chairman and continue with the business[24].

7-09 Informal Resolutions

Before considering the passing of Resolutions at general meetings, we may take note of the extent to which they can be passed without formality or the need for a formal meeting at all. The position is as follows:—

(a) If all the members are present and assent to a proposal, it does not matter that there has been no formal resolution[25].

(b) It appears that unanimous assent of the members to any proposal will suffice, without any meeting at all. Thus in *Re Duomatic Ltd.*[26] the agreement of the two sole shareholders could amount to ratification of improperly paid salaries even though there was no shareholders' meeting.

(c) Notice can be shortened or dispensed with altogether, in the case of

    (i) the Annual General Meeting by the consent of all voting members (s.133(3), 1948 Act),

  and (ii) An Extraordinary General Meeting by the consent of a majority in number representing 95% of the voting shares, (s.133(3)).

This applies also to a Special Resolution, (s.141(2), 1948 Act).

(d) Article 5 of Part II of Table A provides, for *private* companies, that a resolution in writing signed by all the voting members shall be as *valid* as if passed at a general meeting. This seems to be envisaged even for Special and Extraordinary Resolutions by s.143(4) of the 1948 Act. The tendency of the courts is

---

24. *National Dwellings Society v Sykes* [1894] 3 Ch. 159 and even where he properly exercises his power to adjourn as a last resort because of disorder, he must not adjourn for longer than is reasonably necessary. An adjournment *sine die* is unlikely to be justified (*John v Rees* [1969] 2 All E.R. 274).

25. *Re Express Engineering Works* [1920] 1 Ch. 466.

26. [1969] 1 All E.R. 161.

to regard a company as bound by any unanimous act of the members; no matter when or how it is carried out[27].

Moreover, in the case of private companies it is clear that meetings may be dispensed with by the authority of Article 5, Part II of Table A. For public companies there should be a physical meeting of the members since Article 5 will not apply; but again, notice can be dispensed with entirely by unanimous consent (or 95% in the case of Special Resolutions and E.G.M's generally). In practice, unanimous consent to short notice is always sought and a form of consent is signed by all the members[28].

7-10 Resolutions

Resolutions passed at General Meetings are of three types, *Special* and *Extraordinary* (75% majorities) for certain specified purposes and *Ordinary* (bare majority) for all other purposes. Thus, wherever the consent of the members is required, and nothing more is stipulated by the Acts or the Articles, a bare majority will suffice.

(a) *Extraordinary Resolutions* are required for:—

    (i) liquidation on the grounds of insolvency (s.278(i)(c), 1948 Act)

    (ii) sanctioning *arrangements* with creditors (s.306),

    (iii) authorising a *liquidator* to pay creditors in full or to make compromises (ss.245, 303(1)(a)).

    (iv) disposing of *books and papers* in a liquidation (s.341).

The only common type of Extraordinary Resolution is the resolution to go into liquidation on the ground of insolvency. Its only practical difference from a *Special* Resolution is that it normally requires *fourteen,* instead of *twenty-one* days' notice[29]. The resolution must be set out *verbatim* in the notice of the meeting and a copy must be filed with the Registrar within fifteen days. The required majority is *three-quarters* of those who vote[30].

---

27. *Parker and Cooper Ltd. v Reading* [1926] Ch. 975, where an unauthorised debenture was ratified by the members separately and on different occasions.
28. This can be implied where all the members in fact attend, even if they do not all vote (*Re Bailey Hay & Co. Ltd.* [1971] 3 All E.R. 693).
29. s.133(2) and Article 50, Table A. Its sole purpose thus appears to be the saving of one week.
30. ss.141, 143, 1948 Act.

(b) *Special Resolutions* are similar in all respects to Extraordinary Resolutions except that *twenty-one* days' notice is specifically required by s.141, 1948 Act. They are required for (*inter alia*):—

(i) change of name (s.18)

(ii) change of objects (s.5)

(iii) change of Articles (s.10)

(iv) reducing capital (s.66)

(v) winding-up Voluntarily (s.278(1)(b)) (except where insolvent, when an extraordinary resolution is usually passed),

(vi) authorising a sale of assets by a liquidator in exchange for shares (s.287)

All the provisions in respect of Extraordinary Resolutions (apart from notice) apply, so that the resolution must be set out *verbatim* in the notice, and a copy must be filed with the Registrar within fifteen days[30]. Moreover, as a result of s.9(5) and 9(6) of the *European Communities Act 1972,* the company must also file a copy of the amended document where the resolution makes an alteration to the Memorandum or Articles. Every Special or Extraordinary Resolution must also be included in or attached to any copy of the Articles which is afterwards issued[31].

(c) *Ordinary Resolutions* are required for all other cases. A bare majority of those who vote is sufficient, and the length of notice depends on the type of meeting.

Thus an Ordinary Resolution will serve for:—

(i) increase of capital (s.61, 1948 Act)

(ii) removal of a director (s.184)

(iii) appointment of a new director

(iv) appointment of auditor

(v) issue of shares

(vi) increasing directors' borrowing powers (Art. 79, Table A).

---

31. s.143(1), 1948 Act.

(d) *Amendments,* and resolutions from the floor are a source of difficulty. Board resolutions are commonly proposed by the Chairman himself and Table A does not require a seconder. The position then is as follows:—

    (i) The Chairman should allow a reasonable opportunity to *speak* to any member who wishes to do so.

    (ii) *Amendments* from the floor must be accepted and put to the vote before the resolution itself, provided they are within the *scope of the notice* calling the meeting. Thus where notice was properly given of Special Resolutions to wind-up and to appoint a named liquidator, a different liquidator could be proposed at the meeting in place of the second resolution since it was within the scope of the notice and the name of the liquidator need not be stated anyway[31a] nor included in a Special Resolution. The same would have applied to a resolution to appoint directors.

    (iii) *No amendments* to Special and Extraordinary resolutions can be accepted, since these resolutions must be set out *verbatim* in the notice (s.141, 1948 Act).

    (iv) *Failure* to put to the vote amendments or resolutions which are within the scope of the notice or the ordinary business of the meeting (in the case of the A.G.M.) may invalidate a resolution which has been passed.

    (v) *Resolutions* from the floor must also be put to the vote if they satisfy the same criteria, i.e. if they have been included in the notice to members under s.140, 1948 Act, or are within the scope of that notice or of the ordinary business of an A.G.M. At an E.G.M. all business is special business and so the notice is the deciding factor. Moreover, any special requirements of the Act or Articles, such as Special Notice of a resolution to dismiss a director or auditor must have been given (see paragraph 7-06 above).

    (vi) In a *Public* company, resolutions to appoint directors must be proposed separately unless a resolution to the contrary is approved nem. con. (s.183, 1948 Act).

31a. *Re Trench Tubeless Tyre Co.* [1900] 1 Ch. 408.

7-10 Resolutions

(e) *Majorities*

As we have seen the majorities required for these resolutions are *never* majorities of the entire voting membership. They are majorities of those who *actually vote* in person or by proxy, at the meeting in question. Thus it does not matter how few they are, so long as there is a quorum.

7-11 Voting

Voting rights at general meetings depend upon the provisions of the Articles. The right to vote (where it exists) is something which will be enforced by the court[32]. The usual provisions are as follows:—

(a) In the absence of any special rights or restrictions[33], Article 62 of Table A provides that

    (i) on a *show of hands,* members present in person have *one vote each*—i.e. proxies do not count—and the size of a member's shareholding is irrelevant,

    (ii) on a *Poll,* members (in person or by proxy) have *one vote per share*. If the Articles make no provision, s.134(e) of the 1948 Act also gives one vote for each share or for each £10 of stock.

(b) *Article 58* provides that voting in the first instance is by *show of hands,* the result of which is declared by the Chairman. His declaration is conclusive, unless a Poll is demanded (either then or earlier). The advantage of this procedure is that it enables non-contentious business to be disposed of quickly, and indeed contentious business also, if the result is in accordance with the wishes of the majority shareholders. In that event they do not need to ask for a poll and time and trouble is saved. Where there is a seriously disputed issue, however, a show of hands is clearly inadequate and therefore the Articles (and the common law) always provide the right to demand a *Poll*.

(c) *Article 58* allows a Poll to be demanded (on or before the declaration of the result of the show of hands) by:

---

32. *Osborne v Amalgamated Society of Railway Servants* [1911] 1 Ch. 540.
33. The Articles can prescribe any pattern of voting rights that is desired, i.e. excluding some shares from voting altogether ("A" shares) and giving multiple rights to others.

(a) the Chairman

or (b) three members

or (c) any member who represents one-tenth of the voting rights

or (d) any member who represents one-tenth of the paid up voting capital[34].

For these purposes *proxies* have the same rights as their members[35]. A valid demand for a Poll does away with the show of hands which need not then be taken[36].

(d) The Poll is *taken* as directed by the Chairman, except where it is demanded on the election of the Chairman or the adjournment of the meeting. In that case it must be taken at once. In other cases the Chairman can decide the time of the Poll, and meanwhile proceed with the other business. He may well decide that the preparation of polling cards and the arrangements for counting require the Poll to be taken at a later date. In that event the Poll is complete and the resolution carried or defeated, only when the result is ascertained[36].

He should fix the hours for polling and may give notice to all the shareholders if there is sufficient time. Members may vote at the Poll even though they did not attend the meeting, but Proxies may only do so if their proxy forms were lodged in time. Table A, Article 69 requires them to be lodged 48 hours before a meeting and 24 hours before a Poll. Voting should always be in writing and the member's or proxy's signature and the number of shares should appear on each card. Members and Proxies may cast their votes in different directions, as they may have to do where they hold shares on trust for beneficiaries whose interests vary (s.138, 1948 Act). There are no provisions in Table A for postal votes so the members or their proxies must attend. The Chairman and other directors may vote their own shares in their own interests, provided there is no majority oppression of the minority[37]. The Chairman has his usual *casting* vote[38].

---

34. The Articles *cannot* require more than *five members* or the voting strength mentioned in (c) and (d); s.137, 1948 Act.
35. Where the chairman is holding Proxies it may be his duty to demand a Poll (*Second Consolidated Trust v Ceylon etc. Estates* [1943] 2 All E.R. 567.
36. *Holmes v Keyes* [1958] 2 All E.R. 129.
37. *Carruth v I.C.I. Ltd.* [1937] A.C. 707.
38. Article 60, Table A.

7-11 Voting

(e) The *result* is declared by the Chairman but he will naturally want scrutineers who are either independent or representative of both sides. The result, whether of a show of hands or of a Poll, will always be minuted[39]. The importance of strict compliance with the Polling requirements cannot be exaggerated, as if the Chairman wrongly excludes a voter, the Poll may be invalidated[40]. However, *objections* to a voter's qualifications cannot be raised after the meeting and the Chairman's decision is conclusive in respect of objections which are referred to him in due time. This is provided by Article 66 of Table A but it would not prevent the *member* himself from applying to the court if his right to vote had been wrongly denied[40].

7-12 Proxies

Every director should be familiar with the Proxy machinery which is as follows:—

(a) *Statutory Right:* The right to appoint a representative to *attend and vote* is guaranteed for every voting member by s.136 of the 1948 Act.

(b) s.136 also provides that

   (i) the proxy may also *speak* in the case of a private company,

   (ii) a member of a private company can be restricted to *one* proxy,

   (iii) the proxy's voting rights can be restricted to a *Poll* (i.e. not a show of hands),

   (iv) the notice of meeting must state the *right* to appoint the proxy (penalty £50),

   (v) the lodging of the proxy form cannot be required more than *48 hours* before the meeting,

   (vi) if proxy forms are sent out at the company's expense they must be sent to *all* the members, i.e. the directors cannot simply solicit their known supporters (except where the latter request the form and it is available to all); penalty £100.

---

39. Which makes the Chairman's declaration conclusive in the case of a show of hands (Act 58).
40. *R. v Lambeth* (1838) 8 A. & E. 356.

(c) *Listed Companies*

In practice, proxy forms are always sent out by *Listed Companies* and for this purpose the Stock Exchange requires:—

    (i) that the forms should be sent to all those entitled to vote and should provide for *two-way* voting[41],

    (ii) that the Articles must not preclude two-way proxies,

    (iii) that corporate shareholders may execute proxy forms by the signature of an authorised officer,

    (iv) that preference shareholders are given "adequate voting rights . . . in appropriate circumstances"[42].

(d) *Usual Provisions: Table A*

In the light of s.136, *Table A provides*;

    (i) proxies do not vote on a show of hands (Art. 62) but only on a Poll (Art. 67),

    (ii) the *proxy form* shall be in writing signed by the shareholder (Art. 68),

    (iii) the proxy *need not* be a member (Art. 68),

    (iv) the form must be lodged at the registered office:—
48 hours before a meeting or adjourned meeting
24 hours before a Poll (Art. 69),

    (v) the *forms* of proxy are specified in Articles 70 and 71[43].

    (vi) the proxy form confers authority to demand a Poll (Art. 72),

    (vii) the proxy is *not* affected by the member's death, insanity or revocation as long as written notice has not reached the company's office before the meeting, or adjourned meeting.

(e) *Companies: Representatives* of corporate shareholders, appointed by resolution of their boards, have the status of *members* not proxies[44].

(f) *Circulation* of proxy forms by the board at the company's expense is not objectionable[45], provided (as we have seen) the

---

41. *Listing Agreement,* paragraph 5.

42. Schedule VII Part A of App. 34 of *Stock Exchange Rules and Regulations* requires that (ii), (iii) and (iv) must be contained in the Articles.

43. See Appendix B. The two forms are a "general" proxy where the proxy votes *as he* thinks fit and a special "proxy" where he is instructed which way to vote.

44. s.139, (1948 Act) and Art. 74.

45. *Peel v London and N.W. Rly. Co.* [1907] 1 Ch. 5.

forms are sent out to all members, and are "two-way" proxies in the case of Listed Companies. Such circulation can be a two-edged weapon, as the nominated director is then under a *duty* to demand a Poll and to exercise the vote as instructed[46] unless the proxy form gives him discretion[47].

(g) *Validity* of proxies is decided by the Chairman whose decision is final (Art. 66) in the absence of fraud or bad faith[48]. Stamp duty is not required except where the proxy extends for more than one meeting, when it is 50p. The Chairman should not reject a proxy where the defect amounts to no more than a clerical error[48a], and he should bear in mind that a member can still attend in person even when he has given a proxy. In that event either of them may vote[49].

7-13 Directors' Meetings: Notice

As we have seen (paragraph 3-12) the Directors act collectively as a board and the usual procedure under Table A for calling meetings is as follows:—

(a) Directors may meet and regulate their meetings as they think fit (Art. 98).

(b) Any director may call a meeting at any time and the Secretary must do so at his request (Art. 98).

(c) *Reasonable* notice must be given unless the meetings are held at predetermined intervals. What is reasonable depends on company practice, and may be as short as a few minutes if there is nothing to prevent the director attending. If he wishes to object, he must do so at once[50]. However, a casual encounter cannot be converted into a Board meeting against the wishes of a director[51]. Notice need not be given to a director who is abroad (Art. 98).

46. *Second Consolidated Trust Ltd. v Ceylon etc. Estates Ltd.* [1943] 2 All E.R. 567
47. see para. 7-11(e) above.
48. *Wall v Exchange Investments Co.* [1926] Ch. 143.
48a. *Oliver v Dalgleish* [1963] 3 All E.R. 330, where the proxies wrongly referred to "Annual" instead of "Extraordinary" General Meeting. There was no possibility of confusion as the date was correctly stated.
49. *Cousins v International Brick Co. Ltd.* [1931] 2 Ch. 90.
50. *Browne v La Trinidad* (1888) 37 Ch.D. 1.
51. *Barron v Potter* [1914] 1 Ch. 895.

(d) In the absence of proper notice, the meeting is *void*, as where a few hours' notice was given, which was far shorter than normal and did not even reach one director until the day after the meeting[52].

7-14 Directors' Meetings: Quorum

(a) The Quorum is fixed by Table A Article 99 as *two*, unless some other figure is decided by the board. For a directors' meeting the quorum can be *one,* since private companies need only one director[53].

(b) Article 100, Table A, allows the continuing directors to act when they cannot make up a quorum, for the sole purpose of increasing their number or calling a general meeting.

(c) If, exceptionally, there is no provision in the Articles, the quorum is a *majority* of the board in the absence of some other practice[54].

(d) The quorum for directors' meetings is a more complicated matter than that for general meetings, in that the question may arise at any time during the meeting and not simply at the outset. When a director has an interest in a contract the Articles (e.g. Table A, Art. 84) may exclude him both from voting and from counting in the quorum. In that case the quorum must be looked at separately for each item of business in which a director has an interest[55]. The transaction must not be artificially split up so as to defeat the requirements[56]. However, there is nothing to prevent a subsequent meeting with an effective quorum from ratifying an invalid resolution and outsiders will not usually be affected, because of the rule in *Royal British Bank v Turquand*[57].

7-15 Directors' Meetings: Procedure

As we have seen, the directors regulate their own procedure and Table A, Article 101 allows them to elect a Chairman for such period as they think fit. If he is absent five minutes after the appointed time

52. *Re Homer Gold Mines* (1888) 39 Ch.D. 546.
53. s.176, 1948 Act.
54. *Cork Tramways Co. v Willows* (1882) 8 Q.B.D. 685.
55. see paragraphs 4-07, 4-09.
56. *Re North Eastern Insurance Co. Ltd.* [1919] 1 Ch. 198.
57. (1856) 6 E. & B. 327.

any director may be elected.   The following matters may be noted:—

(a) An *attendance book* is often signed but this is not compulsory, unless the Articles require it (as does Article 86 of Table A).

(b) An *agenda* will normally be circulated a little before the meeting with the minutes of the last meeting and other items, such as Accounts, which require prior study.

(c) *Voting* is normally on the basis of a simple majority on a show of hands with a casting vote for the Chairman (Article 98). Thus size of shareholdings is normally irrelevant, but there is nothing to prevent special voting rights from being given by the Articles.

(d) A meeting may be *dispensed* with altogether, under Article 106, if the resolutions are signed by *all* the directors.

(e) No director *must* be *excluded*, unless the members have so resolved[58].   They can in any case remove a director at any time under s.184, 1948 Act.

7-16 Minutes

After a general meeting or a directors' meeting it is the duty of the secretary to record the decisions taken in the form of minutes.

In some large companies, it is the practice, following approval of draft board minutes by the chairman, for copies of certain draft minutes to be circulated to other directors who may be particularly concerned with the subject matter.   Any amendments made by such directors will then be communicated to the chairman and agreed by him before the minutes are finally recorded in the minute book.   The duty to keep proper minutes is imposed by section 145(i) of the 1948 Act which provides that:—

"Every company shall cause minutes of all proceedings of general meetings, all proceedings at meetings of its directors and, where there are managers, all proceedings at meetings of its managers to be entered in books kept for that purpose."

Failure to comply with this obligation involves the company and every officer of the company who is in default to liability to a fine of up to £5 for every day while the default continues.

---

58. *Hayes v Bristol Plant Hire Ltd.* [1957] 1 All E.R. 685.

The statutory obligation is reinforced by Article 86 of Table A which requires minutes of:

(a) all appointments of officers,

(b) attendances at meetings,

(c) resolutions and proceedings at all general and directors' meetings.

7-17 Minutes as Evidence

In addition to the statutory penalty, however, failure to keep adequate minutes may have even more serious consequences if it results in the company's being unable to prove that a particular decision was taken or that the proper requirements were observed in relation to some action.

Although unrecorded business may be proved by other evidence, if available, the best evidence that can be offered is a duly signed minute. This is the result of subsections (2) and (3) of section 145, which provide that:—

"(2) Any such minute if purporting to be signed by the chairman of the meeting at which the proceedings were had or by the chairman of the next succeeding meeting, shall be *evidence* of the proceedings.

"(3) Where minutes have been made in accordance with the provisions of this section of the proceedings at any general meeting of the company or meeting of directors or managers, then, until the contrary is proved, the meeting shall be deemed to have been duly held and convened, and all proceedings had thereat to have been duly had, and all appointments of directors, managers or liquidators shall be deemed to be valid."

It will be noted that the signed minutes are simply "Evidence", not "conclusive evidence". This means that while a Court will accept them as *prima facie* proof of what was done at the meeting in the absence of evidence to the contrary, other evidence, such as the testimony of someone present, can be admitted to show that the minutes are incomplete or inaccurate. It was held in *Fireproof Doors Ltd*[59] that decisions not recorded in the minutes may be proved by other evidence.

---

59. [1916] 2 Ch. 142.

7-17 Minutes as Evidence

Sometimes the Articles go further than the section and provide that signed minutes shall be *conclusive* evidence. For example, Article 58 of Table A, which deals with the demand for a Poll following the declaration of the result of a vote by show of hands at a general meeting, contains the following:

"Unless a poll be so demanded a declaration by the chairman that a resolution has on a show of hands been carried or carried unanimously, or by a particular majority, or lost and an entry to that effect in the book containing the minutes of the proceedings of the company shall be *conclusive evidence* of the fact without proof of the number or proportion of the votes recorded in favour of or against such resolution."

It was held in *Kerr v John Mottram Ltd.*[60] that such an Article is indeed conclusive (as between the members) in the absence of fraud or bad faith. This means that contrary evidence cannot normally be admitted.

7-18 Signature of Minutes

For minutes to be evidence of the proceedings they must be signed by the chairman of the meeting of which they are a record[61], or, alternatively, by the chairman of the next succeeding meeting. There is no rule of law that the minutes must be submitted to the meeting for "confirmation", "verification" or "adoption"—all that is required is that they shall be signed by the chairman and he can, if he wishes, do so entirely on his own responsibility and without reference to his colleagues. As a matter of prudence, however, it is invariable practice to submit the minutes to the meeting at which they are to be signed and obtain approval of them as a correct record. This is sometimes described as "confirming" the minutes, but the word should be avoided as all that is involved is the question whether the proceedings have been correctly recorded, the decisions taken not requiring any "confirmation".

It follows that no question regarding the merits of any decision stated in the minutes should be raised when the signature of the minutes is being decided upon, and that only members present at the previous meeting should take part in any discussion as to whether or not the minutes of that meeting are a true record. If the

---

60. [1940] Ch. 657.
61. s.145(2).

meeting considers that a particular decision, while correctly recorded in the minutes, ought not to have been taken, the proper course is to leave the minutes as a true record of what was done but pass a new resolution rescinding the decision. Where, on the other hand, it is decided that a minute does not accurately record what happened, the necessary correction should be made and initialled by the chairman when he signs the minutes. No alteration should ever be made after the minutes have been signed[62] and mutilation of any minute book will give rise to suspicions of bad faith[63].

The fact that a meeting approves the minutes of a previous meeting does not of itself make a director who is present at the second meeting, but who was absent from the previous meeting, responsible for the decisions recorded in the minutes. This is a further reason for avoiding the word "confirmed" which might suggest the contrary.

The usual procedure for submitting board minutes for approval is to circulate a copy to the members of the board in advance of the meeting; thus saving time as well as giving the directors an opportunity to consider them carefully before the meeting.

It is also usual for the minutes of a general meeting of a company to be signed at the next meeting of the board of directors, rather than to leave them unsigned until the next general meeting, possibly a year later. This is quite in order provided they are signed by the chairman who presided at the general meeting. If, however, the chairman of the board meeting is not the same person as the chairman who presided at the general meeting, it would seem that he is not competent to sign the minutes of the general meeting for the "next succeeding meeting", for the purpose of section 145(2) is the next general meeting, not the next board meeting. In most cases, the chairman of the board will have presided at the general meeting and will be competent to sign its minutes by that fact alone.

7-19 Contents of Minutes

Minutes are not intended to be a report of the meeting but are a record of decisions taken, preceded by a very short narrative where necessary, to lead up to the decision.

When there has been a conflict of opinion on any part of the business of the meeting it is not necessary to record the names of

---

62. *Re Cawley and Co.* (1889) 42 Ch.D. 209.
63. *Hearts of Oak Assurance Co. v James Flower and Sons* [1936] Ch. 76.

those voting against the decision taken by the majority unless this is specially requested. If, therefore, a director feels strongly that a wrong decision has been taken, he should ask that his objections be recorded in the minutes[64].

The books containing the minutes of *general* meetings must be kept at the registered office of the company and must be open for inspection by any member of the company without charge. In addition, any member is entitled to be furnished, within seven days after request, with a copy of such minutes at a charge not exceeding 2½p for every hundred words (section 146, 1948 Act).

Shareholders have no right to inspect or have copies of the minutes of *directors'* meetings and these should, therefore, be kept in separate books from those containing the minutes of general meetings. The auditors are entitled to access to the minutes of both general meetings and directors' meetings. A director has a common law right to inspect minutes of Board meetings though there is no provision in the Acts[65].

Section 436 of the 1948 Act provides that any register, index, minute book or book of account required by the Act to be kept by a company may be kept either by making entries in bound books or by recording the matters in question in any other manner. When entries are made in some manner other than bound books (e.g. loose-leaf books) adequate precautions must be taken for guarding against falsification and for facilitating its discovery, otherwise the company and every officer of the company who is in default will be liable to a penalty.

Precautions which are usually regarded as adequate for loose-leaf minute books are for the chairman, when signing the minutes, to initial each page, and for the book to be provided with a lock, the key being kept by a responsible official. An alternative method is for the typewritten sheets to be initialled or signed and stuck into a bound book.

7-20 Irregularities at Meetings

We have looked at the effect of failure to comply with some of the requirements for calling and conducting meetings. The general principle under *Foss v Harbottle*[66] is that the court, will not interfere in

---

64. see paragraph 6-02 above.
65. *McCusker v McRae* (1966), S.C. 253.
66. (1843), 2 Hare 461.

internal irregularities at the request of the minority. The argument is that it is futile to allow the minority to litigate on such matters when the majority can cure the defect at any time by going through the correct procedure[67]. However, this principle is subject to the exceptions to *Foss v Harbottle* which are discussed in paragraph 5-17 above. In particular, the rule does not apply, and any member may ask the court for an injunction or a declaration that the proceedings are invalid, where:—

(a) his personal rights of membership are being denied, e.g. the right to vote[68], or to object to short notice of the A.G.M.[69]

(b) what is being done could not be satisfied by *a bare majority* as where rights in the Articles are being infringed, which it would need a special Resolution to change[70].

(c) the matter complained of is *illegal* or *ultra vires* or a *fraud* on the minority[71] or even where a notice is merely *misleading* because it conceals some benefit which is to be conferred on the directors[72]. Where the objectors consider that the irregularity falls outside *Foss v Harbottle*, they will normally sue on behalf of themselves and the other minority shareholders and, as a preliminary, either side can seek a "declaration of rights" so as to ascertain whether the minority have the right to sue[73]. Where the objectors are in a majority, the rule presents them with no problem as they can call another general meeting and reverse the disputed resolution, remove the directors and cause the company to sue them for breach of duty.

Even where a dissatisfied member or director is unable or unwilling to apply to the court he has alternative remedies which may be available including:—

---

67. *Bentley-Stevens v Jones* [1974] 2 All E.R. 653, where the irregularity was a defect in calling an E.G.M. to remove a director. Hence an injunction was refused.
68. *Pender v Lushington* (1877) 6 Ch.D. 70.
69. s.133(3), 1948 Act.
70. *Edwards v Halliwell* [1950] 2 All E.R. 1064.
71. *Cook v Deeks* [1916] 1 A.C. 554, where the directors were passing a resolution to appropriate the company's property for their own benefit.
72. *Normandy v Ind Coope and Co.* [1908] 1 Ch. 84.
73. *Rules of Supreme Court,* Order 15 Rule 16—as in *Edwards v Halliwell* above.

(a) a request to the Department of Trade for *an investigation* (paragraph 5-18 above),

(b) a request for *criminal proceedings,* as some of the statutory requirements for meetings carry criminal sanctions, e.g. s.136 of the 1948 Act which requires the Notice to state the right to appoint a *proxy,*

(c) a *requisition* for an E.G.M. under s.132, if he can obtain the support of one-tenth of the paid-up voting capital.

Chapter 8

TERMS OF SERVICE FOR DIRECTORS

8-01 Remuneration—Determined by Articles

Directors' remuneration is commonly of two kinds—"fees" for non-executive services and "salary" for full or part time service as an executive. These are not technical terms but are a convenient means of distinguishing two forms of payment which differ in several respects.

The first point which a director should impress on his mind is the fact that he has *no* right to remuneration by virtue of his office[1]. He must therefore be able to show the authority for remuneration before he can safely accept or pay it. Otherwise it is liable to be reclaimed by the Company or by a Liquidator[2].

The question depends primarily on the terms of the articles and the usual position is as follows:—

(a) Article 76 of Table A provides that:—

  (i) The remuneration shall be determined by the Company (i.e. members) in *General Meeting*.

  (ii) It accrues from day to day (so that a broken period can be apportioned).

  (iii) Expenses can be paid including those of attending board meetings[3].

(b) If Article 76 is adopted the board cannot fix remuneration for themselves[2]. This is clearly unsatisfactory and is widely disregarded in private companies where the directors normally include their remuneration in the accounts[4] which then are

---

1. *Re George Newman & Co.* [1895] 1 Ch. 674.
2. *Kerr v Marine Products Limited* (1928) 44 T.L.R. 292, where the board acted *ultra vires* in sending a director to Australia in a salaried post.
3. Otherwise these cannot be paid and are regarded as being covered by the remuneration.
4. As they must do to comply with the Acts; see below.

submitted to the members at the A.G.M. It is doubtful whether approval of such accounts is sufficient in itself to comply with Article 76, although members might find it difficult to complain if they approved the accounts after being made aware that they were also approving the remuneration[5]. Approval by *all* the voting shareholders would suffice, without any resolution at the A.G.M.[6], and the accounts must draw attention to the directors' remuneration in order to comply with s.6 of the 1967 Act.

(c) Article 76 should therefore be supplemented by a Special Article, which meets business requirements by authorising the Board to fix remuneration. Article 84 of Table A moves in this direction by allowing a director to take an "office of profit" (as contrasted with his fee earning position as a non-executive director) on such terms as to salary and otherwise as the board may decide. But this article is really concerned with a director's interests in contracts and some more specific authority is desirable. What is often found is a special article providing for:—

    (i) a *fee* for non-executive services of £X per annum

and (ii) a *salary* and/or commission for any *executive* services at a rate fixed by the board, which is also given full power to settle the general terms of any such employment.

It is not, therefore, common to find a resolution to approve the Directors' remuneration at the A.G.M., and indeed Article 52 of Table A does not include it as one of the items of ordinary business at that meeting.

(d) The Article should also specify, as does Article 76, that remuneration accrues from day to day, so that an apportionment can be made, if a Director serves for only part of the year[7].

(e) Whatever the procedure, the Courts will construe it strictly and against the directors who are remunerating themselves. Thus in a case where a resolution to pay remuneration was passed at a general meeting without a quorum those responsible were made jointly and severally liable to repay[8].

5. *Felix Hadley & Co. Ltd. v Hadley* (1897) 77 L.T. 131.
6. *Re Duomatic Limited* [1969] 1 All E.R. 161.
7. Otherwise a fee of "£X per annum", may imply that a full year must be served; *Salton v New Beeston Cycle Co.* [1899] 1 Ch. 775.
8. *Re J. Franklin & Sons Ltd.* [1937] 4 All E.R. 43.

(f) Where the authority is given to the Directors, care must also be taken to comply with the requirements of the Articles as to *interests in contracts* (see para. 4-07 above). In Table A, this means Article 84 which provides *inter alia* that he *may* be counted in the quorum when his office is being considered but he *may not vote* upon it. If he complies with this, he may be appointed to any office of profit under the company, in conjunction with his office as director, on such terms as the board may decide (Article 84(3)).

(g) The Articles may include provisions for remuneration by way of commission or *share of profits* and in this case it is again desirable to leave the details to the discretion of the Directors. If the Articles attempt to define the terms too closely, difficult questions of definition may arise, which can only be resolved by an alteration of the Articles or an application to the Court[9].

8-02 Taxation

(a) *Tax-free* payments to directors are prohibited by s.189 of the 1948 Act, which provides that any agreement for payment of a net sum, after deduction of tax shall be treated as though the net sum were *gross*. Thus the director must bear tax on the net sum.

(b) The directors' personal liability to tax on remuneration falls under *Schedule E* and P.A.Y.E. applies, as it does for employees. The company is therefore liable to account to the Inland Revenue and if it fails to deduct, its remedy is to debit the director and deduct the debt from further remuneration[10]. The P.A.Y.E. deductions include higher rates of income tax, as well as the basic rate, with effect from 6th April 1973[11].

(c) *Expenses and benefits in kind,* are *prima facie* taxable in the hands of directors and the onus is on them to justify any deductions[12] (see 8-07 below).

---

9. *Johnston v Chestergate Hat Manufacturing Co. Ltd.* [1915] 2 Ch. 338 where 'Net Profits' had to be defined by the Court. It was held that they meant profits *before* tax.
10. *Bernard Shaw Limited v Shaw & Rubin* [1951] 2 All E.R. 267.
11. Finance Act 1971 (Part II, Chapter III).
12. Income and Corporation Taxes Act 1970 ss. 195–203.

(d) *Compensation* for loss of office is also *prima facie* taxable
except
(i) on loss of office through death or disability,
and (ii) to the extent of the first £5,000; provided it is a
gratuitous payment at or after termination of employment[13].

8-03 Share Incentive Schemes

Many companies have rewarded the efforts of their directors and
employees by giving them *options* to acquire shares at a favourable
price. This has been done either by means of an option in the true
sense or by issuing shares on which a very small part of the Capital
is paid up or by the provision of loan facilities. Such Schemes do not
conflict with the prohibition on *option dealing* in s.25 of the 1967 Act
which does not apply to options to subscribe for shares from the
company itself.

The tax treatment of these benefits has changed from time to time
and will, no doubt, change again in the future. They were attacked
in 1966, rescued in 1972 and attacked again in 1974. At the time of
writing, the position in most cases is that the benefits derived from the
schemes (whether by directors or other employees) are taxed, not as
capital gains, but as *earned income*[14].

Listed Companies who introduce such schemes must obtain the
approval of the members in General Meeting and the schemes must
provide:—
(i) details of qualified participants
(ii) the total amount of securities affected
(iii) the maximum entitlement of any participant
(iv) details of the terms of issue;

Moreover, alteration cannot be made to the advantage of the
participants without the shareholders' prior approval[15].

8-04 Loans to Directors

Loans to directors are *prohibited* by s.190, 1948 Act, as are
guarantees or *securities* provided by the company for loans to directors

---

13. Finance Act 1960 ss.37, 38 and see *G. J. Smith & Co. Ltd. v Furlong* [1969] 2 All
E.R. 760.
14. s.20, Finance Act 1974; s.186, *Income and Corporation Taxes Act 1970*.
15. *Admission of Securities to Listing*; Chapter 1, para 30 (Stock Exchange
Council).

by third parties. So a company cannot, for example, lend money to a director to enable him to buy a house, nor can it guarantee his mortgage[16].

The following points may be noted

(a) The prohibition extends to directors of the company's *holding* company.

(b) It does not apply to loans by a subsidiary to its parent, where that parent is a director.

(c) It does not apply to loans to enable a director to perform his duties[17].

(d) It does not preclude loans by money lending or banking companies, where the lending of money for general purposes forms part of their ordinary business[18].

(e) If the company does lend money to a director for the purpose of his duties under (c), instead of simply reimbursing him for his expenses (as it should), it must either get the prior approval of the members or have the loan repaid six months after the next A.G.M. if it is not then approved. Failing this the responsible Directors are liable to indemnify the company. The absurdity of these provisions is apparent, when one remembers that if the board made an outright payment to the director instead of a loan, they would not need to refer to the general meeting at all.

(f) When a loan is made in one of the exceptional cases (b) (c) and (d) above it must be *disclosed* in the *accounts* under s.197, 1948 Act. This section makes it necessary to show, in the accounts, the amount of any loans made during the financial year to any *officer* of the company or any person who, after the making of the loan, became during that year, an officer of the company. Not only loans by the company itself must be disclosed, but loans by a subsidiary or by any person under a guarantee from, or on a security provided by, the company or its subsidiary. It is not however, necessary to show loans by a

---

16. The reason for this rule was stated by the Jenkins Committee, para. 58— "If the director can offer good security it is no hardship to him to borrow from other sources. If he cannot offer good security, it is undesirable that he should obtain from the company credit which he would not be able to obtain elsewhere" (quoting Cohen Committee Report).

17. This is hardly a concession; under Table A, Article 76 such expenditure can be discharged by the company in any event.

18. *Steen v Law* [1963] 3 All E.R. 770.

parent company to the officer of its subsidiary provided he was not also an officer of the parent company.

Particulars must also be given of any such loans which were repaid during the year and the amount of any such loans made at any time before the company's financial year and outstanding at the end of that year.

The following are, however, expressly excepted from the requirement to disclose:

"(a) A loan made in the ordinary course of its business by the company or a subsidiary thereof where the ordinary business of the company or, as the case may be, the subsidiary, included the lending of money.

(b) A loan made by the company or a subsidiary thereof to an officer who is an employee (*not a director*) of the company or subsidiary, as the case may be, if the loan does not exceed £2,000 and is certified by the directors of the company or subsidiary, as the case may be, to have been made in accordance with any practice adopted by the company or subsidiary with respect to loans to its employees."

In both the above cases the loan must not be made by the company under a guarantee from, or a security provided by a subsidiary, or by the subsidiary under a guarantee from or a security provided by the company or any fellow subsidiary.

For the purposes of the section, a subsidiary means a company which was a subsidiary at the end of the company's financial year, irrespective of what it was when the loan was made.

If the requirements of the section are not complied with, the auditors must include the particulars in a statement in their report, so far as they are reasonably able to do so, as in the case of failure to comply with section 196 (particulars of remuneration). Under section 198 directors and officers are under an obligation to give to the company notice of the required particulars in respect of loans to themselves.

(g) s.190 says that loans to directors "shall not be *lawful*", not that they are *invalid*. No criminal penalty or civil liability is specified and the effect of such a loan cannot be stated with any certainty. What is certain however, is that the company is entitled to recover the money one way or another—either by

(i) suing the director for repayment if the contract of the loan is valid,

or (ii) suing him for breach of duty in taking the loan,

or (iii) suing the co-directors for breach of duty in consenting to it[19].

As the loan is unlawful, it cannot, of course, be authorised in advance or ratified afterwards by the board or by the members.

(h) Loans to directors of *"exempt private companies"* were permitted until the abolition of such companies by s.2 of the 1967 Act, which took effect on 27th January 1968. However, existing loans did not become unlawful and could be left outstanding. Directors of such companies (which formed the great majority of private companies) were in the habit of operating current accounts with their companies, on which their drawings would be set against the dividends or remuneration which were credited to them. These accounts would get into debit from time to time and the question which arises, is whether s.190 *prohibits a debit balance* on a director's account. The answer must surely be that it does not. If a man is debited with a sum of money, as where he buys goods on credit this does not mean that he is being *lent* that sum. Likewise, it would seem that occasional debits on a director's current account cannot strictly be described as loans[20], for example where the company pays his car expenses in full and then debits him with that proportion which relates to his private use. However, the question may be one of degree and the only source of complete safety is to avoid such debits altogether[21].

(i) It will be noted that although loans to directors of a holding company are excluded there is nothing to prevent a loan to a director of a subsidiary.

8-05 Remuneration May be Sued For

When properly voted, in accordance with the Articles, directors' remuneration is a debt which can be sued for like any other[22],

---

19. *Wallersteiner v Moir* (No. 1) [1974] 3 All E.R. 217, where Lord Denning M.R· also indicated that s.190 could not be evaded by lending money to a "puppet" company controlled by the director.
20. *Potts Executors v I.R.C.* [1951] 1 All E.R. 76.
21. Especially as loans to exempt private company directors were treated as dividends and taxed accordingly.
22. *Nell v Atlanta Gold etc. Mines* (1895) T.L.R. 407.

regardless of whether the company has made a profit[23]. However, the director's position is, in some respects, different from that of other employees:—

(a) In the absence of a resolution by the appropriate body, they cannot claim a reasonable sum (*quantum meruit*) where the articles provide for the remuneration to be fixed by the board or by the members. If no sum is fixed, then none is payable[24]. An outsider, on the other hand, is entitled to reasonable remuneration if he works for the company without agreeing his remuneration in advance.

(b) The Articles, although not of themselves a contract between the directors and the company, are evidence of the terms on which a director has accepted office, in the absence of express terms in a service contract. Thus, if they say that a director shall be paid £1,000 per annum he may sue for it in the company's liquidation[25]. However, by the same token, he takes the risk that the Articles may be altered by the members at any time.

(c) If remuneration is wrongly paid it may be reclaimed, even though the directors acted in good faith and honestly believed that it was payable[26].

(d) On *liquidation,* properly awarded directors' remuneration ranks equally with the other unsecured debts. It is not, therefore, a *deferred* debt, as are the claims of members for unpaid dividends[27]. Is it on the other hand a *preferred* debt, on the ground that the director is a *clerk or servant?*[28] The Courts have rejected this view in the case of a Managing Director[29], but accepted it in the case of a Secretary[30], and a Director[31] employed as an editor of a paper. The logical distinction would appear to be that between a fee earning non-executive Director who would not qualify, and a salaried

23. *Re Lundy Granite Co.* (1872) 26 L.T. 673.
24. *Re Richmond Gate Property Co. Ltd.* [1964] 3 All E.R. 936.
25. *Re New British Iron Co.* [1898] 1 Ch. 324.
26. *Brown & Green Ltd. v Hays* (1920) 36 T.L.R. 330.
27. s.212(1)(g), 1948 Act
28. s.319(1)(b), 1948 Act — preference limited to 4 months' salary up to £200 and holiday pay.
29. *Re Newspaper Proprietary Syndicate Ltd.* [1900] 2 Ch. 349.
30. *Cairney v Black* [1906] 2 K.B. 746.
31. *Re Beeton & Co. Limited* [1913] 2 Ch. 279.

executive who would[32].   He is certainly an "employee" so why
not a "Clerk or Servant"?

(e) A claim for remuneration may, like any other claim, be barred
by *lapse of time* after six years, or twelve, when the director has
a contract under seal[33].   Normally such a debt will be shown
year by year in the balance sheet, and this may be sufficient
acknowledgement to prevent the time from starting to run[34].
Where the debt is barred, the liquidator cannot pay it, even if
the Company is solvent, unless all the members consent[35].

(f) *Waiver* of remuneration is binding, if resolved by the board[36]
or agreed with the liquidator[37], but a resolution to take no
fees may always be rescinded at a later date.[36]

   Particulars of waived remuneration are required to be shown
in the accounts (by s.7 of the 1967 Act) of all companies
which are parent or subsidiary companies, or whose total
directors' emoluments exceed £15,000.

8-06 Disclosure in Accounts

Disclosure of directors' earnings is secured by requiring the
following particulars in the accounts:

(a) The *Total* amount of directors emoluments, aggregated into
a single figure.   This includes fees, commissions, expenses
which are charged to tax, pension contributions, and the
estimated cash value of benefits in kind.   The totals for
individual directors are not shown but the aggregate figure
must be divided between *directors' fees* and other emoluments
such as *executive salaries* (s.196, 1948 Act.)

(b) The total of directors' or past directors' *pensions,* excluding
those paid under a scheme where the contributions are substantially adequate for maintaining it, but *including* pensions
to widows or dependants (s.196).

(c) The total compensation paid to directors or past directors for
loss of office including sums paid on retirement, and
distinguishing between payments by the company, its subsidiaries and other parties (s.196).

---

32. *Boulting v A.C.T.A.T.* [1963] 1 All E.R. 716.
33. Limitations Act *1939.*
34. *Jones v Bellgrave Properties Limited* [1949] 2 All E.R. 198.
35. *Re Art Reproductions Limited* [1951] 2 All E.R. 984.
36. *Re Consolidated Nickel Mines* [1914] 1 Ch. 883.
37. *West Yorkshire Darracq Agency v Coleridge* [1911] 2 K.B. 326.

All these sums must include payments by the company's subsidiaries and other parties, and must be the amounts receivable in the financial year whether or not they were actually paid.

(d) The emoluments of the *Chairman* (or chairmen if more than one during the year) so far as attributable to his period of office, unless his duties were mainly performed abroad (s.6(1)(a), 1967 Act).

(e) The *number* of directors whose emoluments were in the bands of:—nil to £2,500, £2,500 to £5,000, £5,000 to £7,500 and so on; but excluding those whose service was mainly abroad (s.6(1)(b), 1967 Act).

(f) The emoluments of the *highest paid* director if more than the chairman's (s.6(2), 1967 Act).

(g) Similar information is required for employees earning more than £10,000 a year (s.8, 1967 Act).

Emoluments for the purpose of s.6 are the same as in s.196 of the 1948 Act (para. (a) above) *except* that they omit contributions under a *pension scheme*.

(h) The number of directors who have waived emoluments and the total amount so waived (s.7, 1967 Act).

Sections 6 and 7 of the 1967 Act do not apply to companies which are neither holding nor subsidiary companies and whose total directors' emoluments, as disclosed under s.196 do not amount to £15,000 in the financial year[38]. So we find that pension fund contributions have to be *included* when deciding whether sections 6 and 7 apply, but *excluded* when actually applying them.

(i) If the accounts do not comply with sections 6 and 7 the *Auditors* must state the information (if they can) in their report.

(j) Every director is under a duty to *notify* the company in writing of his own emoluments, etc., so as to enable the company to show the required information in the accounts. The penalty is £50[39]. There is, however, no requirement in the section that the notice should be in writing or in any particular form nor that it should repeat information which is clearly apparent in the company's books. It should disclose

---

38. s.6(6), 1967 Act as amended by The Company (Accounts) Regulations 1971 S.I. 1971 No. 2044.
39. s.198, 1948 Act; ss.6 and 7, 1967 Act.

facts which are unknown to the company, such as payments from other parties and expenses which have been charged to income tax.

(k) In any *Prospectus*, provisions as to directors' remuneration in the articles must usually be disclosed[40] and *Listed* Companies must give details of waived remuneration and dividends with the Directors' Report[41].

(l) *Trustee Directors*, i.e. those whose appointment is due to a trust shareholding, are under a quite separate duty to disclose and *account* for their directors' fees to the Trust estate[42]. However, this will not apply if the trust gives them specific authority to retain them. Where they have the usual professional charging clause they may still have to pay over their director's fees, but can render an account for their time spent on board duties.

8-07 Expenses

The payment of directors' expenses may give rise to several questions:—

(a) Remuneration is regarded as covering travelling expenses and other expenses[43]—unless the Articles specifically permit an additional payment or the members so resolve.

(b) The *Articles* usually give such authority and Article 76 of Table A provides that "Directors may also be paid all travelling, hotel and other expenses properly incurred by them in attending and returning from Meetings of the Directors or any committee of the Directors or General Meetings of the company or in connection with the business of the company".

(c) If the Articles are drawn more narrowly than Table A and restrict directors' expenses to those incurred "in the execution of their offices" then travelling expenses must not be paid[44].

(d) The *Taxation* treatment of expenses naturally changes from year to year, but the position of directors at the time of writing is as follows:

---

40. 4th Schedule paras 2 and 22, 1948 Act.
41. *Listing Agreement*; para. 9(i) and (j).
42. *Re Macadam, Dallow v Codd* [1946] Ch. 73.
43. *Young v Naval and Military Co-op Society* [1905] 1 K.B. 687.
44. *Marmor Limited v Alexander* (1908) 15 S.L.T. 515.

(i) Directors, whether fee earning or salaried, are holders of an office or employment and are taxed under *Schedule E* like any other employee. P.A.Y.E. will normally apply and will extend to the higher as well as the basic rates of tax.

(ii) No matter how low their earnings, payments made by way of reimbursement of directors' expenses or of lump sum allowances or of benefits in kind, must be notified to the Inland Revenue.

(iii) Such payments are then assessable under Schedule E as emoluments[45] *unless* the director can show that they are *wholly exclusively* and *necessarily* incurred in performing his duties[46].

(iv) Exceptions are in respect of staff meals, business accommodation and approved pension and retirement benefits.

(v) Where the Inland Revenue are satisfied that the company's practice is such that the amount would be entirely offset by an allowable deduction, they may notify the company accordingly. These provisions will not then apply until the notice is revoked.

(vi) Any expenses which *are* chargeable to income tax must be disclosed to the accounts as part of the directors' emoluments under s.196[47].

8-08 National Insurance

National Insurance, like expenses and option-schemes, is a political football which is liable to be kicked in a different direction at any time. At the time of writing the director's position under the *Social Security Act 1973* with effect from 6th April 1975 is as follows:[48]

(a) All directors, whether fee earning or salaried are treated as class 1 employees for this purpose, in their capacity as *office holders*.

---

45. Income and Corporation Taxes Act 1970, ss. 195–200.
46. Thus a director's assessment for a benefit in respect of a company house, larger than he would have otherwise occupied, was reduced by one-quarter because of his extensive entertaining of company guests and foreign buyers. *Westcott (Inspector) v Bryan* [1969] 3 All E.R. 564.
47. See para. 8-06 above.
48. See Department of Health and Social Security Leaflet N.P. 15 *Employer's Guide to National Insurance Contributions*.

(b) Stamped Cards and graduated contributions are abolished. They are replaced by earnings related payments which are collected, together with income tax, under the P.A.Y.E. procedure[49].

(c) Secondary contributions are paid by the company as a further percentage of gross earnings.

(d) If the director has more than one directorship he has a separate liability to contribute in respect of *each office* up to the maximum level of contributions for that year (currently 5·5% of £3,588). Moreover, there is no such limit to the *employer's* contributions which are made at the full level for every employee; no matter how many other jobs he may have, nor how large the contributions made for him by other employees.

(e) The State *Graduated Pension Scheme*, remains guaranteed at the relevant level for each individual as it was at 6th April 1975. No further contributions are payable and no further benefits will accrue. It should have been replaced at that date by a Reserve Pension Scheme which would have continued the build-up of a second pension in addition to the basic state pension. However, this part of the policy of the 1970–74 Conservative Administration did not commend itself to the 1974 Labour Administration. The result is that the Graduated Scheme has been cancelled, nothing has replaced it, and there will be a hiatus until an alternative scheme is introduced.

(f) The fact that only payments and not benefits are now related to earnings and that a separate liability arises for every single employment means that the last vestiges of the contributory system have disappeared. For directors and employees the contributions are simply an additional form of Income Tax on a specific part of their earnings. For employers they are a form of graduated pay roll tax. It might be better if their true nature were openly acknowledged.

8-09 Service Contracts

Any executive director has a service contract whether or not it is reduced to writing. There is everything to be said for incorporating

---

49. For the tax year 1975–76 the rates are
   (a) Director (Employees' primary contribution) 5·5% of earnings.
   (b) Company (Employers' secondary contribution) 8·5% of earnings.
This applies over the range of earnings between £11 and £69 per week.

the more important provisions in a written agreement, however short or informal, particularly in view of the requirements of the *Contracts of Employment Act 1972* and section 26 of the *Companies Act 1967*. A specimen form of agreement is in Schedule A. The following points may be noted:

(a) *The Contracts of Employment Act 1972* (which consolidated the relevant parts of the *Contracts of Employment Act 1963*, the *Redundancy Payments Act 1965* and the *Industrial Relations Act 1971*) provides minimum periods of notice as follows:—

    (1) An *employee* who has served for 13 weeks must give not less than *one week* (s.1).

    (2) An *Employer* must give periods of notice depending on the length of the employee's continuous service:

0–2 years	1 Week
2–5 Years	2 Weeks
5–10 Years	4 Weeks
10–15 Years	6 Weeks
More than 15 years	8 Weeks (s.1)

    (3) These periods are *minima,* so that they will not apply if a longer period of reasonable notice would be implied by law.

    (4) Executive directors with a contract of service, express or implied, are employees for this purpose, but the minimum period of notice will not usually affect them, since *reasonable* notice in their case will almost certainly be longer[50].

    (5) Either side may still terminate the contract without notice where this is justified, e.g. for dishonesty or some other grave breach of the contract.

    (6) "Notice" means an actual period of notice or salary in lieu, and the period of weeks must exclude the day of service and the day on which it is to take effect.

    (7) s.4 provides that *written particulars* of the terms of employment must also be given to employees (including employed directors) whose hours of work are normally at least 21 per week.

---

50. Probably between 6 and 12 months; *Adams v Union Cinemas Limited* [1939] 3 All E.R. 136.

(8) The *particulars* must include remuneration, pay periods, hours, holidays, sick pay, pensions, trade union membership, redress of grievances and *notice* on either side.

(9) Since the period of notice must be stated it will usually be *longer* than the statutory period in the case of directors.

(10) The requirements of s.4 do not apply where the director or other employee has a written *service contract* containing all the relevant matters.

(b) *Disclosure*

Section 26 of the 1967 Act provides as follows:

(1) A *copy* of the Director's service agreement, or a memorandum of the terms, if not in writing, is to be kept at an appropriate place.

(2) *Appropriate place* means either:
   (i) Registered Office
or (ii) where the register of members is kept
or (iii) principal place of business in England of an English company, and in Scotland of a Scottish Company;
   in the case of (ii) or (iii) the Registrar of Companies must be notified of the address.

(3) The Copies and Memoranda must be open to inspection by *members* (not the public) without charge for not less than 2 hours per day. There is no right to demand copies.

(4) In *default* there are fines on the Company and every officer in default of up to £500 and £5 per day.

(5) Two classes of contract are *excepted*:
   (i) Where the director works wholly or mainly abroad,
and (ii) Where his contract expires within 12 months or can be terminated by the company within 12 months without compensation. This can give rise to difficulty, such as what is the position of a director who has no specific agreement as to the length of notice on termination? In such cases he must be given "reasonable" notice, and for a senior

executive director this might be as much as 12 months. In such cases, therefore, the relevant disclosure should be made unless the director is willing to acknowledge that he is entitled to something less than 12 months' notice.

(c) *Notice to Terminate*

We have seen that this question is relevant to the disclosure liability under s.26 of the 1967 Act, and that in the absence of specific agreement, notice must be *"reasonable"* on both sides[51]. This applies where the director is an employee, but the question of termination of employment in relation to his office as a director involves other matters which are discussed in Chapter 9. In any event the meaning of "reasonable" notice, would depend on the circumstances in each case and certainty is clearly preferable[52]. The parties should therefore specify in the Service Agreement either the fixed term of that agreement, or the period of notice required to terminate, or some combination of the two.

When deciding on the period of service agreements, the board must always bear in mind that they are exercising their discretion in the interests of the company and not of the individual directors. The director's position is clearly strengthened by a long-term agreement, particularly in the event of a change of control, but it is rarely in the interests of the company to enter into a fixed contract for more than five years[53]. The Stock Exchange require *Listed* companies to obtain the member's approval to contracts of *ten* years or more[54]. They must also make contracts available for inspection during the A.G.M. period unless terminable within a year, and must notify members accordingly when calling the A.G.M. This is in addition to the statutory requirements of section 26.

(d) *Duties* in the Service Agreement should be specified as far as possible but, from the company's point of view, it is desirable

---

51. *James v Thomas H. Kent & Co. Limited* [1950] 2 All E.R. 1099.
52. The Institute of Directors suggest that reasonable notice for an executive director in a typical case is currently six to nine months; *Guidelines for Directors*, p. 63.
53. See *Guidelines for Directors*, pp. 62–64.
54. *Listing Agreement*, Cl. 10.

to give wide discretion to the board, i.e. "such duties as the board may from time to time require".

This is particularly useful in a group where the board may wish to move the director from one subsidiary to another, as circumstances require[55]. The contract should contain the usual power to terminate in the event of breach of duties or failure to carry them out by reason of ill-health or absence, as well as for bankruptcy or conviction of a crime.

(e) *Patents and Inventions* should be reserved for the company's benefit where they relate to the company's business, and are taken out or made during the director's period of service. This may well be implied, in any event, from his fiduciary duties as a director[56] but it is better to spell it out. The agreement should also allow the company to make the patent application if it so wishes.

(f) *Restrictive Convenants*

Naturally a director acquires knowledge, experience and goodwill, and it would be very damaging to the company if, on leaving, he took these to a competitor. Accordingly, a service agreement may contain a "restrictive covenant" whereby he undertakes that for a specified period after he leaves the company he will not be engaged in the same kind of business. If such a covenant is to be of any use, however, it must be very carefully drafted, as all covenants of this kind are *prima facie* in restraint of trade and are accordingly void unless it can be established that having regard to all the circumstances they are reasonable, and the onus of proving that a particular covenant is reasonable is on the party seeking to enforce it[57]. Whether or not a covenant is reasonable depends upon whether it is necessary for the protection of the company's legitimate interests and is not injurious to the public. A covenant which is merely designed to protect the company from legitimate competition by a former director is going beyond the protection of legitimate interests[58]. In deciding whether a

---

55. *Harold Holdsworth and Co. (Wakefield) Ltd. v Caddies* [1955] 1 All E.R. 725, where such a power served to defend the board against an action by a disgruntled director who objected to having his powers restricted to one of the subsidiaries.

56. *Fine Industrial Commodities Limited v Powling* (1954) 71 R.P.C. 253.

57. *Nordenfelt v Maxim Nordenfelt Guns & Ammunition Co. Ltd.* [1894] A.C. 535.

58. *Morris (Herbert) Ltd. v Saxelby* [1916] 1 A.C. 688.

particular covenant should or should not be enforced the Courts attach importance to such factors as its geographical extent and its duration in point of time; if in either respect it is beyond what is reasonable the whole covenant will be held void—the Courts will not enforce it to the extent only that would be reasonable—for that would be to make a new contract between the parties. Provided, however, that it can be shown that a restrictive covenant is reasonable, it can be enforced by injunction[59].

A restriction on the director engaging in any other business or occupation *while he is serving* the company may be inserted in his service agreement, and it may also be provided that he shall account to the company for any remuneration he may receive as director of any other company. In the absence of any clause of this kind he is entitled to retain such remuneration, just as he is entitled to retain any other profits or earnings so long as they are not "secret profits" made by virtue of his office and for which he is under a fiduciary obligation to account to the company (see para. 4-06 above).

(g) *Pensions*

The Service Agreement will usually contain provisions for membership of any pension scheme operated by the company. This is discussed in Chapter 10 below.

(h) *Enforcement*

Contracts for personal services are not normally enforced by orders of specific performance. In other words neither the company nor the director will be compelled to *perform* the service contract against their wishes. The remedy is, therefore, a claim for damages and if one party refuses to perform his obligations, the loss to the other must be quantified and claimed accordingly.

However, where a company has agreed to give a service contract to a third party, then it may be ordered to *enter* into the agreement. It was so decided in *C. H. Giles & Co. Limited v Morris*;[60] the mere fact that the contract itself was not one which would be specifically enforced, was not a ground for

---

59. *Masons v Provident Clothing & Supply Co. Ltd.* [1913] A.C. 724.
60. [1972] 1 All E.R. 960.

refusing to decree that the contract should be entered into. The Judge added that it should not be assumed that as soon as any elements of personal service or continuous service can be discerned in a contract, the Court will, without more evidence, refuse specific performance.

8-10 Special Directors

The office of director is a single entity as far as the law is concerned. Either a man is a director in the full sense or he is not one at all. However, different categories of director are found in practice and it may be useful to take note of them here and to consider what they mean:—

(a) *Managing Directors* are those appointed by the board under the provisions of Articles 107–109 of Table A or similar provisions. Without such an Article the appointment cannot be made[61]. Table A leaves the duties, powers and remuneration of the Managing Director entirely to the discretion of the board. The only distinction between him and the other directors, which is recognised by the law, is his implied authority to bind the company by contracts in the ordinary course of business[62].

(b) *Alternate* Directors are those appointed by the members of the board to act and speak on their behalf during periods of absence or incapacity. A special Article is needed and there is no such provision in Table A. During his appointment, the Alternate Director, is certainly a *de facto* director (see below) and the Article should therefore provide that he is an Officer of the company for all purposes.

(c) *De facto* directors are those who have not been properly appointed but who are "occupying the position of a director" and are therefore treated as directors by s.455 of the 1948 Act. They therefore bear all the responsibilities of directors without enjoying any of the authority[63].

(d) *Special, Executive, Local, Regional, Assistant* and *Divisional* Directors are titles which are seen with some frequency,

---

61. *Boschoek Proprietary Co. Limited v Fuke* [1906] 1 Ch. 148.
62. *Freeman & Lockyer v Buckhurst Park Properties Mangal Limited* [1964] 1 All E.R. 630. See para, 3-15 above.
63. Thus the dominating group chairman in the *First Reinvestment Trust Limited* investigation was treated by the Inspectors as a *de facto* director of six group companies on whose boards he did not serve. He was, therefore, in breach of his duties to those companies as well as to the others (H.M.S.O. 1974).

particularly in large companies. The object is usually to give enhanced status to senior executives, without at the same time admitting them to the main board. They are, therefore, the opposite of *de facto* directors in that they are directors in name but not in fact.

The problem here is that it may not be possible both to have one's cake and to eat it. It is the use of the name alone which is wanted but the responsibilities and powers which go with it cannot be disregarded. Unless the position is absolutely clear from the articles, an outsider can hardly be expected to know that the "Special Director" with whom he is dealing is not really a director at all and the very use of the word must involve a strong likelihood that a *de facto* directorship will arise under s.455. The prospective holder of such an office should, therefore, be aware that the full rigours of the Acts may well apply to him, particularly as he is bound to be an officer, for the purpose of the criminal penalties on an "officer in default". Where there is a group of companies the solution to the problem is to appoint the executive to the board of the particular subsidiary with which he is most concerned. In that case there is no doubt about his status as a full director of the subsidiary but not of the parent[64]. Where, however, a special directorship is desired for senior employees, there must be an enabling provision in the Articles. This is not found in Table A and so a special article will be needed. In the light of the problems discussed above, this should give complete discretion to the board with regard to his appointment, removal, duties and title, and should expressly provide, if that is the intention, that he is *not* a director for the purposes of the Companies Acts.

8-11 Directors as Employees

The dual capacity of directors as board members on the one hand, and executives or employees on the other, has already been noted[65]. To the question:— is a director an employee?—the answer must unfortunately be—yes—for some purposes and—no—for others.

It may be useful to summarise some of the situations in which a director's status as an *employee* may be relevant:—

---

64. See also the comments in *Guidelines for Directors*, p. 59.
65. Paras 1-12(c) and 8-05(d) above.

(a) The 1948 Act clearly envisages that a director may be an employee, for s.54(1)(b) uses the phrase "any director holding a salaried *employment* or office in the company". This seems to point to a logical distinction between a salaried executive director who forms part of the "labour force" under a contract of employment and would qualify as an employee, and a fee earning non-executive who would not[66]. This distinction is not, however, drawn in every situation and the failure to keep the two capacities separate has led to some confusion.

(b) A Managing Director has been held *not* to be a "clerk or servant" so as to have *preference* on winding up[67], but there seems no reason why this principle should not be restricted to his *fees*, leaving him free to claim preference in respect of his salary.

(c) *All* directors *are* treated as employees or office holders for the purpose of their liability to *Schedule E Income Tax* under P.A.Y.E. and *National Insurance* Class 1 contributions under the *Social Security Act 1973*[68].

(d) Under the *Trade Union & Labour Relations Act 1974,* the right not to be "*unfairly dismissed*" applies to those who work under a "contract of employment" which is defined as a "*contract of service*"[69].

Here we seem to have the distinction correctly applied. A non-executive director will not have a contract of employment but a salaried executive director will, and should therefore have the protection of the "unfair dismissal" provisions.

(e) Similar definitions are used in the *Redundancy Payments Act 1965* and the *Contracts of Employment Act 1972* and directors

---

66. *Boulting v A.C.T.A.T.* [1963] 1 All E.R. 716.
67. *Re Newspaper Proprietary Syndicate Ltd.* [1900] 2 Ch. 349.
68. Under the pre-1973 National Insurance Scheme, the distinction was drawn between a director as such, who was treated as Class 2 self-employed, and a director "working for the Company in some capacity which is separate from his directorship" who was a class 1 employee for the purpose of his contributions (D.H.S.S. Booklet N.I. 35.)
69. Trade Union and Labour Relation Act 1974 s.30 and Schedule 1, para. 4, re-enacting s.22 of the Industrial Relations Act 1971. It should be noted that although T.U.L.R.A. commences with the words "The Industrial Relations Act 1971 is hereby repealed" (s.1(i)), it then proceeds to re-enact large parts of it.

with *contracts of service,* whether express or implied, should fall within their provisions, as employees.

(f) For some purposes directors are specifically set apart from other employees, for example:—

    (i) s.54(1)(c) of the 1948 Act allows the company to make loans for the purchase of its own shares, to *bona fide* employees *"other than directors"*,

    (ii) the more favourable taxation treatment of expenses and benefits for employees earning less than £5,000 p.a. does not apply to directors, even if they are full-time employees[70].

(g) Strong authority for the treatment of an executive director as an employee is to be found in the case of *Lee v Lee's Air Farming Limited*[71], where the managing and controlling director of a one man company was killed in an air crash while carrying out a crop spraying contract for the company. The Privy Council held that he had entered into a *contract of service* and was therefore a "worker" for the purpose of the New Zealand Workers Compensation Act 1922.

---

70. Income and Corporation Taxes Act 1970, ss.195–197. However, these employees are themselves due to lose their advantage in the year 1976/77.
71. [1960] 3 All E.R. 420.

Chapter 9

RESIGNATION, REMOVAL AND RETIREMENT

9-01 Vacation of Office

Vacation of a director's office may occur for several different reasons:—

(a) *Resignation* (Table A, Article 88(e)),
(b) *Removal* by the members under s.184 (whether or not involving a breach of any service agreement),
(c) *Disqualification* by Law (e.g. s.182 or s.188)
(d) *Automatic* vacation under provisions in the Articles (e.g. Table A, Article 88).
(e) *Retirement* (e.g. Article 89 and s.185).

We now consider these events separately.

9-02 Resignation

Article 88(e) of Table A allows a director to resign *in writing*.   With or without such an Article, the position is as follows:—

(a) A director may always resign and (unless the Articles forbid or impose specific restrictions) notice to the Secretary or to the company completes his resignation.
(b) Once given, the resignation cannot be withdrawn, even though there has been no formal acceptance[1].
(c) Despite the reference to *written* notice to the company in Article 88, a verbal notice submitted and accepted at a general meeting is effective[2].

9-03 Removal under s.184

Section 184 of the 1948 Act provides that "A company may by *ordinary*[3] resolution, remove a director before the expiration of his

---

1. *Glossop v Glossop* [1907] 2 Ch. 370.
2. *Latchford Premier Cinema Ltd. v Ennion* [1931] 2 Ch. 409.
3. This is the only section which prescribes an Ordinary Resolution, i.e. a bare majority at a General Meeting.

period of office, *notwithstanding* anything in its *Articles* or in any *agreement* between it and him."

The importance of this section can scarcely be exaggerated—it is the key to shareholder control and the statutory expression of the principle that the majority must ultimately have their way[4]. It means that those who can gather together a bare majority of the votes can remove the *entire board at any time* and replace them with directors of their own choosing.

Several features of this section should be noted:—

(a) The power to remove, is that of the *members* in general meeting. The *board* has no such power unless the Articles specifically provide it (Table A does not)[5].

(b) The procedure to be followed in implementing this section is:—

   (i) The proponents of the resolution must give *Special Notice* to the *company* of their intention to propose it at the next general meeting[6]. Since this must be given 28 days before the meeting and they may not know when it will take place, it is sufficient for them to state "the next general meeting" without specifying the date. If, after receipt of the notice the directors call a meeting for less than 28 days thereafter, the notice is still valid (s.142, 1948 Act).

   (ii) The company must give notice of the resolution to the members and if this cannot be included with the notice of the meeting (e.g. because it has already been sent out) they must *advertise* at least 21 days before the meeting.

   (iii) If the directors fail to call a meeting, the advocates of the resolution may require them to so do, or (finally) call it themselves, by mustering the required *tenth* of the paid-up voting capital[7].

   (iv) A copy of the Special Notice must be sent by the company to the director, who is entitled to have his written representations circulated or read out at the

---

4. In the absence of such a provision in the Act or Articles there is no *inherent* power to remove a director before his period of office has expired, *Imperial Hydropathic Hotel Co., Blackpool v Hampson* (1882) 23 Ch.D. 1.

5. Thus the board must not attempt to exclude a fellow director unless he has been properly removed by the members. *Hayes v Bristol Plant Hire Ltd.* [1957] 1 All E.R. 685.

6. see para. 7-06 above.

7. ss.132 and 134, 1948 Act; see para, 7-02 above.

meeting[8], and to be heard on the resolution at the meeting (s.184(2) and (3)).

    (v) At the meeting, the Ordinary Resolution for the removal of the director (with or without the appointment of a replacement) is decided by a bare majority of the votes cast, either by a show of hands or (if demanded) on a poll[9].

(c) Although s.184 *overrides* anything in the Articles, so that an Ordinary Resolution is always sufficient to remove a director, it does not require that all the shares shall have equal voting rights. Thus the Articles are free to give special rights to special shares, even if such rights are confined to cases where a s.184 resolution is being proposed. Thus it was held by the House of Lords in *Bushell v Faith*[10] that an Article which gave a director additional voting rights when his own removal was being proposed, was valid and did not infringe s.184, even though it would enable him to defeat any such resolution. If the case had been decided otherwise, the problem would have been to draw the line between acceptable and unacceptable variations in voting rights. There is nothing in statute or common law to prescribe absolute equality and numerous variations are found in practice, including shares which lack any voting rights at all ("A shares"). Thus the House of Lords was acknowledging that s.184 *could* be effectively overridden by appropriately weighted voting rights and there was nothing they could do about it. The remedy is only to be found in an amendment to the Acts and cl.44 of the 1973 Companies Bill would have provided that on a s.184 resolution, no share should carry *any more votes* than it would have carried on other matters of business. This would prevent special rights of the *Bushell v Faith* type, although it would not prevent the conferring of loaded voting rights on particular shares for *all* purposes. Such rights are less likely to be found, however, except in close family companies, as the majority of the contributors of share capital will not normally accept a situation where they are put into a permanent minority. The

---

8. Except where the court is satisfied that the privilege is being abused so as to give needless publicity to defamatory matter (s.184(3)).
9. see paras 7-10, 7-11 above.
10. [1970] 1 All E.R. 53.

right way to give protection to directors is by means of service contracts of reasonable length.

(d) The *Special Notice* procedure where a director is being removed under s.184, applies also to any resolution to appoint a replacement at the same meeting (s.184(2)). If there is no replacement, the vacancy may later be filled as a *casual vacancy* (s.184(4)) by the board under Article 95 of Table A. Alternatively, the next General Meeting may make the appointment by Ordinary Resolution under Article 97, either on a recommendation of the board, or on twenty-one days' notice by a member under Article 93. These requirements for Special Notice and for notice of resolutions to be proposed from the floor are intended to prevent the springing of sudden and unexpected proposals at meetings and also to ensure that there is time for consideration by all the parties.

(e) Removal under section 184 *does not deprive* a director of any compensation or damages to which he may be entitled in respect of termination of his office or of any other appointment (s.184(6)). Nor does the Section derogate from any other power to remove which may exist separately. Thus Article 96 of Table A expressly confers a power of removal similar to that in s.184[11], but there is nothing to prevent the Articles from conferring wider powers.

The question of compensation depends upon the existence of some separate contract which is broken by the removal from office and this is discussed in para. 9-05.

(f) Section 184 does not apply to the director of a *private* company holding office for *life* on 18th July 1945. Provisions to this effect were not uncommonly found in the Articles of closely controlled private companies and indeed there is nothing to prevent such appointments being made now. The only difference in the case of post-1945 appointments is that "Life" or "Governing" or "Permanent" directors may be removed, if the s.184 procedure is followed.

---

11. *Listed* Companies *must* contain an Article of this type (Admission of Securities to Listing, Sched. VII, Part A) and, in addition, they often give a power of removal by Extraordinary Resolution (75% majority), which does not require the Special Notice procedure.

9-04 Restrictions on Use of s.184

Section 184(6) envisages that removal of a director under the provisions of the section may amount to a breach of any separate service contract which he may have. It therefore provides that his right to claim compensation or damages is not affected and such claims are considered in the next paragraph. What it does not say is that he has any right to restrain or object to his removal, as such. Are there then, any circumstances in which removal may be questioned, in so far as it deprives him of any *right* to hold office as a *director*, as opposed to his right to serve his contract as an employee?

The answer seems to be as follows:—

(a) He cannot prevent the *passing* of the resolution. This is a legal right of the majority under s.184 and cannot be restrained by injunction or otherwise[12].

(b) Nor can he complain of oppression by means of a petition to the *court* under s.210 of the 1948 Act. This section protects petitioners in their capacity as *members* and not as directors or employees[13].

(c) If, however, he can show the sort of *quasi-partnership situation*, which commonly exists in private companies, he may be able to petition for *compulsory winding-up* under the "just and equitable" ground in s.222(f) of the 1948 Act. The Court will make such an order where the facts show an underlying obligation that he should *participate* in management as long as the business continues[14]. Such a situation might arise where three equal shareholders jointly own and manage the business and where two of them combine together to expel the third, leaving him locked in as a shareholder but excluded from management remuneration. Such remuneration, rather than dividends, is often the return which owner-managers of this type expect to see on the capital and effort which they have invested. The risk of precipitating a winding-up may prove an effective deterrent against such conduct and may limit, in practice, the theoretical freedom of the majority under section 184.

---

12. *Bentley-Stevens v Jones* [1974] 2 All E.R. 653.
13. *Re Five Minute Car Wash Limited* [1966] 1 All E.R. 242.
14. *Re Westbourne Galleries* [1972] 2 All E.R. 492.

(d) Apart from situations of the *Westbourne Galleries* type, where the company is, in substance, a partnership, there may be an express agreement between the parties for continued participation in management. If this is broken, and one party is excluded there may again be grounds for "just and equitable" winding-up[15].

9-05 Removal from Office as Breach of Contract

We have seen that removal under section 184 does not deprive the dismissed director of any compensation or damages to which he may otherwise be entitled. Under what circumstances, then may he have such a claim?

(a) The distinction must be made between the directors' roles first as a *director* and second as an *employee*. This is discussed above in paragraph 8-11 and must be clearly borne in mind if the law is to be understood. The right of removal under s.184 relates solely to the director's statutory position as a member of the board. If he is also employed by the company under a contract of service, express or implied, that contract may have been broken by the removal and a claim may arise. It follows that in the absence of some separate contract or appointment, there can be no such claim, except in the limited circumstances where there is a *right* to a place on the board under the *Westbourne Galleries* principle, referred to in paragraph 9-04 above.

(b) A director who is faced or threatened with removal under s.184, or some familiar provision in the Articles must, therefore, consider the terms of his own service contract and see if they are broken. If he is serving in an executive capacity he should have either a written agreement or written particulars under the provisions of the *Contracts of Employment Act 1972*.

(c) It is possible that his *employment* will not be affected by his removal from the board, for example if he has a service contract as Accountant or Works Manager. If this contract can be performed without a seat on the board (and it does not guarantee him such a seat) then his removal will not affect that contract. No question of damages or compensation will arise as no contract has been broken.

---

15. *Re A. & B.C. Chewing Gum Ltd.* [1975] 1 All E.R. 1071.

(d) On the other hand his position on the board may be a requirement of his service contract, as where he is the Managing *Director*. In this case, removal from the board will also terminate the service contract and will lead to a claim for damages, if it breaks the terms of that contract. Thus the question in every case is; are the terms of the contract broken?

(e) The general principle is that a director will be able to make such a claim only if he has a separate contract (i.e. outside the Articles) which is *inconsistent with removal under* the Articles or s.184. Thus, an unconditional contract to serve as Managing Director for a fixed term of ten years, is inconsistent with a right of removal under the Articles, and such a removal before the end of the period will entitle him to damages for breach of contract[16]. It is an implied term of the service contract that the company will do nothing of its own volition to prevent the director from carrying it out.

(f) Where no period of office or of notice is specified in the contract, there is *nothing inconsistent* with the general right of removal and the director cannot complain if he is dismissed, without notice, under a power in the Articles[17].

(g) The provisions in Table A, and normally adopted, are:—

   (i) *Article 96,* authorising removal as under s.184, without prejudice to any claim for damages for breach of *any contract of service* .

   Thus, if the contract contains nothing inconsistent with Article 96, there is no breach of contract and no claim for damages.

   (ii) *Article 107,* authorising the appointment of a Managing Director on such terms as the Board think fit with power to *revoke* the appointment, *subject* to the terms of any service agreement. This does not give the directors power to terminate his directorship, merely his appointment as Managing Director. Termination in either case will be a breach of contract if it is inconsistent with the express terms of his agreement,

---

16. *Shindler v Northern Raincoat Co. Ltd.* [1960] 2 All E.R. 239.
17. *Read v Astoria Garage (Streatham) Ltd.* [1952] 2 All E.R. 292.

as it will be if the Directors have exercised their powers by giving a fixed term contract[18]. Moreover where the member terminates his directorship, this amounts to an automatic termination of his appointment as Managing Director under Article 107.

(h) The Articles do not of themselves constitute a contract with the director, although they may be evidence of the terms on which he has agreed to serve. If the director relies entirely on the provisions of the Articles, however, he runs the risk that they may be changed at any time by Special Resolution (75% majority) even if the change results in his instant removal from office[19]. He can only complain if the alteration is inconsistent with an express term of some separate contract, *outside* the Articles[20].

(i) The conclusion to be drawn from these cases is that it will usually be in the director's interest to secure a long-term service contract, outside the Articles with no provision for premature termination. Otherwise he is at the mercy of those who can command a majority of the members' votes at any time, and his position may well be weaker than that of employees who are not on the board. However, the directors must bear in mind when giving such contracts to their own colleagues, that their duty is to the *company* and not to themselves, and that it will rarely be in the interest of the company to bind itself by service contracts of excessive length[21]. Indeed, such contracts may actually depress the value of the shareholders' interests, since any buyer of the shares would have to calculate the cost of terminating the contracts when making his valuation.

9-06 Compensation for Loss of Office. The Position at Law.

Where removal from office amounts to a breach of the director's service contract on the principles discussed above, the position is as follows:—

---

18. *Nelson v James Nelson and Sons Ltd.* [1914] *2 K.B. 770.*
19. *Shuttleworth v Cox Bros. and Co. (Maidenhead) Ltd.* [1927] 2 K.B. 9.
20. *Southern Foundries (1926) Ltd. v Shirlaw* [1940] A.C. 701 (House of Lords).
21. The Institute of Directors, suggests that 5 years is usually long enough (*Guidelines for Directors*, p. 63).

(a) As we have seen, the director cannot prevent the passing of the resolution, nor can he insist on the performance of the service contract since the court does not order specific performance of contracts for personal services.

(b) His remedy, therefore, is damages for breach of contract. Damages are intended to compensate for what has been lost, subject to a discount for earlier payment, and the director may therefore have a claim in respect of salary, commission, reduction in pension, loss of life insurance cover, loss of car and other items[22].

(c) As in all contractual claims for damages, the director is under a duty to *mitigate* his loss, by seeking and taking alternative employment where he might be reasonably expected to do so. His damages will thus be reduced by the value of any such employment which was open to him. He is, however, entitled to look for something reasonably commensurate with his status, and a Managing Director was held justified in refusing a job as assistant managing director at the same salary[23]. His liability for Income Tax (basic and higher rates) must also be taken into account in calculating the damages[24].

(d) An executive director who has no entitlement to damages, because there is nothing in his service contract which is inconsistent with a right of instant dismissal under the Articles may, as a last resort, fall back on the statutory right to minimum periods of notice under the *Contracts of Employment Act 1972*[25].

(e) Such a director may also qualify under the *Redundancy Payments Act 1965*, for a payment related to pay, length of service and age. A rebate (currently 50%) may be claimed by the company from the Redundancy Fund[26]. The director must make his own claim against the company within 6 months of dismissal.

---

22. *Bold v Brough, Nicholson and Hall Ltd.* [1963] 3 All E.R. 849.
23. *Yetton v Eastwoods Froy Ltd.* [1966] 3 All E.R. 353.
24. *British Transport Commission v Gourlay* [1956] A.C. 185 (House of Lords).
25. see para. 8-09(a) above.
26. For the up-to-date position under this Act, the latest revision of the booklet "*The Redundancy Payments Scheme*" should be obtained from the Department of Employment.

(f)   He may also be able to make a claim for "unfair dismissal" under the *Trade Unions and Labour Relations Act 1974*. For this purpose the burden of proof of fairness is on the *company* and the maximum compensation which can be awarded by the Industrial Tribunal is £5,200. The director cannot normally qualify both for Redundancy and for Unfair Dismissal, since dismissal for redundancy is usually "fair" and will thus satisfy the employer's burden of proof. Since, in the case of dispute, the employee will not know whether he was redundant or unfairly dismissed (or neither), until the Tribunal has decided the point, he should apply on both grounds.

9-07 Compensation for Loss of Office. Negotiated Settlements

A dismissed director who does qualify for common law damages will normally expect to resolve his claim by negotiation with the company, rather than by litigation. His former colleagues on the board will therefore face the task of considering both the merits of the claim and also their own powers and duties in the matter.

(a)   If the Articles include the power (as does Table A, Articles 84 and 107) to give service contracts to their fellow members, then the power to settle a legal claim for compensation for loss of office must be implied and the board is free to negotiate accordingly. They will, no doubt, take professional advice to satisfy themselves that they are dealing with a "*bona fide* payment by way of damages for breach of contract or by way of pension in respect of past services".[27]

(b)   *Section 191:*

Where, however, they cannot satisfy themselves that they are dealing with such a legally enforceable claim (e.g. because the director has no service agreement which has been broken), so that there is an element of *gratuity* in the proposed payment, then the position is different. Section 191 of the 1948 Act provides that it is *unlawful* to make to a director any payment by way of compensation for loss of office, or as consideration for or in connection with retirement, unless particulars are *disclosed*[28] to and *approved* by the *members*. This means that an *Ordinary Resolution* of the members in general

---

27. s.194(3), 1948 Act.
28. Disclosure must be to all members including non-voting members, *Re Duomatic Ltd.* [1969] 1 All E.R. 161.

meeting must be obtained, unless *unanimous* approval is obtained in some other way[29]. This section is drawn so widely that it can apply equally to cases where a director is removed altogether from the board, and to those where he remains on the board but loses some other job, such as Managing Director or Secretary.

(c) Where there is such a gratuitous element in the proposed compensation the board require not only the consent of the members, but power in the *Memorandum* as otherwise the payment may be *ultra vires*. Such a power is normally conferred by a well-drafted objects clause, and may be *implied* by the court on the ground that generous treatment of former employees is in the best interests of the company's business and therefore incidental to its main objects[30]. However, this cannot be the case where the company is ceasing business or going into liquidation, and in these situations, gratuitous payments cannot be justified[31].

(d) *Section 192:*

Where the whole or part of the company's undertaking is being transferred to a third party, particulars of compensation for a director's loss of office must again be disclosed and approved by the members under section 192. If not, the director holds the compensation on *trust* for the company, so that he must pay it over to the company on demand. If the company itself were making the payment, it would fall within s.191, so s.192 must apply to cases where the *transferee* or some other party is doing so. The object of the section is to ensure that there is no question of secret payments to the directors, as an incentive for facilitating the transfer of assets.

(e) *Section 193:*

Where there is a conventional *takeover* by transfer of the company's shares, resulting from:

    (i) an offer to the general body of shareholders,

or (ii) an offer with a view to the company's becoming a subsidiary,

---

29. *Re Gee and Co. (Woolwich) Ltd.* [1974] 2W.L.R. 515.
30. *Cyclists Touring Club v Hopkinson* [1910] 1 Ch. 179.
31. *Parke v Daily News Ltd.* [1962] 2 All E.R. 959. This principle was to have been overturned by Cl. 7 of the *1973 Companies Bill* and will no doubt be dealt with in the next reform of Company Law.

or (iii) an offer for control of not less than one-third of the voting power,

or (iv) any other conditional offer,

and a payment is to be made to a director for loss of office or retirement, he must take all reasonable steps to ensure that particulars are *sent* to the shareholders together with the offer. The penalty in default is a fine of £25 (s.193).

If this is not done or the payment is not approved by *Ordinary Resolution* of the members before the transfer of shares, the director holds the compensation on trust for those who sell their shares as a result of the offer.

He must therefore divide it amongst them.

(f) *Section 194:*

As we have already seen, these provisions (ss. 191–3) do not apply where the director has a legal claim to damages and a *bona fide* payment is made in settlement (s.194). However, s.194 goes on to provide that ss.192 and 193 cannot be evaded by the simple expedient of the bidder's paying more for the director's shares than for those of the other shareholders. The excess is to be treated as compensation for loss of office.

Moreover, payments are *prima facie* to be treated as falling within ss.192 and 193, where they

(a) form part of the takeover arrangement or are *agreed* during the *three* year period beginning one year before and ending two years after,

and (b) the company or the transferee was *privy* to the arrangement.

(g) Where gratuitous payments of this type are duly made, the first £5,000 will normally be *exempt* from Income Tax[32].

9-08 Disqualification by Law

The 1948 Act disqualifies[33]:—

(a) an undischarged *bankrupt,* unless authorised by the Court (s.187),

---

32. *Finance Act 1960*, ss.37, 38.
33. Discussed in paras 2-11 and 2-13 above.

(b) a person *prohibited* by the court as a result of conviction of company offences (s.188),

(c) the *Auditor* or his partner or employee (s.161)

(d) a person who fails to acquire his *qualification* shares (if required) within two months (s.182). Sections 187 and 188 disqualify the director from *acting,* not from *being* a member of the board. However, the Articles normally remove him from office (see paragraph 9-09 below).

9-09 Vacation of Office under the Articles

The Articles normally contain a list of events which serve equally to *remove* a disqualified director automatically from office, and to *prevent* him from being appointed[34].

Table A, Article 88 lists the following:—

(a) *failure* to obtain *qualification* shares (if required) under s.182, 1948 Act or vacation of office at *age 70* under s.185[35],

(b) *bankruptcy* or composition with creditors,

(c) *prohibition* by Order of the Court under s.188,

(d) *insanity,*

(e) *resignation* in writing,

(f) *absence* from meetings for more than six months without the consent of the board[36].

The Articles are free to add to and subtract from this list and the following variations may be found:—

(a) provision for a *resolution* of the board in cases (d) and (f) above, as otherwise there may be doubt as to whether and when the disqualifying event has occurred,

(b) exclusion of s.185 (retirement at age 70) in a public company or its subsidiary,

---

34. Discussed in para. 2-15 above.
35. s.185 does not apply to private companies (except subsidiaries of public companies) and even where it does apply, it can be excluded by the Articles (see para. 2-11 above). Moreover, the director can be re-appointed on Special Notice.
36. This will not include involuntary absence through ill-health, *Mack's Claim* [1901] 1 Ch. 728.

9-09 Vacation of Office under the Articles

(c) removal from office by some procedure additional to that in s.184, e.g. Extraordinary Resolution (75% majority) not requiring Special Notice,

(d) disqualification on *conviction* of a crime other than in connection with a motoring offence,

(e) resolution by a specified majority of the board or by other specified parties,

(f) the holding of conflicting directorships, with some procedure for certification by the Chairman or resolution by the Board as to the existence of the conflict.

The effect of these Articles is automatic and cannot be waived by the Board[37] or by an Ordinary Resolution of the members. It can only be nullified by a Special Resolution (75% majority) altering the Articles.

9-10 Retirement by Rotation

There is no need to provide for the retirement by rotation of directors. It is, however, usual for Articles of Association to prescribe that a proportion of the directors shall retire from office at each annual general meeting, but shall be eligible for re-election, and that those to retire shall be the directors who have been longest in office since their last appointment or election. For example, Table A, Articles 89–90 provides that at the first annual general meeting all the directors shall retire from office and that at the annual general meeting in every subsequent year one-third of them, or if their number is not three or a multiple of three, then the number nearest one-third shall retire.

In *Re David Moseley & Sons Ltd*[38], the articles differed from Table A in that where the number of directors was not three or a multiple thereof, then the number nearest to *but not exceeding* one-third had to retire. At a particular general meeting only two directors were subject to retirement by rotation, and it was held that on a proper construction of the articles neither of them need retire. It would have been otherwise had the articles simply stated that *the number nearest* one-third should retire as does Article 89. In that case one of the two directors would have retired.

37. Re *The Bodega Co. Ltd.* [1904] 1 Ch. 276.
38. [1939] 2 All E.R. 791.

It is usual for Articles to provide that a managing director shall not be subject to retirement by rotation and shall not be taken into account when computing the number of directors who are to retire. This is because a managing director usually has a contract of service for a fixed term of years. Article 107 provides accordingly. The Articles may also name specified individuals as permanent directors, to avoid the need for periodical retirement and in many private companies there is much to be said for dispensing with the rotation provisions altogether.

When choosing the directors to retire by rotation at an annual general meeting it is often found that a number of them have an equal period of service. Article 90 deals with such a situation by providing that as between persons who become directors on the same day, those to retire shall be determined by lot unless they agree among themselves which of them are to retire. In *Eyre v Milton Proprietary Ltd.*, the articles stated that they should be chosen by "ballot". The Court held that this meant by lot.

Article 94 contains a provision commonly adopted to the effect that the company may from time to time by ordinary resolution increase or reduce the number of directors and determine in what rotation the increased or reduced number is to go out of office.

Article 92 should also be noted, which provides that if the retiring director offers himself for re-election at the A.G.M., he is *deemed* to have been re-elected unless

    (a) another person is elected

or (b) a resolution not to fill the vacancy is passed

or (c) a resolution for his re-election is lost.

So if no action is taken, he will be re-elected.

9-11 Retirement under Age Limit (Public Companies only)

Another contingency which may terminate a director's appointment is the attainment of any age limit imposed by the Articles or, if the company is subject to section 185 of the Act, the statutory age limit of seventy prescribed by that section.

Briefly, the effect of section 185 is that, as a general rule, no one over seventy years of age shall be a director but that there shall be machinery whereby, if with a full knowledge of the facts the shareholders agree, a man aged over seventy can be a director as a special case. Alternatively, the section can be excluded by the Articles altogether.

9-11 Retirement under Age Limit (Public Companies only)

The first point to note is that the section has no application to a private company *unless* it is a subsidiary of a company incorporated in the United Kingdom which is not itself a private company. To put it in another way, the statutory age limit applies only to public companies and their subsidiaries and only to them if they do not exclude it.

In a company which is subject to section 185, no person can be appointed as a director if he has attained seventy years of age unless the company has excluded the operation of the section or his appointment is approved by the shareholders in general meeting by an Ordinary Resolution of which "Special" Notice, stating his age, has been given. "Special Notice" is defined in paragraph 7-06 above.

Where, in a company to which the section applies, an existing director attains seventy years of age, he must vacate office at the conclusion of the next annual general meeting after he attains that age. This is, however, subject to the same exceptions as apply to the rule against appointing directors over the age limit, that is to say it does not take place if the company has "contracted out" of the section and, even if the company has not contracted out, the director may be retained in office by a resolution in general meeting of which Special Notice, specifying his age, has been given.

If such a resolution is passed, the Act does not impose any express limit on the period for which he shall continue in office; and the resolution may, therefore, either provide that he shall hold office for a specified time or leave this open. In the latter event, unless the company's Articles contain provisions for the rotation of directors, the director can hold office without further reference to the shareholders for the rest of his life, or until he is removed. If, however, the usual rules for the retirement of a proportion of the directors each year are contained in the articles, then when next his turn comes to retire by rotation he can only be reappointed by the procedure of special notice in which his age is disclosed again.

In this connection subsection (6) of section 185 is important.

A person reappointed director on retiring by virtue of subsection (2) of this section, or appointed in place of a director so retiring, shall be treated, for the purpose of determining the time at which he or any other director is to retire, as if he had become director on the day on which the retiring director was last appointed before his retirement; but, except as provided by this subsection, the retirement of a director out of turn by virtue of the said subsection (2) shall be disregarded in determining when any other directors are to retire.

The effect of this is best explained by an example. Let it be assumed that there are eight directors, two of whom have to retire each year under the articles, those to retire being the directors who have been longest in office since their last election.

"A" is over seventy at the annual general meeting in 1975 but is not one of the two directors who have been longest in office since their last election and is not, therefore, due to retire by rotation until 1977. He must, however, retire in 1975 under the age limit (together with the two others who retire by rotation) and if he is reappointed under Special Notice his reappointment will not alter the rotation of directors, so that he must submit himself for re-election again in 1977 despite his reappointment in 1975. In 1977 his reappointment, if made, must be carried out with the same formalities as regards special notice as in 1975. If, on the other hand, he was due for retirement *by rotation,* as well as under the age limit, in 1975, then he will count as one of the two to retire by rotation and he need not retire again by rotation until the normal period has expired; i.e. in 1979, as he did not retire "out of turn" in 1975. The same principle is applied in relation to a director appointed in place of one retiring under the age limit—if the latter retires "out of turn" the director taking his place steps into his shoes for purposes of rotation, but not otherwise.

Where a director retires because of his attaining the age of seventy, no provision for the automatic reappointment of retiring directors in default of another appointment applies. If at the meeting at which he retires the vacancy is not filled, it may be filled later as a casual vacancy.

Reference has been made to the power to "contract out" of section 195. If it is a new company it may adopt Articles which contain a clause to the effect that section 185 shall not apply, or that directors shall not be obliged to retire on account of age, or that the retiring age shall be some age other than seventy (e.g. sixty, or eighty); any of these provisions, being inconsistent with section 185, will be sufficient to exclude the statutory age-limit. Similarly, an existing company may, by Special Resolution (75% majority), alter its articles in order to include one of these provisions so as to exclude the age limit of seventy. So articles which are inconsistent with the statutory age limit prevail over that limit; the only exception is where articles were in existence on the 1st January 1947, and which have not been amended in the manner described above. Here the section prevails *except* to the extent to which the articles themselves impose an age limit. If,

9-11 Retirement under Age Limit (Public Companies only)

therefore, such articles provide that a director shall hold office for life, the statutory age limit will apply to him, but if they provide that he shall hold office until aged eighty, for example, that limit will apply instead of the statutory one.

Section 186 of the 1948 Act requires a person, who has attained the age limit imposed by the Act or the company's Articles, and who is appointed or to his knowledge is proposed to be appointed director of the company, to give *notice* of his *age* to the company. Failure to do so, or acting as director under any appointment which is invalid or has terminated on account of age, involves liability to a fine of up to £5 for every day while the failure continues or while he continues to act. The obligation to inform the company of his age does not, however, apply in relation to a reappointment on the termination of a previous appointment as director of the company—presumably because his age would be already known. Under section 200 of the Act a company to which section 185 applies must include the date of birth of each director among the particulars shown in its register of directors and in the returns of directors made to the Registrar of Companies.

It is provided in subsection (2) of section 185 that acts done by a person as a director shall be valid notwithstanding that it is afterwards discovered that his appointment had terminated by his attaining seventy years of age. This would not, however, apply where his appointment was from the beginning invalid under the section.

9-12 Winding Up

In a winding up of a company all the powers of the directors cease on the appointment of a liquidator, except in so far as the company in general meeting or the liquidator sanctions their continuance in a members' voluntary winding up, or in a creditors' voluntary winding up, except in so far as the committee of inspection or, if there is no such committee, the creditors, sanction such continuance (section 285 and 296, 1948 Act).

Chapter 10

DIRECTORS' PENSIONS

10-01 Power to Pay Pensions

Executive directors will expect their company to provide them with pensions and the question of pension provision for directors, staff and employees is one which absorbs a growing proportion of the time of the board and of the profits of the company. This difficult and continuously changing subject naturally demands specialist advice, which must be regularly up-dated. In this chapter we attempt only to draw attention to some of the more important features of the scene at the time of writing in June 1975.

Before considering the alternatives, the director must first satisfy himself that the company and board have power to pay pensions at all. The usual position is that the Memorandum confers an express power to pay pensions upon the company and the Articles then delegate that power to the board. Both Memorandum and Articles should specifically include the directors as potential pensioners, as it has been held that reference to employees alone is not sufficient[1]. If the power is omitted from the Objects Clause in the Memorandum, the power to provide pensions for employees is probably to be implied as incidental to the business. The Article normally adopted is Article 87 of Table A which provides as follows:—

> "The directors on behalf of the company may pay a gratuity or pension or allowance on retirement to any Director who has held any other salaried office or place of profit with the Company or to his widow or dependants and may make contributions to any fund and pay premiums for the purchase or provision of any such gratuity, pension or allowance."

The Board must, however, bear in mind that these powers must be exercised only in the interests of the Company's business and not otherwise. Thus a pension awarded to a directors' widow, five years

---

1. *Normandy v Ind Coope & Co.* [1908] 1 Ch. 84.

10-01 Directors' Pensions

after his death was not justified, as there was no evidence that it was for the benefit of the Company[2].

When implementing a scheme the Board may either set up their own fund and administration, if the size of the scheme will be sufficient or contract the scheme out, in whole or in part, to an Insurance Company. There are many company schemes but the advantages of size, administrative expertise and investment management which the Insurance Companies can offer are clearly significant.

10-02 State Pension Schemes

The contributions to the flat-rate National Insurance Pension are discussed in paragraph 8-08 above. These contributions are related to earnings but at the time of writing (June 1975), there is no earnings related scheme of benefits in operation and there is unlikely to be until 1977.

Successive schemes for second or reserve pensions have failed to reach the post and the current favourite is the scheme for "earnings related-pensions *fully protected* against inflation at all times" set out in the White Paper "*Better Pensions*"[3] and the *Social Security Pensions Bill 1975*. Whether this Utopian vision will materialise and whether future contributors can afford to pay for it, remains to be seen[4].

The scheme is intended to provide a £ for £ replacement of earnings up to a base level (£10 per week in 1974 terms) and thereafter a quarter of average earnings up to seven times the base level. On this basis, a married man earning £70 per week would start off, on 1974 figures, with a pension of £25 per week. Inflation proofing, both before and after retirement, is to be achieved by expressing the contributor's earnings in any year as a fraction of *average* earnings in that year. The pension when awarded will relate to the fraction at that time. The base level (i.e. flat rate part) will then be up-rated in line with average earnings ("growth-proofed") while the earnings-related part will follow increases in the price-level ("inflation proofed"). Inflation protection will be extended to the present graduated pensions, both those currently being paid and the accumulated rights (as at April 1975) of those who have not yet retired.

---

2. *Re Lee Behrens & Co.*, [1932] 2 Ch. 46 and see also para. 9-07(c).
3. September 1974 Cmnd. 5713. The scheme also aims to provide equal treatment for women.
4. The Government Actuary's calculations of the cost of the scheme in the White Paper were based on inflation at 5%!

Provisions for contracting out members of occupational pension schemes remain to be settled but are likely to require full contributions up to the base level and a reduced contribution thereafter. The occupational schemes will also have to provide an accrual of at least one-eightieth of salary per annum and a widow's pension of half that rate. The minimum pension for each individual must be at least as much as the pension forgone in the state scheme on his upper band earnings. Clearly the eventual outcome of these proposals will have a critical effect on what is noted below with regard to directors' participation in occupational schemes.

10-03 Private Schemes for Directors

At present directors may find their pension arrangements falling under one of several categories:—

(a) The board, in exercise of its powers, may simply *grant* them a pension on retirement. This is a deductible expense for the Company but it has to be borne entirely during the retirement period and has none of the advantages of the statutory schemes.

(b) There may be a staff scheme *approved* by the Inland Revenue under what is known as the *New Code,* introduced by the *Finance Act 1970* and in which all directors were allowed to participate by the *Finance Act 1973.*

(c) There may be older schemes under the *Old Code* (pre-1970) which must be approved under the *New Code* by not later than 5th April 1980.

(d) There may be private provision by the director himself for a *Retirement Annuity* under the *Finance Act 1956*[5].

We can now look at some of the significant features of (b), (c), and (d).

10-04 The New Code

The *Finance Act 1970* introduced a new code of approval and tax treatment of staff pension and death benefit arrangements which will (by 1980) supersede the previous system. Controlling directors, with more than 5% of the shares in Companies controlled by the

5. As consolidated in the Income and Corporation Taxes Act 1970 and amended by the Finance Act 1971.

board, were excluded from participation until they were admitted by the *Finance Act 1973*. They are now in the same position as other employees, except that 20% shareholders must average their pensionable remuneration over any three years within the last ten, and cannot therefore give their salary a boost in the final year, simply to establish a high level for pension purposes. The following features may be noted:—

(a) The directors' *maximum benefits* are essentially:—

 On death before normal retirement age:

 (i) Life Assurance Benefit

 (a) 4 × final salary (or £5,000 if greater)

 and (b) a refund of his own contributions

 (ii) Widows Pension[6] — 4/9 × final salary.

 On Retirement:

 (i) Personal Pension — $\frac{2}{3}$ × final salary.

 (ii) Tax Free Cash Sum. — $1\frac{1}{2}$ × final salary (reducing the pension accordingly.)

 (iii) Widow's Pension[6]. — 4/9 × final salary.

(b) *Minimum Service* for receipt of these maximum benefits is 10 years, except that 20 years is required for the maximum cash commutation. Lesser periods reduce the benefits.

(c) Pensions from *previous sources*, must be taken into account when arriving at the permitted limits.

(d) *Increases* in pensions in course of payment are permitted by a percentage not greater than the percentage rise in the cost-of-living index.

(e) There is no limit on the amount of *contributions* as the limits are imposed only on the emerging benefits. However, the directors' personal contributions must not exceed 15% of his relevant earnings.

(f) For calculating the limits, directors' *fees* may be included and "remuneration" means basic salary, with an average (e.g. over 3 years) of fees, commissions, bonuses and fluctuating payments. "Final remuneration" means remuneration in any of the last 5 years of employment or an average of 3 successive

---

6. Separate pensions may also be provided for children or other dependants but the total must not exceed the maximum director's pension, $\frac{2}{3}$rds i.e. generally of final salary.

years in the last 10 for Directors with shareholdings of more than 20%.

(g) The scheme must usually be set up under *irrevocable trusts*, and all employees, whether staff or directors, may participate either in an all embracing scheme, or in one limited to specific categories or individuals.

(h) *Retiring dates* must normally be in the age range of 60–70 for men and 55–65 for women.

(i) The company *must contribute* and contributions both of company and director are *fully deductible* from their respective taxable earnings. The pensions, when paid are taxable as earned income under P.A.Y.E.. The lump sum benefits on retirement and death are tax-free. The Trustees of the scheme are often given discretion as to the application of the death benefit and Estate Duty (and, it is believed Capital Transfer Tax) is not normally payable. Where, in the usual case, the death benefit passes to the spouse, C.T.T. does not apply in any event.

(j) The position on *leaving employment* is that the *Social Security Act 1973* requires that any employee aged 26 or over with at least 5 years' pensionable service must *retain* the right to any pension earned up to the date of leaving. The benefits may be preserved as they are, or transferred to any suitably approved scheme of the new employer.

Alternatively the employee may take a refund of his own contributions (less tax at 10%) if his remuneration has not exceeded £5,000 per annum. However, this does not apply in respect of contributions paid after April 1975 for an employee leaving after April 1980 who is aged 26 or over and has 5 years of pensionable service.

(k) In cases of *late retirement*, the director may either postpone and thus increase his pension, or take it and continue working.

(l) The *Pension Fund* itself is exempt from Income Tax and Capital Gains Tax.

(m) *Approval* and *supervision* of schemes is dealt with by the Joint Office of the Inland Revenue Superannuation Funds Office and the Occupational Pensions Board, at Apex Tower, High Street, New Malden, Surrey KT3 4DN, from whom practice notes can be obtained on all aspects of occupational schemes.

10-05 The Old Code

(a) What is known as the *Old Code* consisted, basically, of two types of pre-1970 scheme, Staff Superannuation Schemes (s.208 Schemes) and Directors' Special Pension Schemes ("Top Hat Schemes"). They must both be converted to New Code schemes and approved as such by April 1980, or on the making of any major change before that date. All schemes introduced after 1970 must comply with the New Code from their inception. Pending approval, the Old Code schemes continue, although if directors take advantage of the *Finance Act 1973* and join their staff scheme, this will necessitate re-approval under the New Code.

(b) *Staff Superannuation Schemes* (s.208):
Staff schemes were approved under S.208 of the *Income and Corporation Taxes Act 1970* and some of their main characteristics (and differences from New Code schemes) were as follows:—

   (i) Controlling directors were *excluded*. This meant directors holding 5% of the shares of a director controlled company, and ruled out most directors of family companies.

   (ii) There was full Tax relief on contributions, and pensions were received as earned income, but there was no right to a *cash commutation* of any part of the pension.

   (iii) *Death benefit* was usually a maximum of seven times remuneration up to £25,000 or the capital value of the maximum approvable pension if higher.

   (iv) *Widows pension* was limited to half the husband's.

   (v) The *maximum* pension was two-thirds of final remuneration after 20 years' service, with a limit of £3,000 p.a. in contributory schemes.

   (vi) *Refunds* of contributions were not available to those earning over £4,500 p.a. unless the pension was restricted to £3,000 p.a.

   (vii) Directors' *fees* could not be included in calculations of remuneration.

   (viii) *Build-up* of funds was tax free as under the New Code.

(c) *Directors' Special Pension Schemes* (*"Top Hat Schemes"*, s.220):

As a result of the limit of £3,000 p.a. special arrangements were often made for directors under what were known as "Top Hat Schemes". The characteristics were as follows:—

(i) *Approval* of the Inland Revenue was again required—this time under s.222 of the *Income & Corporation Taxes Act 1970.*

(ii) The arrangements could take the form of a collective scheme or individual arrangements for each Director.

(iii) Unlike s.208 Schemes, there could be a *commutation* of part (usually one-quarter) of the total benefits for cash.

(iv) The company's payments normally took the form of premiums (which were not taxable as receipts of the Director) securing an endowment policy, which included life cover as well as the pension.

(v) The pension could not exceed $\frac{2}{3}$ salary for which there had to be at least 20 years' service.

(vi) Membership was normally available to those with at least 5 years to go before retirement, and salary was stabilised at that point for the purpose of calculating the pension. Directors' fees were excluded. Part-time directors required special approval.

10-06 Retirement Annuities under the Finance Act 1956

Facilities for such annuities were provided by the 1956 Act (now Ch. III, Part IV, of the *Income and Corporation Taxes Act 1970* as amended by the *Finance Act 1971*) for controlling directors and self-employed persons who could not participate in approved schemes. These facilities are still fully effective and still available to directors, but they must choose between them and the option, which is now open to them, of joining their staff scheme. If they choose the latter, they can make no further payments towards a retirement annuity and the benefits they have already acquired must be taken into account in determining their maximum benefits. Retirement Annuities are purchased by the director, by the payment of premiums, which may vary from year to year. The following points may be noted:—

(i) *Premiums* up to 15% of earned income with a limit of £1,500 p.a. are fully deductible for Income Tax. When received the pension is taxed as earned income.

(ii) The pension itself is not limited, as the limiting factor is the contributions. It may be taken at any age between 60 and 70.

(iii) There can be a *cash* commutation at pension age of *three times* the annual pension then remaining.

(iv) The pension cannot be assigned or surrendered, and on death before pension age, the contributor gets only the return of his contributions without interest, or alternatively an annuity for his dependants.

(v) The pension can be guaranteed for up to 10 years and part can be given up in return for a widow's or dependants' pension for life.

10-07 Insurance Cover

The advantages to directors of joining their staff schemes under the New Code will often outweigh all other factors except in circumstances where income is likely to fluctuate very widely, when retirement annuities may offer the most flexible solution. They should also bear in mind the benefits which the staff schemes can give them in respect of group life cover, *regardless* of state of health and permanent sickness cover up to three-quarters of their income. Such cover can also provide their contributions to the main scheme until they reach retirement, when they can retire on full pension, even though they may have been incapacitated for many years.

10-08 Disclosure in Accounts

Section 196 of the Act requires the aggregate amount of Directors' or past directors' pensions to be disclosed in the accounts of a company or in a statement annexed thereto, on the same lines as directors' remuneration is disclosed (see para. 8-06). "Pension" includes any superannuation allowance, superannuation gratuity or similar payment, but it is not necessary to include in the total any pensions under a contributory pension scheme if the contributions are substantially adequate for the maintenance of the scheme, for in that case any contributions paid by the company, if separately ascertainable, will have been disclosed as part of the directors' remuneration. A pension, paid in respect of a director's services to a dependant or nominee of his, must be included in the total, unless paid under a contributory scheme. Pensions in respect of services as a director, whether of the company or its subsidiary, must be distinguished from other pensions.

Appendix A

**Specimen Form of Director's Service Agreement
(copyright of the Institute of Directors)**

THIS AGREEMENT is made the   day of   One thousand nine
hundred and   BETWEEN   LIMITED (hereinafter
called "the Company") whose registered office is situate at
of the one part and   of
(hereinafter called "Mr.   ") of the other part

WHEREAS the Board of Directors of the Company (hereinafter called "the
Board") has approved the terms of this Agreement

IT IS HEREBY AGREED as follows:

1. The Company shall employ Mr.   **and Mr.**
        shall serve the Company as a full-time   Director
of the Company for the period stipulated in Clause 2 hereof

2. This Agreement shall commence on the   day of
One thousand nine hundred and   and shall (subject as hereinafter
provided) continue until the   day of
One thousand nine hundred and   and thereafter from year to year subject
to the right of either party to determine this Agreement on the said   day of
        One thousand nine hundred and   or at any time thereafter
by giving to the other party not less than six month's previous notice in writing to
that effect

3. During the continuance of this Agreement Mr.   shall well
and faithfully serve the Company and use his utmost endeavours to promote the
interests thereof and shall perform such duties and exercise such powers in relation
to the conduct and management of the affairs of the Company and of such subsidiary
companies of the Company as may from time to time be assigned to or vested in
him by or at the direction of the Board and shall give to the Board such information
concerning the affairs of the Company and its subsidiaries as the Board shall
require and at all times shall conform to the reasonable directions of the Board

4. Mr   shall devote the whole of his time and attention and abilities
during normal business hours and at such other times as the Company or his duties
reasonably require to the business and affairs of the Company (and if applicable the
subsidiaries of the Company) unless prevented by ill-health from so doing and shall
not during the continuance of this Agreement directly or indirectly enter into or be
concerned or interested in any other business whatsoever except with the prior
consent in writing of the Company but Mr.   may nevertheless
be or become a minority holder of any securities which are quoted and dealt in on
any recognised Stock Exchange

APPENDIX A

5. Mr.   shall receive as remuneration for his services hereunder a salary at the rate of £   per annum, or at such higher rate as the Company shall from time to time decide, to be paid by equal monthly instalments on the last day of each calendar month. The said salary shall unless otherwise agreed in writing with the Company be inclusive of all fees and other remuneration which Mr.   may receive for his services from the Company and any subsidiary companies of the Company

6. In addition to his remuneration hereunder Mr.   shall be reimbursed the amount of all reasonable travelling hotel entertainment and other expenses properly and necessarily incurred and defrayed by him in the discharge of his duties hereunder

7. Mr.   shall be entitled (in addition to Public Holidays) to   weeks' holiday in every year at such times as shall be convenient to the Company and such additional holidays as the Board shall approve. The entitlement to holiday (and on termination of employment holiday pay in lieu of holiday) accrues pro rata throughout each year of the appointment

8. Mr.   shall not either during the continuance of this Agreement (otherwise than in the performance of his duties hereunder) or thereafter without the consent in writing of the Board being first obtained divulge to any person firm or company and shall during the continuance of this Agreement use his best endeavours to prevent the publication or disclosure of any confidential information concerning the business accounts affairs or finances of the Company and its subsidiary companies (if any) or any of their secrets dealings or transactions which have or may come to his knowledge during the continuance of this Agreement or previously or otherwise

9. (a) If Mr.   shall be guilty of any grave misconduct or any breach or non-observance of any of the provisions of this Agreement or shall neglect or fail (otherwise than by reason of accident or ill-health) or shall refuse to carry out the duties required of him hereunder or shall commit any act of bankruptcy or shall take advantage of any statute for the time being in force offering relief for insolvent debtors then and immediately thereupon it shall be lawful for the Company by notice in writing to Mr. summarily to determine his services hereunder

    (b) If Mr.   shall at any time become or be unable properly to perform his duties hereunder by reason of ill-health accident or otherwise for a period or periods aggregating at least 180 days in any period of 12 consecutive calendar months the Company may by not less than three months notice in writing determine this Agreement but any such notice of determination shall be given by the Company within three months after such period or periods totalling 180 days

10. Upon the expiration or sooner determination of this Agreement Mr. shall deliver up to the Company or its authorised representative all plans statistics documents records or papers which may be in his possession or control and relate in any way to the business or affairs of the Company or any of its subsidiary companies and no copies shall be retained by him

11. The determination of this Agreement shall be without prejudice to any right the Company may have in respect of any breach by Mr. of any of the provisions of this Agreement which may have occurred prior to such determination

12. Any notice given under this Agreement shall be deemed to have been duly given if despatched by either party hereto by registered post addressed to the other party at in the case of the Company its registered office and in the case of Mr. his last known address and any such notice shall be deemed to have been given on the day on which in the ordinary course of post it would be delivered

13. From the date when this Agreement shall take effect all other Agreements or arrangements between Mr.   and the Company and any subsidiary Company of the Company relating to his services shall be deemed to have been cancelled

14. In this Agreement the expression "subsidiary company" shall have the same meaning as "subsidiary company" in Section 154 of the Companies Act, 1948 or any statutory modification or re-enactment thereof for the time being in force

    AS WITNESS whereof the parties have hereunto set their hands the day and year first before written

SIGNED by a Director
for and on behalf of

LIMITED in the
presence of:

SIGNED by the said

in the presence of:

APPENDIX A

The accompanying Service Agreement is drafted in a form which covers the usual terms and conditions in a Contract of Service between a Director and his Company—but of course circumstances arise which require special consideration and possibly special provisions in the Agreement. While it is not practicable to deal with all such situations in the specimen Agreement or accompanying Notes, the Institute will be glad to answer questions on points not specifically covered.

---

1. Before entering into any commitment the Company and the Director are strongly recommended to consult their respective Solicitors to obtain independent professional advice. A Service Agreement is an important document. The financial obligations and the duties laid down in the Agreement can be onerous to both parties.

2. A Service Agreement may be verbal, incorporated in an exchange of letters or comprise a formal document in accordance with the attached Specimen. Each one is legally binding—but the disadvantage of a verbal agreement is that with the passage of time memories fade and arguments arise concerning the exact terms which were earlier agreed upon.

3. In each case, notice under the Contracts of Employment Act 1972 should be given by the Company to the Director. Under this Act the notice must also contain particulars relating to "grievance procedure" and holiday entitlement. The grievance procedure for a Director must, as for any other employee, set out to whom, in the first instance, application for redress of a grievance should be made, and also the steps open to the Director consequent upon any such application. A suggested grievance procedure for a Director relating to his employment would be application, in the first instance, to the Company's Managing Director, and thereafter to the Chairman of the Board.

4. A Director is normally entitled to nominal Directors' fees for attending Board Meetings. A full-time Director is usually paid a salary for the executive services he renders, in his executive capacity, to the Company. The Articles of Association of the Company normally authorise the Board to appoint Directors to executive office at remuneration (as distinct from Directors' fees) determined by the Board.

5. It should be stated in the Agreement whether a Director's remuneration, in an executive capacity, is to be inclusive or exclusive of Directors' fees.

6. It is normal practice for Directors' remuneration to be subject to periodical review by the Board or a Committee of the Board (if possible comprised of non-Executive Directors). The Agreement can provide that the salary shall be increased annually by reference to any increase in the General Index of Retail Prices.

7.   The attached Specimen Agreement is for a fixed term and thereafter from year to year subject to determination by a period of notice.   Accordingly, after the expiry of the fixed term, the Agreement will continue until notice is served by one party on the other or a fresh Agreement is negotiated.   Service Agreements are normally for a fixed term of three years and in exceptional circumstances, depending upon the age of the Director, five or seven years.   It is unusual for a Service Agreement to be for any longer fixed term.   In the case of a public company whose capital is listed on the Stock Exchange, it is a Stock Exchange requirement that a Director's Service Agreement for a term of more than ten years must be approved by the shareholders in general meeting.   It is a further Stock Exchange requirement for such a public company that a Director's Service Agreement which does not expire or cannot be determined without payment of compensation within one year must be available for inspection by the public from the date of the notice convening an Annual General Meeting to the conclusion of that meeting.   This latter obligation is additional to that contained in Section 26 of the Companies Act 1967 (which applies to all companies) that Directors' Service Agreements must be available during normal business hours for inspection by Shareholders.

8.   Under the Redundancy Payments Act 1965 and under the Trade Union and Labour Relations Act 1974 the Company can in a Service Agreement for a fixed term of two years or more exclude any liability to make a payment of compensation for unfair dismissal or a redundancy payment where such liability, if any, arises only by virtue of the expiry of the fixed term without the employment in question being renewed.   If it is wished to exclude such liability Clause 2 of the Agreement should be amended by deleting the words from "and thereafter from year to year" to the end of Clause 2 and inserting a new clause as follows:
"Mr.   hereby agrees to exclude:

(a)   any right to a redundancy payment under the Redundancy Payments Act 1965 (or any statutory modification or re-enactment thereof) in the event of the expiry of the term of the employment provided in Clause 2 hereof without its being renewed; and

(b)   any claim in respect of rights under Paragraph 4 of Schedule 1 of the Trade Union and Labour Relations Act 1974 (or any statutory modification or re-enactment thereof) in relation to this Agreement".

9.   If a Director is to receive commission or a share of profits, the clause expressing the method of calculation of such profits or commission will require to be drafted with care, and professional advice is essential.

10. If not contrary to the Company's employment policy a clause may be inserted in the Agreement that the Director shall be provided with a car at the expense of the Company (including road tax, insurance, repairs and fuel etc.) which may also be used for private purposes.

11. The Specimen Agreement provides that the duties to be performed by the Director in his executive capacity shall be determined by the Board from time to time.   If the executive duties of the Director are detailed in the Agreement the freedom of the Board to make administrative changes at some future time may be restricted.

12. Any restraint on competition by the Director after the determination of his Service Agreement requires professional advice, since such restraints are very frequently unenforceable because their scope is wider than the minimum necessary to protect the interests of the Company in the particular circumstances of the case. Even if unenforceable such restraints can however impose a strong moral obligation on the Director.

13. Service Agreements may be under Seal or under hand as a matter of choice (each has the same effect) and do not attract Stamp Duty. The Agreement must be approved by a Resolution of the Board of the Company (or by a Resolution of an expressly authorised Committee of the Board) and the Director concerned should normally not vote on his own Agreement.

14. If a whole-time Director is to be permitted to hold other Directorships or to indulge in other (non-competing) business activities they can be made the subject matter of an express letter of consent from the Board.

15. If a Director, by reason of his duties, is likely to discover any inventions which might be of use to the Company or a subsidiary, an express clause can be inserted in his Service Agreement to the effect that all such inventions belong to the Company without additional payment by the Company. Here again, such a clause would need to be drafted by the Company Solicitors to suit the particular circumstances.

16. An Executive Director can be required by the Board to perform his duties in any new location unless his Service Agreement stipulates that he shall not be obligated to perform duties in a location which necessitates changing his permanent residence from a particular area.

17. Pension provisions are normally incorporated in an entirely separate document or letter; if the Company is obligated by such letter (or in the actual Service Agreement) to pay premiums or make contributions during the continuance of the Agreement to provide the Director with a pension then the value thereof will be reflected by an increase in any compensation for loss of office payable to the Director in the case of his wrongful dismissal.

A Director may surrender a part of his remuneration so that it may be applied by the Company in the provision of a pension or increased pension; subject to various limitations the amount so surrendered will not be treated as part of the Director's taxable income.

18. The execution of a Service Agreement imposes obligations and duties on both the Company and the Director and accordingly if either party determines the Agreement prematurely such party may be liable for wrongful breach. If the Director subsequently carries on a competitive business contrary to a restrictive covenant in the Service Agreement which he has breached or if the Company incurs considerable expense in finding a replacement, the Director may be liable in damages to his previous company who may alternatively seek by injunction to prevent him from competing. Where a company breaches an Agreement, in addition to its potential liability to pay to the Director compensation for unfair dismissal under the Trade Union and Labour Relations Act 1974 the Director may claim damages based upon the remuneration payable for the unexpired period of the Agreement, although the Director has a duty to mitigate his loss by seeking and if possible obtaining suitable alternative employment. The tax position of the Director in these circumstances should be considered in each case and expert advice taken. Unless the Agreement otherwise provides, a change in the ownership of the shares of the Company (e.g. as a result of a takeover) or major changes in the Board will not normally terminate the Agreement with the result that the obligations of both parties will continue after such changes.

Appendix B

**1. Specimen Memorandum and Articles of Association
(copyright Model Form "D"**

form D
for a private Company

The Companies Acts 1948 to 1967
COMPANY LIMITED BY SHARES

Draft

Memorandum and
Articles of Association

Limited

Settled by
RICHARD SYKES, B.A.
of Lincoln's Inn, Barrister-at-Law

Jordan & Sons Limited
Legal and Information Services, Printers and Publishers
Jordan House 47 Brunswick Place London N1 6EE
Telephone: 01–253 3030   Telex No. 261010   ©1971

APPENDIX B1

INTRODUCTION

This form is primarily for the use of solicitors and others concerned in the formation of private companies limited by shares under the Companies Acts 1948 to 1967. It is intended to provide a convenient draft on which the Memorandum and Articles of Association of a private company may be based.

For purposes of registration copies of the drafts after settlement can be printed either by letterpress or type-lithography for signature by Subscribers and for supplying to Members in accordance with Section 24 of the Companies Act 1948. Jordan & Sons Limited are specially equipped to prepare expeditiously prints from drafts settled from this form.

This form was entirely resettled by Counsel in 1970 and accords with the latest enactments and judicial decisions.

COMMENTARY ON THE FORM

Notes to Memorandum

Clause 3 (a)—*see draft form.*

Clause 5.

Even if the share capital is to be divided into different classes of shares it is advisable, and usual, to omit any such division or reference to special classes in the Memorandum.

Notes to Articles

These Articles are suitable for use in connection with any private company limited by shares under the Companies Acts and, appropriately altered, may be adopted as new Articles in substitution for the existing Articles of a Company.

Article 1.

All the Clauses in Parts I and II of Table A (save for Clauses 24 and 53 in Part I of Table A for which Clauses 3 and 4 in Part II of Table A are substituted) apply except where any such Clauses are prefaced by any of the following special articles.

Article 2.

(b) If the Articles are not to specify the maximum and minimum number of Directors the second alternative **(b)** should be deleted.

(c) If the first Directors are not to be named the first alternative **(c)** should be included and the second alternative **(c)** should be deleted. If the first Directors are not named in this form the Declaration of Compliance will need to be made by a Solicitor engaged in the formation of the company.

(d) Although it may be provided that Directors shall be Permanent Directors i.e. not liable to retirement by rotation, any such Director is liable to be removed by Ordinary Resolution (Section 184 of the Companies Act 1948). Accordingly where Paragraph **(d)** is used it may be thought desirable to include Paragraph **(e)** which confers on a Permanent Director enhanced voting rights, but the inclusion of such Paragraph may constitute "control" of the company for purposes of estate duty. It should be noted that unless a Permanent Director holds, or has the support of, at least 26% of the Voting Capital he will not be able to prevent a Special Resolution being passed to delete this Paragraph which would consequently remove the protection afforded thereby.

The final sentence in each alternative Paragraph **(b)** is designed to remove any doubts as to the ability of a sole Director (where the minimum number is stated to be one) to act as the Board of Directors, but it should be noted that a sole Director may not also act as Secretary.

Article 3.

Although this Clause places the allotment of shares in the hands of the Directors and does not require that unissued shares be offered pro rata to existing Members they must act *bona fide* in the exercising of their powers.

Article 4.

In a private company it is usual to extend the powers of a company's lien conferred by Clause 11 in Part I of Table A to include fully paid as well as partly paid shares and also shares held by joint holders.

Article 5.
This Clause removes the somewhat restricted limit on calls imposed by Table A.

Article 6.
This states the law (Section 1 of the Stock Transfer Act 1963).

Article 7.
This Clause serves as a reminder of the statutory requirements (in Section 136 of the Companies Act 1948 and Section 14 of the Companies Act 1967).

Article 8.
This Clause is designed to avoid argument as to the inability of one Member to constitute a quorum even at an adjourned Meeting.

Article 9.
This Clause extends Table A to enable a resolution in writing to consist of several documents.

Article 10.
Section 185 of the Companies Act 1948 as to appointment and retirement of Directors over the age of 70 does not apply to a private company unless it is the subsidiary of a public company but the inclusion of this Clause is regarded as a useful reminder.

Article 11.
This Clause is thought to be useful in view of the increasing tendency for Directors to be absent for various reasons and enables an absent Director to be represented at Board Meetings.

Article 12.
This Clause varies Table A to enable Directors to vote at Board Meetings without restriction on matters in which they have an interest and is commonly included in the Articles of private companies.

Article 13.
The powers of the company as to payment of pensions conferred by Clause 3 (q) of the Memorandum is wide and includes Directors whether or not they hold any salaried office. This Clause enables the Directors to exercise these powers, whereas Clause 87 in Part I of Table A limits payment of pensions to Directors holding salaried office.

Article 14.
In the case of a private company the signing of the Minute Book at Directors Meetings is generally considered unnecessary.

Article 15.
This Article has the same result for resolutions of Directors as Article 9 has for resolutions of General Meetings.

Article 16.
This Article gives the Directors unlimited borrowing powers which is usual in a private company, whereas under Clause 79 in Part I of Table A they are limited.

Article 17.
The addition to Clause 126 in Part I of Table A serves as a reminder of the statutory provisions.

Article 18.
The indemnity given by this Clause is wider than that provided by Clause 136 in Part I of Table A.

Transfer Articles.
If no special Article is included the Directors will have an absolute right to refuse to register transfers under Clause 3 in Part II of Table A.
Alternative transfer Article A provides a free right of transfer to relatives and, subject thereto, the Directors' right to refuse to register a transfer applies.
Under transfer Article B in addition to a free right of transfer to relatives there is also a right of pre-emption and provision for the compulsory transfer of shares held by employees of the Company.

APPENDIX B1

Special Note.
If any variations of the specimen transfer provisions are desired or if any special provisions are required as regards the Share Capital these may be included and the publishers will be pleased to assist in the settling of such provisions which will necessarily increase the formation expenses by an amount commensurate with the additional printing required and the technical assistance provided.

Table A to the Companies Act 1948
as amended by the Companies Act 1967.
A print of Table A to the Companies Act 1948 as amended is appended to this form as the Articles adopt Table A with modifications.
It is advisable to have copies of Table A bound up with the special Articles so that the whole of the regulations governing the company may be accessible in a convenient form under one cover, and copies of Memorandum and Articles printed and supplied by the publishers will have copies of Table A attached.

Note: Attention is directed to the fact that these draft forms are the copyright of Jordan & Sons Limited and may not be reproduced without the express permission of the publishers.

The standard charge offered by Jordan & Sons Limited is based on the adoption of Memorandum and Articles of Association based on their Form D. Any alteration whatsoever to the model form, other than the alternatives already offered in the draft, will involve additional expenses.

The Companies Acts 1948 to 1967

COMPANY LIMITED BY SHARES

Memorandum of Association of

Limited

1. The name of the Company is "
LIMITED."

2. The registered office of the Company will be situate in England.

3. The objects for which the Company is established are:—

(a)

Note: If the form is returned to the Publishers with a note as to the principal business to be carried on by the Company they will insert a suitable main objects Clause. Please specify if an existing business is being acquired; if a claim for relief from Capital Duty pursuant to Para 10 Schedule 19 of the Finance Act 1973 is to be made, reference to the acquisition may be necessary.

(b) To carry on any other business which may seem to the Company capable of being conveniently carried on in connection with the above objects, or calculated directly or indirectly to enhance the value of or render more profitable any of the Company's property.

(c) To purchase or by any other means acquire and take options over any freehold, leasehold or other real or personal property for any estate or interest whatever, and any rights or privileges of any kind over or in respect of any real or personal property.

(d) To apply for, register, purchase, or by other means acquire and protect, prolong and renew, whether in the United Kingdom or elsewhere, any patents, patent rights, brevets d'invention, licences, secret processes, trade marks, designs, protections and concessions and to disclaim, alter, modify, use and turn to account and to maunfacture under or grant licences or privileges in respect of the same, and to expend money in experimenting upon, testing and improving any patents, inventions or rights which the Company may acquire or propose to acquire.

(e) To acquire and undertake the whole or any part of the business, goodwill, and assets of any person, firm, or company carrying on or proposing to carry on any of the businesses which this Company is authorised to carry on, and as part of the consideration for such acquisition to undertake all or any of the liabilities of such person, firm or company, or to acquire an interest in, amalgamate with, or enter into partnership or into any arrangement for sharing profits, or for co-operation, or for mutual assistance with any such person, firm or company, or for subsidising or otherwise assisting any such person, firm or company, and to give or accept, by way of consideration for any of the acts or things aforesaid or property acquired, any Shares, Debentures, Debenture Stock, or securities that may be agreed upon, and to hold and retain, or sell, mortgage, and deal with any shares, debentures, debenture stock, or securities so received.

(f) To improve, manage, construct, repair, develop, exchange, let on lease or otherwise, mortgage, charge, sell, dispose of, turn to account, grant licences, options, rights and privileges in respect of, or otherwise deal with all or any part of the property and rights of the Company, both real and personal.

(g) To invest and deal with the moneys of the Company not immediately required in such manner as may from time to time be determined and to hold, sell or otherwise deal with any investments made.

(h) To lend and advance money or give credit on such terms as may seem expedient and with or without security to customers and others, to enter into guarantees, contracts of indemnity and suretyships of all kinds, to receive money on deposit or loan upon such terms as the Company may approve and to become security for any persons, firms, or companies.

(i) To borrow and raise money in such manner as the Company shall think fit and to secure the repayment of any money borrowed, raised, or owing, by mortgage, charge, lien or other security upon the whole or any part of the Company's property or assets (whether present or future), including its uncalled capital, and also by a similar mortgage, charge, lien or security to secure and guarantee the performance by the Company of any obligation or liability it may undertake or which may become binding on it.

(j) To draw, make, accept, endorse, discount, negotiate, execute and issue promissory notes, bills of exchange, bills of lading, warrants, debentures, and other negotiable or transferable instruments.

(k) To apply for, promote, and obtain any Act of Parliament, Provisional Order, or Licence of the Department of Trade and Industry or other authority for enabling the Company to carry any of its objects into effect, or for effecting any modification of the Company's constitution, or for any other purpose which may seem expedient, and to oppose any proceedings or applications which may seem calculated directly or indirectly to prejudice the Company's interests.

(l) To enter into any arrangements with any Governments or authorities (supreme, municipal, local, or otherwise) that may seem conducive to the attainment of the

Company's objects or any of them, and to obtain from any such Government or authority any charters, decrees, rights, privileges or concessions which the Company may think desirable and to carry out, exercise, and comply with any such charters, decrees, rights, privileges, and concessions.

(m) To subscribe for, take, purchase, or otherwise acquire and hold shares or other interests in or securities of any other company having objects altogether or in part similar to those of the Company or carrying on any business capable of being carried on so as directly or indirectly to benefit the Company or enhance the value of any of its property and to co-ordinate, finance and manage the businesses and operations of any company in which the Company holds any such interest.

(n) To act as agents or brokers and as trustees for any person, firm or company, and to undertake and perform sub-contracts, and also to act in any of the businesses of the Company through or by means of agents, brokers, sub-contractors, or others.

(o) To remunerate any person, firm or company rendering services to this Company either by cash payment or by the allotment to him or them of Shares or other securities of the Company credited as paid up in full or in part or otherwise as may be thought expedient.

(p) To pay all or any expenses incurred in connection with the promotion, formation and incorporation of the Company, or to contract with any person, firm or company to pay the same, and to pay commissions to brokers and others for underwriting, placing, selling, or guaranteeing the subscription of any Shares or other securities of the Company.

(q) To support and subscribe to any charitable or public object, and to support and subscribe to any institution, society, or club which may be for the benefit of the Company or its employees, or may be connected with any town or place where the Company carries on business; to give or award pensions, annuities, gratuities, and superannuation or other allowances or benefits or charitable aid to any persons who are or have been Directors of, or who are or have been employed by, or who are serving or have served the Company, or of any company which is a subsidiary of the Company or the holding company of the Company or of the predecessors in business of the Company or of any such subsidiary or holding company and to the wives, widows, children and other relatives and dependants of such persons; to make payments towards insurance; and to set up, establish, support and maintain superannuation and other funds or schemes (whether contributory or non-contributory) for the benefit of any such persons and of their wives, widows, children and other relatives and dependants; and to set up, establish, support and maintain profit sharing or share purchase schemes for the benefit of any of the employees of the Company or of any such subsidiary or holding company and to lend money to any such employees or to trustees on their behalf to enable any such share purchase schemes to be established or maintained.

(r) To promote any other company for the purpose of acquiring the whole or any part of the business or property and undertaking any of the liabilities of the Company, or of undertaking any business or operations which may appear likely to assist or benefit the Company or to enhance the value of any property or business of the Company, and to place or guarantee the placing of, underwrite, subscribe for, or otherwise acquire all or any part of the shares or securities of any such company as aforesaid.

(s) To sell or otherwise dispose of the whole or any part of the business or property of the Company, either together or in portions, for such consideration as the Company may think fit, and in particular for shares, debentures, or securities of any company purchasing the same.

(t) To distribute among the Members of the Company in kind any property of the Company of any kind.

(u) To procure the Company to be registered or recognized in any part of the world.

(v) To do all or any of the things or matters aforesaid in any part of the world and

APPENDIX B1

either as principals, agents, contractors or otherwise and by or through agents or otherwise and either alone or in conjunction with others.

(w) To do all such other things as may be deemed incidental or conducive to the attainment of the above objects or any of them.

The objects set forth in each sub-clause of this Clause shall not be restrictively construed but the widest interpretation shall be given thereto, and they shall not, except where the context expressly so requires, be in any way limited or restricted by reference to or inference from any other object or objects set forth in such sub-clause or from the terms of any other sub-clause or by the name of the Company. None of such sub-clauses or the object or objects therein specified or the powers thereby conferred shall be deemed subsidiary or ancillary to the objects or powers mentioned in any other sub-clause, but the Company shall have as full a power to exercise all or any of the objects conferred by and provided in each of the said sub-clauses as if each sub-clause contained the objects of a separate company.

4. The liability of the Members is limited.

5. The Share Capital of the Company is £   divided into   Shares of £   each.

We, the several persons whose names, addresses, and descriptions are subscribed, are desirous of being formed into a Company in pursuance of this Memorandum of Association, and we respectively agree to take the number of Shares in the Capital of the Company set opposite our respective names.

Names, addresses and descriptions of Subscribers	Number of Shares taken by each Subscriber (a)

Dated   19

Witness to the above signatures:—

(a) *The Subscribers should insert in their own hand-writing the number of Shares agreed to be taken by them respectively and if the Capital is divided into Shares of different classes, the class subscribed for should also be stated.*

The Memorandum of Association of a Private Company must be signed by at least two Subscribers and their signatures must be duly attested. (The Companies Act 1948, Section 1.)

The subscription of the Memorandum by a person resident outside the Scheduled Territories, or by a nominee for another person so resident, unless he subscribes with the permission of the Treasury, is invalid, so far as it would, on registration of the Memorandum, have the effect of making him a Member of or Shareholder in the Company (Exchange Control Act 1947, Section 8 (2)).

The Companies Acts 1948 to 1967

COMPANY LIMITED BY SHARES

Articles of Association of

Limited

Preliminary.

1. The regulations contained or incorporated in Parts I and II of Table A in the First Schedule to the Companies Act 1948 (such Table being hereinafter called "Table A") shall apply to the Company save in so far as they are excluded or varied hereby and such regulations (save as so excluded and varied) and the Articles hereinafter contained shall be the regulations of the Company.

First Directors.

2. (a) Clause 75 in Part I of Table A shall not apply to the Company.

(b) The number of the Directors shall be determined in writing by the Subscribers of the Memorandum of Association or a majority of them. In the event of the minimum number of Directors fixed by or pursuant to these Articles or Table A being one a sole Director shall have authority to exercise all the powers and discretions by Table A or these Articles expressed to be vested in the Directors generally.

***Alternative**

(b) Unless and until the Company in General Meeting shall otherwise determine, the number of Directors shall not be less than   nor more than   . In the event of the minimum number of Directors fixed by or pursuant to these Articles or Table A being one a sole Director shall have authority to exercise all the powers and discretions by Table A or these Articles expressed to be vested in the Directors generally.

(c) The first Directors of the Company shall be appointed by the Subscribers of the Memorandum of Association or a majority of them. Until the appointment of the first Directors the Subscribers hereto may exercise all the powers of the Directors.

***Alternative**

(c) The following persons shall be the first Directors of the Company:

****Delete if not required**

[and each of them shall be a Permanent Director of the Company].

(d)*[Any Director appointed by the Subscribers hereto may if the instrument of appointment so provides be appointed a Permanent Director of the Company.] A Permanent Director shall, subject to the provisions of Clause 88 in Part I of Table A, be entitled to hold such office so long as he shall live unless he shall be removed from office under Clause 96 in Part I of Table A; and accordingly Clauses 89 to 94 in Part I of Table A shall not apply to any Permanent Director.

(e) If at any General Meeting a poll is duly demanded on a resolution to remove a Permanent Director from office, such Director shall on the poll being taken be entitled to ten votes for each Share of which he is the holder; and Clause 62 in Part I of Table A shall be modified accordingly. Any motion for the removal of two or more Permanent Directors from office shall be submitted to the Meeting as a separate resolution in respect of each of such Directors.

****Paragraphs** (d) and (e) may be deleted. Paragraph (e) cannot be used unless Paragraph (d) is also retained. * [ ] Delete if first alternative (c) is not used.

Shares.

3. The Shares shall be under the control of the Directors, who may allot and dispose of or grant options over the same to such persons, on such terms, and in such manner as they think fit.

4. The lien conferred by Clause 11 in Part I of Table A shall attach to fully paid up Shares and to all Shares registered in the name of any person indebted or under liability to the Company, whether he shall be the sole registered holder thereof or shall be one of two or more joint holders.

5. Clause 15 in Part I of Table A shall be read and construed as if there were omitted from such Clause the words "provided that no Call shall exceed one-fourth of the nominal value of the Share or be payable at less than one month from the date fixed for the payment of the last preceding Call".

6. A transfer of a fully paid Share need not be executed by or on behalf of the transferee; and Clause 22 in Part I of Table A shall be modified accordingly.

General Meetings and Resolutions.

7. Every notice convening a General Meeting shall comply with the provisions of Section 136(2) of the Companies Act 1948 as to giving information to Members in regard to their right to appoint proxies; and notices of and other communications relating to any General Meeting which any Member is entitled to receive shall be sent to the Auditor for the time being of the Company.

8. Clause 54 in Part I of Table A shall be read and construed as if the words "Meeting shall be dissolved" were substituted for the words "Members present shall be a quorum".

9. A resolution in writing pursuant to Clause 5 in Part II of Table A may consist of two or more documents in like form each signed by one or more of the Members in such Clause referred to; and the said Clause 5 shall be modified accordingly.

Directors.

10. No Director shall vacate or be required to vacate his office as a Director on or by reason of his attaining or having attained the age of 70 or any other age and any Director or any person may be re-appointed, as the case may be, as a Director notwithstanding that he has then attained the age of 70, and no special notice need be given of any resolution for the re-appointment or appointment, or approval of the appointment of a Director at any age, and it shall not be necessary to give the Members notice of the age of any Director or person proposed to be so re-appointed or appointed; and Sub-Sections (1) to (6) inclusive of Section 185 of the Companies Act 1948 shall be excluded from applying to the Company.

11. A Director may at any time appoint any other person (whether a Director or Member of the Company or not) to act as Alternate Director at any Meeting of the Board at which the Director is not present, and may at any time revoke any such appointment. An Alternate Director so appointed shall not be entitled as such to receive any remuneration from the Company, but shall otherwise be subject to the provisions of Table A and of these presents with regard to Directors. An Alternate Director shall be entitled to receive notices of all Meetings of the Board and to attend and vote as a Director at any such Meeting at which the Director appointing him is not personally present, and generally to perform all the functions, rights, powers and duties of the Director by whom he was appointed. An Alternate Director shall ipso facto cease to be an Alternate Director if his appointer ceases for any reason to be a Director: Provided that if a Director retires by rotation and is re-elected by the Meeting at which such retirement took effect, any appointment made by him pursuant to this Article which was in force immediately prior to his retirement shall continue to operate after his re-election as if he had not so retired. Where a Director who has been appointed to be an Alternate Director is present at a Meeting of the Board in the absence of his appointer such Alternate Director shall have one vote in addition to his vote as Director. Every appointment and revocation of appointment of an Alternate Director shall be made by instrument in writing under the hand of the Director making or revoking such appointment and such instrument shall only take effect on the service thereof at the registered office of the Company. The remuneration of any such Alternate Director shall be payable out of the remuneration payable to the Director appointing him and shall consist of such portion of the last mentioned remuneration as shall be agreed between the Alternate Director and the Director appointing him.

12. A Director may vote as a Director in regard to any contract or arrangement in which he is interested or upon any matter arising thereout, and if he shall so vote his vote shall be counted and he shall be reckoned in estimating a quorum when any such contract or arrangement is under consideration; and Clause 84 in Part I of Table A shall be modified accordingly.

13. (a) The Directors may exercise the powers of the Company conferred by Clause 3(q) of the Memorandum and shall be entitled to retain any benefits received by them or any of them by reason of the exercise of any such powers.

(b) Clause 87 in Part I of Table A shall not apply to the Company.

14. It shall not be necessary for Directors to sign their names in the Minute Book; and Clause 86 in Part I of Table A shall be modified accordingly.

15. A resolution in writing pursuant to Clause 106 in Part I of Table A may consist of two or more documents in like form each signed by one or more of the Directors in such Clause referred to: and the said Clause 106 shall be modified accordingly.

Borrowing Powers.

16. (a) The Directors may exercise all the powers of the Company to borrow money, and to mortgage or charge its undertaking, property and uncalled capital, or any part thereof, and to issue Debentures, Debenture Stock, and other securities, whether outright or as security for any debt, liability or obligation of the Company or of any third party.

(b) Clause 79 in Part I of Table A shall not apply to the Company.

Accounts.

17. In Clause 126 in Part I of Table A after the words "157 of the Act" shall be added the words "and Sections 16 to 22 inclusive of the Companies Act 1967".

Indemnity.

18. (a) Every Director or other officer of the Company shall be entitled to be indemnified out of the assets of the Company against all losses or liabilities which he may sustain or incur in or about the execution of the duties of his office or otherwise in relation thereto, including any liability incurred by him in defending any proceedings, whether civil or criminal, in which judgment is given in his favour or in which he is acquitted or in connection with any application under Section 448 of the Companies Act 1948, in which relief is granted to him by the Court, and no Director or other officer shall be liable for any loss, damage or misfortune which may happen to or be incurred by the Company in the execution of the duties of his office or in relation thereto.   But this Article shall only have effect in so far as its provisions are not avoided by Section 205 of the Companies Act 1948.

(b) Clause 136 in Part I of Table A shall not apply to the Company.
Special transfer Articles, either alternative A or B, can be added here as Article 19 if required in substitution for Clause 3 in Part II of Table A.

SPECIAL TRANSFER ARTICLES
ALTERNATIVE A

Transfer and Transmission of Shares.

19. (a) (i) Any Member may transfer or by Settlement settle or by Will bequeath any Shares held by him or her to or upon trust for a member or members of his or her family as hereinafter defined and in the case of such Settlement or bequest the Shares so settled or bequeathed may be transferred to the Trustees of the Settlement or Will or to any beneficiary or beneficiaries thereunder, being a member or members of the family of the Settlor or Testator and any Shares of a deceased Member may be transferred by his legal personal representatives to any person entitled under Sections 46 and 47 of The Administration of Estates Act, 1925, as amended by the Intestates' Estates Act, 1952, to share in the estate of the deceased Member; provided that such person is a member of the family of the deceased Member. For the purposes hereof, a member of the family of any Member shall include a wife, husband, son-in-law, daughter-in-law, father or mother of such Member, or any direct lineal descendant of such father or mother but no other person.

(ii) Where any Shares are held upon the trusts of any Deed or Will a transfer thereof may be made upon any change or appointment of new trustees to the new trustees thereof, unless the change is made in connection with the acquisition of any beneficial interest under such trusts by a person not a member of the family of a Settlor or Testator, but the Directors may require evidence to satisfy themselves of the facts in relation to such transfer.

(iii) A Share may at any time be transferred to any Member of the Company.

(b) The Directors may, in their absolute discretion and without assigning any reason therefor, decline to register any transfer of Shares other than a transfer made pursuant to Sub-Article (a) hereof. Clause 3 in Part II of Table A shall not apply.

(c) The Directors shall not have any right to decline or suspend the registration of the legal personal representatives of a deceased Member as Members of the Company in respect of the Shares of the said deceased; and Clause 30 in Part I of Table A shall be modified accordingly.

SPECIAL TRANSFER ARTICLE
ALTERNATIVE B
Transfer of Shares.

19. (a) Any Share may be transferred by a Member to any child or other issue, son-in-law, daughter-in-law, father, mother, brother, sister, nephew, niece, wife or husband of such Member; and any Share of a deceased Member may be transferred by his or her legal personal representatives to any child or other issue, son-in-law, daughter-in-law, father, mother, brother, sister, nephew, niece, widow, or widower of such deceased Member; and Shares standing in the names of the trustees of the Will of any deceased Member may be transferred upon any change of trustees to the trustees for the time being of such Will unless the change is made in connection with the acquisition of any beneficial interest under the trusts of the Will by any person not a beneficiary under the Will. A Share may at any time be transferred to any Member of the Company.

(b) Save as aforesaid, no Share shall be transferred unless and until the rights of pre-emption hereinafter conferred shall have been exhausted.

(c) Except where the transfer is made pursuant to Sub-Article (a) hereof, the person proposing to transfer any Share (hereinafter called "the proposing transferor") shall give notice in writing (hereinafter called "the transfer notice") to the Company that he desires to transfer the same, and such notice shall specify the sum he fixes as the fair value, and shall constitute the Company his agent for the sale of the Share to any Member of the Company (or any person selected by the Directors as one whom it is desirable in the interests of the Company to admit to Membership) at the price so fixed or, at the option of the purchaser, at the fair value to be fixed by the Auditor in accordance with Sub-Article (e) of this Article. The transfer notice may include two or more Shares, and in such case shall operate as if it were a separate notice in respect of each. The transfer notice shall not be revocable except with the sanction of the Directors.

(d) If the Company shall within the period of twenty-eight days after being served with the transfer notice find a Member (or person selected as aforesaid) willing to purchase the Share (hereinafter called "the purchaser") and shall give notice thereof to the proposing transferor, he shall be bound upon payment of the fair value to transfer the Share to the purchaser, who shall be bound to complete the purchase within fourteen days from the service of the last-mentioned notice.

(e) In case any difference arises between the proposing transferor and the purchaser as to the fair value of a Share the Auditor shall, on the application of either party, certify in writing the sum which in his opinion is the fair value, and such sum shall be deemed to be the fair value, and in so certifying the Auditor shall be considered to be acting as an expert and not as an arbitrator; and accordingly the Arbitration Act, 1950, shall not apply.

(f) If in any case the proposing transferor after having become bound as aforesaid makes default in transferring the Share the Company may receive the purchase money on his behalf, and may authorise some person to execute a transfer of the Share in favour of the purchaser, who shall thereupon be registered as the Holder of the Share. The receipt of the Company for the purchase money shall be a good discharge to the purchaser, and after his name has been entered in the Register of Members in purported exercise of the aforesaid power the validity of the proceedings shall not be questioned by any person.

(g) If the Company shall not within the period of twenty-eight days after being served with the transfer notice find a Member (or person selected as aforesaid) willing to purchase the Share and give notice in manner aforesaid, the proposing transferor shall at any time within three calendar months afterwards be at liberty, subject to Sub-Article (i) hereof, to sell and transfer the Share, or in case more than one Share is included in the transfer notice the Shares not placed, to any person and at any price.

(h) The Shares included in any transfer notice given to the Company as aforesaid shall be offered by the Company in the first place to the Members (other than the proposing transferor) as nearly as may be in proportion to the existing Shares held by them respectively, and the offer shall in each case limit the time within which the same, if not accepted, will be deemed to be declined, and may notify to the Members that any Member who desires to purchase a number of Shares in excess of his proportion should in his reply state how many excess Shares he desires to have; and if all the Members do not claim their proportions the unclaimed Shares shall be used for satisfying the claims in excess in proportion to the existing Shares held by the claimants respectively. If any Shares shall not be capable without fractions of being offered to the Members in proportion to their existing holdings, the same shall be offered to the Members, or some of them, in such proportions or in such manner as may be determined by lots drawn in regard thereto, and the lots shall be drawn in such manner as the Directors think fit.

(i) The Directors may refuse to register any transfer of a Share (a) where the Company has a lien on the Share, or (b) where the Directors are of opinion that the transferee is not a desirable person to admit to Membership; but Paragraph (b) of this Sub-Article shall not apply to a transfer made pursuant to Sub-Article (a) hereof. Clause 3 in Part II of Table A shall not apply.

(j) Whenever any Member of the Company (other than a Director) who is employed by the Company in any capacity is dismissed from such employment or ceases to be employed by the Company, the Directors may at any time within twenty-eight days after his dismissal or his ceasing to be employed resolve that such Member do retire, and [thereupon] [at the expiration of twenty-eight days from the passing of such resolution] he shall (unless he has already served a transfer notice) be deemed to have served the Company with a transfer notice pursuant to Sub-Article (c) hereof, and to have specified therein the amount paid up on his Shares as the fair value. Notice of the passing of any such resolution shall forthwith be given to the Member affected thereby.

Alternatives delete as required. The latter gives the opportunity for the employer to serve a transfer notice voluntarily.

Names, addresses and descriptions of Subscribers (a)

Dated   19   .

Witness to the above signatures:—

(a) *The Articles of Association must be signed by the Subscribers of the Memorandum of Association* (*The Companies Act 1948, Section 6*).

2. Table "A"—The Companies Acts 1948 to 1967.

The Companies Acts 1948 to 1967

FIRST SCHEDULE

TABLE A

PART I

Regulations for Management of a Company Limited by Shares, not being a Private Company.

Interpretation.

1. In these Regulations:—

"the Act" means the Companies Act 1948.

"the Seal" means the Common Seal of the Company.

"Secretary" means any person appointed to perform the duties of the Secretary of the Company.

"the United Kingdom" means Great Britain and Northern Ireland.

Expressions referring to writing shall, unless the contrary intention appears, be construed as including references to printing, lithography, photography, and other modes of representing or reproducing words in a visible form.

Unless the context otherwise requires, words or expressions contained in these Regulations shall bear the same meaning as in the Act or any statutory modification thereof in force at the date at which these Regulations become binding on the Company.

Share Capital and Variation of Rights.

2. Without prejudice to any special rights previously conferred on the holders of any existing Shares or class of Shares, any Share in the Company may be issued with such preferred, deferred or other special rights or such restrictions, whether in regard to dividend, voting, return of Capital or otherwise as the Company may from time to time by Ordinary Resolution determine.

3. Subject to the provisions of Section 58 of the Act, any Preference Shares may, with the sanction of an Ordinary Resolution, be issued on the terms that they are, or at the option of the Company are liable, to be redeemed on such terms and in such manner as the Company before the issue of the Shares may by Special Resolution determine.

4. If at any time the Share Capital is divided into different classes of Shares, the rights attached to any class (unless otherwise provided by the terms of issue of the Shares of that class) may, whether or not the Company is being wound up, be varied with the consent in writing of the holders of three-fourths of the issued Shares of that class, or with the sanction of an Extraordinary Resolution passed at a separate General Meeting of the holders of the Shares of the class.   To every such separate General Meeting the provisions of these Regulations relating to General Meetings shall apply, but so that the necessary quorum shall be two persons at least holding or representing by proxy one-third of the issued Shares of the class and that any holder of Shares of the class present in person or by proxy may demand a poll.

5. The rights conferred upon the holders of the Shares of any class issued with preferred or other rights shall not, unless otherwise expressly provided by the terms of issue of the Shares of that class, be deemed to be varied by the creation or issue of further Shares ranking pari passu therewith.

Note: Marginal Notes refer to the Articles set out in the model form "D".

6. The Company may exercise the powers of paying commissions conferred by Section 53 of the Act, provided that the rate per cent. or the amount of the commission paid or agreed to be paid shall be disclosed in the manner required by the said section and the rate of the commission shall not exceed the rate of 10 per cent. of the price at which the Shares in respect whereof the same is paid are issued or an amount equal to 10 per cent. of such price (as the case may be). Such commission may be satisfied by the payment of cash or the allotment of fully or partly paid Shares or partly in one way and partly in the other. The Company may also on any issue of Shares pay such brokerage as may be lawful.

7. Except as required by law, no person shall be recognised by the Company as holding any Share upon any trust, and the Company shall not be bound by or be compelled in any way to recognise (even when having notice thereof) any equitable, contingent, future or partial interest in any Share or any interest in any fractional part of a Share or (except only as by these Regulations or by law otherwise provided) any other rights in respect of any Share except an absolute right to the entirety thereof in the registered holder.

8. Every person whose name is entered as a Member in the Register of Members shall be entitled without payment to receive within two months after allotment or lodgment of transfer (or within such other period as the conditions of issue shall provide) one Certificate for all his Shares or several Certificates each for one or more of his Shares upon payment of 12½p for every Certificate after the first or such less sum as the Directors shall from time to time determine. Every Certificate shall be under the Seal and shall specify the Shares to which it relates and the amount paid up thereon. Provided that in respect of a Share or Shares held jointly by several persons the Company shall not be bound to issue more than one Certificate, and delivery of a Certificate for a Share to one of several joint holders shall be sufficient delivery to all such holders.

9. If a Share Certificate be defaced, lost or destroyed, it may be renewed on payment of a fee of 12½p or such less sum and on such terms (if any) as to evidence and indemnity and the payment of out-of-pocket expenses of the Company of investigating evidence as the Directors think fit.

10. The Company shall not give, whether directly or indirectly, and whether by means of a loan, guarantee, the provision of security or otherwise, any financial assistance for the purpose of or in connection with a purchase or subscription made or to be made by any person of or for any Shares in the Company or in its holding company nor shall the Company make a loan for any purpose whatsoever on the security of its Shares or those of its holding company, but nothing in this Regulation shall prohibit transactions mentioned in the proviso to Section 54 (1) of the Act.

Lien.
11. The Company shall have a first and paramount lien on every Share (not being a fully paid Share) for all moneys (whether presently payable or not) called or payable at a fixed time in respect of that Share, and the Company shall also have a first and paramount lien on all Shares (other than fully paid Shares) standing registered in the name of a single person for all moneys presently payable by him or his estate to the Company; but the Directors may at any time declare any Share to be wholly or in part exempt from the provisions of this Regulation. The Company's lien, if any, on a Share shall extend to all dividends payable thereon.

12. The Company may sell, in such manner as the Directors think fit, any Shares on which the Company has a lien, but no sale shall be made unless a sum in respect of which the lien exists is presently payable, nor until the expiration of fourteen days after a notice in writing, stating and demanding payment of such part of the amount in respect of which the lien exists as is presently payable has been given to the registered holder for the time being of the Share, or the person entitled thereto by reason of his death or bankruptcy.

See Article 4.

13. To give effect to any such sale the Directors may authorise some person to transfer the Shares sold to the purchaser thereof. The purchaser shall be registered as the holder of the Shares comprised in any such transfer, and he shall not be bound to see to the application of the purchase money, nor shall his title to the Shares be affected by any irregularity or invalidity in the proceedings in reference to the sale.

14. The proceeds of the sale shall be received by the Company and applied in payment of such part of the amount in respect of which the lien exists as is presently payable, and the residue, if any, shall (subject to a like lien for sums not presently payable as existed upon the Shares before the sale) be paid to the person entitled to the Shares at the date of the sale.

Calls on Shares.

15. The Directors may from time to time make calls upon the Members in respect of any moneys unpaid on their Shares (whether on account of the nominal value of the Shares or by way of premium) and not by the conditions of allotment thereof made payable at fixed times, provided that no call shall exceed one-fourth of the nominal value of the Share or be payable at less than one month from the date fixed for the payment of the last preceding call, and each Member shall (subject to receiving at least fourteen days' notice specifying the time or times and place of payment) pay to the Company at the time or times and place so specified the amount called on his Shares. A call may be revoked or postponed as the Directors may determine.

See Article 5

16. A call shall be deemed to have been made at the time when the resolution of the Directors authorising the call was passed and may be required to be paid by instalments.

17. The joint holders of a Share shall be jointly and severally liable to pay all calls in respect thereof.

18. If a sum called in respect of a Share is not paid before or on the day appointed for payment thereof, the person from whom the sum is due shall pay interest on the sum from the day appointed for payment thereof to the time of actual payment at such rate not exceeding 5 per cent. per annum as the Directors may determine, but the Directors shall be at liberty to waive payment of such interest wholly or in part.

19. Any sum which by the terms of issue of a Share becomes payable on allotment or at any fixed date, whether on account of the nominal value of the Share or by way of premium, shall for the purposes of these Regulations be deemed to be a call duly made and payable on the date on which by the terms of issue the same becomes payable, and in case of non-payment all the relevant provisions of these Regulations as to payment of interest and expenses, forfeiture or otherwise shall apply as if such sum had become payable by virtue of a call duly made and notified.

20. The Directors may, on the issue of Shares, differentiate between the holders as to the amount of calls to be paid and the times of payment.

21. The Directors may, if they think fit, receive from any Member willing to advance the same, all or any part of the moneys uncalled and unpaid upon any Shares held by him, and upon all or any of the moneys so advanced may (until the same would, but for such advance, become payable) pay interest at such a rate not exceeding (unless the Company in General Meeting shall otherwise direct) 5 per cent. per annum, as may be agreed upon between the Directors and the Member paying such sum in advance.

Transfer of Shares.

22.* The instrument of transfer of any Share shall be executed by or on behalf of the transferor and transferee, and, the transferor shall be deemed to remain a holder of the Share until the name of the transferee is entered in the Register of Members in respect thereof.

See Article 6

23. Subject to such of the restrictions of these Regulations as may be applicable, any Member may transfer all or any of his Shares by instrument in writing in any usual or common form or any other form which the Directors may approve.

24. The Directors may decline to register the transfer of a Share (not being a fully paid Share) to a person of whom they shall not approve, and they may also decline to register the transfer of a Share on which the Company has a lien.

This clause is replaced by clause 3 in Part II of Table A, and see pages 13 to 15 of model form

25. The Directors may also decline to recognise any instrument of transfer unless:—
(a) a fee of 12½p or such lesser sum as the Directors may from time to time require is paid to the Company in respect thereof;
(b) the instrument of transfer is accompanied by the Certificate of the Shares to which it relates, and such other evidence as the Directors may reasonably require to show the right of the transferor to make the transfer; and
(c) the instrument of transfer is in respect of only one class of Share.

26. If the Directors refuse to register a transfer they shall within two months after the date on which the transfer was lodged with the Company send to the transferee notice of the refusal.

27. The registration of transfers may be suspended at such times and for such periods as the Directors may from time to time determine, provided always that such registration shall not be suspended for more than thirty days in any year.

28. The Company shall be entitled to charge a fee not exceeding 12½p on the registration of every probate, letters of administration, certificate of death or marriage, power of attorney, notice in lieu of distringas, or other instrument.

Transmission of Shares.

29. In case of the death of a Member the survivor or survivors where the deceased was a joint holder, and the legal personal representatives of the deceased where he was a sole holder, shall be the only persons recognised by the Company as having any title to his interest in the Shares; but nothing herein contained shall release the estate of a deceased joint holder from any liability in respect of any Share which had been jointly held by him with other persons.

30. Any person becoming entitled to a Share in consequence of the death or bankruptcy of a Member may, upon such evidence being produced as may from time to time properly be required by the Directors and subject as hereinafter provided, elect either to be registered himself as holder of the Share or to have some person nominated by him registered as the transferee thereof, but the Directors shall, in either case, have the same right to decline or suspend registration as they would have had in the case of a transfer of the Share by that Member before his death or bankruptcy, as the case may be.

* *as amended by the Companies Act 1967 Schedule VIII Part III.*

31. If the person so becoming entitled shall elect to be registered himself, he shall deliver or send to the Company a notice in writing signed by him stating that he so elects. If he shall elect to have another person registered he shall testify his election by executing to that person a transfer of the Share. All the limitations, restrictions and provisions of these Regulations relating to the right to transfer and the registration of transfers of Shares shall be applicable to any such notice or transfer as aforesaid as if the death or bankruptcy of the Member had not occurred and the notice or transfer were a transfer signed by that Member.

32. A person becoming entitled to a Share by reason of the death or bankruptcy of the holder shall be entitled to the same dividends and other advantages to which he would be entitled if he were the registered holder of the Share, except that he shall not, before being registered as a Member in respect of the Share, be entitled in respect of it to exercise any right conferred by Membership in relation to Meetings of the Company;

Provided always that the Directors may at any time give notice requiring any such person to elect either to be registered himself or to transfer the Share, and if the notice is not complied with within ninety days the Directors may thereafter withhold payment of all dividends, bonuses or other moneys payable in respect of the Share until the requirements of the notice have been complied with.

Forfeiture of Shares.

33. If a Member fails to pay any call or instalment of a call on the day appointed for payment thereof, the Directors may, at any time thereafter during such time as any part of the call or instalment remains unpaid, serve a notice on him requiring payment of so much of the call or instalment as is unpaid, together with any interest which may have accrued.

34. The notice shall name a further day (not earlier than the expiration of fourteen days from the date of service of the notice) on or before which the payment required by the notice is to be made, and shall state that in the event of non-payment at or before the time appointed the Shares in respect of which the call was made will be liable to be forfeited.

35. If the requirements of any such notice as aforesaid are not complied with, any Share in respect of which the notice has been given may at any time thereafter, before the payment required by the notice has been made, be forfeited by a resolution of the Directors to that effect.

36. A forfeited Share may be sold or otherwise disposed of on such terms and in such manner as the Directors think fit, and at any time before a sale or disposition the forfeiture may be cancelled on such terms as the Directors think fit.

37. A person whose Shares have been forfeited shall cease to be a Member in respect of the forfeited Shares, but shall, notwithstanding, remain liable to pay to the Company all moneys which, at the date of forfeiture, were payable by him to the Company in respect of the Shares, but his liability shall cease if and when the Company shall have received payment in full of all such moneys in respect of the Shares.

38. A statutory declaration in writing that the declarant is a Director or the Secretary of the Company, and that a Share in the Company has been duly forfeited on a date stated in the declaration, shall be conclusive evidence of the facts therein stated as against all persons claiming to be entitled to the Share. The Company may receive the consideration, if any, given for the Share on any sale or disposition thereof and may execute a transfer of the Share in favour of the person to whom the Share is sold or disposed of and he shall thereupon be registered as the holder of the Share, and shall not be bound to see to the application of the purchase money, if any, nor shall his title to the Share be affected by any irregularity or invalidity in the proceedings in reference to the forfeiture, sale or disposal of the Share.

39. The provisions of these Regulations as to forfeiture shall apply in the case of non-payment of any sum which, by the terms of issue of a Share, becomes payable at a fixed time, whether on account of the nominal value of the Share or by way of premium, as if the same had been payable by virtue of a call duly made and notified.

Conversion of Shares into Stock.
40. The Company may by Ordinary Resolution convert any paid-up Shares into Stock, and reconvert any Stock into paid-up Shares of any denomination.

41. The holders of Stock may transfer the same, or any part thereof, in the manner, and subject to the same regulations, as and subject to which the Shares from which the Stock arose might previously to conversion have been transferred, or as near thereto as circumstances admit; and the Directors may from time to time fix the minimum amount of Stock transferable but so that such minimum shall not exceed the nominal amount of the Shares from which the Stock arose.

42. The holders of Stock shall, according to the amount of Stock held by them, have the same rights, privileges and advantages as regards dividends, voting at Meetings of the Company and other matters as if they held the Shares from which the Stock arose, but no such privilege or advantage (except participation in the dividends and profits of the Company and in the assets on winding up) shall be conferred by an amount of Stock which would not, if existing in Shares, have conferred that privilege or advantage.

43. Such of the regulations of the Company as are applicable to paid-up Shares shall apply to Stock, and the words "Share" and "Shareholders" therein shall include "Stock" and "Stockholder".

Alteration of Capital.
44. The Company may from time to time by Ordinary Resolution increase the Share Capital by such sum, to be divided into Shares of such amount, as the Resolution shall prescribe.

45. The Company may by Ordinary Resolution—
(a) consolidate and divide all or any of its Share Capital into Shares of larger amount than its existing Shares;
(b) sub-divide its existing Shares, or any of them, into Shares of smaller amount than is fixed by the Memorandum of Association subject, nevertheless, to the provisions of Section 61(1)(*d*) of the Act;
(c) cancel any Shares which, at the date of the passing of the Resolution, have not been taken or agreed to be taken by any person.

46. The Company may by Special Resolution reduce its Share Capital, any Capital Redemption Reserve Fund or any Share Premium Account in any manner and with, and subject to, any incident authorised, and consent required, by law.

General Meeting.
47. The Company shall in each year hold a General Meeting as its Annual General Meeting in addition to any other Meetings in that year, and shall specify the Meeting as such in the notices calling it; and not more than fifteen months shall elapse between the date of one Annual General Meeting of the Company and that of the next. Provided that so long as the Company holds its first Annual General Meeting within eigtheen months of its incorporation, it need not hold it in the year of its incorporation or in the following year. The Annual General Meeting shall be held at such time and place as the Directors shall appoint.

48. All General Meetings other than Annual General Meetings shall be called Extraordinary General Meetings.

49. The Directors may, whenever they think fit, convene an Extraordinary General Meeting, and Extraordinary General Meetings shall also be convened on such requisition, or, in default, may be convened by such requisitionists, as provided by Section 132 of the Act. If at any time there are not within the United Kingdom sufficient Directors capable of acting to form a quorum, any Director or any two Members of the Company may convene an Extraordinary General Meeting in the same manner as nearly as possible as that in which Meetings may be convened by the Directors.

Notices of General Meetings.

50. An Annual General Meeting and a Meeting called for the passing of a Special Resolution shall be called by twenty-one days' notice in writing at the least, and a Meeting of the Company other than an Annual General Meeting or a Meeting for the passing of a Special Resolution shall be called by fourteen days' notice in writing at the least. The notice shall be exclusive of the day on which it is served or deemed to be served and of the day for which it is given, and shall specify the place, the day and the hour of meeting and, in case of special business, the general nature of that business, and shall be given, in manner hereinafter mentioned or in such other manner, if any, as may be prescribed by the Company in General Meeting, to such persons as are, under the regulations of the Company, entitled to receive such notices from the Company:

Provided that a Meeting of the Company shall, notwithstanding that it is called by shorter notice than that specified in this Regulation, be deemed to have been duly called if it is so agreed—

(a) in the case of a Meeting called as the Annual General Meeting, by all the Members entitled to attend and vote thereat; and

(b) in the case of any other meeting, by a majority in number of the Members having a right to attend and vote at the Meeting, being a majority together holding not less than 95 per cent. in nominal value of the Shares giving that right.

51. The accidental omission to give notice of a Meeting to, or the non-receipt of notice of a Meeting by, any person entitled to receive notice shall not invalidate the proceedings at that Meeting.

Proceedings at General Meetings.

52. All business shall be deemed special that is transacted at an Extraordinary General Meeting, and also all that is transacted at an Annual General Meeting, with the exception of declaring a dividend, the consideration of the accounts, balance sheets, and the reports of the Directors and Auditors, the election of Directors in the place of those retiring and the appointment of, and the fixing of the remuneration of, the Auditors.

53. No business shall be transacted at any General Meeting unless a quorum of Members is present at the time when the Meeting proceeds to business; save as herein otherwise provided, three Members present in person shall be a quorum.

This clause is replaced by clause 4 in Part II of Table A.

54. If within half an hour from the time appointed for the Meeting a quorum is not present, the Meeting, if convened upon the requisition of Members, shall be dissolved; in any case it shall stand adjourned to the same day in the next week, at the same time and place or to such other day and at such other time and place as the Directors may determine, and if at the adjourned Meeting a quorum is not present within half an hour from the time appointed for the Meeting, the Members present shall be a quorum.

See Article 8.

55. The Chairman, if any, of the Board of Directors shall preside as Chairman at every General Meeting of the Company, or if there is no such Chairman, or if he shall not be present within fifteen minutes after the time appointed for the holding of the Meeting or is unwilling to act the Directors present shall elect one of their number to be Chairman of the Meeting.

56. If at any Meeting no Director is willing to act as Chairman or if no Director is present within fifteen minutes after the time appointed for holding the Meeting, the Members present shall choose one of their number to be Chairman of the Meeting.

57. The Chairman may, with the consent of any Meeting at which a quorum is present (and shall if so directed by the Meeting), adjourn the Meeting from time to time and from place to place, but no business shall be transacted at any adjourned Meeting other than the business left unfinished at the Meeting from which the adjournment took place. When a Meeting is adjourned for thirty days or more, notice of the adjourned Meeting shall be given as in the case of an original Meeting. Save as aforesaid it shall not be necessary to give any notice of an adjournment or of the business to be transacted at an adjourned Meeting.

58. At any General Meeting a resolution put to the vote of the Meeting shall be decided on a show of hands unless a poll is (before or on the declaration of the result of the show of hands) demanded—

(a) by the Chairman; or

(b) by at least three Members present in person or by proxy; or

(c) by any Member or Members present in person or by proxy and representing not less than one-tenth of the total voting rights of all the Members having the right to vote at the Meeting; or

(d) by a Member or Members holding Shares in the Company conferring a right to vote at the Meeting being Shares on which an aggregate sum has been paid up equal to not less than one-tenth of the total sum paid up on all the Shares conferring that right.

Unless a poll be so demanded a declaration by the Chairman that a resolution has on a show of hands been carried or carried unanimously, or by a particular majority, or lost and an entry to that effect in the book containing the minutes of the proceedings of the Company shall be conclusive evidence of the fact without proof of the number or proportion of the votes recorded in favour of or against such resolution.

The demand for a poll may be withdrawn.

59. Except as provided in Regulation 61, if a poll is duly demanded it shall be taken in such manner as the Chairman directs, and the result of the poll shall be deemed to be the resolution of the Meeting at which the poll was demanded.

60. In the case of an equality of votes, whether on a show of hands or on a poll, the Chairman of the Meeting at which the show of hands takes place or at which the poll is demanded, shall be entitled to a second or casting vote.

61. A poll demanded on the election of a Chairman or on a question of adjournment shall be taken forthwith. A poll demanded on any other question shall be taken at such time as the Chairman of the Meeting directs, and any business other than that upon which a poll has been demanded may be proceeded with pending the taking of the poll.

Votes of Members.
62. Subject to any rights or restrictions for the time being attached to any class or classes of Shares, on a show of hands every Member present in person shall have one vote, and on a poll every Member shall have one vote for each Share of which he is the holder.

63. In the case of joint holders the vote of the senior who tenders a vote, whether in person or by proxy, shall be accepted to the exclusion of the votes of the other joint holders; and for this purpose seniority shall be determined by the order in which the names stand in the Register of Members.

64. A Member of unsound mind, or in respect of whom an order has been made by any court having jurisdiction in lunacy, may vote, whether on a show of hands or on a poll, by his committee, receiver, curator bonis, or other person in the nature of a committee, receiver or curator bonis appointed by that court, and any such committee, receiver, curator bonis or other person may, on a poll, vote by proxy.

65. No Member shall be entitled to vote at any General Meeting unless all calls or other sums presently payable by him in respect of Shares in the Company have been paid.

66. No objection shall be raised to the qualification of any voter except at the Meeting or adjourned Meeting at which the vote objected to is given or tendered, and every vote not disallowed at such Meeting shall be valid for all purposes. Any such objection made in due time shall be referred to the Chairman of the Meeting, whose decision shall be final and conclusive.

67. On a poll votes may be given either personally or by proxy.

68. The instrument appointing a proxy shall be in writing under the hand of the appointor or of his attorney duly authorised in writing, or, if the appointor is a corporation, either under seal, or under the hand of an officer or attorney duly authorised. A proxy need not be a Member of the Company.

69. The instrument appointing a proxy and the power of attorney or other authority, if any, under which it is signed or a notarially certified copy of that power or authority shall be deposited at the registered office of the Company or at such other place within the United Kingdom as is specified for that purpose in the notice convening the Meeting, not less than 48 hours before the time for holding the Meeting or adjourned Meeting, at which the person named in the instrument proposes to vote, or, in the case of a poll, not less than 24 hours before the time appointed for the taking of the poll, and in default the instrument of proxy shall not be treated as valid.

70. An instrument appointing a proxy shall be in the following form or a form as near thereto as circumstances admit—

        ``   Limited

I/We   of   ,
       in the County of   being a Member/Members
       of the above-named Company, hereby appoint
       of
       or failing him,   of   ,
       as my/our proxy to vote for me/us on my/our behalf at the (Annual or Extraordinary, as the case may be) General Meeting of the Company, to be held on the   day of   19 ,
       and at any adjournment thereof.

Signed this   day of   19 ''

71. Where it is desired to afford Members an opportunity of voting for or against a resolution the instrument appointing a proxy shall be in the following form or a form as near thereto as circumstances admit—

        ``   Limited

I/We   of
       in the County of   being a Member/Members

of the above-named Company, hereby appoint
of ,
or failing him, of ,
as my/our proxy to vote for me/us on my /our behalf at the (Annual or
Extraordinary, as the case may be) General Meeting of the Company,
to be held on the   day of   19 ,   and
at any adjournment thereof.

Signed this   day of   19

This form is to be used $\frac{\text{*in favour of}}{\text{against}}$ the resolution.

Unless otherwise instructed, the proxy will vote as he thinks fit.

*Strike out whichever is not desired."

72. The instrument appointing a proxy shall be deemed to confer authority to demand or join in demanding a poll.

73. A vote given in accordance with the terms of an instrument of proxy shall be valid notwithstanding the previous death or insanity of the principal or revocation of the proxy or of the authority under which the proxy was executed, or the transfer of the Share in respect of which the proxy is given, provided that no intimation in writing of such death, insanity, revocation or transfer as aforesaid shall have been received by the Company at the office before the commencement of the Meeting or adjourned Meeting at which the proxy is used.

Corporations Acting by Representatives at Meetings.

74. Any corporation which is a Member of the Company may by resolution of its Directors or other governing body authorise such person as it thinks fit to act as its representative at any Meeting of the Company or of any class of Members of the Company, and the person so authorised shall be entitled to exercise the same powers on behalf of the corporation which he represents as that corporation could exercise if it were an individual Member of the Company.

Directors.

75. The number of the Directors and the names of the first Directors shall be determined in writing by the Subscribers of the Memorandum of Association or a majority of them.

See Article 2.

76. The remuneration of the Directors shall from time to time be determined by the Company in General Meeting. Such remuneration shall be deemed to accrue from day to day. The Directors may also be paid all travelling, hotel and other expenses properly incurred by them in attending and returning from Meetings of the Directors or any Committee of the Directors or General Meetings of the Company or in connection with the business of the Company.

77. The shareholding qualification for Directors may be fixed by the Company in General Meeting, and unless and until so fixed no qualification shall be required.

78. A Director of the Company may be or become a Director or other officer of, or otherwise interested in, any company promoted by the Company or in which the Company may be interested as shareholder or otherwise, and no such Director shall be accountable to the Company for any remuneration or other benefits received by him as a Director or officer of, or from his interest in, such other company unless the Company otherwise direct.

APPENDIX B2

Borrowing Powers.

79.   The Directors may exercise all the powers of the Company to borrow money, and to mortgage or charge its undertaking, property and uncalled Capital, or any part thereof, and to issue Debentures, Debenture Stock, and other securities whether outright or as security for any debt, liability or obligation of the Company or of any third party:

Provided that the amount for the time being remaining undischarged of moneys borrowed or secured by the Directors as aforesaid (apart from temporary loans obtained from the Company's Bankers in the ordinary course of business) shall not at any time, without the previous sanction of the Company in General Meeting, exceed the nominal amount of the Share Capital of the Company for the time being issued, but nevertheless no lender or other person dealing with the Company shall be concerned to see or enquire whether this limit is observed.   No debt incurred or security given in excess of such limit shall be invalid or ineffectual except in the case of express notice to the lender or the recipient of the security at the time when the debt was incurred or security given that the limit hereby imposed had been or was thereby exceeded.

See Article 16.

Powers and Duties of Directors.

80.   The business of the Company shall be managed by the Directors, who may pay all expenses incurred in promoting and registering the Company, and may exercise all such powers of the Company as are not, by the Act or by these regulations, required to be exercised by the Company in General Meeting, subject, nevertheless, to any of these Regulations, to the provisions of the Act and to such regulations, being not inconsistent with the aforesaid Regulations or provisions, as may be prescribed by the Company in General Meeting; but no regulation made by the Company in General Meeting shall invalidate any prior act of the Directors which would have been valid if that regulation had not been made.

81.   The Directors may from time to time and at any time by power of attorney appoint any company, firm or person or body of persons, whether nominated directly or indirectly by the Directors, to be the attorney or attorneys of the Company for such purposes and with such powers, authorities and discretions (not exceeding those vested in or exercisable by the Directors under these regulations) and for such period and subject to such conditions as they may think fit, and any such powers of attorney may contain such provisions for the protection and convenience of persons dealing with any such attorney as the Directors may think fit and may also authorise any such attorney to delegate all or any of the powers, authorities and discretions vested in him.

82.   The Company may exercise the powers conferred by Section 35 of the Act with regard to having an official seal for use abroad, and such powers shall be vested in the Directors.

83.   The Company may exercise the powers conferred upon the Company by Sections 119 to 123 (both inclusive) of the Act with regard to the keeping of a Dominion Register, and the Directors may (subject to the provisions of those sections) make and vary such regulations as they may think fit respecting the keeping of any such Register.

84.—(1)   A Director who is in any way, whether directly or indirectly, interested in a contract or proposed contract with the Company shall declare the nature of his interest at a Meeting of the Directors in accordance with Section 199 of the Act.

(2)   A Director shall not vote in respect of any contract or arrangement in which he is interested, and if he shall so do his vote shall not be counted, nor shall he be counted in the quorum present at the Meeting, but neither of these prohibitions shall apply to—

(a) any arrangement for giving any Director any security or indemnity in respect of money lent by him to or obligations undertaken by him for the benefit of the Company; or

(b) to any arrangement for the giving by the Company of any security to a third party in respect of a debt or obligation of the Company for which the Director himself has assumed responsibility in whole or in part under a guarantee or indemnity or by the deposit of a security; or

(c) any contract by a Director to subscribe for or underwrite Shares or Debentures of the Company; or

(d) any contract or arrangement with any other company in which he is interested only as an officer of the Company or as holder of Shares or other securities;

and these prohibitions may at any time be suspended or relaxed to any extent, and either generally or in respect of any particular contract, arrangement or transaction, by the Company in General Meeting.

(3) A Director may hold any other office or place of profit under the Company (other than the office of Auditor) in conjunction with his office of Director for such period and on such terms (as to remuneration and otherwise) as the Directors may determine, and no Director or intending Director shall be disqualified by his office from contracting with the Company either with regard to his tenure of any such other office or place of profit or as vendor, purchaser or otherwise, nor shall any such contract or arrangement entered into by or on behalf of the Company in which any Director is in any way interested, be liable to be avoided, nor shall any Director so contracting or being so interested be liable to account to the Company for any profit realised by any such contract or arrangement by reason of such Director holding that office or of the fiduciary relation thereby established.

(4) A Director, notwithstanding his interest, may be counted in the quorum present at any Meeting whereat he or any other Director is appointed to hold any such office or place of profit under the Company or whereat the terms of any such appointment are arranged, and he may vote on any such appointment or arrangement other than his own appointment or the arrangement of the terms thereof.

(5) Any Director may act by himself or his firm in a professional capacity for the Company, and he or his firm shall be entitled to remuneration for professional services as if he were not a Director; provided that nothing herein contained shall authorise a Director or his firm to act as Auditor to the Company.

See Article 12.

85. All cheques, promissory notes, drafts, bills of exchange and other negotiable instruments, and all receipts for moneys paid to the Company, shall be signed, drawn, accepted, endorsed, or otherwise executed, as the case may be, in such manner as the Directors shall from time to time by resolution determine.

86. The Directors shall cause minutes to be made in books provided for the purpose—

(a) of all appointments of officers made by the Directors;

See Article 14.

(b) of the names of the Directors present at each Meeting of the Directors and of any Committee of the Directors;

(c) of all resolutions and proceedings at all Meetings of the Company, and of the Directors, and of Committees of Directors;

and every Director present at any Meeting of Directors or Committee of Directors shall sign his name in a book to be kept for that purpose.

87. The Directors on behalf of the Company may pay a gratuity or pension or allowance on retirement to any Director who has held any other salaried office or place of profit with the Company or to his widow or dependants and may make contributions to any fund and pay premiums for the purchase or provision of any such gratuity, pension or allowance.

Disqualification of Directors.

88. The office of Director shall be vacated if the Director—

(a) ceases to be a Director by virtue of Section 182 or 185 of the Act; or

(b) becomes bankrupt or makes any arrangement or composition with his creditors generally; or

(c) becomes prohibited from being a Director by reason of any order made under Section 188 of the Act; or

(d) becomes of unsound mind; or

(e) resigns his office by notice in writing to the Company; or

(f) shall for more than six months have been absent without permission of the Directors from Meetings of the Directors held during that period.

Rotation of Directors.

89. At the first Annual General Meeting of the Company all the Directors shall retire from office, and at the Annual General Meeting in every subsequent year one-third of the Directors for the time being, or, if their number is not three or a multiple of three, then the number nearest one-third, shall retire from office.

90. The Directors to retire in every year shall be those who have been longest in office since their last election, but as between persons who became Directors on the same day those to retire shall (unless they otherwise agree among themselves) be determined by lot.

91. A retiring Director shall be eligible for re-election.

See Article 13.

92. The Company at the Meeting at which a Director retires in manner aforesaid may fill the vacated office by electing a person thereto, and in default the retiring Director shall if offering himself for re-election be deemed to have been re-elected, unless at such Meeting it is expressly resolved not to fill such vacated office or unless a resolution for the re-election of such Director shall have been put to the Meeting and lost.

93. No person other than a Director retiring at the Meeting shall unless recommended by the Directors be eligible for election to the office of Director at any General Meeting unless not less than three nor more than twenty-one days before the date appointed for the Meeting there shall have been left at the registered office of the Company notice in writing, signed by a Member duly qualified to attend and vote at the Meeting for which such notice is given, of his intention to propose such person for election, and also notice in writing signed by that person of his willingness to be elected.

94. The Company may from time to time by Ordinary Resolution increase or reduce the number of Directors, and may also determine in what rotation the increased or reduced number is to go out of office.

95. The Directors shall have power at any time, and from time to time, to appoint any person to be a Director, either to fill a casual vacancy or as an addition to the existing Directors, but so that the total number of Directors shall not at any time exceed the number fixed in accordance with these Regulations. Any Director so appointed shall hold office only until the next following Annual General Meeting, and shall then be eligible for re-election but shall not be taken into account in determining the Directors who are to retire by rotation at such Meeting.

APPENDIX B2

96. The Company may by Ordinary Resolution, of which special notice has been given in accordance with Section 142 of the Act, remove any Director before the expiration of his period of office notwithstanding anything in these Regulations or in any agreement between the Company and such Director. Such removal shall be without prejudice to any claim such Director may have for damages for breach of any contract of service between him and the Company.

97. The Company may by Ordinary Resolution appoint another person in place of a Director removed from office under the immediately preceding Regulation, and without prejudice to the powers of the Directors under Regulation 95 the Company in General Meeting may appoint any person to be a Director either to fill a casual vacancy or as an additional Director. A person appointed in place of a Director so removed or to fill such a vacancy shall be subject to retirement at the same time as if he had become a Director on the day on which the Director in whose place he is appointed was last elected a Director.

Proceedings of Directors.

98. The Directors may meet together for the despatch of business, adjourn, and otherwise regulate their Meetings, as they think fit. Questions arising at any Meeting shall be decided by a majority of votes. In case of an equality of votes, the Chairman shall have a second or casting vote. A Director may, and the Secretary on the requisition of a Director shall, at any time summon a Meeting of the Directors. It shall not be necessary to give notice of a Meeting of Directors to any Director for the time being absent from the United Kingdom.

99. The quorum necessary for the transaction of the business of the Directors may be fixed by the Directors, and unless so fixed shall be two.

100. The continuing Directors may act notwithstanding any vacancy in their body, but, if and so long as their number is reduced below the number fixed by or pursuant to the regulations of the Company as the necessary quorum of Directors, the continuing Directors or Director may act for the purpose of increasing the number of Directors to that number, of or summoning a General Meeting of the Company, but for no other purpose.

101. The Directors may elect a Chairman of their Meetings and determine the period for which he is to hold office; but if no such Chairman is elected, or if at any Meeting the Chairman is not present within five minutes after the time appointed for holding the same, the Directors present may choose one of their number to be Chairman of the Meeting.

102. The Directors may delegate any of their powers to Committees consisting of such member or members of their body as they think fit; any Committee so formed shall in the exercise of the powers so delegated conform to any regulations that may be imposed on it by the Directors.

103. A Committee may elect a Chairman of its Meetings; if no such Chairman is elected, or if at any Meeting the Chairman is not present within five minutes after the time appointed for holding the same, the members present may choose one of their number to be Chairman of the Meeting.

104. A Committee may meet and adjourn as it thinks proper. Questions arising at any Meeting shall be determined by a majority of votes of the members present, and in the case of an equality of votes the Chairman shall have a second or casting vote.

105. All acts done by any Meeting of the Directors or of a Committee of Directors or by any person acting as a Director shall, notwithstanding that it be afterwards discovered that there was some defect in the appointment of any such Director or person acting as aforesaid, or that they or any of them were disqualified, be as valid as if every such person had been duly appointed and was qualified to be a Director.

106. A resolution in writing, signed by all the Directors for the time being entitled to receive notice of a Meeting of the Directors, shall be as valid and effectual as if it had been passed at a Meeting of the Directors duly convened and held.

See Article 15.

Managing Director.

107. The Directors may from time to time appoint one or more of their body to the office of Managing Director for such period and on such terms as they think fit, and, subject to the terms of any agreement entered into in any particular case, may revoke such appointment. A Director so appointed shall not, whilst holding that office, be subject to retirement by rotation or be taken into account in determining the rotation of retirement of Directors, but his appointment shall be automatically determined if he cease from any cause to be a Director.

108. A Managing Director shall receive such remuneration (whether by way of salary, commission or participation in profits, or partly in one way and partly in another) as the Directors may determine.

109. The Directors may entrust to and confer upon a Managing Director any of the powers exercisable by them upon such terms and conditions and with such restrictions as they may think fit, and either collaterally with or to the exclusion of their own powers and may from time to time revoke, withdraw, alter or vary all or any such powers.

Secretary.

110. The Secretary shall be appointed by the Directors for such term, at such remuneration and upon such conditions as they may think fit; and any Secretary so appointed may be removed by them.

111. No person shall be appointed or hold office as Secretary who is—

(a) the sole Director of the Company; or

(b) a corporation the sole Director of which is the sole Director of the Company; or

(c) the sole Director of a corporation which is the sole Director of the Company.

112. A provision of the Act or these Regulations requiring or authorising a thing to be done by or to a Director and the Secretary shall not be satisfied by its being done by or to the same person acting both as Director and as, or in place of, the Secretary.

The Seal.

113. The Directors shall provide for the safe custody of the Seal, which shall only be used by the authority of the Directors or of a Committee of the Directors authorised by the Directors in that behalf, and every instrument to which the Seal shall be affixed shall be signed by a Director and shall be countersigned by the Secretary or by a second Director or by some other person appointed by the Directors for the purpose.

Dividends and Reserve.

114. The Company in General Meeting may declare dividends, but no dividend shall exceed the amount recommended by the Directors.

115. The Directors may from time to time pay to the Members such interim dividends as appear to the Directors to be justified by the profits of the Company.

116. No dividend shall be paid otherwise than out of profits.

117. The Directors may, before recommending any dividend, set aside out of the profits of the Company such sums as they think proper as a reserve or reserves which shall, at the discretion of the Directors, be applicable for any purpose to which the profits of the Company may be properly applied, and pending such application may, at the like discretion, either be employed in the business of the Company or be invested in such investments (other than Shares of the Company) as the Directors may from time to time think fit. The Directors may also without placing the same to reserve carry forward any profits which they may think prudent not to divide.

118. Subject to the rights of persons, if any, entitled to Shares with special rights as to dividend, all dividends shall be declared and paid according to the amounts paid or credited as paid on the Shares in respect whereof the dividend is paid, but no amount paid or credited as paid on a Share in advance of calls shall be treated for the purposes of this Regulation as paid on the Share. All dividends shall be apportioned and paid proportionately to the amounts paid or credited as paid on the Shares during any portion or portions of the period in respect of which the dividend is paid; but if any Share is issued on terms providing that it shall rank for dividend as from a particular date such Share shall rank for dividend accordingly.

119. The Directors may deduct from any dividend payable to any Member all sums of money (if any) presently payable by him to the Company on account of calls or otherwise in relation to the Shares of the Company.

120. Any General Meeting declaring a dividend or bonus may direct payment of such dividend or bonus wholly or partly by the distribution of specific assets and in particular of paid up shares, debentures or debenture stock of any other company or in any one or more of such ways, and the Directors shall give effect to such resolution, and where any difficulty arises in regard to such distribution, the Directors may settle the same as they think expedient, and in particular may issue fractional certificates and fix the value for distribution of such specific assets or any part thereof and may determine that cash payments shall be made to any Members upon the footing of the value so fixed in order to adjust the rights of all parties, and may vest any such specific assets in trustees as may seem expedient to the Directors.

121. Any dividend, interest or other moneys payable in cash in respect of Shares may be paid by cheque or warrant sent through the post directed to the registered address of the holder or, in the case of joint holders, to the registered address of that one of the joint holders who is first named on the Register of Members or to such person and to such address as the holder or joint holders may in writing direct. Every such cheque or warrant shall be made payable to the order of the person to whom it is sent. Any one of two or more joint holders may give effectual receipts for any dividends, bonuses or other moneys payable in respect of the Shares held by them as joint holders.

122. No dividend shall bear interest against the Company.

Accounts.
123. The Directors shall cause proper books of account to be kept with respect to:—

(a) all sums of money received and expended by the Company and the matters in respect of which the receipt and expenditure takes place;

(b) all sales and purchases of goods by the Company; and

(c) the assets and liabilities of the Company.

Proper books shall not be deemed to be kept if there are not kept such books of account as are necessary to give a true and fair view of the state of the Company's affairs and to explain its transactions.

124. The books of account shall be kept at the registered office of the Company, or, subject to Section 147(3) of the Act, at such other place or places as the Directors think fit, and shall always be open to the inspection of the Directors.

125. The Directors shall from time to time determine whether and to what extent and at what times and places and under what conditions or regulations the accounts and books of the Company or any of them shall be open to the inspection of Members not being Directors, and no Member (not being a Director) shall have any right of inspecting any account or book or document of the Company except as conferred by statute or authorised by the Directors or by the Company in General Meeting.

126. The Directors shall from time to time, in accordance with Sections 148, 150 and 157 of the Act, cause to be prepared and to be laid before the Company in General Meeting such profit and loss accounts, balance sheets, group accounts (if any) and reports as are referred to in those sections.
See Article 17.

127. A copy of every balance sheet (including every document required by law to be annexed thereto) which is to be laid before the Company in General Meeting, together with a copy of the Auditors' report, shall not less than twenty-one days before the date of the Meeting be sent to every Member of, and every holder of Debentures of, the Company and to every person registered under Regulation 31. Provided that this Regulation shall not require a copy of those documents to be sent to any person of whose address the Company is not aware or to more than one of the joint holders of any Shares or Debentures.

Capitalisation of Profits.

128. The Company in General Meeting may upon the recommendation of the Directors resolve that it is desirable to capitalise any part of the amount for the time being standing to the credit of any of the Company's reserve accounts or to the credit of the profit and loss account or otherwise available for distribution, and accordingly that such sum be set free for distribution amongst the Members who would have been entitled thereto if distributed by way of dividend and in the same proportions on condition that the same be not paid in cash but be applied either in or towards paying up any amounts for the time being unpaid on any Shares held by such Members respectively or paying up in full unissued Shares or Debentures of the Company to be allotted and distributed credited as fully paid up to and amongst such Members in the proportion aforesaid, or partly in the one way and partly in the other, and the Directors shall give effect to such resolution:

Provided that a Share Premium Account and a Capital Redemption Reserve Fund may, for the purposes of this Regulation, only be applied in the paying up of unissued Shares to be issued to Members of the Company as fully paid bonus Shares.

129. Whenever such a resolution as aforesaid shall have been passed the Directors shall make all appropriations and applications of the undivided profits resolved to be capitalised thereby, and all allotments and issues of fully paid Shares or Debentures, if any, and generally shall do all acts and things required to give effect thereto, with full power to the Directors to make such provision by the issue of fractional certificates or by payment in cash or otherwise as they think fit for the case of Shares or Debentures becoming distributable in fractions, and also to authorise any person to enter on behalf of all the Members entitled thereto into an agreement with the Company providing for the allotment to them respectively, credited as fully paid up, of any further Shares or Debentures to which they may be entitled upon such capitalisation, or (as the case may require) for the payment up by the Company on their behalf, by the application thereto of their respective proportions of the profits resolved to be capitalised, of the amounts or any part of the amounts remaining unpaid on their existing Shares, and any agreement made under such authority shall be effective and binding on all such Members.

Audit.

130.* Auditors shall be appointed and their duties regulated in accordance with Sections 159 to 161 of the Act and Section 14 of the Companies Act 1967.

Notices.

131. A notice may be given by the Company to any Member either personally or by sending it by post to him or to his registered address, or (if he has no registered address within the United Kingdom) to the address, if any, within the United Kingdom supplied by him to the Company for the giving of notice to him. Where a notice is sent by post, service of the notice shall be deemed to be effected by properly addressing, prepaying, and posting a letter containing the notice, and to have been effected in the case of a notice of a Meeting at the expiration of 24 hours after the letter containing the same is posted, and in any other case at the time at which the letter would be delivered in the ordinary course of post.

132. A notice may be given by the Company to the joint holders of a Share by giving the notice to the joint holder first named in the Register of Members in respect of the Share.

133. A notice may be given by the Company to the persons entitled to a Share in consequence of the death or bankruptcy of a Member by sending it through the post in a prepaid letter addressed to them by name, or by the title of representatives of the deceased, or trustee of the bankrupt, or by any like description, at the address, if any, within the United Kingdom supplied for the purpose by the persons claiming to be so entitled, or (until such an address has been so supplied) by giving the notice in any manner in which the same might have been given if the death or bankruptcy had not occurred.

134. Notice of every General Meeting shall be given in any manner hereinbefore authorised to—

(a) every Member except those Members who (having no registered address within the United Kingdom) have not supplied to the Company an address within the United Kingdom for the giving of notices to them;

(b) every person upon whom the ownership of a Share devolves by reason of his being a legal personal representative or a trustee in bankruptcy of a Member where the Member but for his death or bankruptcy would be entitled to receive notice of the Meeting; and

(c) the Auditor for the time being of the Company.

No other person shall be entitled to receive notices of General Meetings.

Winding-Up.

135. If the Company shall be wound up the Liquidator may, with the sanction of an Extraordinary Resolution of the Company and any other sanction required by the Act, divide amongst the Members in specie or kind the whole or any part of the assets of the Company (whether they shall consist of property of the same kind or not) and may, for such purpose set such value as he deems fair upon any property to be divided as aforesaid and may determine how such division shall be carried out as between the Members or different classes of Members. The Liquidator may, with the like sanction, vest the whole or any part of such assets in trustees upon such trusts for the benefit of the contributories as the Liquidator, with the like sanction, shall think fit, but so that no Member shall be compelled to accept any Shares or other securities whereon there is any liability.

* *as amended by Section 14* **(8)** *(c) of the Companies Act 1967.*

APPENDIX B2

Indemnity.

136. Every Director, Managing Director, Agent, Auditor, Secretary and other officer for the time being of the Company shall be indemnified out of the assets of the Company against any liability incurred by him in defending any proceedings, whether civil or criminal, in which judgment is given in his favour or in which he is acquitted or in connection with any application under Section 448 of the Act in which relief is granted to him by the court.

See Article 18.

PART II.

Regulations for the Management of a Private Company Limited by Shares.

1. The Regulations contained in Part I of Table A (with the exception of Regulations 24 and 53) shall apply.

2. The Company is a Private Company and accordingly—

(a) the right to transfer Shares is restricted in manner hereinafter prescribed;

(b) the number of Members of the Company (exclusive of persons who are in the employment of the Company and of persons who having been formerly in the employment of the Company were while in such employment and have continued after the determination of such employment to be Members of the Company) is limited to fifty. Provided that where two or more persons hold one or more Shares in the Company jointly they shall for the purpose of this Regulation be treated as a single Member;

(c) any invitation to the public to subscribe for any Shares or Debentures of the Company is prohibited;

(d) the Company shall not have power to issue Share Warrants to bearer.

3. The Directors may, in their absolute discretion and without assigning any reason therefor, decline to register any transfer of any Share, whether or not it is a fully paid Share.

4. No business shall be transacted at any General Meeting unless a quorum of Members is present at the time when the Meeting proceeds to business; save as herein otherwise provided two Members present in person or by proxy shall be a quorum.

5. Subject to the provisions of the Act, a resolution in writing signed by all the Members for the time being entitled to receive notice of and to attend and vote at General Meetings (or being corporations by their duly authorised representatives) shall be as valid and effective as if the same had been passed at a General Meeting of the Company duly convened and held.

See Article 9.

Note—Regulation 3 is in substitution for Regulation 24 of Part I.
Regulation 4 is in substitution for Regulations 53 of Part I.
Regulation 6 of this Part was repealed by the Companies Act 1967 Schedule VIII Part III.

Appendix C

Department of Trade*
COMPANIES REGISTRATION OFFICE

1. Notes for the guidance of Registered Companies

With reference to the Companies Acts 1948 to 1967 and the European Communities Act 1972

This pamphlet is intended to serve as a guide to some of the requirements of the Companies Acts 1948 to 1967 and the European Communities Act 1972, but, as much of it is set out in an abbreviated form, reference should be made at all times to the relevant provisions of those Acts for fuller information.

All enquiries relating to the registration of companies having their registered offices in England and Wales should be addressed to the Registrar of Companies, Companies House, 55–71 City Road, London EC1Y 1BB (Telephone: 01-253 9393) (nearest station—Old Street). Those in Scotland should enquire of The Registrar of Companies, Exchequer Chambers, 102 George Street, Edinburgh EH2 3DJ (Telephone: 031-225 5774/5).

Northern Ireland operates its own entirely independent Companies Acts and all enquiries about companies registered there should be addressed to The Registrar of Companies, Ministry of Commerce, Chichester House, 64 Chichester Street, Belfast BT1 4JX Telephone: Belfast 34488).

The attention of directors, secretaries and other officers of registered companies is called to the matters listed under the following alphabetical headings:

1. Accounts

The general provisions as to the balance sheet and profit and loss account are set out in Schedule 8 of the Companies Act 1948. This Schedule was in effect replaced from the 27th January 1968 by Schedule 2 of the Companies Act, 1967, and any accounts laid before a general meeting in respect of a financial year ending after this date will need to meet the requirements of the Act of 1967. This Act also calls for certain information to be given in those accounts or in a statement annexed to the accounts.

The information to be given is as follows:

(a) Particulars of the shares a company holds in its subsidiaries (*Section 3*)

(b) Particulars of shares of any class a company holds in another company which is not its subsidiary, if the shareholding is one-tenth or more of the share capital of that class, or if the shares held in the other company exceed one-tenth of its own assets (*Section 4*)

---

*The material in this Appendix is reproduced by permission of the Controller of Her Majesty's Stationery Office.

(c) The name and country of incorporation of a company's ultimate holding company if the company is itself a subsidiary (*Section 5*)

(d) Particulars of the emoluments of individual directors, unless the company is neither a holding company nor a subsidiary company *and* the aggregate amount of the directors' emoluments shown in the accounts under *Section 196* of the 1948 Act does not exceed £15,000 (*Sections 6 and 7* as amended by the Companies (Accounts) Regulations 1971)

(e) Particulars of salaries of employees receiving more than £10,000 in the year (*Section 8*)

In the case of items (d) and (e) figures for the immediately preceding financial year are also required (*Section 11*).

Accounts must be laid before the company in general meeting not later than 18 months after incorporation and subsequently once at least in every calendar year. The accounts must be made up to a date not earlier than 9 months (12 months in the case of a company carrying on business or having interests abroad) before the the date of the meeting (*Section 148 of the Act of 1948*). See also under 'Annual Return'.

2. Allotments

If a limited company having a share capital makes an allotment of shares it must file a return of the allotment with the Registrar of Companies within a month on form no. **PUC2.** If shares are allotted for a consideration other than cash the the return must be made on form no. **PUC3** and the company must also file a contract in writing constituting the title of the allottee to the allotment, together with any contract of sale or a contract for services relative to the making of the allotment. Where the contract is not in writing the prescribed particulars of the contract stamped with the same stamp duty as on a contract should be given on form no. 52 (*Section 52 of the 1948 Act*).

Forms **PUC2** and **3** bear Inland Revenue Capital Duty at the rate of £1 per £100 or part of £100 on the greater of (a) the total nominal value of the shares allotted or (b) the total amount paid, or due and payable, or treated as paid in respect of the shares allotted. A return of bonus shares should be made on form **PUC7** on which Capital Duty is not payable.

3. Alteration of Memorandum or Articles of Association

A company may alter its objects within the limits laid down in Section 5 of the 1948 Act. It must pass a special resolution to do so, a copy of which has to be sent to the Registrar within 15 days of it being passed (*Section 143 of the 1948 Act*).

If there is no application to the Court for the alteration to be cancelled the company must, not earlier than 21 days or later than 35 days after the date of the resolution, send the Registrar a printed copy of its memorandum as altered. An application to the Court for the alteration to be cancelled must be made within 21 days of the date of passing the resolution, and notice of the application given to the Registrar forthwith on form no. **101.** An office copy of the Court Order cancelling or confirming the alteration must be sent to the Registrar within 15 days of the order. If the order confirms the alteration, the office copy thereof, when sent to the Registrar, must be accompanied by a printed copy of the memorandum as altered (*Section 5 of the 1948 Act*).

When any alteration is made in a company's memorandum or articles of association under Section 5 of the 1948 Act, a copy of the document making or evidencing the alteration must be sent to the Registrar within 15 days of it having been passed together with a printed copy of the memorandum and articles as altered (*Section 9) 5 (of the European Communities Act*).

4. Annual General Meeting

Every company must hold a general meeting as its annual general meeting every calendar year and there should not be a period of more than 15 months between annual general meetings. If a company holds its first annual general meeting within 18 months of its incorporation it need not hold it in the year of its incorporation or in the following year (*Section 131 of the 1948 Act*).

5. Annual Return

In each calendar year every company must send to the Registrar of Companies an annual return made up to the fourteenth day after the annual general meeting. The return must be filed within 42 days of the meeting (*Sections 124, 125 and 126 of the 1948 Act*). Form no. **6A** should be used for companies having a share capital and form no. 7 for those not having a share capital. Form no. **6B** (Annual Return Guide) contains notes on the completion of the returns. The registration fee on an annual return is £3.

All limited companies and certain unlimited companies (see paragraph 39) must attach to the return a certified copy of all accounts laid before the company in general meeting since the date of the last return, together with a copy of the auditors' and directors' reports (*Section 127 of the 1948 Act*). Annexure of accounts, etc., depends on their being laid and should not be delayed if they are not approved at that meeting.

If, despite the provisions mentioned in paragraph 4, no annual general meeting has been held in a particular calendar year, an annual return must still be submitted, made up to the 31st December of that year, endorsed 'no meeting held' and filed forthwith. In such a case, a copy of the company's accounts and directors' report should still be annexed to the annual return, otherwise default under Section 127 may also arise, which will be pursued by the Registrar. This copy of the accounts clearly cannot be certified as a true copy of those 'laid before the company in general meeting' (*Section 127(1(a))*, but the Registrar is normally prepared to accept uncertified accounts for filing, provided that they have been audited and are accompanied by the auditors' report.

If an annual general meeting has been held, but no accounts have been presented since the date of the last annual return, then the company should either:

(a) Attach copies of its latest audited accounts and directors' report, even though these cannot be certified as true copies of those laid in general meeting (see above), or

(b) Endorse the annual return 'no accounts yet presented' (this presumes that accounts will be presented some time during the remainder of the calendar year). Such an endorsement appearing on two successive annual returns will, almost certainly, indicate default under either Section 148 or 127 of the 1948 Act, which will be pursued by the Registrar.

For guidance as to what documents the Registrar will accept as annexes to the annual return in the case of certain 'non-trading companies' see under that heading (paragraph 20).

6. Auditors

In general, only persons who are members of certain bodies of accountants may be appointed as auditors of a company but others may be specifically authorised to be so appointed by the Secretary of State for Trade.

7. Change of Name

A company may by special resolution and with the approval of the Secretary of State change its name. The resolution should be accompanied by a remittance of £40 in payment of the registration fee (*Section 18(1) of the 1948 Act and Schedule 3 of the 1967 Act*).

8. Commencing Business
A 'public' company having a share capital must obtain the Registrar's certificate that it is entitled to commence business before it commences or exercises any borrowing powers (*Section 109 of the 1948 Act*).

9. Defaults
The Companies Acts and the European Communities Act provide for the imposition of penalties for various defaults both in carrying out the requirements of the Acts and in sending the Registrar of Companies returns and notices as they become due. Directors and officers of a company are personally responsible if such defaults occur, whether or not the preparation of returns, etc., has been deputed to accountants or other parties.

10. Defunct Companies
The Registrar has power to strike companies off the register when he has reason to believe that they are not carrying on business or in operation (*Section 353 of the 1948 Act*).

11. Directors and Secretaries
Every company must send to the Registrar a return containing particulars of its directors and secretary within 14 days of their appointment on form no. **9** and details of any subsequent changes on form no. **9A** within 14 days of the changes occurring (*Section 200 of the 1948 Act*).

12. Directors' Service Contracts
If copies of directors' service contracts, or memoranda thereof, are kept at an address other than the registered office of the company, notification of this address should be sent to the Registrar on form no. **R5** (*Section 26 of the 1967 Act*).

13. Directors' Report
In their report, the directors should deal with the state of the company's affairs and indicate the dividend they recommend and amount they propose to carry to reserves (*Section 157(1) of the 1948 Act*).

The matters of a general nature to be dealt with in the directors' report are set out in Section 16 of the 1967 Act (previously Section 157(2) of the 1948 Act applied) and other matters are prescribed in Sections 17 to 20. Broadly, the information required by Sections 16 to 20 is as follows (the circumstances in which the information has to be given vary and, for details, reference should be made to the Sections of the 1967 Act which are mentioned against each item):

(a) The names of persons who have been directors during the financial year (*S.16(1)*)

(b) The principal activities of the company and its subsidiaries during the year and any significant changes therein (*S.16(1)*)

(c) Particulars of any significant changes in the fixed assets of the company or any of its subsidiaries (*S.16(1)(a)*)

(d) Details of shares and debentures issued during the year and the reasons for the issues (*S.16(1)(b)*)

(e) Particulars of significant contracts with the company in which a director thereof has a direct or indirect interest (*S.16(1)(c)*)

(f) A statement of the arrangements to which the company is a party under which directors of the company are or were during the year enabled to acquire shares or debentures in the company or any other body corporate (*S.16(1)(d)*)

(g) Information regarding directors' interests if existing at the end of the year, in shares or debentures of the company or its holding company's subsidiaries, etc. (*S.16(1)(e)*)

(h) Particulars of any other matters material for the appreciation of the state of the company's affairs (*S.16(1)(f)*)

(i)   If the company has carried on business of two or more classes that differ substantially from each other, the turnover and the profit (or loss) attributable to each of those classes unless the company is neither a holding company nor a subsidiary company *and* its turnover does not exceed £250,000 (Section 17 and para 13A of the Schedule as amended by the Companies (Accounts) Regulations 1971)

(j)   If the number of employees of the company exceeds 100, the average number employed during the year must be stated together with their aggregate re-muneration (*S.18*)

(k)   Particulars of contributions made by the company for political or charitable purposes (or both) if the total exceeds £50 in the year (*S.19*)

(l)   If the company supplies goods, the value of goods exported by the company during the year or a statement that no goods were exported *UNLESS*

(a)   it is neither a holding company nor a subsidiary company *and* its turnover does not exceed £250,000
OR
(b)   it is a subsidiary company but not a holding company *and* its turnover as shown in the accounts does not exceed £50,000
OR
(c)   it is a holding company, whether or not it is also a subsidiary company, which presents consolidated accounts *and* its consolidated turnover as shown in the accounts does not exceed £50,000
(*Section 20,* and para 13A of the Schedule as amended by the Companies (Accounts) Regulations 1971.)

Every member of a company and any other person entitled to receive notice of a general meeting is entitled to receive a copy of the directors' report (*S.24*).

14.   Forms
The forms prescribed by the Companies (Forms) Order 1949 (S.I. 1949 No. 382), and the Companies (Forms) Regulations 1967 (S.I. 1967 No. 1442), and other authorised forms may be obtained from the Registrar of Companies or from most law stationers.   A list of forms in use is given at the end of this pamphlet.

15.   Increase of Capital
A company may increase its capital by passing a resolution authorising the increase (*Section 63 of the 1948 Act*).   A copy of the resolution must be sent to the Registrar within 15 days of its being passed, together with a notice on form no. **10** giving particulars of the increase.

16.   Increase of Members
Where an unlimited company or a company limited by guarantee has increased the number of its members beyond the registered number (*Section 7 of the 1948 Act*), it must within 15 days after the increase was resolved upon (or took place), send a notice of the increase on form no. **11**.

17.   Inspection of Documents
All documents kept by the Registrar of Companies relative to individual companies may be inspected at Companies House, 55–71 City Road, London EC1Y 1BB, at a cost of 5p for each company file searched.   The office is open to the public from 9.45 a.m. to 4 p.m. on Mondays to Fridays.   Photocopies of documents on the files can be supplied at a cost of 5p per page (up to 9″ × 14″).

18.   Letters, Trade Catalogues, etc.
Companies are required to show the present and any former names of their directors and their nationality if not British in their letter-heads, trade catalogues, trade circulars, etc. (*Section 201 of the 1948 Act*).

Germany, France, Republic of Ireland, Italy, Luxembourg, Netherlands are exempt from this requirement (Section 201 of the 1948 Act) and The Companies (Disclosure of Directors' Nationality) (Exempting Order 1974).

APPENDIX C1

In addition companies are required to show on business letters and order forms:
(a) the place of registration of the company, and the number with which it is registered. It is recommended that the place of registration should be indicated by the words 'registered in England', or 'registered in Scotland' as appropriate. 'Registered in London' or 'registered in Edinburgh' would, however, be acceptable. The registered number of a company is shown on its certificate of incorporation.
(b) the address of its registered office. If a business letter or an order form shows more than one address it must indicate which of them is the address of the registered office. Where it shows only the address of the registered office the fact that that is the address of the registered office must be indicated.
(c) in the case of a limited company which is exempt under Section 19 of the Companies Act 1948 from the obligation to use the word 'limited' as part of its name, the fact that it is a limited company. This does not alter the company's right to omit the word 'limited' from its name.

If there is on the stationery used for business letters or on the order forms a reference to the amount of share capital, the reference must be to paid-up share capital. A reference to capital is not, however, obligatory (*Section 9(7) of the European Communities Act*).

19. Mortgages and Debentures

Particulars of certain mortgages or charges created by a company must be sent (on either form no. **47** or **47A**) to the Registrar within 21 days after the date of their creation, together with the relevant instrument (if any) creating the charge (*Section 95 of the 1948 Act*). Particulars of certain mortgages or charges on property which is acquired by a company must also be sent to the Registrar on form no. **47B**, with certain limited exceptions, within 21 days of the acquisition, together with a certified copy of the instrument (if any) creating the charge (*Section 97 of the 1948 Act*).

Failure to send particulars (and relevant instruments) to the Registrar within the 21-day time limit mentioned above, will result in the charge becoming void against the liquidator and any creditor of the company in respect of charges created by the company (*Section 95*) and in penalties on the directors in other cases (*Section 97*). The Court may in appropriate circumstances and subject to such conditions as thought fit extend the time (*Section 101*).

Where more than one issue is made of debentures in a series, particulars of each further issue must be sent to the Registrar on form no. **48**.

When a charge is wholly or partly satisfied, or the property charged is released or no longer forms part of the undertaking of the company, a memorandum of satisfaction may be filed under Section 100 of the 1948 Act on either form no. **49, 49A** or **49B**, as appropriate.

A certificate is issued in respect of every charge registered under the 1948 Act (*Section 98*) and a copy of this certificate is to be endorsed on debentures or certificates of debenture stock (*Section 99*).

A copy of every instrument creating a charge requiring registration under the Act is to be kept at the company's registered office (*Section 103*).

The register of charges kept by a company and the copies of instruments creating mortgages and charges are available for public inspection (*Section 104 and 105*).

The registration of mortgages and charges by companies registered at the Edinburgh Office and on property, etc., situated in Scotland may involve other requirements about which the Registrar for Scotland (*see page ii*) should be consulted.

20. Non-trading Companies

Companies that are operating but have not at any time since incorporation traded on their own account may, in seeking to satisfy the requirements of Section 127 of the 1948 Act, attach a statement to this effect, signed by a responsible officer of the company, in lieu of accounts, and where such a statement is received the Registrar will not take default action.

Companies which have not traded during the period since the date of the last annual return and have previously lodged a set of accounts, may, provided that assets and liabilities remain as disclosed in the balance sheet therein, lodge with their annual return a statement to that effect, in lieu of accounts required under Section 127.

In these cases the directors should still report on all relevant matters required by Section 157(1) of the 1948 Act and Section 16 of the 1967 Act (*see under Directors' Report, paragraph 13*).

21. Overseas Companies

Companies incorporated outside Great Britain which have established a place of business in Great Britain are obliged to register certain documents with the Registrar of Companies (*Section 407 of the 1948 Act*). Detailed information as to these requirements can be obtained on request from the Registrar.

22. Printing Requirements

The following documents are required to be printed:

(a) Articles of Association (*Section 9 of the 1948 Act*)

(b) Altered Articles of Association (*Section 9(5) of the European Communities Act*)

(c) Altered Memoranda of Association (*Sections 5(7) of the 1948 Act and 9(5) of the European Communities Act*)

The Registrar of Companies is prepared to regard the printing stipulation as satisfied by the following processes:

> Letterpress, gravure, lithography.
> Stencil duplicating using waxed stencils and black ink, offset lithography, 'office' type-set.
> Electrostatic photocopying.
> 'Photostat' or similar processes properly processed and washed.

Certain documents which under the 1948 Act were required when submitted for registration to be printed may now be in a form approved by the Registrar. Such documents are:

(a) Ordinary Resolutions increasing the capital of any company

(b) Notices of any such increases (*Section 63 of the 1948 Act*)

(c) Special and Extraordinary Resolutions and Agreements as specified in Section 143 of the Companies Act 1948.

The Registrar acting under the powers given by Section 51 of the 1967 Act, is prepared to accept for registration such copy Resolutions and Agreements if produced by any process named above or if typed.

The Registrar's present practice is to accept copies of the memorandum and articles amended in accordance with the following rules. Where the amendment is small in extent, e.g. a change of name or a change in the nominal capital, a copy of the original document may be amended by rubber stamp, 'top copy' typing or in some other permanent manner (but not a manuscript amendment). An alteration of a few lines or a complete short paragraph may be similarly dealt with if the new version is satisfactorily permanently affixed to a copy of the original in such a way as to obscure the words to be amended. Where more substantial amendments are involved, the pages amended may be removed from a copy of the original, the amended text inserted and the pages securely collated. The inserted material must be 'printed' as defined above but need not be produced by the same process as the original. In all cases the alterations must be validated by the seal or an official stamp of the company.

No document will be accepted if in general appearance, legibility, format or durability it is unsuitable for publication and use on the company's public file.

It has been found by experience that documents produced by a semi-dry developed dye line (diazo) system, by spirit duplicating or by thermo-copying do not satisfy the general condition.

23. Private Companies becoming Public

On becoming public a private company must within 14 days file with the Registrar a 'Statement in lieu of prospectus' on form no. 55A, unless a prospectus (*see below*) has been issued in this period (*Section 53 of the 1948 Act*).

24. Prospectus

Sections 37 to 46 of the 1948 Act deal with the issue of a prospectus and a copy of every prospectus, duly dated and signed, must be filed with the Registrar on or before the date of its publication. In certain circumstances, the copy of the prospectus has to be accompanied by the directors' consents in writing to act as directors and by their undertakings in writing to take and pay for their qualification shares, if any.

A document containing an offer of shares or debentures for sale to the public may be deemed to be a prospectus.

25. Prospectus—Statement in lieu of

A public company, having a share capital, which does not issue a prospectus on its formation, or has issued a prospectus but has not allotted any of the shares offered, must file with the Registrar a statement in lieu of prospectus on form no. 55, accompanied by the consents and undertakings by directors mentioned in the previous paragraph (unless these have already been presented for filing). The first allotment of shares must not take place until 3 days after filing the statement in lieu of prospectus (*Section 48 of the 1948 Act*).

26. Protection afforded to persons dealing with a company

A company may not rely against other persons on

(i)   the making of a winding-up order;

(ii) any alteration in its memorandum or articles;

(iii) any change in its directors or in the address of its registered office;

(iv) the appointment of a liquidator in a voluntary winding-up;

if the event has not been officially notified at the material time, unless the company can prove that it was known at the material time to the other party. If the event is officially notified less than 15 days before the material time the other party may treat it as ineffective against him by showing that he was unavoidably prevented knowing of it.

'Officially notified' means, as regards (i), (ii) and (iii) above, notice in the *London Gazette* by the Registrar of Companies of the receipt of documents evidencing the event and as regards (iv) notice in the *London Gazette* by the liquidator of his appointment.

27. Register of Debenture Holders

If a company keeps its register of debenture holders at an address other than its registered office, notification of the address at which it is kept, and any changes in that address, must be sent to the Registrar on form no. 102 (*Section 86 of the 1948 Act*).

28. Register of Directors' Interests

Every company must keep a register for the purposes of Section 27 of the 1967 Act (which requires directors to notify the company of any interests they have in shares in or debentures of the company, its holding company or any subsidiary interests of directors, spouses and infant children must also be stated (*Section 31*). If this register is not kept at the registered office of the company, then a notification of the address at which it is kept, and any changes in that address, must be sent to the Registrar on form no. **R6.** Section 28 contains provisions for giving effect to Section 27 and explains what 'interests' means.

29. Register of Members

Every company must keep a register of members containing the names and addresses of members and particulars of shares held by each (*Section 110 of the 1948 Act*). The date on which each person was entered in the register, and when he ceased to be a member, must also be shown.

The register is normally kept at the registered office of the company but, if not, the Registrar must be notified on form no. **103** of the address at which it is kept (or any changes in that address).

30. Register of Substantial Interests in a Company

Section 33 of the Act of 1967 requires all persons having an interest in shares of a company with a Stock Exchange quotation for any of its shares of a nominal value equal to one-tenth or more of the nominal value of the issued share capital of a class having unrestricted voting rights to notify the company accordingly. Every company to which the section applies must keep a register for the purpose of recording these particulars. The register must be kept at the same address as the place where the register of directors' interests is kept (*see paragraph 28 above*). The provisions of Section 28 are applied with certain variations to Section 33.

31. Registered Office

Every company must notify the Registrar of the situation of its registered office within 14 days of the date of incorporation on form no. **4.** Any subsequent change in the address of the registered office must similarly be notified to the Registrar on this form.

32. Remittances

All remittances should be made payable to the Registrar of Companies and crossed 'A/C Payee'.

Remittances in payment of Inland Revenue stamp duties in connection with return of allotments may be sent to the Registrar of Companies, who will arrange for the documents to be stamped by the Inland Revenue. Registrants may, however, themselves get the documents stamped by the Inland Revenue. Facilities are provided in London at the Inland Stamp Office, Bush House (S.W. Wing), Strand London WC2R 1LB, and 61 Moorgate, London CE2R 1BB, and at the Inland Revenue Stamp Offices in Birmingham, Bristol, Cardiff, Leeds, Liverpool, Manchester, Newcastle upon Tyne, Nottingham and Sheffield. When forms are presented they can be denoted with Inland Revenue duty stamps on payment of the appropriate amount in cash.

33. Re-registration as Limited

Section 44 of the Act of 1967 provides for the re-registration of an unlimited company as limited. Such a company cannot re-register in this way if it has previously been converted from a limited to an unlimited company under Section 43 of the Act (*see paragraph 34*).

The first step in conversion is for the unlimited company to pass a special resolution that it shall be re-registered as limited. The resolution should also state the particulars as to share capital, how the company is to be limited and so on (*Section 43(2)*). The application to the Registrar of Companies to re-register as limited should be made on form no. **R3**, and this should be accompanied by a copy of the resolution mentioned above. The companies registration fees payable are the same as for the incorporation of a new company. Capital duty is payable on a Statement (form no. **PUC 6**) to be delivered to the Controller of Stamps (or in Scotland, to the Controller of Stamps and Taxes (Special Section)) Inland Revenue.

A fresh certificate of incorporation will be issued by the Registrar on the re-registration of a company as limited.

34. Re-registration as Unlimited

Section 43 of the Act of 1967 provides for the re-registration of a limited company as unlimited. Such a company cannot re-register in this way if it has previously been converted from an unlimited to a limited company under Section 44 of the Act (*see paragraph 33*).

The application to the Registrar to re-register as unlimited should be made on form no. **R1**. This form has to bear a flat registration fee of £5, which will cover any additional share capital or membership. No Inland Revenue Capital Duty is payable irrespective of whether or not the company, when unlimited, is to have a share capital. The form no. **R1** must be accompanied by the signed assents of all members of the company to the proposed re-registration (on form no. **R2**), together with a statutory declaration by all the directors (on form no. **R4**) to the effect that the members giving assent constitute the whole of the membership of the company. Printed copies of the memorandum and articles of association, revised to correspond with the proposed new status of the company, must be forwarded with the application.

A fresh certificate of incorporation will be issued by the Registrar on the re-registration of a limited company as unlimited.

35. Resolutions

Where a company is required to file with the Registrar a copy of a resolution it has passed (these are, in the main, special or extraordinary resolutions and ordinary resolutions increasing capital), filing must take place within fifteen days of the passing of the resolution (*Sections 63 and 143 of the 1948 Act, Section 9(5) of the European Communities Act*).

36. Share Capital—Consolidation, Conversion into Stock

If a company having a share capital has consolidated any shares into stock, etc., it must within one month give notice to the Registrar on form no. **28** (*Section 62 of the 1948 Act*).

37. Share transfers

A company should not register a transfer of shares in or debentures of the company unless a proper instrument of transfer has been produced (*Section 75 of the 1948 Act*).

38. Statutory meeting and statutory report

A public company having a share capital must hold its 'statutory meeting' within a period of not less than one month and not more than three months from the date on which it is entitled to commence business (*see paragraph 8*). A copy of the 'statutory report' must be sent to every member at least 14 days before the day on which the meeting is held and a certified copy sent to the Registrar at the same time (*Section 130 of the 1948 Act*).

39. Unlimited Companies

An unlimited company is excepted, by Section 47 of the 1967 Act, from the requirement to file its accounts and the directors' report with its annual return, provided that the company is not:
(a) A subsidiary of one (or more) limited companies
(b) A holding company of a limited company
(c) Carrying on business as a promoter of a trading stamp scheme.

40. Winding Up

The winding up of a company may be either:
(a) By the Court (*Section 222 of the 1948 Act*)
(b) Members' voluntary (*Section 184 to 291*)
(c) Creditors' voluntary (*Sections 292 to 300*)
(d) Subject to the supervision of the Court (*Section 211*)

Notice of a meeting of creditors called for the purposes of Section 293 must be advertised once in the *London Gazette* (in the case of companies registered in England and Wales) and once at least in two local newspapers circulating in the district of the registered office or principal place of business of the company. Notice of all resolutions to wind up voluntarily must be given within 14 days after their passing, by advertisement in the *London Gazette* (in the case of companies registered in England and Wales) (*Section 279*). A copy of the resolution to wind up voluntarily must be filed with the Registrar within 15 days of the passing of the resolution (*Section 143*).

In the case of a proposal to wind up a company as a members' voluntary winding up, a meeting of the directors should first be called at which a 'declaration of solvency' must be made. This declaration should include a statement of the company's assets and liabilities as at the latest practicable date before the declaration is made. This document is a preliminary to the members of the company formally resolving to wind up (*Section 283*).

The declaration of solvency must:
(a) be made within 5 weeks before the date of passing the resolution to wind up, and
(b) be filed with the Registrar of Companies before the resolution is passed.

Failure to comply with (a) and (b) above will, in view of the provisions of Section 283, result in an intended members' voluntary winding up having to be treated as a creditors' voluntary winding up.

Notes for guidance on voluntary liquidation may be obtained from the Registrar on request.

LIST OF FORMS

Form no.	Description	Section of 1948 Act
4	Notice of situation of registered office or of any change therein	107
6A	Annual return of company having a share capital	124 and 126
6B	Annual return guide	—
7	Annual return of company not having a share capital	125 and 127
9A	Change in directors or secretary	200
10	Notice of increase in capital	63
11	Notice of increase in members	7(3)
17	Application to register an existing company as limited	384
18	Application to register an existing company as unlimited	384
19	List of members to be filed on registration of of an existing company	384
21	Statement of capital to be filed on registration of an existing company	384
22	Copy resolution to register an existing company	382 and 384
23	Declaration verifying documents on registering an existing company	386
24	Statement of places of business of banks	432
28	Notice of consolidation, etc.	62
29	Notice of situation where a dominion register kept	119
39C	Notice of appointment of liquidator (members')	305(1)
39D	Notice of appointment of liquidator (creditors')	305

APPENDIX C1

Form no.	Description	Section of 1948 Act
39E	Notice of appointment of liquidator (for insertion in *London Gazette*)	305
42	Consent to act as director of a company	181(1)(a)
43	List of persons who have consented to act as directors	181(4)
44	Declaration to be filed before issue of certificate to commence business (prospectus companies)	109(1)(d)
44A	Declaration to be filed before issue of certificate to commence business for companies filing statement in lieu of prospectus	109(2)(c)
47	Particulars of a mortgage or charge	95
47A	Particulars of a series of debentures	95
47B	Particulars of a mortgage or charge on property acquired	97
47C	Certificate of registration in Scotland or Northern Ireland of a charge comprising property situate there	95(5)
48	Particulars of an issue of debentures in a series	95(8)
49	Declaration verifying memorandum of satisfaction of a registered mortgage or charge	100
49A 49B	Declarations verifying memorandum relating to a registered mortgage or charge	100
52	Particulars of a contract where shares are issued for a consideration other than cash	52(2)
53	Notice of appointment of a receiver or manager	102(1)
55	Statement in lieu of prospectus	48
55A	Statement in lieu of prospectus by a private company on becoming a public company	30(1)
57	Receiver or manager's abstract of receipts and payments	372(2) and 374(1)
57A	Notice of ceasing to act as receiver or manager	102(2)
58	Statement relating to the payment of commission	53(1)(c)(ii) and (d)
101	Notice of application made to the Court for an alteration in a company's memorandum to be cancelled	5(7)
102	Notice of place where register of debenture holders is kept	86(3)
103	Notice of place where register of members is kept	110(3)
108	Declaration of solvency	283
110/111	Liquidator's statement of accounts and return of final meeting (members' winding up)	290
110/112	Liquidator's statement of accounts and return of final meeting (creditors' winding up)	300
1F	List of documents delivered for registration by a company incorporated overseas	407
2F	List of particulars of directors and secretary of an overseas company	407

Form no.	Description	Section of 1948 Act
3F	List of names and addresses of persons resident in Great Britain authorised to accept service for an overseas company	407
4F	Notice of alteration in the Charter, Statutes, memorandum or articles of association of an overseas company	409
5F	Notice of alteration in the list of directors and secretary of an overseas company	409
6F	Notice of alteration in the names or addresses of persons resident in Great Britain authorised to accept service for an overseas company	409
8F	Particulars of a mortgage or charge created by an overseas company on property in England	95 and 106
9F	Particulars of a mortgage or charge on property acquired by an overseas company	97 and 106
10F 11F	Particulars of an issue of debentures in a series by an overseas company	95(8) and 106
12F 12AF 12BF	Declarations verifying memorandum of satisfaction of a registered mortgage or charge created by an overseas company	100
PUC2	Return of Allotments of Shares issued for cash	52(1)
PUC3	Return of Allotments of Shares issued wholly or in part for a consideration other than cash	52(1)
PUC7	Return of Allotments of Shares issued by way of capitalisation of Reserves (Bonus Issues)	52(1)

Form no.	Description	Section of 1967 Act
R1	Application by a limited company to be re-registered as unlimited	43
R2	Members' assent to company being re-registered as unlimited	43
R3	Application by an unlimited company to be re-registered as limited	44
R4	Declaration by directors as to members' assent to re-registration of a company as unlimited	43(3)(b)
R5	Notice of place where copies of directors' written service contracts are kept	26(3)
R6	Notice of place where register of directors' interests in shares is kept	29(8)

C.55a
(6th revise)

October 1974

APPENDIX C2

2. Incorporation of New Companies—Notes for Guidance*

DEPARTMENT OF TRADE
COMPANIES REGISTRATION OFFICE
Companies Acts 1948 to 1967
INCORPORATION OF NEW COMPANIES
notes for guidance

PRIVATE COMPANIES

1.   Any two or more persons may form and carry on a private company.   Under section 28(1) of the Companies Act 1948, a private company must by its articles: (a) restrict the right to transfer its shares; (b) limit the number of its members to fifty (this does not include members who are in the employment of the company); (c) prohibit any invitation to the public to subscribe for any shares or debentures of the company.

2.   The following documents must be lodged with the Registrar of Companies in connection with the registration of a private company:

(a) *Memorandum of Association.* The memorandum, in addition to containing the particulars required by section 2 of the Companies Act 1948, must be signed by at least two persons whose addresses and descriptions must be stated.   Each of them must write opposite to his name in his own handwriting, the number and class of shares taken.   The signatures must be witnessed and the date of execution given. This memorandum forms the company's charter, and indicates the nature of the company's business, its capital and its nationality.   It must be stamped with the appropriate companies registration fee (see page 2). (b) *Articles of Association.* Articles adopting the restrictions mentioned in paragraph 1 must be registered with the memorandum.   In addition, all or any of the regulations contained in Table A in the First Schedule to the Companies Act 1948 may be adopted.   Any of those regulations not specifically excluded or modified by the articles registered will be taken to apply to the company.   The articles must be printed, divided into paragraphs numbered consecutively and must also be executed and dated like the memorandum.   Articles of association are intended to show the regulations for the internal arrangements and the management of the company.   They should not contain anything beyond the powers or rights possessed by the company as stated in the memorandum; (c) *Statement of Capital.* This statement has to be given separately on form No. PUC 1 Inland Revenue capital duty in respect of subscriber shares taken on Incorporation may be payable (see page 2). (d) *Declaration of Compliance.* A statutory declaration by a solicitor engaged in the formation of the company, or by a person named in the articles as a director or secretary of the company that all the requirements of the Companies Acts in respect of registration have been complied with, must be produced to the Registrar (form No. 41). (e) *Notice of Situation of Registered Office.* This notice is required to be lodged with the Registrar (on form No. 4) within 14 days of incorporation. (f) *Particulars of Directors and Secretary.* The names and other particulars of the company's directors and secretary must be lodged (on form No. 9) within 14 days from the appointment of the first directors of the company.   (Note: The notifications on forms No. 4 and No. 9 should if possible, be lodged with the Memorandum and Articles.)

'PUBLIC' COMPANIES

3.   The following documents must be lodged with the Registrar of Companies in connection with the registration of a 'public' company having a share capital: (a) *Memorandum of Association.* The requirements are similar to those for a private company (see paragraph 2), except that the memorandum must be signed

* *Reproduced by permission of the Department of Trade.*

by at least seven persons. (b) *Articles of Association*. The requirements as to articles are also similar to those for private companies. Part II of Table A in the First Schedule to the Companies Act 1948 is not applicable, however. (c) *Statement of Capital*. A statement similar to that required for private companies must be given on form No. PUC 1. (d) *Declaration of Compliance*. A statutory declaration on form No. 41 must be furnished, as with a private company. (e) *Lists of Directors*. There must be delivered with the memorandum a list of the persons who have consented to act as directors of the company (form No. 43). If directors are appointed by the articles the consent in writing of every director appointed by the articles to act as director must be lodged on form No. 42, together with undertakings, in writing, signed by each director appointed by the articles, to take and pay for his qualification shares (if any) where he has not signed the memorandum for at least that number of shares. (f) *Notice of Situation of Registered Office*. The requirements are the same as for a private company (see paragraph 2(e)). (g) *Particulars of Directors and Secretary*. The requirements are the same as for a private company (see paragraph 2(f)).

4. A 'public' company having a share capital must, before it commences business or exercises any borrowing powers, obtain the Registrar's certificate that it is entitled to commence business.

COMPANIES NOT HAVING A SHARE CAPITAL

5. The documents required are those prescribed for private companies, with the exception of the Statement of Capital (form No. PUC 1).

OVERSEAS COMPANIES

6. Companies Incorporated outside Great Britain which have established a place of business in Great Britain are obliged to register certain documents with the Registrar of Companies. Detailed information as to these requirements can be obtained on request from the Registrar.

CHOICE AND APPROVAL OF COMPANY NAMES

7. By virtue of section 17 of the Companies Act 1948, the Secretary of State for Trade is empowered to refuse registration of a company by a name which in his opinion is undesirable. The following notes are given for the guidance of the public though it must be understood that they are in no way exhaustive: (a) A name will be refused if it is too like the name of an existing company or other body corporate; (b) A name will be refused if it is misleading; for example, if the name of a company with small resources suggests that it is trading on a great scale or over a wide field; (c) A name will be refused if it includes the words 'Building Society';

Names will not ordinarily be allowed which:

(a) Suggest a connection with the Crown or member of the Royal Family or suggest royal patronage (including names containing words such as 'Royal', 'King', 'Princess', 'Crown'); (b) Suggest a connection with a Government department, statutory undertaking, local authority, or with any commonwealth or foreign government; (c) The word 'British' is not allowed in a name unless the undertaking is British controlled and entirely or almost entirely British owned; nor will it be allowed where the name of the company taken as a whole, would give the unjustified impression that the company was pre-eminent in its particular field of activity. The same considerations apply to use of the expressions 'National', 'United Kingdom', 'Great Britain', 'Northern Ireland', 'Scotland', 'Europe' and (with appropriate modifications) to 'English', 'Scottish', 'Welsh', and derivates of all these words; (d) Names including the following words will be allowed only where the circumstances justify it: 'Bank', 'Chamber of Commerce', 'Council', 'Co-operative', 'Corporation', 'Institute', 'Insurance', 'International', 'Investment Trust', 'Register', 'Trust', 'Unit Trust': (e) Members of the public are advised that if they wish to form companies whose names include any of the above-mentioned words, then incorporation must necessarily take longer than would otherwise be the case; (f) The words mentioned in this Practice Note should be understood to include all cognate expressions (eg Bank:—Bankers, Banking; Insurance:—Assurance). Although provisional approval of a name may have been given applicants are advised not to incur expenses in connection with the proposed title before the company has been registered and the certificate of incorporation issued.

TRADE MARKS

8. The Registrar does not consult the Trade Marks Index when considering applications for a proposed new company name and the acceptance of a particular name is not an indication that no trade marks rights exist in it. Applicants are therefore advised in their own interests to avoid possible expense and inconvenience by investigating the possibility that others may have trade marks right in the names —or parts of such names—they require before applying to the Registrar. Searches may be made at the Trade Marks Registry, Patent Office, Southampton Buildings, London WC2A 1AY.

ALIEN DIRECTORS

9. Some aliens are under restrictions as to the employment in which they may engage while in this country. If an alien director is in any doubt in this matter he should seek advice from the Aliens Department of the Home Office (Princeton House, 271 High Holborn, London WC1, telephone: 01-405 4321).

EXCHANGE CONTROL REGULATIONS

10. Companies having directors or shareholders who are resident outside the United Kingdom should bear in mind that monies may be transferred abroad only under the terms of Exchange Control Regulations.

FORMS

11. Company forms can be obtained from law stationers, or from Companies Registration Office, 55-71 City Road, London EC1Y 1BB. Specimen memoranda and articles can only be obtained from law stationers.

CAPITAL DUTY

12. On the formation of a company incorporated with limited liability duty at £1 per £100 or part of £100 is charged on the greater of the nominal value of the shares issued or allotted on incorporation and the actual value of assets of any kind contributed less any liabilities which have been assumed or discharged by the company in consideration of the contribution. If duty is to be accounted for when either (a) a call is made on the partly paid (ie NIL paid) subscriber shares or (b) the company proceeds to allot all its shares, including the subscriber shares, to other persons, then form PUC 1 will show the number of shares taken at item C but NIL at E.

FEES

13. A standard registration fee of £50 is payable irrespective of the amount of nominal capital or the number of members in the case of a company without share capital.

REMITTANCES

14. All remittances should be made payable to the Registrar of Companies and crossed 'A/c payee'.

15. Remittances in payment of Inland Revenue stamp duties in connection with new company registrations may be sent, together with the registration fees, to the Registrar of Companies, who will arrange for the documents to be stamped by the Inland Revenue. Registrants may, however, themselves get the documents stamped by the Inland Revenue. Facilities are provided in London at the Inland Revenue Stamp Office, Bush House (SW Wing), Strand, WC2, and 61 Moorgate, EC2, and elsewhere at the Inland Revenue Offices in Birmingham, Bristol, Cardiff,

Edinburgh, Leeds, Glasgow, Liverpool, Manchester, Newcastle upon Tyne, Nottingham and Sheffield, whereby forms presented by an applicant can be denoted with Inland Revenue duty stamps on payment of the appropriate amount in cash.

This leaflet is intended to serve as a guide to the essential requirements for the registration of companies (and other related matters) under the Companies Acts 1948 to 1967, to which reference should be made at all times.

All enquiries relating to the registration of companies having their registered offices in England and Wales should be addressed to the Registrar of Companies, Companies House, 55–71 City Road, London EC1Y 1BB (Telephone 01-153 9393) (nearest station–Old Street).

For companies having registered offices in Scotland, enquiries should be addressed to the Registrar of Companies, Exchequer Chambers, George Street, Edinburgh EH2 3DJ (Telephone 031:225 5774).

C56

(Revised March 1974)

APPENDIX C3

3. Company Law Provisions of the European Communities Act 1972*

SECTION 9 of the European Communities Act 1972 makes changes in company law in order to give effect in Great Britain to an EEC requirement that Member States provide safeguards for persons who deal with companies. This Notice deals only with those changes made by Section 9 which relate to particulars to be given on business letters and order forms and to printed documents for delivery to the registrar of companies.

From the entry date (January 1, 1973), companies will be required to show on business letters and order forms their place of registration, registered number and the address of their registered office. It is recommended that the place of registration should be indicated by the words 'registered in England' or 'registered in Scotland' as appropriate. 'Registered in London' or 'registered in Edinburgh' would also be acceptable. The registered number of a company is shown on its certificate of incorporation.

If a business letter or an order form shows more than one address it must indicate which of them is the address of the registered office. Where it shows only the address of the registered office the fact that that is the address of the registered office must be indicated.

If there is on the stationery used for business letters or on the order forms a reference to the amount of share capital, the reference must be to paid-up share capital. A reference to capital is not, however, obligatory.

Companies holding a licence under s.19 of the Companies Act 1948 authorising them to dispense with the word 'limited' in their name will be required to indicate on letters and order forms that they are limited companies. This does not alter their right to omit the word 'limited' from their name.

The phrase order forms is to be understood to mean forms which the company makes available for other persons to order goods or services from the company. It includes, for example, coupons in newspapers which the public fill in asking for goods to be supplied. The new requirement does not apply to such documents as invoices or delivery notes.

*Reproduced from article "Britain and the E.E.C.—20" in the journal 'Trade and Industry' dated 19th October 1972.

It is not essential for the above information to be included at the top of the letter or order form. If it is found more convenient it may be shown at the foot of the page. In the long term companies will no doubt wish to incorporate the information in a printed layout. In the meantime it can equally well be typed or stamped on as printing is not required by the Act.

Printed documents to be sent to the Registrar

Section 9 requires certain printed documents to be sent to the registrar. The Companies Acts already require certain documents sent to the registrar to be printed. For all these purposes the registrar is prepared to accept as 'printed' documents produced by the following processes:

letterpress, gravure, lithography; 'office' type-set, offset lithography; Electrostatic photocopying; 'Photostat' or similar processes properly processed and washed; Stencil duplicating using wax stencils and black ink.

In all cases this is subject to a general condition that no document will be accepted if in general appearance, format or durability it is unsuitable for publication and use on the company's file. It has been found by experience that documents produced by dye-line copying, spirit duplicating or thermo-copying do no satisfy the general condition.

Up to date copy of memorandum and articles

Companies may need to take action to comply with the requirement that an up to date copy of the memorandum or articles of association has been made. Section 9 requires these documents as altered to be printed. This is already a requirement where the memorandum has been altered by special resolution in accordance with Section 5 of the Companies Act 1948. It is a new requirement where the memorandum has been altered in accordance with some provision or where the articles have been altered.

The registrar will accept copies of the memorandum and articles amended in accordance with the following rules. Where the amendment is small in extent, eg a change of name or a change in the nominal capital, a copy of the original document may be amended by rubber stamp, 'top copy' typing or in some other permanent manner (but not a manuscript amendment). An alteration of a few lines or a complete short paragraph may be similarly dealt with if the new version is satisfactorily permanently affixed to a copy of the original in such a way as to obscure the amended words. Where more substantial amendments are involved, the pages amended may be removed from a copy of the original, the amended text inserted and the pages securely collated. The inserted material must be 'printed' as defined above but need not be produced by the same process as the original. In all cases the alteration must be validated by the seal or an official stamp of the company. The registrar reserves the right to change these arrangements if experience should show them to be unsatisfactory.

Amended copies are required to be delivered to the registrar within one month of the entry date.

Companies to which these provisions apply

The foregoing requirements apply to all companies incorporated in Great Britain under the Companies Acts. They do not apply to branches of companies incorporated outside Great Britain which have an established place of business here.

Similar provisions will be enacted under s.4(3) of the Act for companies incorporated in Northern Ireland.

Appendix D

Extracts from the City Code on Takeovers and Mergers (June 1974)*

Note: These extracts are selective and intended only as illustrations of the nature of the code and of the provisions which particularly concern directors.

1. General Principles

1. It is considered to be impracticable to devise rules in such detail as to cover all the various circumstances which arise in take-over or merger transactions. **Accordingly, persons engaged in such transactions should be aware that the spirit as well as the precise wording of these General Principles and of the ensuing Rules must be observed.** Moreover, it must be accepted that the General Principles and the spirit of the Code will apply in areas or circumstances not explicitly covered by any Rule.

2. While the Boards of an offeror and of an offeree company and their respective advisers and associates have a primary duty to act in the best interests of their respective shareholders, they must accept that there are limitations in connection with takeover and merger transactions on the manner in which the pursuit of those interests can be carried out. Inevitably therefore these General Principles and the ensuing Rules will impinge on the freedom of action of Boards and persons involved in such transactions.

3. Shareholders shall have in their possession sufficient evidence, facts and opinions upon which an adequate judgement and decision can be reached and shall have sufficient time to make an assessment and decision. No relevant information shall be withheld from them.
See Practice Note No. 7.

4. At no time after a *bona fide* offer has been communicated to the Board of an offeree company or after the Board of an offeree company has reason to believe that a *bona fide* offer is imminent shall any action be taken by the Board of the offeree company in relation to the affairs of the company, without the approval in general meeting of the shareholders of the offeree company, which could effectively result in any *bona fide* offer being frustrated or in the shareholders of the offeree company being denied an opportunity to decide on its merits.

5. It must be the object of all parties to a takeover or merger transaction to use every endeavour to prevent the creation of a false market in the shares of an offeror or offeree company.
See Practice Note No. 7.

6. A Board which receives an offer or is approached with a view to an offer being made should normally in the interests of its shareholders seek competent outside advice.

7. Rights of control must be exercised in good faith and the oppression of a minority is wholly unacceptable.

8. All shareholders of the same class of an offeree company shall be treated similarly by an offeror.

9. If, after a takeover or merger transaction is reasonably in contemplation, an offer has been made to one or more shareholders of an offeree company, any subsequent general offer made by or on behalf of the same offeror or his associates to the shareholders of the same class shall not be on less favourable terms.

10. During the course of a takeover or merger transaction, or when such is in contemplation, neither the offeror, the offeree company nor any of their respective advisers shall furnish information to some shareholders which is not made available to all shareholders. This principle shall not apply to the furnishing of information in confidence by an offeree company to a *bona fide* potential offeror or *vice versa,* nor to the issue of circulars by members of The Stock Exchange (who are associates of any party to the transaction) to their own investment clients provided such issue shall previously have been approved by the Panel.
See Practice Note No. 3.

11. Directors of an offeror or an offeree company shall always, in advising their shareholders, act only in their capacity as Directors and not have regard to their personal or family shareholdings or their personal relationships with the companies. It is the shareholders' interests taken as a whole which should be considered, together with those of employees and creditors.

12. Any document or advertisement addressed to shareholders containing information, opinions or recommendations from the Board of an offeror or offeree company or its respective advisers shall be treated with the same standards of care as if it were a prospectus within the meaning of the Companies Act 1948. Especial care shall be taken over profit forecasts.

APPENDIX D2

2. Rules (1 to 13)

THE APPROACH
1. The offer should be put forward in the first instance to the Board of the offeree company or to its advisers.

2. If the offer or an approach with a view to an offer being made is not made by a principal, the identity of the principal must be disclosed at the outset.

3. A Board so approached is entitled to be satisfied that the offeror is or will be in a position to implement the offer in full.

4. Where an offer is being made by a parent company for minority shareholdings in a subsidiary, or in any other case where the offer is not completely at arm's length, it is essential that competent outside advice be obtained in order to ensure, and to satisfy the offeree shareholders, that their interests are fully protected.

EARLY STAGES
5. When any firm intention to make an offer is notified to a Board from a serious source (irrespective of whether the Board views the offer favourably or otherwise), shareholders must be informed without delay by Press notice. A copy of the Press notice, or a circular informing shareholders of the offer, should, on the occasion of the first such Press notice, normally be sent to shareholders promptly after the announcement.
Where there have been approaches which may or may not lead to an offer, the duty of a Board in relation to shareholders is less clearly defined. There are obvious dangers in announcing prematurely an approach which may not lead to an offer. By way of guidance it can be said that an announcement of the facts should be made forthwith as soon as two companies are agreed on the basic terms of an offer and are reasonably confident of a successful outcome of the negotiations.

In any situation which might lead to an offer being made, whether welcome or not, a close watch should be kept on the share market; in the event of any untoward movement in share prices an immediate announcement, accompanied by such comment as may be appropriate, should be made.

6. Joint statements are desirable whenever possible, provided that agreement thereon does not lead to undue delay. The obligation to make announcements lies no less with the potential offeror than with the offeree company.

7. The vital importance of absolute secrecy before an announcement must be emphasised.
See Practice Note No. 7.

8. When an offer is announced, the identity of the offeror must be disclosed and the offeror must also disclose any existing holding in the offeree company which it owns or over which it has control or which is owned or controlled by any person or company acting in concert with the offeror.
Any conditions (including normal conditions relating to acceptances, quotation and increase of capital) to which the offer or the posting of it is subject must be stated in the formal announcement. In particular, where an offer comes within the statutory provisions for possible reference to the Monopolies and Mergers Commission, a condition that the offer will be withdrawn if there is a reference must be included. All conditions must be fulfilled or the offer must lapse within 21 days of the first closing date or the date the offer becomes or is declared unconditional as to acceptances, whichever is the later.
See Practice Note No. 7.

9. If an offeror, which has announced its intention to make an offer, does not proceed with the formal offer within a reasonable time, it must be prepared to justify the circumstances of the case to the Panel. An announced offer cannot be withdrawn without the consent of the Panel, which will be granted only in exceptional circumstances.
See Practice Note No. 7.

BOARD CONSIDERATION OF AN OFFER

10. Directors must always have in mind that they must act in the interests of the shareholders taken as a whole. Shareholders in companies which are effectively controlled by their Directors must accept that in respect of any offer the attitude of their Board will be decisive. There may be good reasons for such a Board rejecting an offer or preferring a lower offer. In the latter case, the Board must very carefully examine its motive for so doing and be prepared to justify its good faith in the context of General Principle 11 and, in such circumstances, competent outside advice must be taken.

11. Except with the consent of the Panel, no sale of shares held by Directors of a company (and their close relatives and related trusts) may be made nor, before formal submission of the offer to the general body of shareholders, may any irrevocable commitment to accept an offer be entered into if the shares the subject of such sale or commitment would, when aggregated with the shareholdings of the purchaser or person to whom such commitment is given (and persons acting in concert with the same), carry 30% or more of the voting rights.
Where such consent to a sale is granted by the Panel of Directors must ensure that as a condition of the sale the purchaser agrees to fulfil his obligations under Rule 34.

12. Any information, including particulars of shareholders, given to a preferred suitor should on request be furnished equally and as promptly to a less welcome but *bona fide* potential offeror.
See Practice Note No. 7.

13. It is essential that after an offer document and a letter setting out the views of the offeree company should be circulated as soon as practicable.

3. Practice Note No. 7 (from commencement to Rule 12)

PRACTICE NOTE NO. 7

The City Code on Takeovers and Mergers

Panel Memoranda of Interpretation and Practice

RULINGS AND INTERPRETATIONS OF GENERAL INTEREST

In Annual Reports issued by the Panel a number of rulings of general interest have been included. Some of these rulings have been taken into account in the edition of the Code published on 6th June, 1974. The remainder still stand but the Rules to which many of them relate have been renumbered: for the convenience of practitioners these rulings, amended or expanded where appropriate, are given below together with a number of further general points of interpretation.

General Principle 3. Financial advisers who own shares in a client company should not deal in such shares contrary to any advice they may have given to shareholders, or to any advice with which it can be reasonably assumed that they were associated, without giving reasonable public notice of their intentions.

General Principle 5. (a) If, after an announcement has been made that takeover or merger discussions are taking place or that an approach or offer is contemplated, the discussions are terminated, or the offeror decides not to proceed with an offer, no dealings in the shares of the offeree company by the offeror or by any person or company privy to the intention to terminate the discussions or to the decision not to proceed with the offer may take place prior to the announcement that the discussions have been terminated or that a decision not to proceed with an offer has been taken.

(b) The exemption of the offeror under Rule 30 from the prohibition on dealings does not apply to cases where the offeror would be precluded from dealing under ordinarily accepted standards of business behaviour, e.g., where the offeror has been supplied by the offeree company with confidential price-sensitive information in the course of takeover or merger discussions.

Rules 30 and 31 should be read in the light of the above interpretations.

Rule 7. Where a cash alternative to an offer is to be provided which involves underwriting, underwriters may be informed of the impending offer immediately before the general announcement provided they are expressly warned of the confidential nature of their advance information.

Rule 8. (a) The language used in press statements should clearly and concisely reflect the position being described. The word "agreement" should be used with the greatest care and, in particular, statements should be avoided which may give the impression that Directors have committed themselves to certain courses of action (e.g., accepting in respect of their own shares) when they have not in fact done so.

(b) If offeree Directors advise their shareholders that they intend to accept an offer but there are qualifications to that intention then words such as "present intention" should be used.

(c) Announcements of offers should not include conditions which depend on subjective judgements by Directors or the fulfilment of which are in the hands of the Directors since these create unnecessary uncertainty; nor should they include a condition that, if the general economic situation deteriorates, the Directors can withdraw the offer. It would normally be acceptable in an announcement for an offer to be expressed as being conditional on statements or estimates being appropriately verified.

Rule 9. (a) A change in economic, industrial or political circumstances would not normally justify the withdrawal of an announced offer. To justify unilateral withdrawal some circumstance of an entirely exceptional nature and amounting to something of the kind which would frustrate a legal contract would normally be required.

(b) An announced offeror need not proceed with his formal offer if a competitor has already posted a higher offer.

Rule 11. (a) It is the practice of the Panel to require the production of competent outside advice in addition to the recommendation of the Board of the company concerned before considering an application for consent to a shut-out bid. Directors of companies who contemplate entering into a shut-out transaction are strongly recommended to obtain such independent advice at an early stage and before reaching an affirmative conclusion on the offer.

(b) Although the requirement to clear a shut-out with the Panel rests on the offeree Directors, offerors should ensure that this action has been taken.

(c) Where more than one approach has been received by an offeree Board, the Panel will normally expect less preferred suitors to be given at least 48 hours to compete before the offeree Directors give a shut-out.

(d) When, after a shut-out has been approved by the Panel, further irrevocable undertakings to accept the offer are obtained from persons subject to Rule 11, such persons should clear the undertakings with the Panel.

Rule 12. The less welcome offeror should specify the questions to which he requires answers. He is not entitled to receive the benefit of his competitor's industry or special knowledge by asking in general terms for all the information supplied to his competitor.

Appendix E

1. Stock Exchange Listing Agreement—Companies*

.... (NAME OF COMPANY) ....

The following is an extract from the minutes of a meeting of the board of directors held the..day of..19..........

In compliance with the requirements of the Council of The Stock Exchange, it was resolved that the company agrees (all such agreements to be read and construed in accordance with and subject to the notes to the Listing Agreement currently appearing in Chapter 2 of the document "Admission of Securities to Listing" published by The Stock Exchange as follows:—

1. To notify the Department in advance of the date fixed for any board meeting at which the declaration or recommendation or payment of a dividend is expected to be determined upon, or at which any announcement of the profits or losses in respect of any financial period or part thereof is to be approved for publication.

2. To notify the Department immediately after the relevant board meeting has been held of:—

(a) any preliminary profits announcements for any year, half-year or other period;

(b) all dividends and other distributions to members recommended or declared or resolved to be paid and of any decision to pass any dividend or interest payment;

(c) short particulars of any proposed change in the capital structure, or redemption of securities.

3. To notify to the Press the basis of allotment of securities in prospectus and other offers and, if applicable, in respect of excess applications, such notice to appear not later than the morning of the business day next after the allotment letters or other relevant documents of title are posted.

4. To notify the Department without delay of:—

(a) particulars of any material acquisitions or realisations of assets comprised in the definition set out in the Chapter on Acquisitions and Realisations contained in "Admission of Securities to Listing";

(b) any information required to be disclosed to The Stock Exchange under the provisions of The City Code on Takeovers and Mergers;

(c) any changes in the directorate;

(d) any proposed change in the general character or nature of the business of the company or of the group;

(e) any information required to be notified to the company under Section 33 of the Companies Act 1967 (or which would be so required if the company were subject to the provisions of that Act);

(f) any change in the status of the company under the close company provisions of the Income and Corporation Taxes Act 1970 (and of any amendments thereto);

*The material in this Appendix is reproduced from "Admission of Securities to Listing" by permission of the Council of the Stock Exchange.

(g) any other information neccessary to enable the shareholders and the public to appraise the position of the company and to avoid the establishment of a false market in its securities.

5. To send with the notice convening a meeting of holders of securities to all persons entitled to vote thereat proxy forms with provision for two-way voting on all resolutions intended to be proposed.

6. To forward to the Department copies of:—

(a) proofs for approval (through the companys' brokers), of all circulars to holders of securities, notices of meetings, forms of proxy and notices by advertisement to holders of bearer securities;

(b) all circulars, notices, reports, announcements or other documents at the same time as they are issued;

(c) all resolutions passed by the company other than resolutions concerning routine business at an annual general meeting.

7. To notify the Department of an explanation for the delay in any case where no annual report and accounts have been issued by the company within the six months following the date of the end of the financial period to which they relate, at the same time indicating when it is expected that such report and accounts will be published.

8. To prepare a half-yearly or interim report which must be sent to the holders of securities or inserted as paid advertisements in two leading daily newspapers not later than six months from the date of the notice convening the annual general meeting of the company.

9. To circulate with the annual report of the directors:—

(a) a statement by the directors as to the reasons for adopting an alternative basis of accounting in any case where the auditors have stated that the accounts are not drawn up in accordance with the standard accounting practices approved by the accountancy bodies;

(b) a geographical analysis of turnover and of contribution to trading results of those trading operations carried on by the company (or group) outside the United Kingdom;

(c) the name of the principal country in which each subsidiary operates;

(d) the following particulars regarding each company in which the group interest in the equity capital amounts to 20% or more:—

(i) the principal country of operation;

(ii) particulars of its issued share and loan capital and, except where the group's interest therein is dealt with in the consolidated balance sheet as an associated company, the total amount of its reserves;

(iii) the percentage of each class of loan capital attributable to the company's interest (direct or indirect);

(e) a statement as at the end of the financial year showing the interests of each director in the share capital of the company appearing in the register maintained under the provisions of the Companies Act 1967 (or which would be required so to appear if the company were subject to the provisions of that Act), distinguishing between beneficial and non-beneficial interests; such statement should include by way of note any change in those interests occurring between the end of the financial year and a date not more than one month prior to the date of the notice of meeting or, if there has been no such change, disclosure of that fact;

(f) a statement showing particulars as at a date not more than one month prior to the date of the notice of meeting of an interest of any person, other than a director, in any substantial part of the share capital of the company and the amount of the interest in question or, where appropriate, a negative statement;

(g) (i) a statement showing whether or not, so far as the directors are aware, the close company provisions of the Income and Corporation Taxes Act 1970 (and of any amendments thereto) apply to the company and whether there has been any change in that respect since the end of the financial year;

    (ii) in the case of an investment trust a statement showing the status of the company under the provisions of the Income and Corporation Taxes Act 1970 (and of any amendments thereto) and of any change in that status since the end of the financial year;

(h) particulars of any contract subsisting during or at the end of the financial year in which a director of the company is or was materially interested and which is or was significant in relation to the company's business;

(i) particulars of any arrangement under which a director has waived or agreed to waive any emoluments;

(j) particulars of any arrangement under which a director has waived or agreed to waive any dividends.

10. (a) To procure that any service contract granted by the company, or any subsidiary of the company, to any director or proposed director of the company not expiring or determinable within ten years by the employing company without payment of compensation (other than statutory compensation) must be made subject to the approval of the company in general meeting.

(b) To make available for inspection at the registered office or transfer office during usual business hours on any weekday (Saturdays and public holidays excluded) from the date of the notice convening the annual general meeting until the date of the meeting and to make available for inspection at the place of meeting for at least 15 minutes prior to the meeting and at the meeting copies of all service contracts, unless expiring or determinable within one year by the employing company without payment of compensation, of any director of the company with the company or any of its subsidiaries and, where any such contract is not reduced to writing, a memorandum of the terms thereof;

(c) To state in a note to the notice convening the annual general meeting that copies or, as the case may be, memoranda of all such service contracts will be available for inspection or, if there are no such contracts, to state that fact.

11. To certify transfers against certificates or temporary documents and to return them on the day of receipt or, should that not be a business day, on the first business day following their receipt and to split and return renounceable documents within the same period.

12. To register transfers and other documents without payment of any fee.

13. To issue, without charge, certificates within:—

(a) one month of the date of expiration of any right of renunciation;

(b) 14 days of the lodgment of transfers.

14. To arrange for designated accounts if requested by holders of securities.

15. Where warrants to bearer have been issued or are available for issue; (i) to issue certificates in exchange for warrants (and *vice versa,* if permitted) within 14 days of the deposit of the warrants (or certificates); and (ii) to certify transfers against the deposit of warrants.

16. In the absence of circumstances which have been agreed by the Council to be exceptional to obtain the consent of the company in general meeting prior to issuing for cash:—

(a) equity capital or capital having an equity element,

(b) securities convertible into equity capital, or

(c) warrants or options to subscribe for equity capital; otherwise than to the equity shareholders of the company and, where appropriate, holders of other equity securities of the company entitled thereto.

17. In the event of a circular being issued to the holders of any particular class of security, to issue a copy or summary of such circular to the holders of all other listed securities unless the contents of such circular are irrelevant to such other holders.

I hereby certify that the above is a true and correct extract from the minutes of the board.

Secretary.

APPENDIX E2

2. Requirements for the Articles of Association of Listed Companies

SCHEDULE VII

Part A

ARTICLES OF ASSOCIATION

The articles of association or other corresponding document must conform with the following provisions and, where necessary, a certified copy of a resolution of the board of directors undertaking to comply with the appropriate provisions must be lodged with the Department:—

A. As Regards Transfer and Registration

1. That transfers and other documents relating to or affecting the title to any shares shall be registered without payment of any fee. (127)

2. That fully-paid shares shall be free from any restriction on the right of transfer and shall also be free from all lien. (128)

3. That where power is taken to limit the number of shareholders in a joint account, such limit shall not prevent the registration of a maximum of four persons. (129)

4. That the closing of the registers shall be discretionary. (130)

B. As Regards Definitive Certificates

1. That all certificates for capital shall be under the common seal, which shall only be affixed with the authority of the directors. (131)

2. That a new certificate issued to replace one that has been worn out, lost or destroyed shall be issued without charge and that where the holder has sold part of his holding, he shall be entitled to a certificate for the balance without charge. (132)

3. Where power is taken to issue share warrants to bearer, that no new share warrant shall be issued to replace one that has been lost, unless the company is satisfied beyond reasonable doubt that the original has been destroyed. (133)

C. As Regards Dividends

1. That any amount paid up in advance of calls on any share may carry interest but shall not entitle the holder of the share to participate in respect thereof in a dividend subsequently declared. (134)

2. Where power is taken to forfeit unclaimed dividends, that power shall not be exercised until twelve years or more after the date of the declaration of the dividend. (135)

D. As Regards Directors

1. Borrowing powers—That the directors shall be under an obligation to (136) restrict the borrowings of the company and exercise all voting and other rights or powers of control exercisable by the company in relation to its subsidiary companies (if any) so as to secure (as regards subsidiary companies so far as by such exercise they can secure) that the aggregate amount for the time being remaining undischarged of all moneys borrowed by the group (exclusive of inter-group borrowings) shall not, except with the consent of the company in general meeting, exceed an ascertainable amount. For the purposes of the said limit the issue of loan capital shall be deemed to constitute borrowing notwithstanding that the same may be issued in whole or in part for a consideration other than cash.

2. That, subject to such exceptions specified in the articles of association (137) as the Committee may approve, a director shall not vote on any contract or arrangement or any other proposal in which he has a material interest.

3. That any person appointed by the directors to fill a casual vacancy on (138) or as an addition to the board shall hold office only until the next following annual general meeting of the company, and shall then be eligible for re-election.

4. That, where not otherwise provided by law, the company in general (139) meeting shall have power by ordinary resolution to remove any director (including a managing director, but without prejudice to any claim for damages under any contract) before the expiration of his period of office.

5. That the minimum length of the period, during which notice to the (140) company of the intention to propose a person for election as a director and during which notice to the company by such person of his willingness to be elected may be given, be at least seven days, the latest date for lodgment of such notices to be not more than seven days prior to the date of the meeting appointed for such election.

E. As Regards Accounts

That a printed copy of the directors' report, accompanied by the balance (141) sheet (including every document required by law to be annexed thereto) and profit and loss account or income and expenditure account, shall, at least twenty-one days previous to the general meeting, be delivered or sent by post to the registered address of every member.

F. As Regards Rights

1. That adequate voting rights are in appropriate circumstances secured to (142) to preference shareholders.

2. That a quorum for a separate class meeting (other than an adjourned (143) meeting) to consider a variation of the rights of any class of shares shall be the holders of at least one-third of the issued shares of the class.

G. As Regards Companies to be Included in the "Investment Trusts" Section of the Official List

That all moneys realised on the sale or other realisation of any capital (144) assets in excess of book value and all other moneys in the nature of accretion to capital shall not be treated as profits available for dividend.

H. As Regards Notices

1. That where power is taken to give notice by advertisement such advertisement shall be inserted in at least one leading London daily newspaper. (145)

2. That where it is provided that notices will be given only to those members whose registered addresses are within the United Kingdom, any member, whose registered address is not within the United Kingdom, may name an address within the United Kingdom which, for the purpose of notices, shall be considered as his address. (146)

I. As Regards Redeemable Shares

That, where power is reserved to purchase for redemption a redeemable share:— (147)

   (a) Purchases not made through the market or by tender shall be limited to a maximum price.

   (b) If purchases are by tender, tenders shall be available to all shareholders alike.

J. As Regards Capital Structure

That the structure of the share capital of the company be stated and where the capital consists of more than one class of share it must also be stated how the various classes shall rank for any distribution by way of dividend or otherwise. (148)

K. As Regards Non-voting or Restricted Voting Shares

1. That, where the capital of the company includes shares which do not carry voting rights, the words "non-voting" must appear in the designation of such shares. (149)

2. That, where the equity capital includes shares with different voting rights, the designation of each class of shares, other than those with the most favourable voting rights, must include the words "restricted voting" or "limited voting". (150)

L. As Regards Proxies

1. That where provision is made in the articles as to the form of proxy this must be so worded as not to preclude the use of the two-way form. (151)

2. That a corporation may execute a form of proxy under the hand of a duly authorised officer. (152)

Appendix F

List of Company Forms Supplied by Jordan & Sons Limited
(*All prices shown are exclusive of value added tax and liable to alteration without notice*)

Draft Form of Memorandum and Articles of Association
Form D: For a private company adopting Table A with modifications
75p each*

Articles of Association
Table A. The Companies Act 1862 (Revised 1906)   £1.25 each*
Table A. The Companies (Consolidation) Act 1908   75p each*
Table A. The Companies Act 1929   50p each*
Table A. The Companies Act 1948   45p each*

Registration of Company
41 Declaration of Compliance with the requirements of the Companies Act in respect of matters precedent and incidental to registration   30p per 10
PUC 1 Statement on formation of a company   30p per 10

Allotment
PUC 2 Return of Allotments of Shares issued for cash   30p per 10
PUC 3 Return of Allotments of Shares issued for consideration other than cash   30p per 10
PUC 5 Statement of further amounts paid on partly paid Shares   30p per 10
PUC 6 Statement relating to a chargeable transaction of a capital company   30p per 10
PUC 7 Return of Allotments of Shares issued by way of capitalisation   30p per 10
45(X) Return of Allotments continuation sheet   30p per 10
CF 45XD Return of Allotments continuation sheet for use with Addressing Machine   30p per 10
52 Particulars of Contract where no Contract in writing and Shares allotted otherwise than for cash   30p per 10

Zero rated for VAT at April 1st 1973.

Consolidation of Share Capital, etc.

28 Notice of Consolidation, Division, Sub-Division, or Conversion of Shares into Stock etc., of the Redemption of Redeemable Preference Shares, or of the Cancellation of Shares   30p per 10

Debentures

On receipt of instructions from solicitors we will be pleased to prepare drafts to suit individual cases

Register of Members

CF 103 Notice of Place where Register of Members is kept, or any change in that place   30p per 10

Increase of Share Capital

10 Notice of Increase in Nominal Capital   30p per 10

CA 51 Form of Extraordinary Resolution   30p per 10

27 Form of Ordinary Resolution   30p per 10

Transfer of Shares and Debentures

CA 10 Stock Transfer Form (under seal) Transferee and Transferor to sign
                                            30p per 10   £1.70 per 100

CA 30 Stock Transfer Form under 1963 Act Transferor to sign only (Stock Exchange Format)   30p per 10   £1.70 per 100

CA 15 Non-Returnable Transfer Receipt—book of 50 in duplicate, £3.65 each

CA 37 Request for Payment of interest or Dividends   30p per 10

CA 15A Notification to Transferor of receipt of Transfer for certification or registration—   book of 50 in duplicate, £3.65 each

CA 17 Balance Receipt—   book of 50 in duplicate, £1.90 each

CA 18 Form of Request by Executors or Administrators to be registered as members
                                                               30p per 10

CA 16A Indemnity in respect of lost or destroyed Share Certificate   30p per 10

CA 16B Indemnity in respect of lost or destroyed Warrant   30p per 10

Registration of Charges

47 Particulars for Registration of a Mortgage or Charge   60p per 10

47A Particulars for Registration of a Series of Debentures   60p per 10

48 Particulars for Registration of a further issue of Debentures in a registered Series   30p per 10

47B Particulars of a Mortgage or Charge subject to which property has been acquired
                                                               30p per 10

47C Certificate of Registration in Scotland or Northern Ireland of a charge comprising property situate there   30p per 10

49 Memorandum of Complete Satisfaction of Mortgage or Charge   30p per 10

APPENDIX F

49A Memorandum of Partial Payment or Satisfaction of Mortgage or Charge or of Release of Part of Property or Undertaking from Mortgage or Charge
30p per 10

49B Memorandum of Fact that part of property or undertaking mortgaged or charged has ceased to form part of property or undertaking of company
30p per 10

CF 53 Notice of Appointment of Receiver or Manager (to Registrar of Companies)
30p per 10

CF 57A Notice of ceasing to act as Receiver or Manager   30p per 10

Annual Return

6A Annual Return of Company having a Share Capital   60p per 10

8(A) List of Past and Present Members—continuation sheets for annual Returns
60p per 10

8AD List of Past and Present Members—continuation sheets for use with an addressing machine   £2.00 per 100

6(B) Additional Certificate to be given in the case of a former exempt private Company   30p per 10

J7 Annual Return of Company not having a Share Capital   60p per 10

Registered Office

4 Notice of Situation of Registered Office, or any change therein   30p per 10

Meetings and Proceedings

CA 45 Notice of Statutory Meeting   30p per 10

CA 47 Notice of Meeting of Directors   30p per 10

CA 43 Proxy Form—General Power   30p per 10

CA 44 Proxy Form—Special or General Power   30p per 10

CA 49 Notice of Extraordinary General Meeting to pass Special Resolution
30p per 10

CA 49A Notice of Extraordinary General Meeting to pass Extraordinary or Ordinary Resolution   30p per 10

CA 51 Form of Extraordinary Resolution   30p per 10

50 Form of Special Resolution   30p per 10

27 Form of Ordinary Resolution   30p per 10

Directors and Other Officers

CA 90 Notification by Director of his interest in Shares or Debentures as at 27th October 1967, or date of appointment if after that date   60p per 10

CA 91 Notification by Director of occurrence of an event affecting his interest in Shares or Debentures   60p per 10

CFR 5 Notice of place where copies of Directors' written Service Contracts or Memorandum thereof are kept or any change in that place   30p per 10

CFR 6 Notice of place where register of Directors' Interests in Shares is or Debentures of, a company or its associated Companies is kept or of any change in that place   30p per 10

9 Return of Particulars of First Directors and Secretary, Fly form   60p per 10

9A Notification of Change or Directors or Secretary or in their particulars, Fly form   60p per 10

Divends

CA 63 Dividend List—suitable for use with Addressing Machine   £3.10 per 100

CA 60 Statement of Dividend and Tax Credit Voucher to accompany cheque for Dividend,   30p per 10

JS 517B Statement of Dividend and Tax Credit Alternative pattern. Book of 50 with counterfoil £1.70 each   30p per 10 sheets

JS 50 Notice of Interest and Tax Voucher to accompany cheque for Interest   30p per 10

Re-Registrations

CFR 1 Application by a Limited Company to be Re-Registered as Unlimited   30p per 10

CFR 2 Members Assent to Company being Re-Registered as Unlimited   30p per 10

CFR 3 Application by an Unlimited Company to be Re-Registered as Limited   30p per 10

CFR 4 Declaration by Directors as to Members' Assent to Re-Registration of a Company as Unlimited   30p per 10

Arrangements and Reconstructions

CF 100 Notice to Dissenting Shareholders, pursuant to Section 209   30p per 10

CF 100A Notice to Non-Assenting Shareholders   30p per 10

FORMS APPLICABLE TO
Members' Voluntary Winding-Up

Summary of Proceedings in a Members' V.W.U.   50p each*

Complete set of forms for Members' Voluntary Winding-Up, in duplicate   89p per set

CA 98 Notice to Members of Meeting when Winding-Up continues for more than a year   30p per 10

WUR 108 Declaration of Solvency, embodying statement of assets and liabilities   30p per 10

APPENDIX F

CA 71 Notice to Members of Meeting to pass Special Resolution to wind up Company voluntarily   30p per 10

CA 70 Special Resolution to wind up Company voluntarily   30p per 10

CA 70A Special Resolution to wind up Company voluntarily (for publication in *London Gazette*)   30p per 10

39C Notice of Appointment of Liquidator (Members' Voluntary Winding-Up)   30p per 10

CA 75 Notice of Final Winding-Up Meeting (to be sent to Members)   30p per 10

CA 75A *Gazette* Notice to Members of Final Winding-Up Meeting   30p per 10

WUR 111/110 Combined Form of Liquidators' Statement of Account (Members' Voluntary Winding-Up) and Return of Final Winding-Up Meeting   60p per 10

51A Form of Extraordinary Resolution re disposal of books   30p per 10

CA 99 Notice to Creditors of Meeting of Creditors on Insolvency of Company   30p per 10

CA 99A *Gazette* Notice of Meeting of Creditors in case of Insolvency   30p per 10

WUR 109 Statement of Assets and Liabilities in case of Insolvency   60p per 10

FORMS APPLICABLE TO
Creditors' Voluntary Winding-Up

Summary of Proceedings in a Creditors' V.W.U.   50p each*

Complete set of forms for Creditors' Voluntary Winding-Up, in duplicate   94p per set

CA 76 Notice of Meeting of Creditors (to be sent to Creditors)   30p per 10

CA 76A *Gazette* Notice of Meeting of Creditors   30p per 10

CA 72 Notice to Members of Meeting to pass Extraordinary Resolution to wind up an Insolvent Company   30p per 10

CA 73 Extraordinary Resolution to Wind-Up (printed for filing, with space for name of Company, etc., to be filled in)   30p per 10

CA 73A Extraordinary Resolution to Wind-Up (for publication in *London Gazette*)   30p per 10

39D Notice of Appointment of Liquidator (Creditors' Voluntary Winding-Up)   30p per 10

CA 77 Notice to Creditors of Final Winding-Up Meeting (to be sent to Creditors)   30p per 10

CA 77A *Gazette* Notice of Creditors' Final Winding-Up Meeting   30p per 10

CA 78 Notice to Members of Final Winding-Up Meeting (to be sent to Members)   30p per 10

CA 78A *Gazette* Notice Members Final Winding-Up Meeting   30p per 10

WUR 112/110 Combined form of Liquidators' Statement of Account (Creditors' Voluntary Winding-Up) and Return of Final Winding-Up Meeting   60p per 10

FORMS APPLICABLE TO
Every Voluntary Winding-Up

CA 79 Notice to Creditors to come in and prove debts and claims   30p per 10

CA 79A *Gazette* Notice to Creditors to come in and prove debts and claims   30p per 10

39 E *Gazette* Notice of Appointment of Liquidator (Creditors' or Members' Voluntary Winding-Up)   30p per 10

CA 74 Notice to send in claims (to be sent to Creditors)   30p per 10

CA 74A *Gazette* Notice to Creditors to send in claims   30p per 10

WUR 92 Liquidator's Statement of Account pursuant to Section 342   60p per 10

WUR 93 Affidavit verifying Liquidator's Statement of Account   30p per 10

WUR 94 Liquidator's Trading Account   60p per 10

Forms applicable to every Voluntary Winding-Up

WUR 95 Lists of Dividends or Compositions   60p per 10

WUR 96 List of Amounts paid or payable to Contributories   60p per 10

WUR 92X Liquidator's Statement Continuation Sheets   60p per 10

WUR 94X Liquidator's Trading Account Continuation Sheets   60p per 10

WUR 95X List of Dividends or Compositions Continuation Sheets   60p per 10

WUR 96X List of Amounts Continuation Sheets   60p per 10

WUR 80/81 General and Special Proxy (Combined form)   30p per 10

WUR 59A Proof of Debt—Voluntary Liquidation   30p per 10

WUR 74 List of Creditors or Contributories to be used at every Meeting   30p per 10

WUR 74X List of Creditors Continuation Sheet   30p per 10

WUR 61 Notice of Rejection of Proof of Debt   30p per 10

WUR 76 Affidavit of Postage of Notices of meetings   30p per 10

Receivers and Managers

CF 108 Notice of Appointment of Receiver or Manager (to the Company)   30p per 10

CF 57 Receiver's or Manager's Abstract of Receipts and Payments   60p per 10

CF 57X Receiver's or Manager's Abstract of Receipts and Payments Continuation Sheets   60p per 10

Probate

PR 8 Oath of Executor   30p per 10

PR 9 Oath of Administrator   30p per 10

PR 12 Oath of Administrator (with will annexed)   30p per 10

Index

INDEX

INDEX

INDEX

INDEX

INDEX

INDEX

Institute of Directors

Incorporated by Royal Charter 1906

The objects and purposes for which the Institute of Directors is constituted are as follows:

1. To promote the interests, and raise the status and professional standards, of Directors and to provide Members with a professional advisory and information service particularly on company law and taxation.

2. To arrange for meetings at important centres at which prominent business and public men can address gatherings of Directors on matters of special interest to them.

PAST PRESIDENTS: SIR PAUL CHAMBERS, K.B.E., C.B., C.I.E., THE LORD PRITCHARD

VICE-PRESIDENT: THE EARL OF DERBY, M.C., C.C., LL.D.

CHAIRMAN OF THE COUNCIL: THE RT. HON. LORD ERROLL OF HALE

LEADER OF PARLIAMENTARY PANEL: CECIL E. PARKINSON, M.P.

COUNCIL

THE HON. JOHN F. H. BARING
L. E. ROWAN BENTALL
M. W. CLARK
A. G. DAVIES
THE EARL OF DROGHEDA, K.G., K.B.E.
EDMUND T. GARTSIDE, T.D.
JAMES GULLIVER
SIR CHARLES HARDIE, C.B.E.
R. T. HARRIS
D. HOLDEN-BROWN
THE EARL OF INCHAPE
R. S. JUKES, C.B.E.
SIR GEOFFREY KITCHEN, T.D.
J. P. KOPPEL
HECTOR LAING
KENNETH MCALPINE
MICHAEL MANDER

SIR WILLIAM MATHER, O.B.E., M.C., T.D.
A. E. S. MENZIES
SIR PETER MENZIES
DENIS M. MOUNTAIN
SIR JOHN MUSKER
SIR DAVID NICOLSON
THE HON. ANGUS OGILVY
SIR HUMPHREY PRIDEAUX, O.B.E.
DENYS RANDOLPH
M. E. RICH
M. J. DE R. RICHARDSON
THE LORD ROOTES
A. THOMSON
NIGEL VINSON
DAVID WOLFSON

DIRECTOR-GENERAL: JAN HILDRETH

DEPUTY DIRECTOR-GENERAL: ROGER D. F. MARLOW, D.S.C.

SOLICITORS: ALLEN & OVERY

BANKERS: BARCLAYS BANK LTD.

AUDITORS: DELOITTE & CO.

The President, Past Presidents, Vice-President, Treasurer, Chairman and Deputy Chairman of the Council, leader of the Parliamentary Panel and Chairmen of Branches are *ex officio* Members of Council.

BRANCHES OF THE INSTITUTE

Cleveland and District: *Chairman:* N. R. M. Moir, D.L., F.I.C.S.; *Honorary Secretary:* P. V. Dickins, A.C.A., M.A., Chipchase Manners & Co., 384 Linthorpe Road, Middlesbrough, Cleveland.

Devon and Cornwall: *Chairman:* R. Petty; *Honorary Secretary:* D. L. Cullum, F.C.A., Cullum, White & Pawley, Torrington Chambers, 58 North Road East, Plymouth, Plymouth 64217.

Eastern: *Chairman:* B. P. Dyer; *Honorary Secretary:* H. F. Adams, 19 Briar Way, Peterborough PE1 5LH. Peterborough 62026.

Hampshire and Dorset: *Chairman:* M. J. Cobham, *Honorary Secretary:* Graham Lockyer, 28 Poole Hill, Bournemouth, Dorset BH2 5PR, 0202 23555.

Leicestershire: *Chairman:* M. P. Tahany; *Honorary Secretary:* H. Leslie Milliard, O.B.E., T.D., J.P., 4 Horsefair Street, Leicester LE1 6HA. Leicester 27171.

Lincolnshire and South Humberside: *President:* The Duke of Rutland; *Chairman:* J. R. J. Mansbridge, *Honorary Secretary:* G. H. Camamile, J.P., F.C.A., 11 Bailgate, Lincoln LN1 3AE. Lincoln 31341.

Liverpool and Merseyside: *President:* The Earl of Derby, M.C., C.C., LL.D.; *Chairman:* Alan Waterworth, J.P.; *Honorary Secretary:* J. Marsden Hanmer, M.B.E., F.C.A., 43 Ballantrae Road, Liverpool L18 6JG. 051–724 1085.

Greater Manchester Area: *Chairman:* G. H. Kenyon, D.L., J.P.; *Honorary Secretary:* Sir Richard Miller, Lloyd's House, 4th Floor, 18 Lloyd Street, Manchester M2 5WA. 061–834 9300.

Midland: *Chairman:* J. C. W. Daniels; *Honorary Secretary:* Edmund C. Blewitt, 67a New Street, Birmingham B2 4DU. 021–643 2811.

Norfolk and Suffolk: *Chairman:* The Lord Mackintosh of Halifax; *Honorary Secretary:* W. H. Greenwood, F.C.A., Rowntree Mackintosh Ltd., Norwich NOR34A. Norwich 26101.

Northamptonshire and Bedfordshire: *President:* The Lord Luke of Pavenham, D.L., J.P.; *Chairman:* R. H. Eaton; *Honorary Secretary:* G. D. Franklin, Footwear Manufacturers' Association, 50 East Park Parade, Northampton, Northampton 31511.

Northern Counties: *Chairman:* G. V. Carr, F.C.A.; *Honorary Secretary:* R. C. Spoor, F.C.A., Norham House, 12 New Bridge Street, Newcastle upon Tyne NE1 8AD. Newcastle 611063.

Northern Ireland: *Chairman:* R. B. Henderson, M.A.; *Honorary Secretary:* E. I. Johnstone, F.C.A. 36 Arthur Street, Belfast BT1 4GL. Belfast 36525.

Nottinghamshire and Derbyshire: *Chairman:* H. Russell; *Honorary Secretary:* J. C. Naake, Calemation Ltd., Unit No. 1, Carey Road, Bulwell, Nottingham NE6 8AT. Nottingham 277611.

Scotland: *Chairman:* Sir Thomas Waterlow, Bt., C.B.E.; *Honorary Secretary:* D. M. Mowat, J.P., M.A., 20 Hanover Street, Edinburgh GH2 2HJ. 031–225 5851.

Sheffield and District: *Chairman:* Col. J. A. H. Nicholson, M.C., T.D., D.L.; *Honorary Secretary:* D. W. Hatfield, Ernest W. Hatfield Ltd., 1 Sidney Street, Sheffield. Sheffield 77651.

Wales: *President:* Neil Taylor; *Chairman:* John Aeron-Thomas, J.P.; *Honorary Secretary:* P. Phillips, Beynon House, Mount Stuart Sq., Cardiff CF1 6QJ. Cardiff 29431.

West of England: *Chairman:* G. T. Gedge, C.B.E.; *Honorary Secretary:* R. Milward, Harveys of Bristol Limited, Harvey House, Whitchurch Lane, Bristol ES99 7JE. Whitchurch 6161.

Yorkshire and North Humberside: *Chairman:* N. J. A. Crosse, D.L.; *Honorary Secretary:* J. Perkins, F.C.A., A.T.I.I., Crown Chambers, 14a Princes Street, Harrogate HG1 1NJ. Harrogate 64446.

CHANNEL ISLANDS
Jersey: *Chairman:* R. G. Maltwood; *Honorary Secretary:* S. Lee-Browne, F.C.I.S., 41 La Motte Street, St. Helier, Jersey, C.I. Jersey Central 35256.

INSTITUTE OF DIRECTORS

OVERSEAS

Cyprus: *Chairman:* C. D. Severis; *Honoray Secretary:* Dr. G. V. Vassilliou, P.O. Box 2098, Nicosia, Cyprus.

Gibraltar: *Honorary Secretary:* C. G. Gaggero, O.B.E., C.ST.J., Saccone & Speed Ltd., 130 Main Street, Gibraltar.

Jamaica: *President:* L. E. Ashenheim; *Chairman:* F. Fox; *Honorary Secretary:* I. M. D. Murphy, P.O. Box 154, Kingston 8.

Malta: G.C.: *Chairman:* Dr. V. A. Mercieca, LL.D.; *Honorary Secretary:* J. A. Grima, Floor 4, Valletta Buildings, South Street, Valletta, Malta, G.C. Telephone 20899. Cables Impact Malta.

Central Africa: *President:* Major-Gen. Sir Peter Bednall, K.B.E., C.B., M.C., F.C.A.; *Chairman:* E. R. Campbell, C.B.E.; *Vice-Chairman:* G. Betts; *Honorary Secretary:* Mrs. F. M. Rowe, P.O. Box 2629, Salisbury, Rhodesia.

New Zealand: *Chairman and President:* Sir Geoffrey Roberts, C.B.E., A.F.C., L. OF M. (U.S.), F.R.A.E.S.; *Honorary Secretary:* A. Ross Brown, P.O. Box No. 10340, Wellington.

South Africa: *President:* Harry Oppenheimer; *Chairman:* H. E. Entwistle; *Honorary Secretary:* W. E. Marsh, B.COM., C.A.(S.A.), P.O. Box 6962, Johannesburg 2000, South Africa.

THE INSTITUTE OF DIRECTORS IN AUSTRALIA

President: Sir Robert Crichton-Brown, C.B.E.; *Vice-Presidents* R. S. Turner, C.B.E., and Sir Roger Darvall, C.B.E.; *Honorary Treasurer:* A. J. White, B.COMM., A.I.A.A.;

Executive Director: P. R. Grogan, B.A., LL.B., B.EC.

Branches

New South Wales: *Chairman:* Sir Robert Crichton-Brown, C.B.E.; *Executive Director:* P. R. Grogan, B.A., LL.B., B.EC.; *Administrative Officer:* Miss Frances Laxen, P.O. Box 1566. Sydney 2001.

South Australia: *Chairman:* B. R. Macklin, O.B.E.; *Honorary Secretary:* R. D. Hastwell, 191 Melbourne St., N. Adelaide 5006.

Queensland: *Chairman:* W. A. Park; *Honorary Secretary/Treasurer:* B. E. Scott; *Executive Secretary:* W. D. Banks, 288 Queen Street, Brisbane 4000.

Victoria: *Chairman:* Sir Roger Darvall, C.B.E.; *Honorary Secretary:* R. A. Everett, 34 Queens Road, Melbourne. Vic 3004. Telegrams: Boardrooms, Melbourne.

Western Australia: *Chairman:* G. D. Wright; *Honorary Secretary:* R. G. Houlding, 15th Floor, 37 St. Georges' Terrace, Perth. W.A. 6000.

Tasmania: *Chairman:* J. B. Piggott, C.B.E.; *Honorary Secretary:* P. Williams, 128 Macquarie Street, Hobart 7000.

Australian Capital Territory: *Chairman:* J. G. Service; *Honorary Secretary:* J. D. Richards, P.O. Box 124, Canberra City ACT 2601.

**Inquiries to the Director-General, Institute of Directors,
10 Belgrave Square, London SW1X 8PW (01-235 3601)**